ANSELM
KIEFER
EARLY WORKS

ANSELM KIEFER

EARLY WORKS

Edited by
Lena Fritsch

CONTENTS

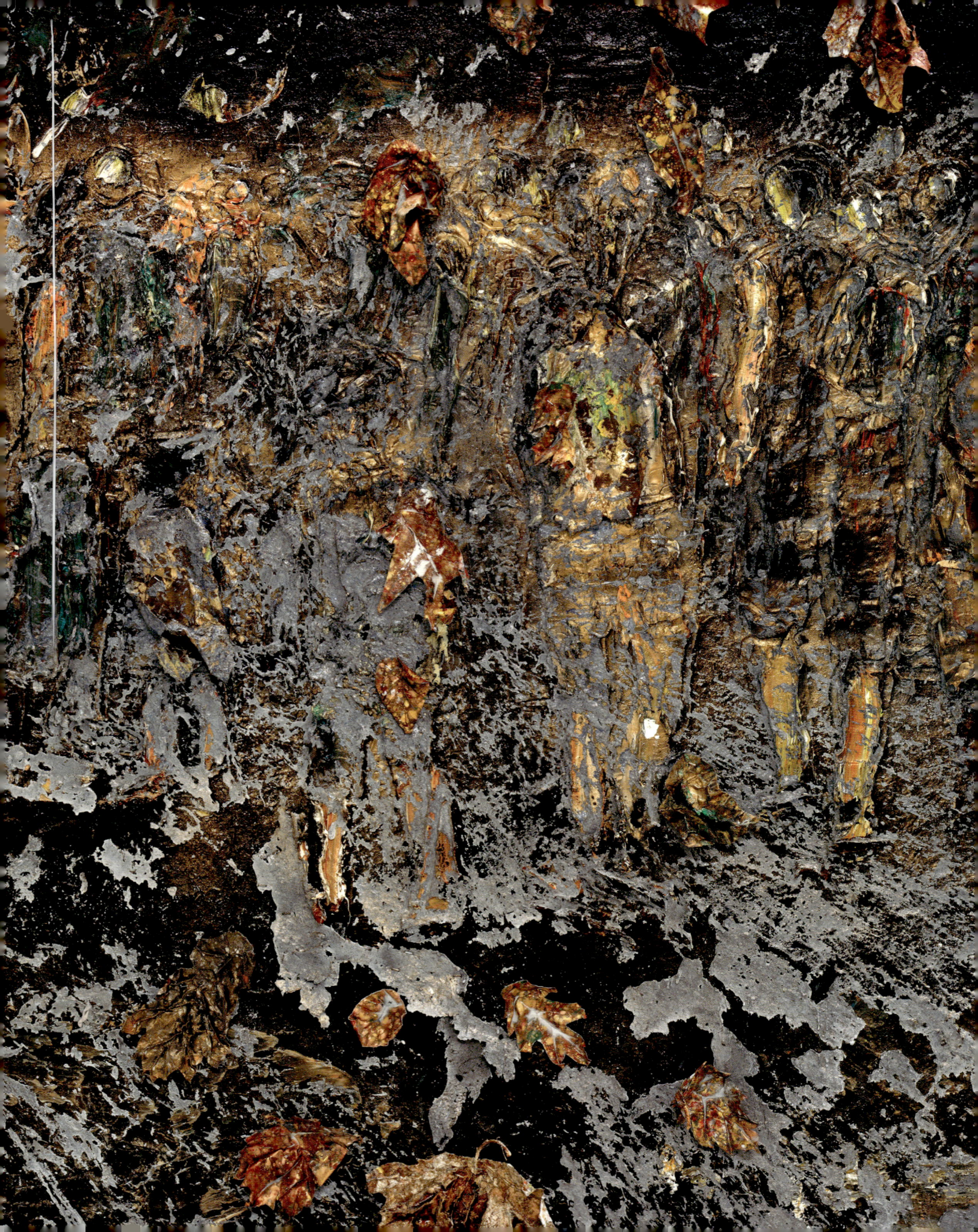

DIRECTOR'S FOREWORD

Alexander Sturgis

This book accompanies a major exhibition at the Ashmolean Museum, of the early works of the internationally acclaimed German artist Anselm Kiefer (b.1945). *Anselm Kiefer: Early Works* looks back to the origins of the artist's practice and the emergence of themes, subjects, and motifs that have been returned to and sustained throughout his long and distinguished career. The exhibition focuses on his paintings, drawings, woodcuts, photographs, and artist books, created between 1969 and 1982, when Kiefer was among the first generation of Germans to confront the country's troubled past and national identity in the wake of the Third Reich, Second World War, and the Holocaust. Incorporating multi-layered references to Germany's past, Kiefer's work explores how history, literature, and myth can be used and transformed; claimed and tainted by the National Socialists on the one hand, but still potent as a means to understand broader themes of civilisation, culture, and spirituality on the other. Three recent works, specially selected for the exhibition by the artist, suggest continuities between Kiefer's early work and his current practice.

The exhibition is a collaboration with the Hall Art Foundation, who mounted an earlier iteration of the show at Kunstmuseum Schloss Derneburg, 2022–3. Sincere thanks are due to Andy and Christine Hall for their exceptional generosity, not only for ending their unique collection of early Anselm Kiefer works to this exhibition, but also for their longstanding support of the Ashmolean including their co-funding of the post of the Ashmolean's Curator of Modern and Contemporary Art. We are also grateful to Maryse Brand and her team at the Hall Art Foundation for all their practical help and support in the mounting of the show.

No exhibition would be possible without support and thanks are due, in particular, to White Cube, Jay Jopling, and the gallery team around Susannah Hyman for their generous financial and logistical support of this exhibition and book. Thanks as well to the patrons of the Ashmolean Museum and other supporters of our exhibition programme.

At the Ashmolean particular thanks are due to the exhibition's curator Dr Lena Fritsch and the exhibition team led by Agnes Valencak, while we are also grateful to all the authors of this catalogue for their insightful contributions, offering new art historical readings of Kiefer's works. Above all, we are indebted to the artist, Anselm Kiefer himself, and to his studio in France for their trust and close collaboration.

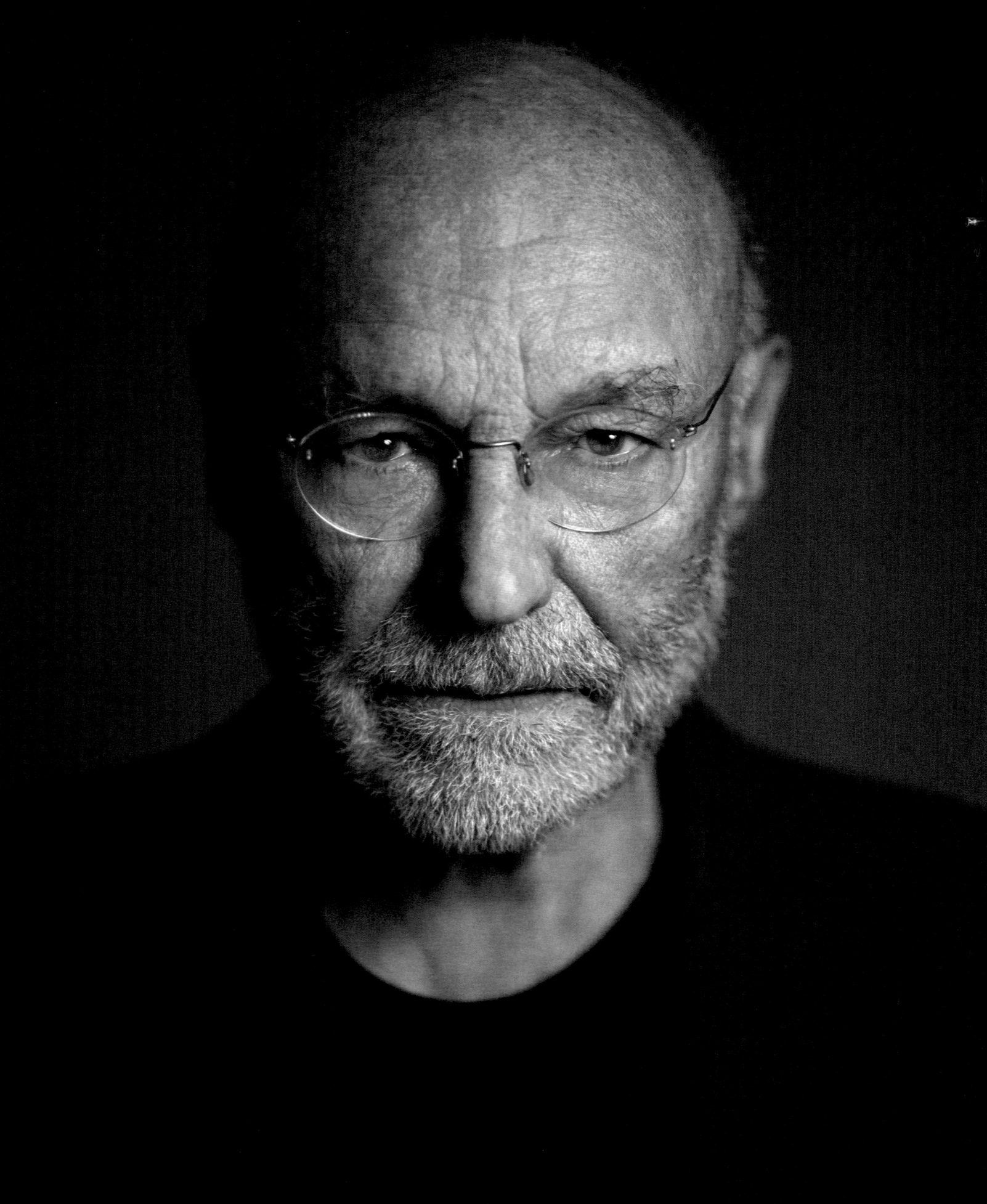

INTRODUCTION

Lena Fritsch

The art of internationa ly acclaimed and celebrated German artist Anselm Kiefer (b.1945, in Donaueschingen) is unique, uncompromising, and instantly recognisable. His monumental body of work – fusing painting, drawing, photography, sculpture, woodcut, and text – represents a microcosm of collective memory, while addressing issues of (national) identity and the convergence of history and mythology. It encapsulates and references a boundless array of cultural, literary, and philosophical allusions, ranging from the Old and New Testaments to Kabbalah mysticism, and from Germanic legends and the operas of Richard Wagner (1813–1883) to the poetry of Rainer Maria Rilke (1875–1926) ard Paul Celan (1920–1970). Kiefer's artistic techniques and supplies – including straw, lead, concrete, fire, and ash – are as expansive as they are symbolically resonant, mirroring the artist's deep interest in different materials and their transformative nature. Many of Kiefer's works have a life of their own, endlessly changing in form.

This publication accompanies a major exhibition of works created by Anselm Kiefer between 1969 and 1982, complemented by three recent paintings chosen specifically by the artist for this project. The exhibition and book showcase the signature themes, subjects, and styles of Kiefer's art, while also providing a more personal context for the large-scale installations with which he is often associated today. The works feature references to recent German history as well as to German Romanticism and Expressionism, ancient Nordic mythology, and wider European philosophy, science, religion, spirituality, art, ard culture. The early works are on loan from the Hall Collection. The Hall Art Foundation was established in 2007 by Andy and Christine Hall to support post-war and contemporary art. The Halls oversee two art museums: Kunstmuseum Schloss Derneburg in Germany and the Hall Art Foundation, housed in a former dairy farm in Reading, Vermont, US. Many of the works by Kiefer were previously in the collection of another German artist-titan: Georg Baselitz (b.1938). Baselitz was one of the first people to collect Kiefer's works, with holdings dating to the 1970s, and later, the two men represented Germany at the 1980 Venice Biennale. The Halls acquired Baselitz's collection in 2005, before also acquiring the old castle, Schloss Derneburg, where Baselitz lived and worked until 2006. Between 2022 and 2023, Kunstmuseum Schloss Derneburg exhibited the majority of the works featured in this book in an exhibition titled *Anselm Kiefer – Frühwerk* (*Early Works*).

Portrait of Anselm Kiefer
by Till Brönner, 2023

For this book, art historians, artists, curators, and experts of Kiefer's work from Germany, Austria, Belgium, Britain, and the US have contributed 'In Focus' texts, presenting original analyses of individual paintings, drawings, photographs, woodcuts, and artist books, organised in a broadly chronological structure. A chronology at the end of the book provides an overview of the artist's early practice and life to help further contextualise these works.

The book begins with Kiefer's seminal photographs, paintings, and artist books that link to the *Besetzungen* and *Heroische Sinnbilder* series, created in 1969 and 1970, which Kiefer views as his first serious works. As part of the 'denazification' of Germany, Nazi symbols and gestures, including the '*Sieg Heil*' salute, had been banned when, as a 24-year-old art student, Kiefer staged a series of performances, both in his studio and at historically significant European locations, in which he raised his right arm. He provocatively and bravely role-played his immediate predecessors, asking himself and his viewers uncomfortable questions that required facing Germany's recent past: what did you do when Germany was under Nazi rule? What would you have done if you had been born twenty years earlier? Can you be certain that you would not have been seduced and infiltrated by the Nazi ideology? Kiefer was among the first generation of German post-war artists to directly address the country's dark past, while also drawing attention to the fact that, although Nazism had been silenced, it had not yet been processed, nor had it been eradicated. Full of complex references to German socio-political history, but also to culture, literature, and his personal life, Kiefer's works carry a unique iconography, linking classic ideas of great art with a distinctive understanding of artistic materiality. The landscapes in his watercolours are historically charged; the handwritten words on paintings are closely linked with poetry and intellectual discourses well-known to most German viewers. Motifs and symbols point to Nazi ideologies and to complicity, as well as to a collective feeling of guilt. Like the poems of Paul Celan, which Kiefer incorporates into some of his works, his art speaks the inner language of the viewer, addressing their subconscious, and often drawing on a collective cultural memory. As a German art historian and curator now based in Britain, I feel a strong sense of responsibility to translate and explain the relevant German contexts and cultural memories that make Kiefer's early works so multi-layered, strong, and poignant.

Acknowledgements

This book and exhibition have depended on the generous support of many individuals. Above all, I would like to thank the artist, Anselm Kiefer, and his studio, particularly Waltraud Forelli, Eva König, and Laura Volkert for their warm guidance and professionalism. They have patiently answered my questions about individual works, dates, and backgrounds; it has been a great joy and honour to work with them. I would also like to express my sincere thanks to Andy and Christine Hall, without whom this exhibition would not have been possible. Not only have they agreed to lend a large number of treasured works from their collections, but they also support my curatorial post at the Ashmolean Museum. At the Hall Art Foundation, Director Maryse Brand, Alex Haviland, Andrew Bernero, and Stephanie Biron have also provided invaluable help and collaboration. White Cube has been immensely generous in their support of this exhibition and book, and it was a pleasure to work with Susannah Hyman from the gallery. I do not underestimate our debt to all exhibition sponsors for their belief in this project. I would also like to thank the authors who have responded so enthusiastically with new readings of Kiefer's works: Stephanie Biron, Richard Calvocoressi, Harriet Häußler, Antonia Hoerschelmann, Liz Rideal, Lisa Saltzman, Sabine Schütz, An Van Camp, and Christian Weikop. Responsible for the insightful and beautifully paced exhibition design is Byung Kim. The elegant design of this book is down to Ocky Murray, and I'm grateful to Lizzy Silverton for the careful copy-editing.

Anselm Kiefer in his studio,
August 1982

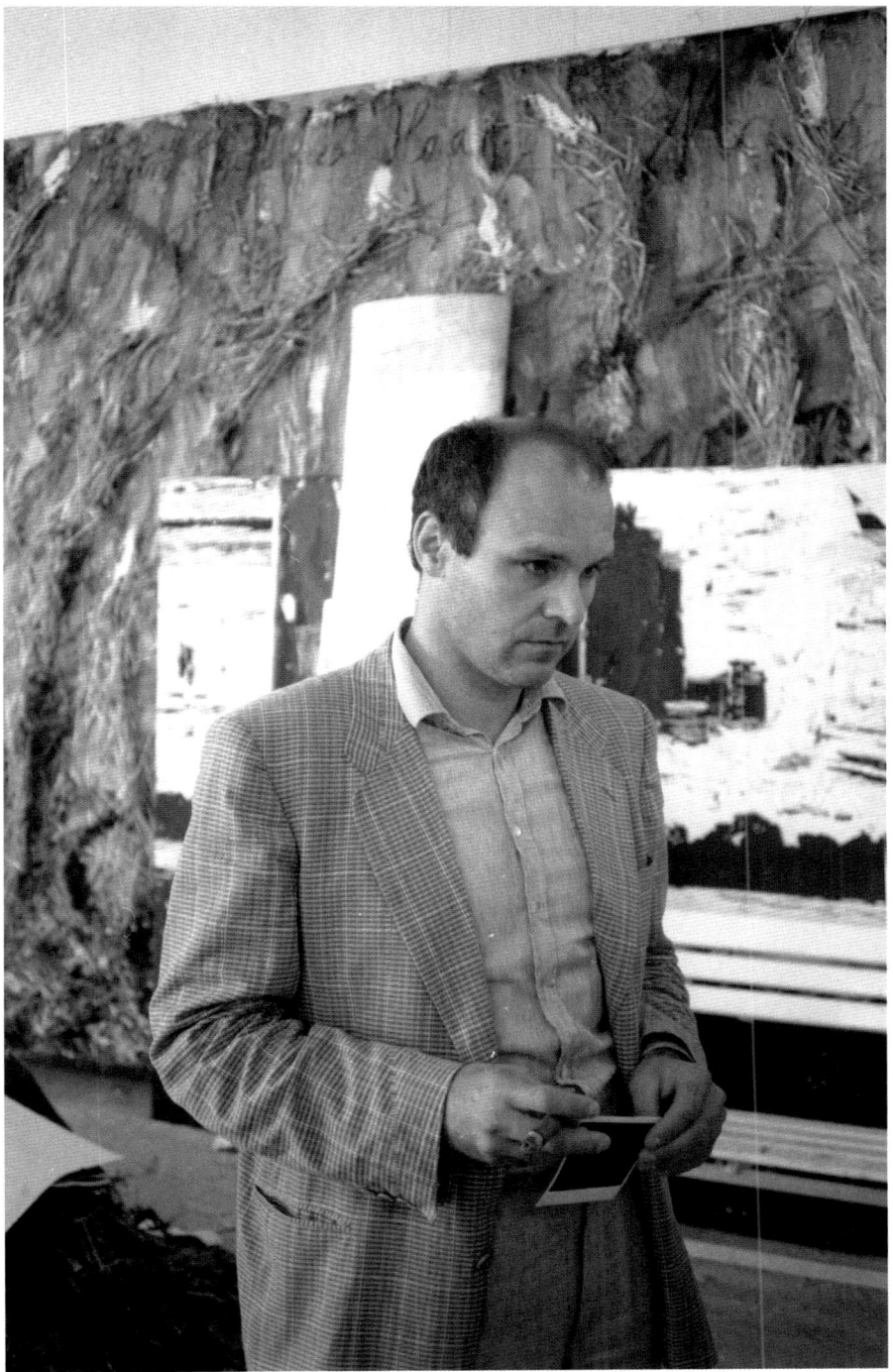

At the Ashmolean, I would like to thank Agnes Valencak and Tegan Rush for capably managing the exhibition logistics. Aisha Burtenshaw and her team of registrars have shepherded the loans, and in Development I am indebted to Emily Magnuson and her team. As always, many thanks go to Dec McCarthy, Head of Publishing and Licensing, for working closely with me on the successful completion of this publication. I would also like to recognise all the work behind the scenes by my colleagues in Art Handling, Commercial, Communication, Conservation, Design, Education and Interpretation, Marketing, Press, Public Programme, Social Media, and Visitor Experience.

IN FOCUS

with contributions by
Richard Calvocoressi
Lena Fritsch
Harriet Häußler
Antonia Hoerschelmann
Liz Rideal
Lisa Saltzman
Sabine Schütz
An Van Camp
Christian Weikop

1

FÜR JEAN GENET (FOR JEAN GENET), 1969

Bound watercolour on paper, graphite,
original photographs, hair and canvas
strips on cardboard (24 pages)
67 × 51 × 4 cm

Hall Collection

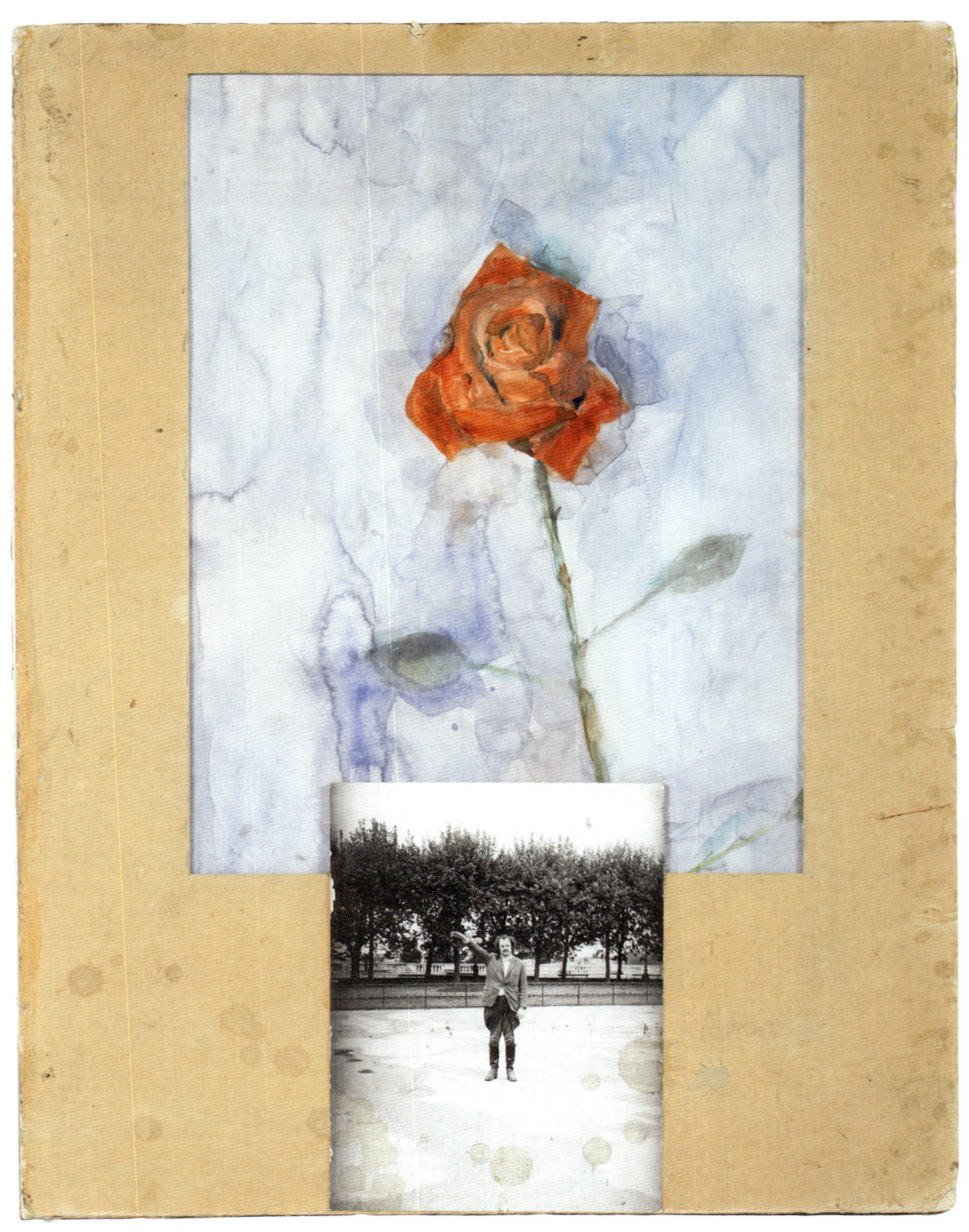

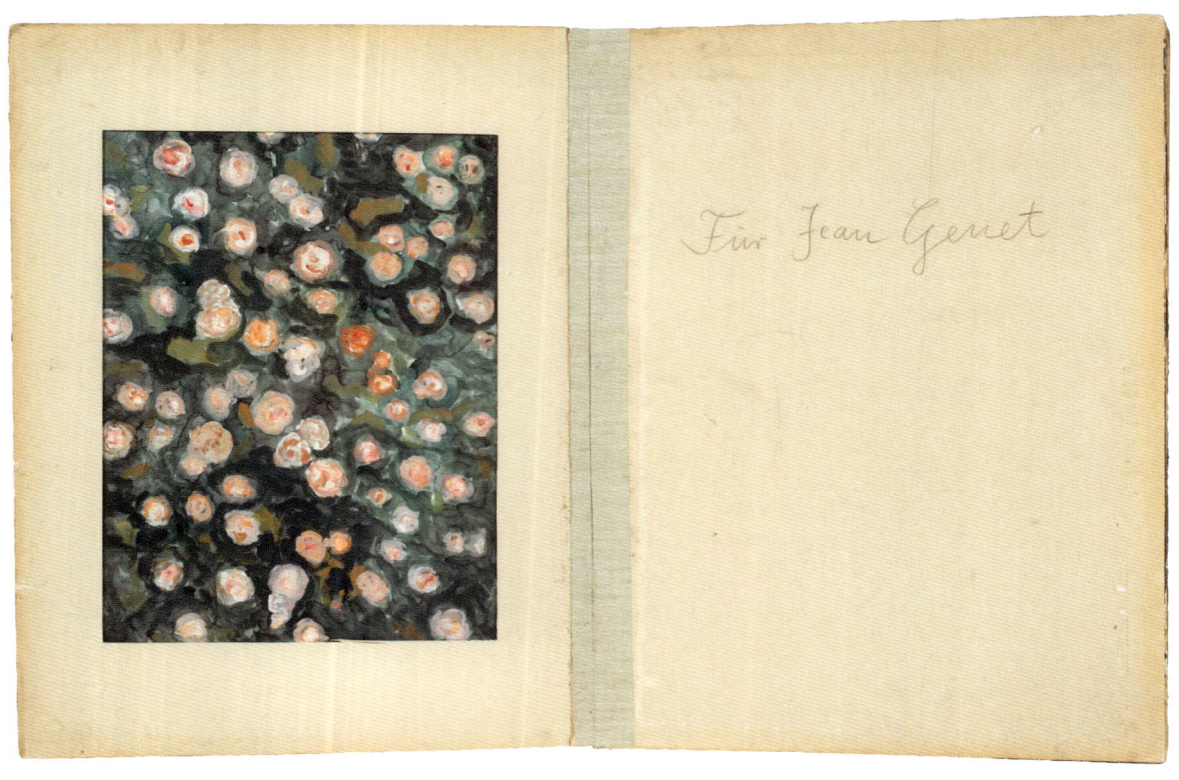

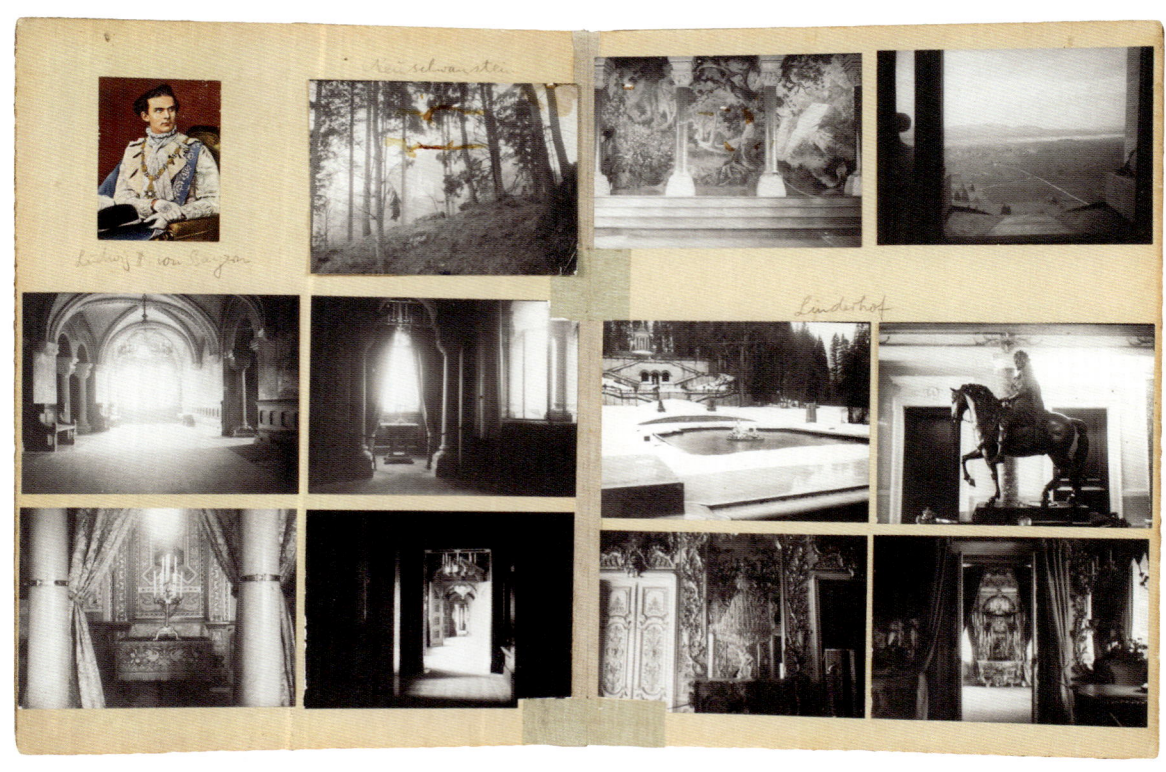

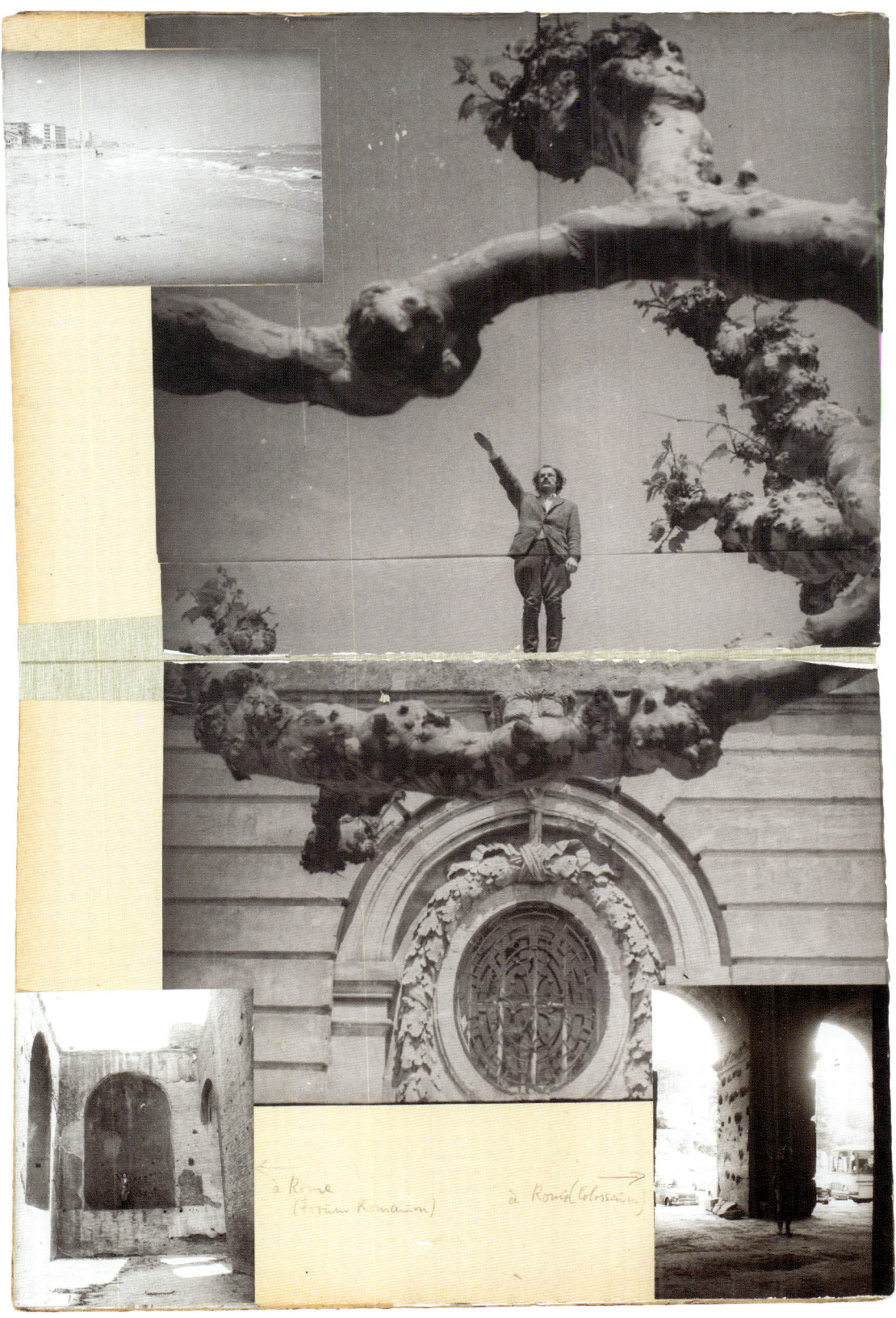

à Rome
(Forum Romanum)   à Rome (Colosseum)

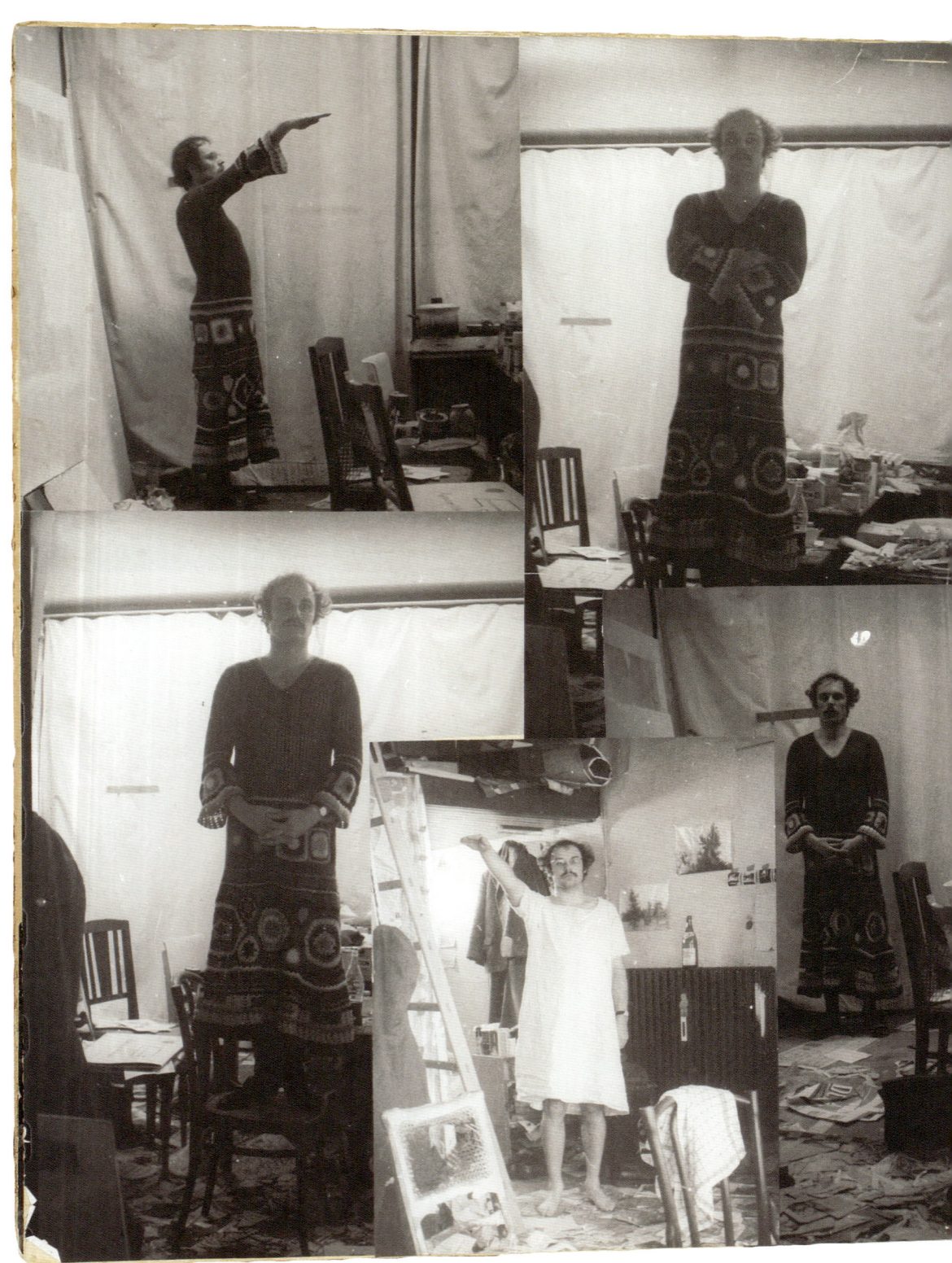

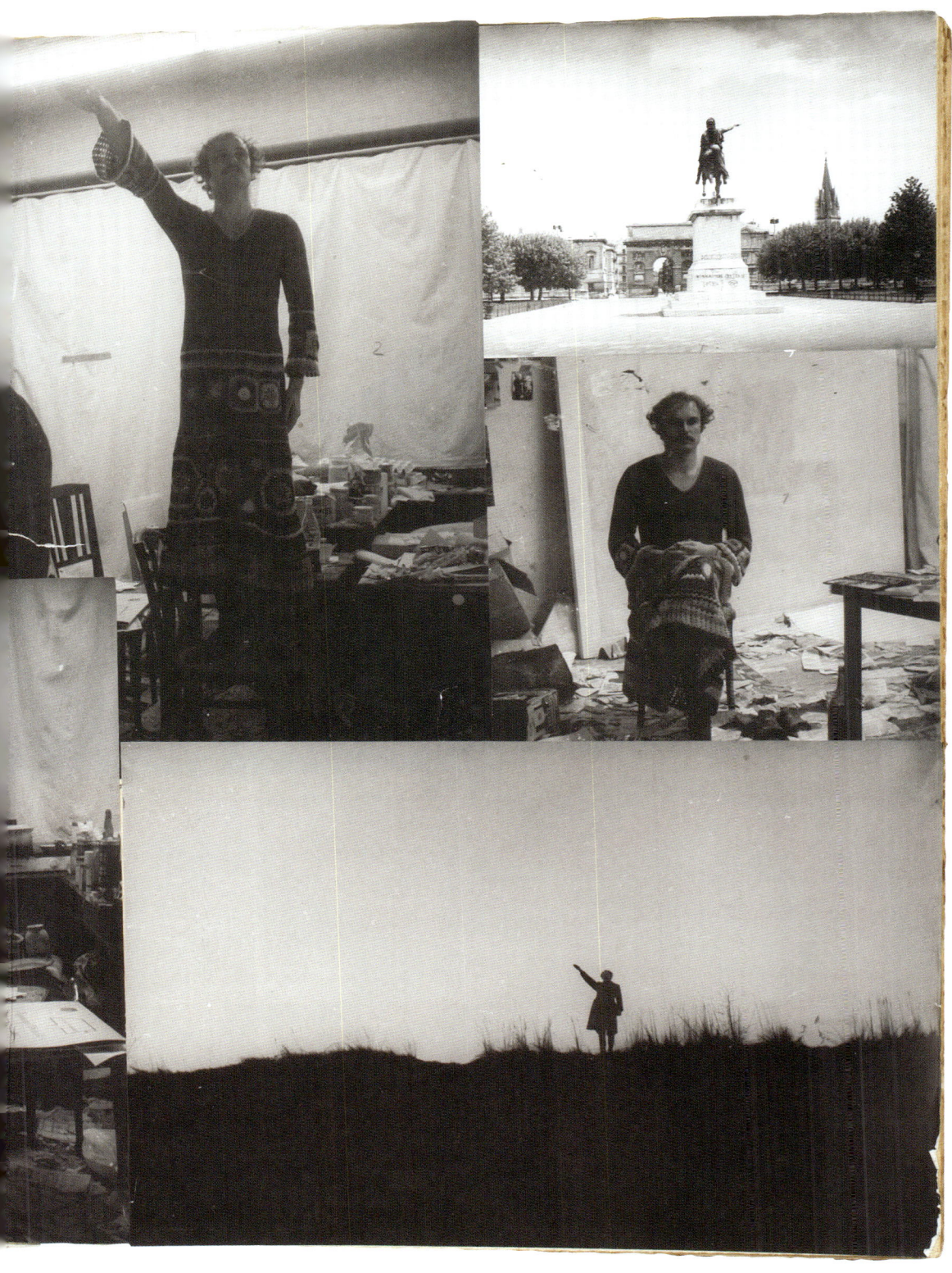

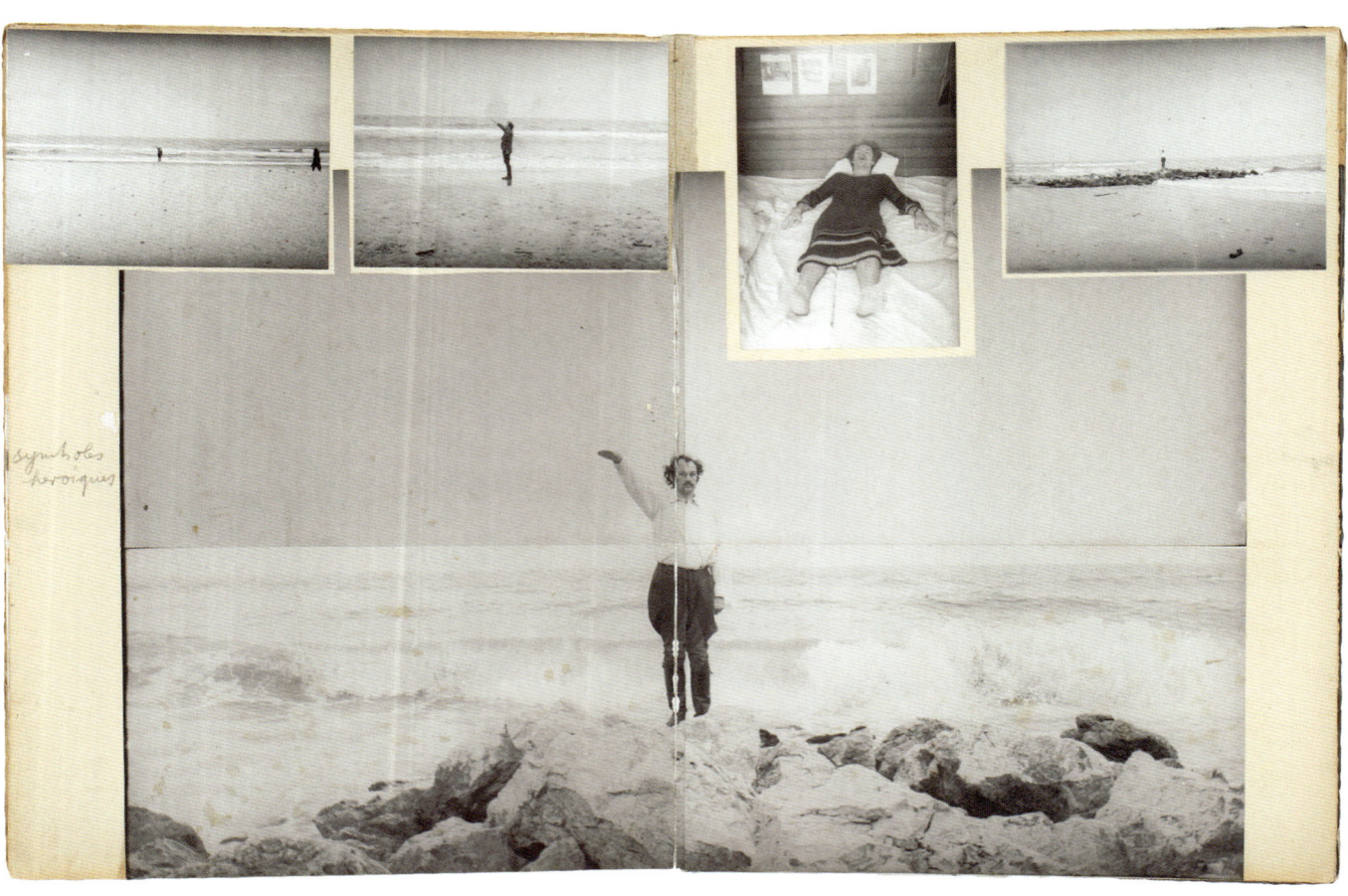

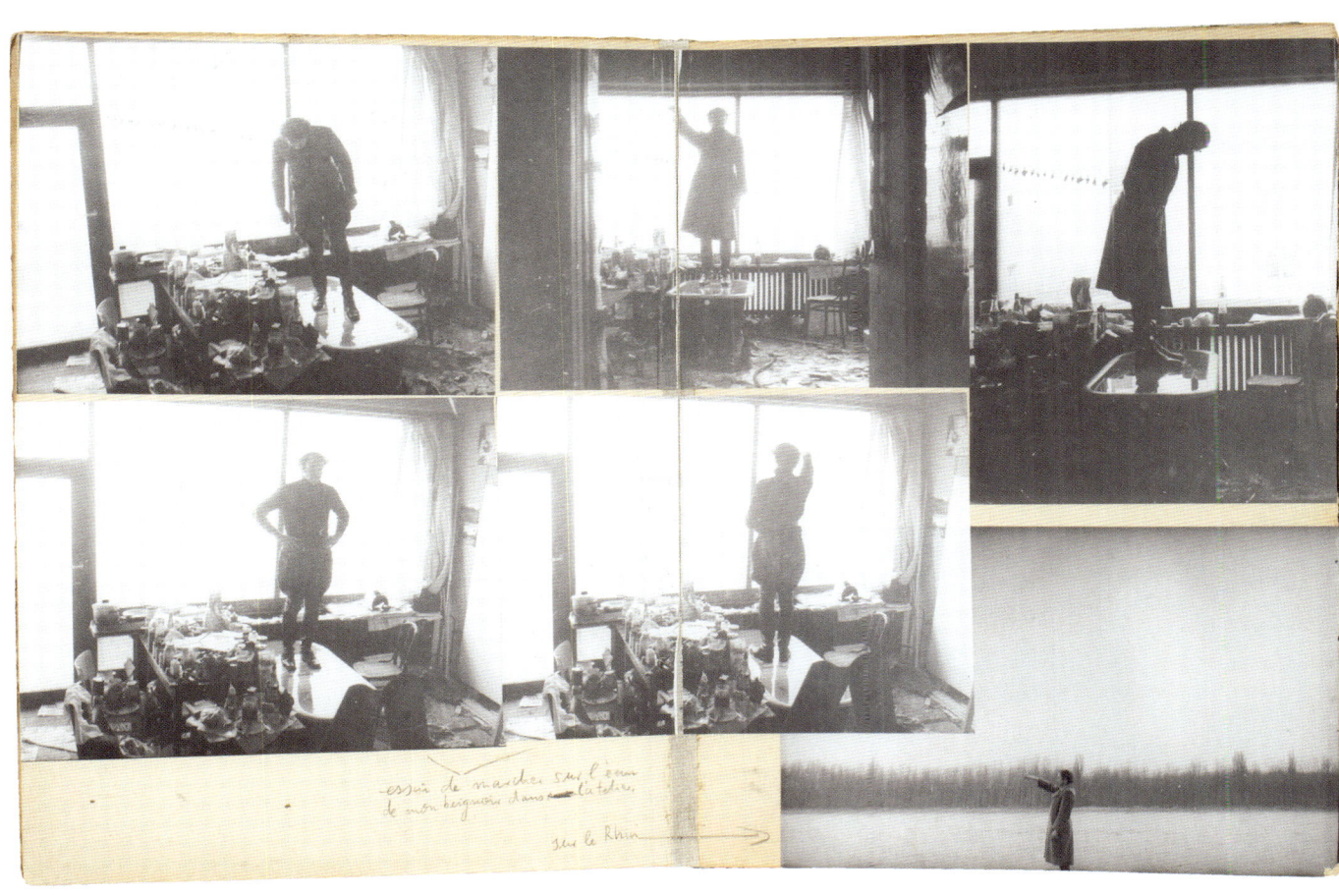

essai de marcher sur l'eau
de mon baignoir dans l'atelier

sur le Rhin

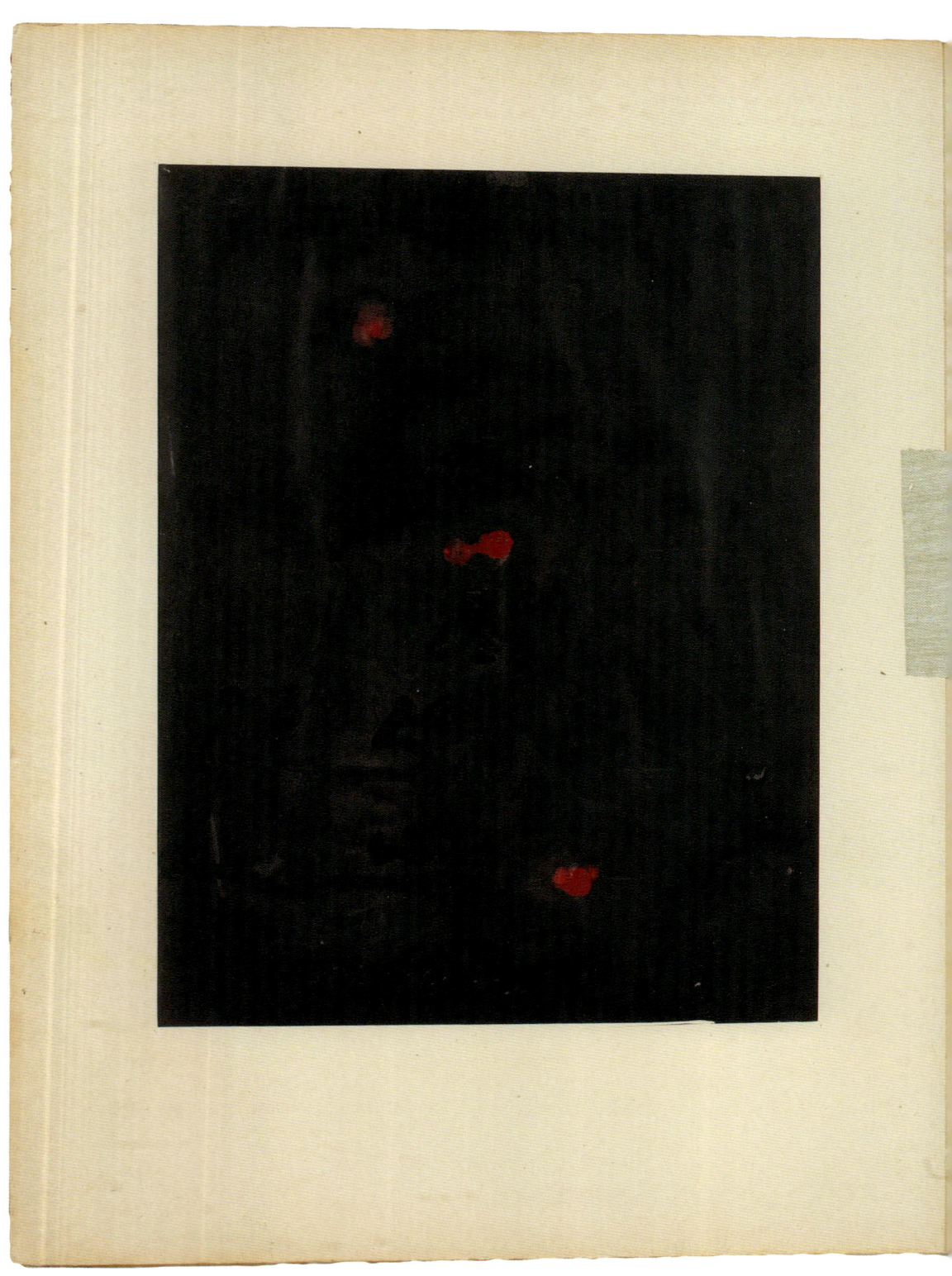

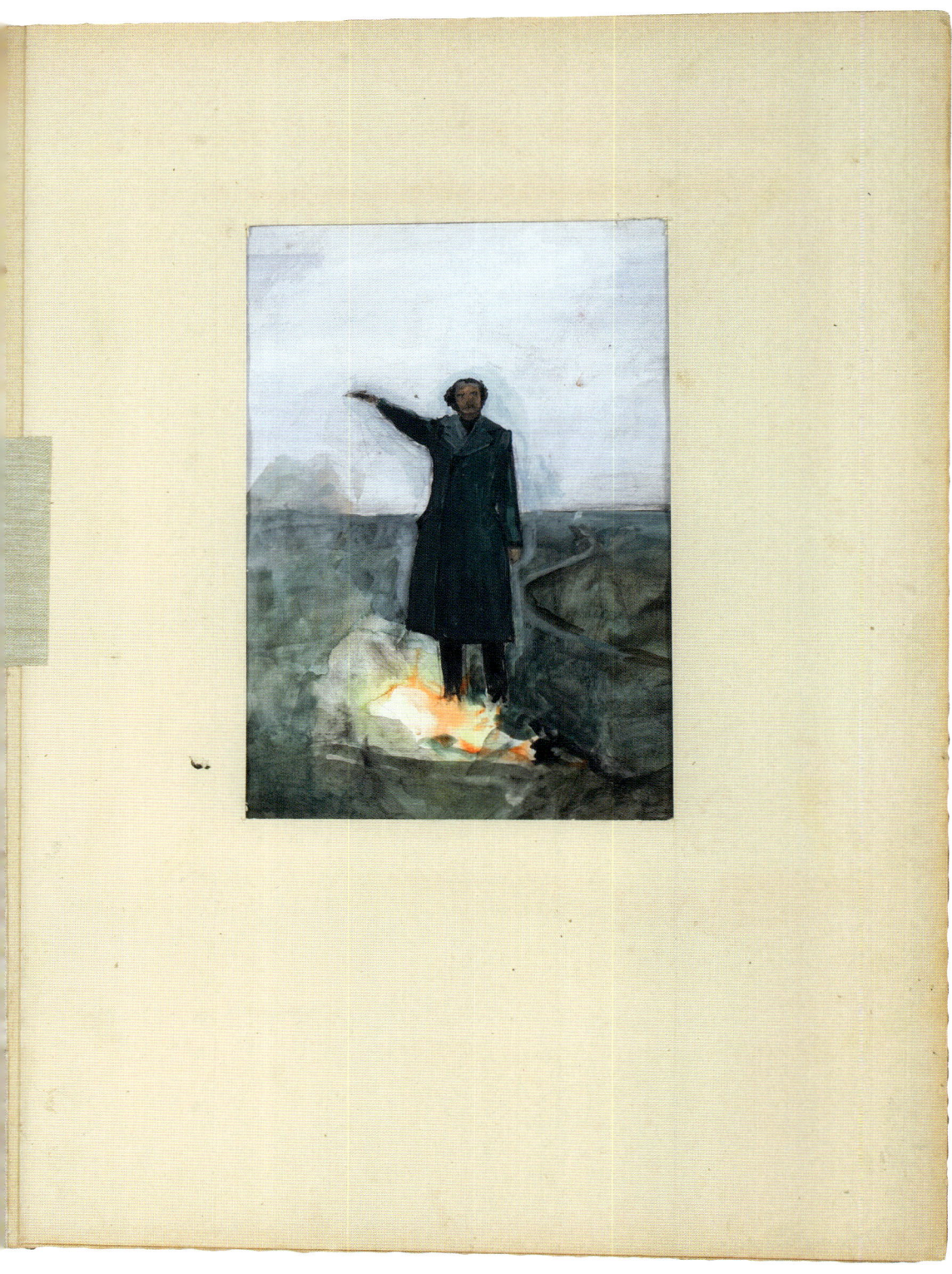

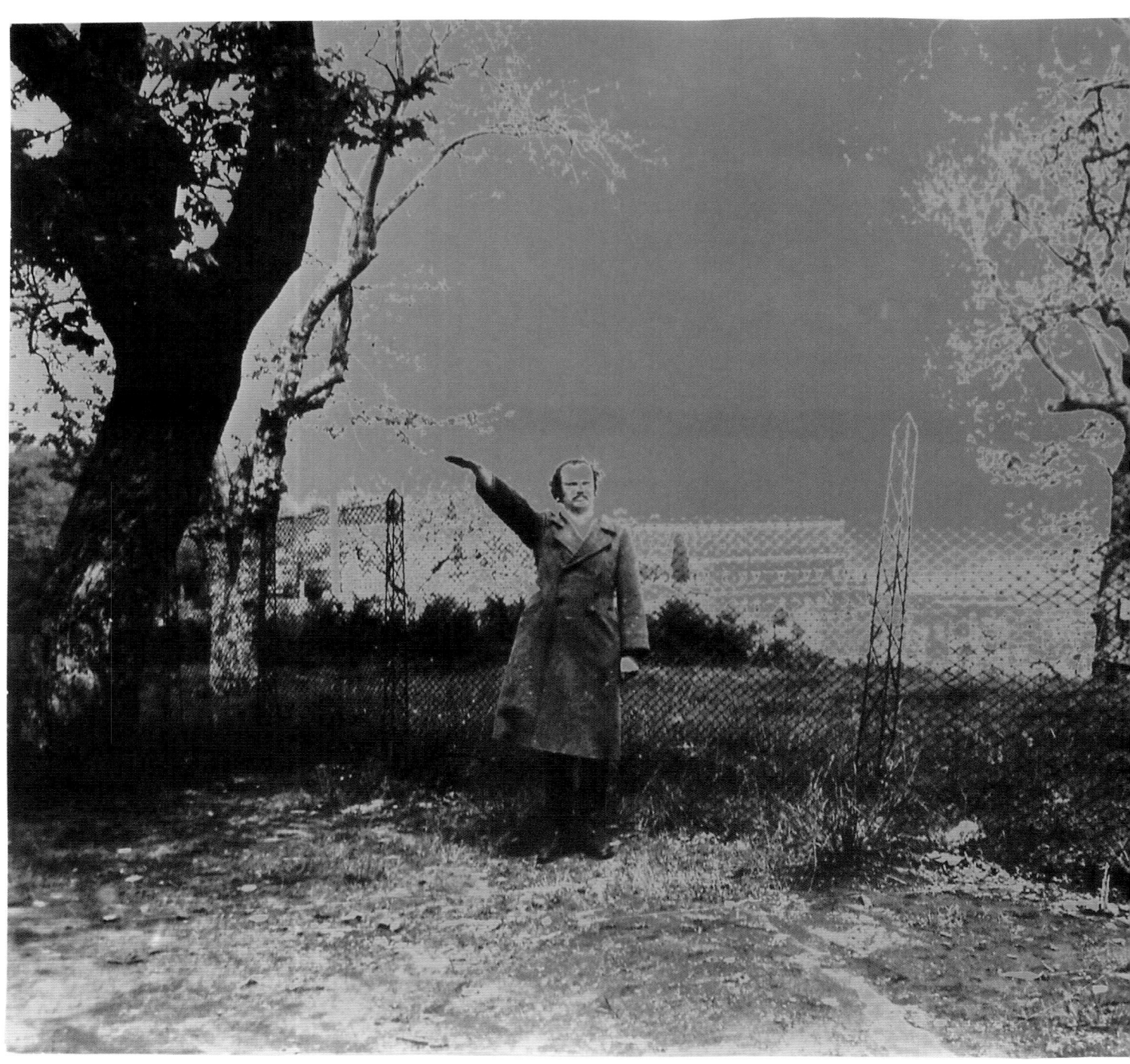

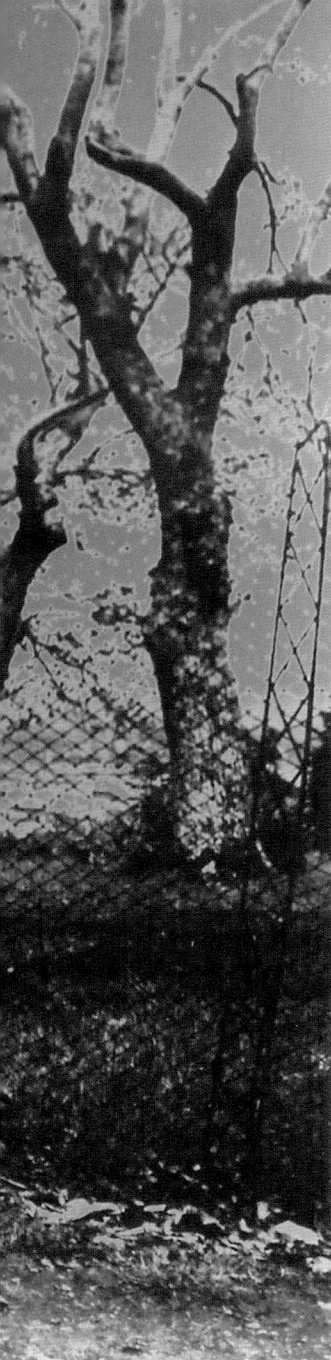

BESETZUNG (OCCUPATION), 1969–2016
Solarised silver gelatin print
30 × 40.5 cm
Hall Collection

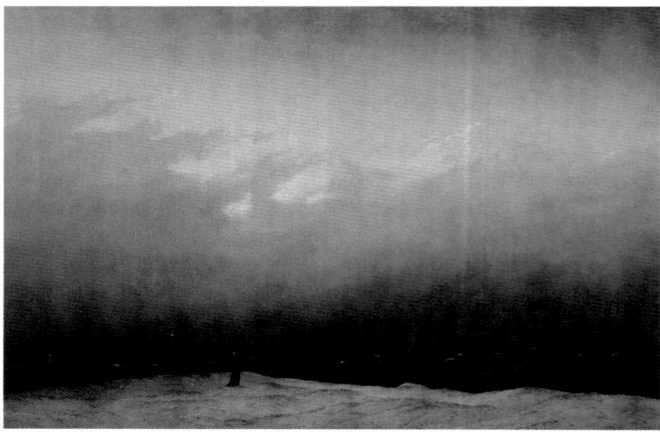

Caspar David Friedrich (1774–1840)
Der Mönch am Meer (*Monk by the Sea*), 1808–10
Oil on canvas, 110 × 171.5 cm

FÜR JEAN GENET (FOR JEAN GENET), 1969

Anselm Kiefer's book, *Für Jean Genet* (1969), formerly in the collection of Georg and Elke Baselitz, comprises 24 pages of original photographs, juxtaposed with watercolours, graphite inscriptions, hair and canvas strips on cardboard. It is closely related to another book by Kiefer, *Heroische Sinnbilder* (*Heroic Symbols*; 1969), and the French translation of the term *Heroische Sinnbilder* as *symboles héroïques* appears as a caption in *Für Jean Genet*, indicating the connection between these projects.

The original photographs shown in both books relate to Kiefer's performance project or 'action', *Occupations*, for which he travelled across Europe. This was no typical student excursion: on this journey, he staged the taboo 'Sieg Heil' salute in a number of historically and culturally charged European locations, many with some trace of an imperial past. These important books – the incubators for ideas that Kiefer has continued to develop throughout his career – were not published in an edition, but unique iterations of each do exist. For instance, there is a version of *Für Jean Genet* in the collection of the Art Gallery of New South Wales, Sydney, which does not include Kiefer's watercolours of roses, but does include actual dried roses; neither does it include any photographs of Kiefer saluting 'on location', but it does include many photographs of the artist rehearsing his *Occupations* 'action' in his Karlsruhe studio, preparing for, or staging, the salute in various outfits, as well as naked, standing over a bathtub.

On the front cover of the Hall Collection version of *Für Jean Genet* – a book that includes both indoor and outdoor photographs – Kiefer is shown giving the salute in the Place Royale du Peyrou in Montpellier, France. This photograph is pasted under one of his watercolours of a rose, a humorous juxtaposition as one of the lateral stems of the rose seems to be echoing Kiefer's saluting gesture. The artist visually alludes to the publications of the French activist, novelist, and playwright Jean Genet (1910–1986), a hero figure of the post-war Existentialist movement, whose transgressive writings, especially his provocative portrayals of homosexuality and criminality, intrigued Kiefer.

Genet's second novel, *Miracle de la rose* (1946), was written while the author was incarcerated during the Second World War, and was also informed by his memories of confinement at the Mettray Penal Colony in the late 1920s. A sense of confinement is effectively conveyed in the claustrophobic studio photographs (pp.20–21) included by Kiefer in the various versions of *Für Jean Genet*, which, in addition to suggesting the secret lair of a megalomaniac, could almost function as a stand-in for Genet's cell. Genet's poetic debut novel, *Notre Dame des Fleurs* (1943), was also written from prison and featured a fictionalised alter ego, a trans woman named Divine, likely the inspiration for Kiefer's cross-dressing in *Für Jean Genet*. Other publications by Genet known to Kiefer included *Funeral Rites* (1948) and *The Thief's Journal* (1949). In the former, the author fantasises about 'sleeping with the enemy' during the Nazi occupation of France. Susan Sontag has observed that this is 'one of the first texts that showed the erotic allure fascism exercised on someone who is not a fascist'. Kiefer reacts to various sources in *Für Jean Genet*, a complex compilation of artistic reflections on Genet's literature, and much more besides.

The absurdist quality of the front cover of *Für Jean Genet* is carried over inside the book. In a double-page spread of photographs of Kiefer saluting in Sète, (p.22), he appears to be responding to the Romantic art of Caspar David Friedrich (1774–1840), notably *Der Mönch am Meer* (*Monk by the Sea*; 1808–10; above), and *Wanderer über dem Nebelmeer* (*Wanderer above the Sea of Fog*; 1818).

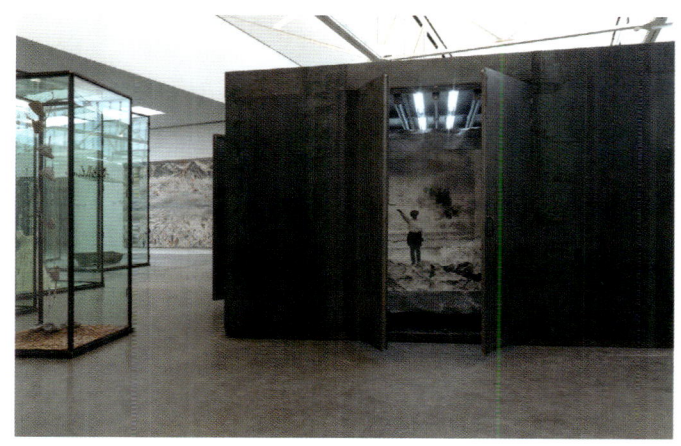

Anselm Kiefer
Occupations, 2010, installation view
at Gagosian gallery, New York

He also includes a photograph of himself in a crocheted dress, lying face up and open-mouthed on an attic-room bed (possibly another reference to Genet's character Divine). This collage arrangement deliberately undercuts the seriousness of the salute and any Friedrich-esque sense of the sublime. Kiefer was also conscious that Friedrich had been misused as a 'showcase' artist for National Socialism; that the reputation of the Romantic artist he so greatly admired had been tainted by association. The Sète sequence of photographs suggest that state of 'contamination'.

There is one page of name inscriptions in *Für Jean Genet*, which at first glance seems quite random. Kiefer groups together 'Caspar David Friedrich', 'Heraklit' (possibly a reference to lectures delivered by the philosopher Martin Heidegger (1889–1976) at the University of Freiburg in 1943/4 on the thoughts of Heraclitus); 'Dollmann' (most likely Friedrich Dollmann (1882–1944), the German general who commanded the 7th Army during the Invasion of France in the Second World War); 'Ludwig II von Bayern' (1845–1886); 'Ernst Jünger' (1895–1998) a decorated soldier and author who turned against Nazi totalitarianism by 1943; 'Richard Wagner'; 'Jean Genet'; 'Schopenhauer' (1788–1860); 'Joseph Beuys' (1921–1986) who would later become Kiefer's mentor when he enrolled at the Kunstakademie Düsseldorf in 1970; 'Adolf Hitler' (1889–1945); 'Hiob' (German for 'Job'); 'Elisabeth von Österreich' (1837–1898); Madame de Staël (1766–1817) the French woman of letters who published the book *De l'Allemagne* in 1813 that championed Romanticism; 'Jeanne d'Arc' (1412–1431); 'Mariana Alcoforado' (1640–1723) associated with the publication *Letters of a Portuguese Nun* of 1669; and finally, 'Jason' (the mythological hero of the Argonauts).

There are some connections between these names. For instance, there is a sequence of photographs in *Für Jean Genet* devoted to the residences of the reclusive 'Swan King' Ludwig II (p.18), who was a fervent devotee of both Louis XIV (1638–1715) and the composer Richard Wagner. Additionally, there are some parallels between the fantasies of the Bavarian king and the fantasies of Hitler, who also adored Wagner, and who envisioned military conquests and occupations in his residence in the Bavarian Alps.

Whether through indoor or outdoor photographs, what comes across in *Für Jean Genet* is an overwhelming sense of isolation. This is derived not just from the lone saluting figure but also from the trappings of monarchism and the ruins and symbols of past regimes. It is a visual exploration of hubris syndrome, a disorder characterised by narcissism, grandiosity, and a conflation of personal interests with those of the nation.

Christian Weikop

2

BESETZUNG (OCCUPATION), 1969–2016

This photograph relates to Anselm Kiefer's notorious performance, or 'action', of 1969, *Occupations*, in which he performed the taboo *'Sieg Heil'* salute in various European locations. On this 'tour' he saluted in front of the statue of Louis XIV in Montpellier; facing the Mediterranean Sea in nearby Sète; as well as at the Roman necropolis in Alyscamps, Arles. In Switzerland he saluted in Bellinzona. In Italy he saluted under the colonnades of the Colosseum and at St Peter's Basilica in Rome; among the ruins of the forum at Paestum; in Caprarola; in Pompeii; and even by the crater of Vesuvius.

This *Occupations* photograph is a re-exposed, solarised image, making it difficult to identify the location

3

HEROISCHE SINNBILDER (SELBSTPORTRÄT) (HEROIC SYMBOLS (SELF PORTRAIT)), 1970

Acrylic and charcoal on wood panel
250 × 122 cm
Hall Collection

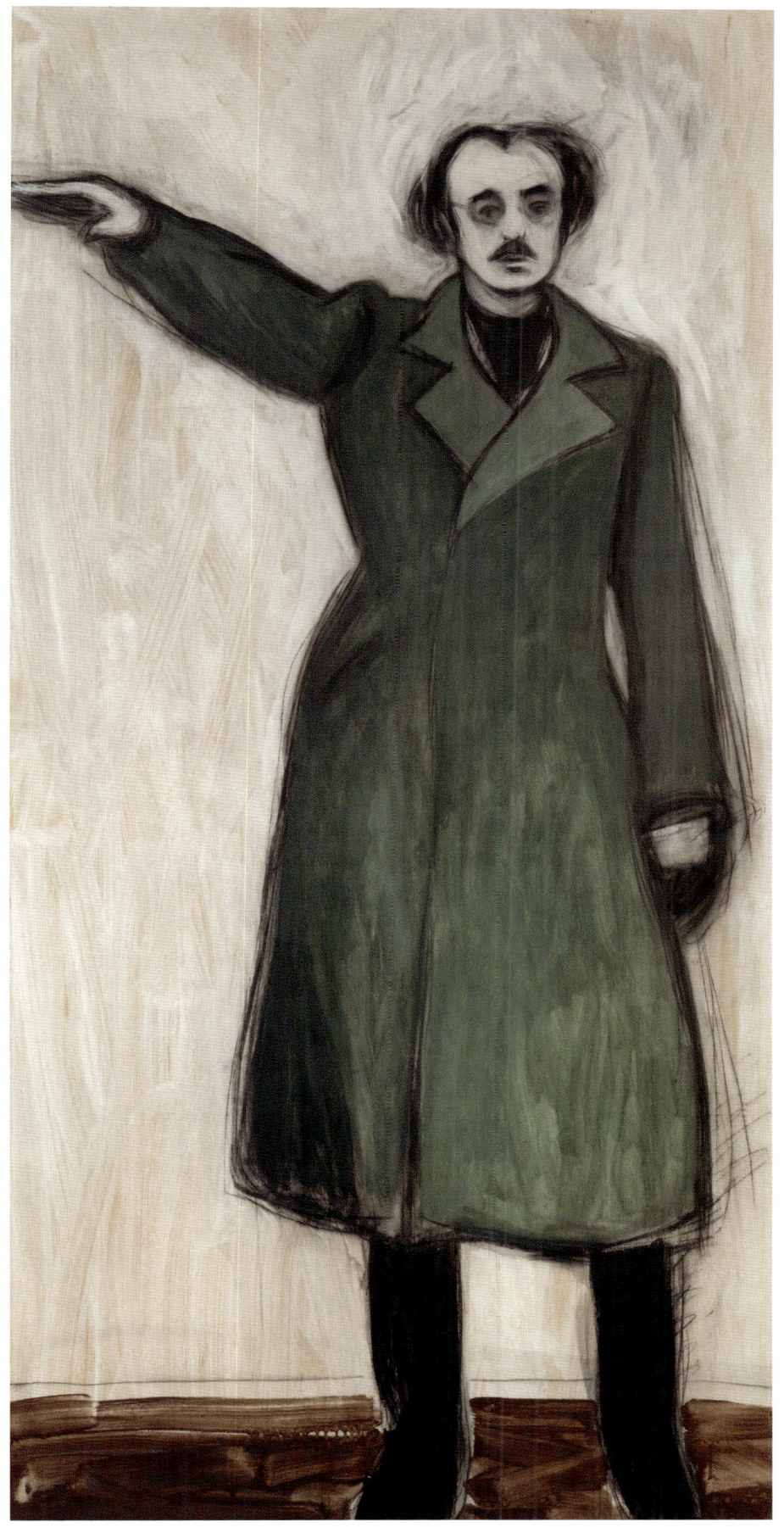

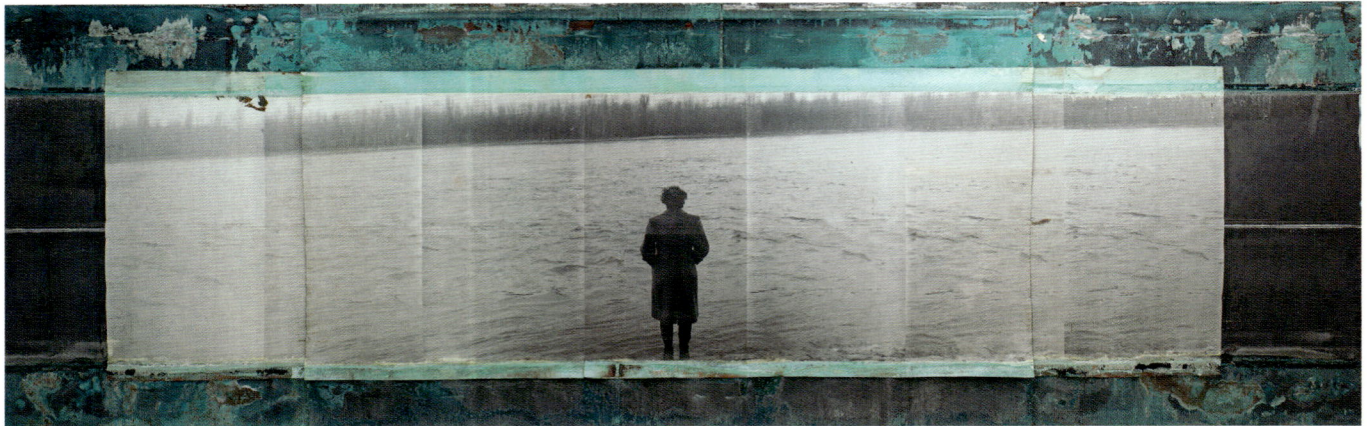

Anselm Kiefer
Der Rhein (The Rhine), 1969–2012
Electrolysis on gelatin silver print
mounted on lead, 380 × 1100 cm

as the topographical details are indistinct. Comparing it with other images from the same sequence makes it easier to ascertain the location, which is in fact Caprarola, a town in the Lazio region of central Italy, 60 kilometres north of Rome. The solarisation bestows a spectral quality to the image. In addition to the saluting Kiefer, the only forms that can be discerned are the ghostly trees and what appears to be a wire fence behind the artist. The photograph is disconcerting because it triggers thoughts of Nazi concentration camps, particularly of the Buchenwald camp in the forest of Ettersberg, with its electrified fences and towers.

In 2010 Kiefer used this image for a work on a much larger scale. He enlarged the photograph to 240 × 430 cm using photographic paper on lead. In this larger work the photograph looks as if it is fading away, just as the use of lead lends a memorial gravity and permanence. Similar blown-up photographs were used in Kiefer's installation *Occupations* (p.29) at the Gagosian gallery, New York. This consisted of 76 *Occupations* photographs, printed on burlap and mounted on lead, placed within a steel container, with the doors sufficiently ajar to catch a glimpse of the saluting Kiefer on the first lead sheet. The installation gave a sense of a forbidden archive, a Pandora's Box of historical memory. Kiefer observed: 'If we don't remember what we have done, we will do the same thing again.'[1]

Although this Hall Collection photograph of Caprarola was not used in Kiefer's 1969 books, *Für Jean Genet* and *Heroische Sinnbilder*, or in his 1975 photoessay, *Besetzungen* (*Occupations*), published in the German neo-avant-garde art magazine *Interfunktionen*, another photograph from Caprarola *was* included in *Interfunktionen*, as the penultimate image of the sequence.[2] It shows Kiefer saluting at the top of the double entrance ramps to the imposing Renaissance mansion, Villa Farnese. In its monumentality, the Villa Farnese

photograph echoes the photograph that opened the *Interfunktionen* essay, with a saluting Kiefer dramatically framed by the pruned branches of a plane tree at the Place Royale du Peyrou in Montpellier, a photograph first used in his book *Für Jean Genet*. This was a low-angle shot that emulated the techniques of the National Socialist cinematographer Leni Riefenstahl (1902–2003), demonstrating that Kiefer was not just documenting a performance, but also exploring the aesthetics of fascism.

The *Occupations* photoessay was a travesty of a travelogue, laid out under the laconic caption: '*Anselm Kiefer. Zwischen Sommer und Herbst 1969 habe ich die Schweiz, Frankreich und Italien besetzt. Ein paar Photos*' ('Anselm Kiefer. Between Summer and Autumn 1969, I occupied Switzerland, France and Italy. A few photos'). Kiefer presented a sequence of eighteen dramatic photographs in which he performed the taboo '*Sieg Heil*' salute. The photoessay alienated some fellow artists, advertisers, and a section of the magazine's readership, who, at this time, all fiercely reacted, without more closely reflecting on what Kiefer was trying to achieve. The withdrawal of support effectively cut off funding for the publication, leading to the dissolution of *Interfunktionen*. Benjamin Buchloh, the last editor of the publication, would later defend the work, stating that *Occupations* was 'a real working through of German history. You have to inhabit it to overcome it'.[3]

When exploring Kiefer's huge studio complex in Croissy-Beaubourg, it is striking how many artworks reference his early *Occupations* action from 1969. Blown-up photographs mounted on lead, or paintings that were based on these photographs, can be seen throughout the studio. Some ghostly images of the saluting Kiefer have even surfaced on the sides of the corrugated concrete towers that can be seen in this studio and elsewhere, like an unsettling avatar of the artist. Kiefer has resurrected his *Occupations*

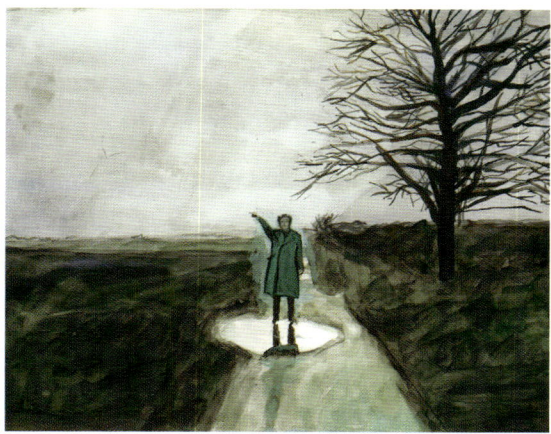

Anselm Kiefer
Ohne Titel (Heroische Sinnbilder)
(*Untitled (Heroic Symbols)*), 1969
Watercolour, gouache and charcoal on paper,
35.8 × 45.4 cm

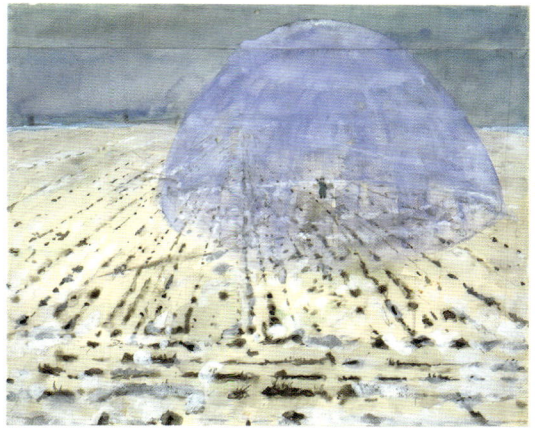

Anselm Kiefer
Jeder Mensch steht unter seiner Himmelskugel
(*Everyone Stands Under His Own Dome of Heaven*), 1970
Watercolour, gouache and graphite on paper, 40 × 48 cm

project many times in different media. His large-scale *Der Rhein* (1969–2012) again blows up a photographic image from 1969 and mounts it on lead (p.32). For this work, Kiefer wore the heavy Wehrmacht overcoat belonging to his father, seen in the *Heroische Sinnbilder (Selbsporträt)* painting in the Hall Collection (pp.30–31).

Facing the much-mythologised Rhine River, Kiefer also adopted the *Rückenfigur* motif made iconic by his hero, the Romantic landscape painter Caspar David Friedrich (see also p.28). Kiefer does not salute in this piece, but stands on the bank of the Rhine with his hands in his pockets. He is located in Germany but looks out to France. The source photograph of this work comes from a sequence he took by the Rhine in 1969, in which he stares out to the opposite bank, or is preparing, or enacting, the '*Sieg Heil*' salute. Another photograph from the same sequence, where he is saluting, can be found in *Für Jean Genet*, captioned in French, *Sur le Rhin* (*On the Rhine*). Undoubtedly, these 1969 photographs that capture his extraordinary 'action' unlock a great deal in Kiefer's universe of eternal recurrence: of history repeating itself. Somehow everything goes back to the beginning.

Christian Weikop

3

HEROISCHE SINNBILDER (SELBSTPORTRÄT) (HEROIC SYMBOLS (SELF PORTRAIT)), 1970

This life-sized self-portrait shows the artist donning his father's Wehrmacht overcoat and delivering a '*Sieg Heil*' salute. Kiefer's moustache makes him look vaguely Hitlerian, but he does not have the same Prussian military crew cut as Hitler. Instead, his hair looks unkempt,

resembling certain photographs of the scientist, Albert Einstein (1879–1955), with his distinctive messy hairstyle. Kiefer's face and saluting hand are deathly white, unnervingly so, as if he were an apparition from Germany's Nazi past. The work has a muted tonality due to being painted on a wood panel. The central figure stands out against the nondescript background, recalling the performative self-portraits of the Austrian Expressionist Egon Schiele (1890–1918), where neutral backdrops provide no distraction from the focus on the figure.

This painting is related to Kiefer's notorious *Occupations* photographs, which first surfaced in his early unique books, such as *Heroische Sinnbilder* and *Für Jean Genet* (pp.17–25), both from 1969. In *Für Jean Genet* there is also a small watercolour self-portrait of Kiefer wearing the same overcoat and delivering a salute in a field, his feet concealed by a burning pyre in an image of potential self-immolation. These books also contain photographs of Kiefer staging the provocative salute wearing alternative outfits – including a white shift, a crocheted dress, and a pair of outlandish nineteenth-century pantaloons – thereby subverting the stiff-shirt identity of the archetypal uniformed Nazi. Equally, Kiefer's changes of attire could suggest that fascism comes in many guises, that it can morph over time, and that it is not set in any one form of representation.

Between 1969 and 1971 Kiefer created a number of oil paintings and watercolours in which he portrayed himself, in both real and imagined settings, delivering the '*Sieg Heil*' salute. For one of these works, now in the collection of the Metropolitan Museum of Art, New York, he painted himself rehearsing his *Occupations* 'action' in a stark landscape near Karlsruhe. Stood next to a single skeletal tree, it appears as if he is commanding nature, with the branch of the tree echoing the angle of his salute (above). It is a bleak image of an isolated figure that deflates all the pomp and ceremony usually evident in photographic or

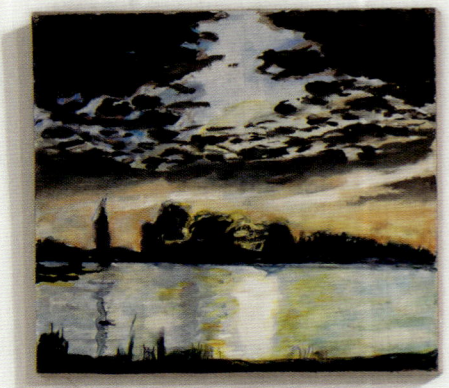

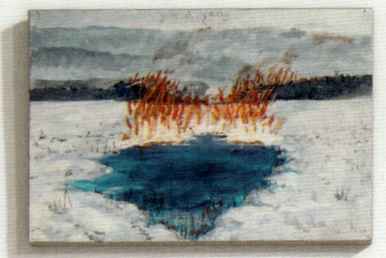

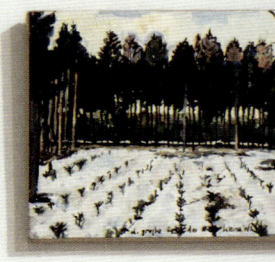

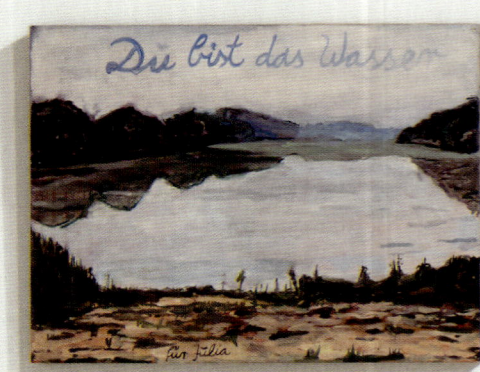

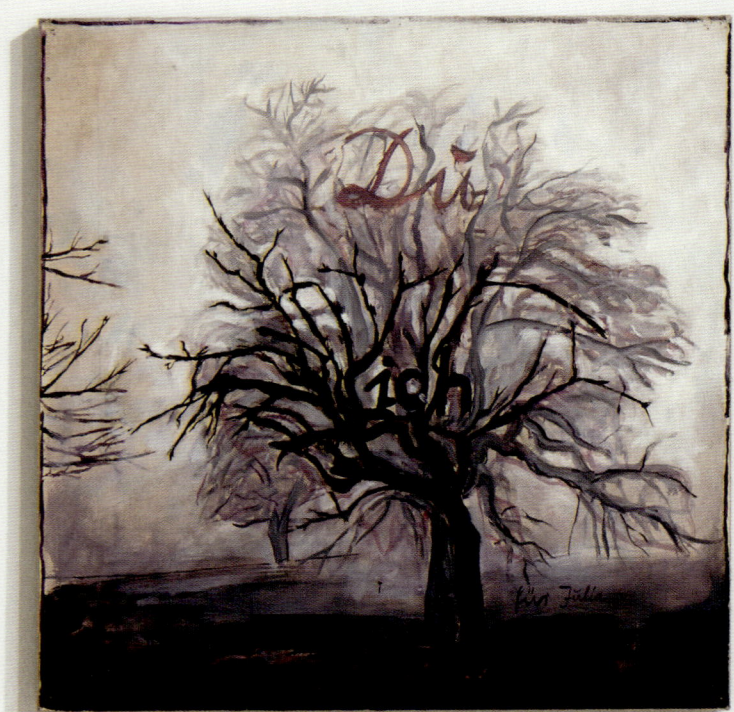

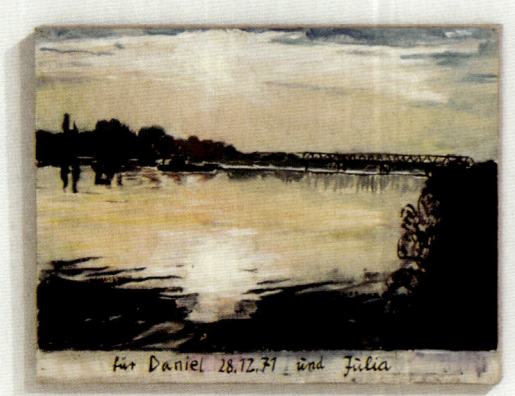

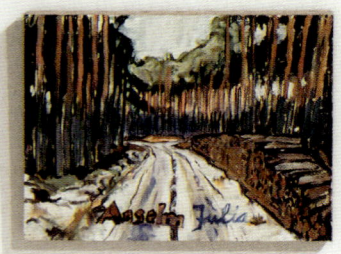

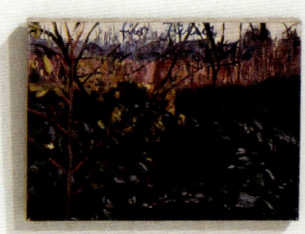

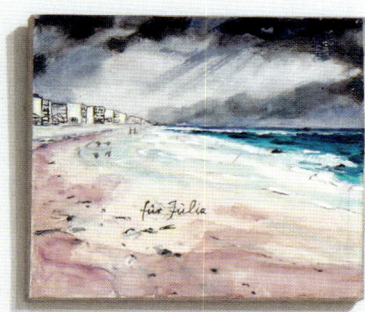

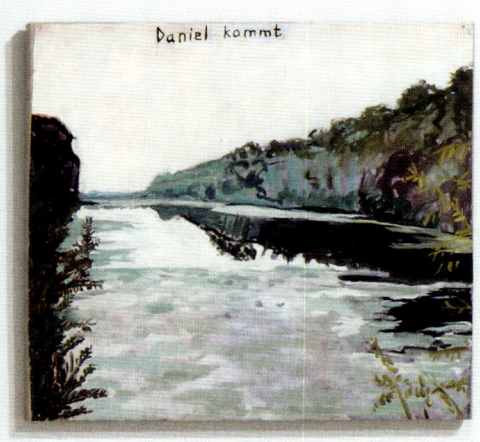

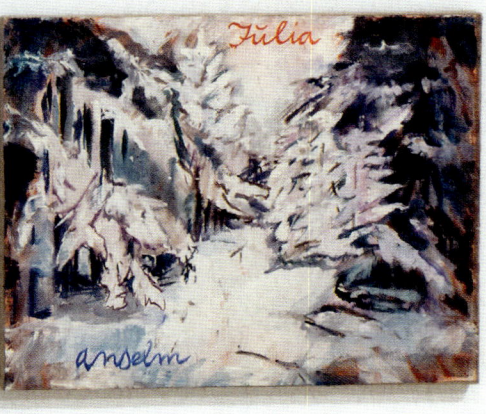

ICH – DU (I – YOU), 1971

Oil on canvas, mounted on canvas
Dimensions of the individual paintings,
clockwise from top left: 51.5 × 56 cm,
33 × 47.5 cm, 32 × 42 cm, 40 × 47 cm,
57 × 62 cm, 98 × 95.5 cm, 53 × 67 cm,
28.5 × 38 cm, 32 × 42.5 cm, 50.5 × 64 cm,
48 × 62 cm; installation dimensions can vary
Hall Collection

film documentation of saluting National Socialists at mass rallies. This isolation is even more evident in the striking watercolour *Everyone Stands Under His Own Dome of Heaven* of 1970 (p.33), which, rather than presenting a life-sized self-portrait, shows a diminutive Kiefer seen from a great distance; a tiny, almost comically condensed figure, donning the same overcoat, and giving a salute in a kind of transparent hemisphere, suggestive of an ideological bubble or microcosm.

In 2007, as Kiefer prepared to move his studio to Paris, he rediscovered a cycle of eight oil paintings from 1970 entitled *Heroic Symbols* (now in the Würth Collection), which are related to the painting under consideration here. These works display a dreamy, almost Surrealist treatment, often imaginatively fusing together 'found' and original photographs present in the *Heroische Sinnbilder* and *Für Jean Genet* books. One of these rediscovered canvases, *Heroic Symbol VIII*, shows Kiefer's saluting figure standing before an enthroned Pope Pius XII (1876–1958), a controversial individual who maintained a public front of indifference and remained silent while German atrocities were committed during the Second World War. The Day-glo colours that the artist used to render the scene makes this a bizarre form of history painting.

In 1971 Kiefer attempted to show some of the *Heroic Symbols* paintings at the *Exhibition of the Association of German Artists* in Stuttgart, but the artworks were rejected, possibly because they were judged to have crossed a line, irrespective of whether or not they could be appreciated as ironic. And certainly, this *Heroische Sinnbilder* work in the Hall Collection cannot be explained solely in terms of it representing an ironic 'action' of 'occupying' Europe, or an act of ridiculing Hitler, as Charlie Chaplin (1889–1977) had done in his film *The Great Dictator* (1940). Especially when wearing his father's Wehrmacht uniform – the long coat, breeches, and boots – Kiefer was in fact attempting to

'occupy', in a bodily and psychological sense, the position of his father and his father's generation. This brings us to the most difficult aspect of this art 'action'. It is important to stress that Kiefer did not identify with fascism, rather, he was staging a performance. In a conversation with the German art historian Götz Adriani, however, the artist stated: 'I wanted to experience, through my own body, what that [National Socialism] was and how I'd behave.'[4] This was a critical process of self-questioning through a staged 're-experiencing'. Indeed, the word *Besetzung* (occupation) not only brings to mind military manoeuvres, or student sit-ins, but can also mean 'cathexis', a psychoanalytic Freudian term for 'holding fast'; an allocation of mental or emotional energy to a person, object, or idea. Kiefer's constant invoking of the saluting gesture in his art over his career suggests that, for him, this historical trauma cannot be emotionally released. The compulsion to repeat the salute over time and in various artistic contexts seems like a form Nietzschean eternal recurrence, bringing to mind Kiefer's own words: 'I think human beings have something not well constructed. There is definitely something wrong, because our conflicts continue ceaselessly.'[5]

Christian Weikop

4

ICH – DU (I – YOU), 1971

An old bare tree is set against a nebulous grey background; dark conifers contrast with snowy clearings; cloudy skies mirror in glittering lakes; horizontal stacks of felled brown timber on the side of a snowy forest path are juxtaposed with vertical tree trunks that suggest life and growth. *Ich – Du* is a group of eleven landscape paintings that deliberately flirt with a simple figurative language. They

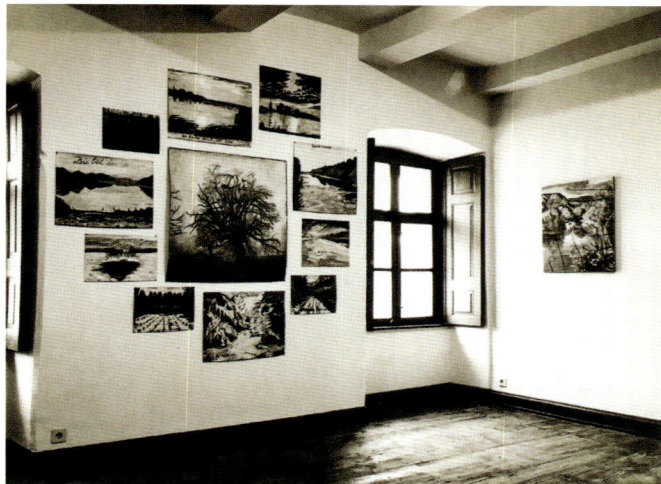

are centred around a roughly square image of a large tree. The bare trees, grey skies, and snow suggest that the paintings were all made in autumn and winter.

With a sense of natural harmony, the balanced compositions present complementary opposites, such as water and sky, light and dark, young and old, life and death, and earth and heaven. On a small painting featuring orange, flame-like structures in juxtaposition with light-blue water and snow, the artist wrote 'ying u. yang', referencing the cosmology concept of harmonious dichotomy in traditional Chinese philosophy. Etymologically, the character 'ying' defines the 'dark' side of the mountain, representing a cool, female, receptive energy, while the 'yang' is the 'light' side of the mountain, linked to a hot, male, active energy. Exhibited in all existence, ying and yang are believed to create a constant balance, connecting the earth with the sky, and the human realms with the cosmos.

There is a long tradition in German art, literature, and music to link landscapes with both the macro and the micro: a natural scene can symbolise the whole universe but also an individual human's inner feelings. In the late eighteenth and early nineteenth centuries, the Romantics placed new emphasis on the awe of nature, viewing emotion as an authentic source of aesthetic experience. The great power, sublimity, and beauty of the landscape took centre stage in paintings by Romantic artists including Caspar David Friedrich and Philipp Otto Runge (1777–1810). Their paintings represent a quiet encounter between the artist and nature, which is often spiritual (for example, see Friedrich's painting *Monk by the Sea*, p.28). The works indicate a pantheistic Christian faith: the mountains, trees, clouds, and the beautiful light speak of God.

The rise of Nazism in the 1930s saw a strong resurgence in the popularity of German Romantic culture. The genre of Romantic landscape painting was, therefore, associated with promoting nationalism and sometimes viewed sceptically. Kiefer painted *Ich – Du* less than 30 years after the end of the Second Word War. The composite work is one of many paintings and watercolours in Kiefer's large oeuvre that points towards the intertwined relationship of German landscapes with history and cultural memory. The paintings can also be interpreted as an invitation to free landscapes from associations with political ideologies, focusing instead on their connection to the universal cosmos and personal life. Like Friedrich's landscapes, *Ich – Du* presents quiet vistas, suggesting an encounter between nature and the artist/viewer in solitude. Painted in 1971 – the year that the artist and his wife at the time, Julia, moved to the village of Horrbach in the mountainous region of Odenwald – the work links Romantic ideas of the landscape with the artist's own biography. This period saw great changes in the artist's life: newly wed and in a new home, he made these paintings shortly before and after his first child, Daniel was born. The title *Ich – Du* as well as the intimate inscriptions – '*für Julia*', '*Anselm Julia*', '*Daniel kommt*', and '*für Daniel 28.12.1971*' – reference the artist's new family and the arrival of his son. Suggesting a private dialogue with nature, the landscape paintings combine universal concepts of harmonious duality that can be found in ancient Chinese cosmology as well as in Christianity, with Kiefer's highly personal experience of entering a marriage and having a child.

Ich – Du was bought by artist Georg Baselitz and his wife Elke in 1973, after it had been included in the *14 mal 14* exhibition at Staatliche Kunsthalle Baden-Baden. This series of group exhibitions, which ran under Director Klaus Gallwitz's reign from 1968 until 1973, featured young and emerging artists. The works of many now internationally acclaimed artists, including Georg Baselitz, Markus Lüpertz (b.1941), Gerhard Richter (b.1932), and

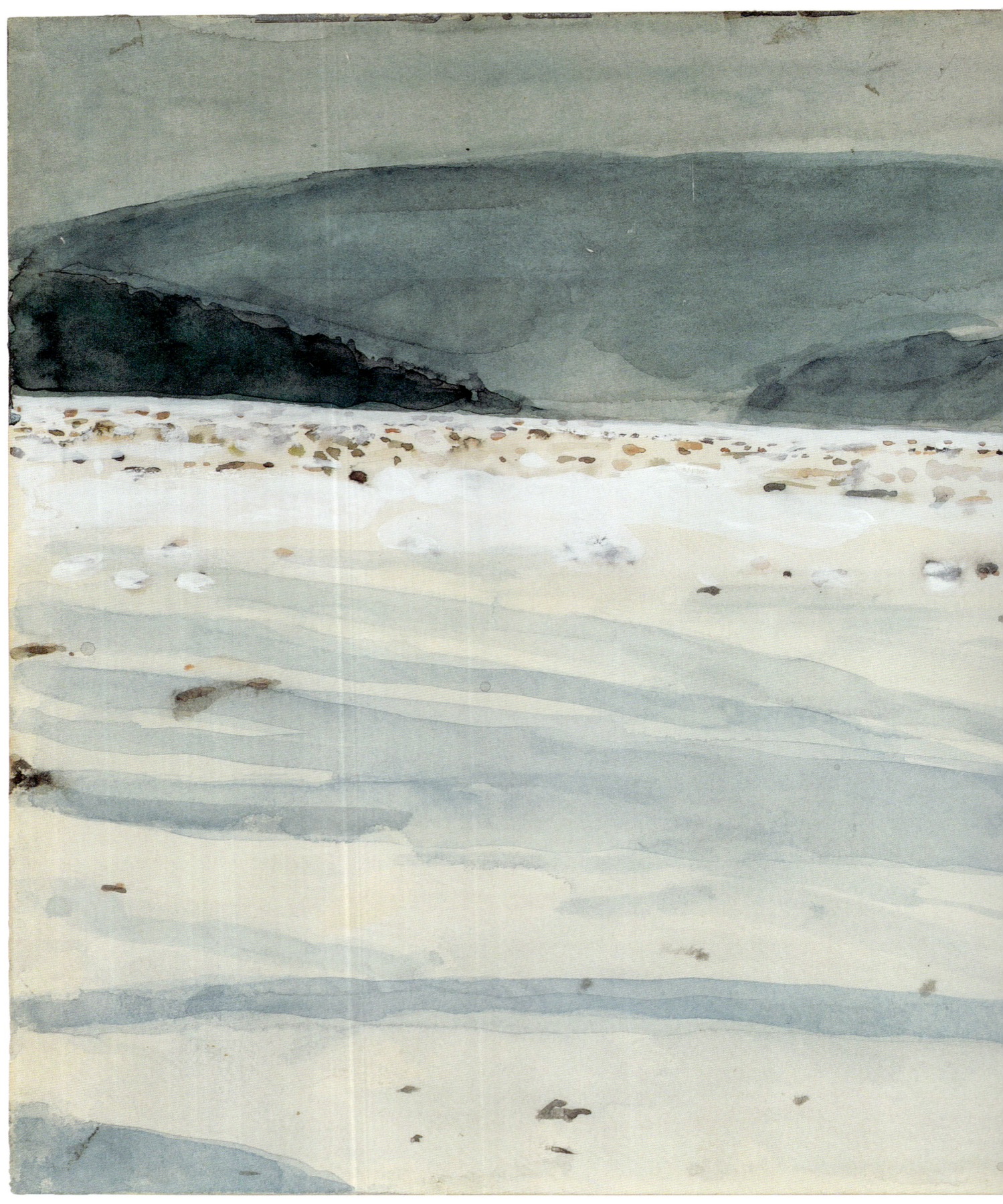

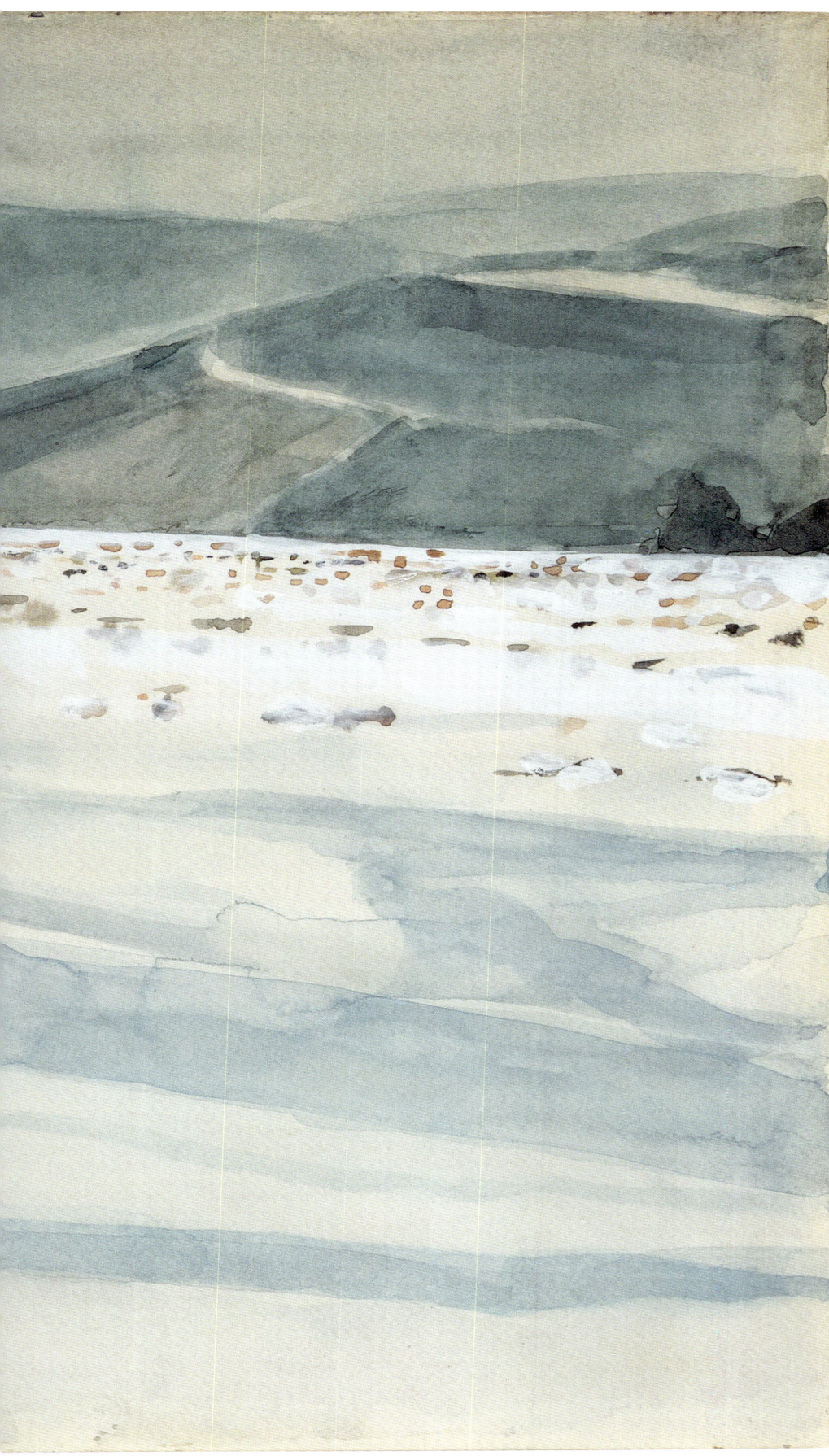

5

LANDSCHAFT BEI BUCHEN (LANDSCAPE NEAR BUCHEN), 1971

Watercolour and gouache on paper
24 × 34 cm
Hall Collection

6

WALD (_FOREST_), 1973–4
Watercolour on paper
17 × 24 cm
Hall Collection

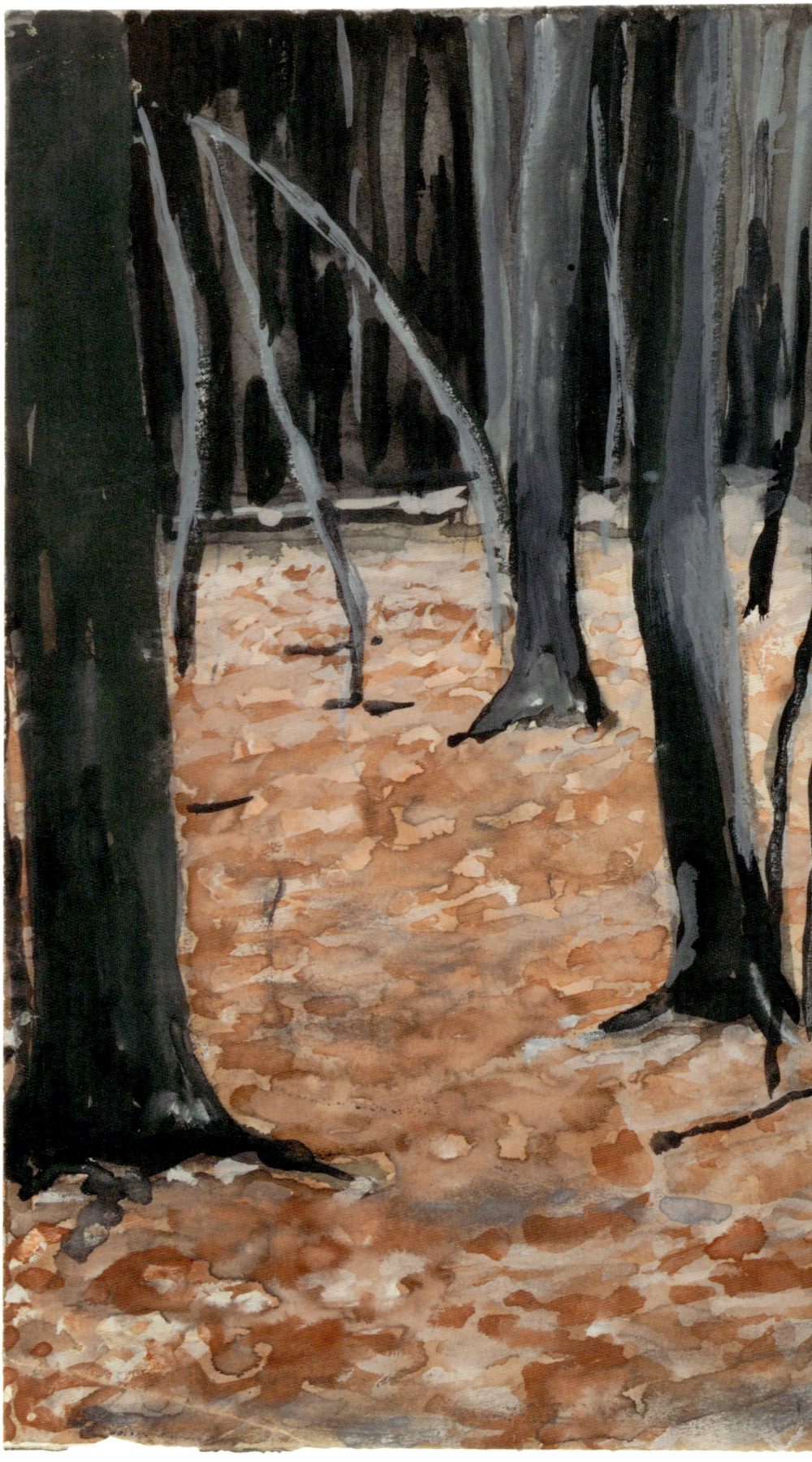

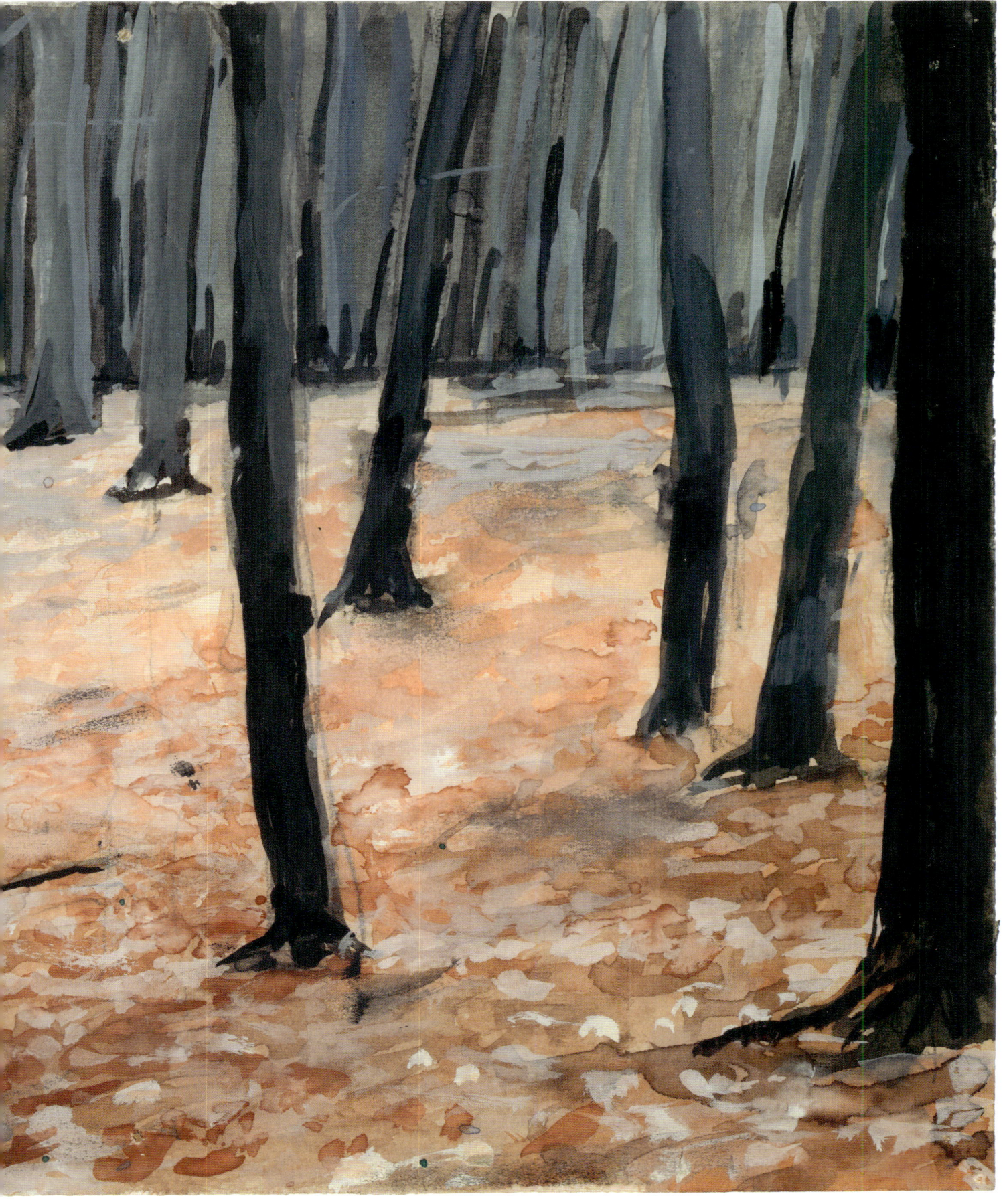

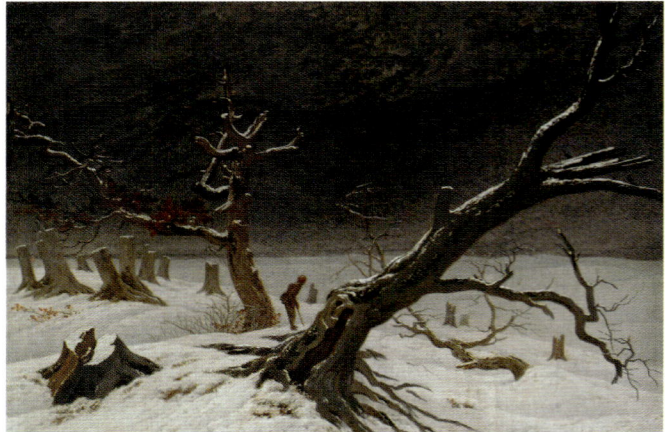

Caspar David Friedrich (1774–1840)
Winterlandschaft (*Winter Landscape*), 1811
Oil on canvas, 32.5 × 45 cm

Günther Uecker (b.1930), were exhibited here at the very beginning of their careers. Before it was acquired by the Halls in 2005, *Ich – Du* hung in Baselitz's home in Schloss Derneburg (p.37).

Lena Fritsch

5

LANDSCHAFT BEI BUCHEN (LANDSCAPE NEAR BUCHEN), 1971

In this small watercolour, a snow-blanketed field, painted in light grey and white watery hues, is juxtaposed with dark-grey mountains and ominous forests in the distance. The harmonious composition conveys an impression of lightness and silence. One can imagine being stood within this endless field of snow, breathing in the fresh, cold air, pervaded by a feeling of harmony with the surrounding landscape.

Landschaft bei Buchen is one of many watercolours by Anselm Kiefer in which he focuses his attention on the landscape. The artist first learnt to paint with watercolours as a child and he has used the medium throughout his career. This work was made in the same year that he and his first wife, Julia, moved to the Odenwald region in the Rhineland-Palatinate, an area known for its natural beauty. The town of Buchen, where Kiefer had his studio, is surrounded by a low, rolling range of mountains, valleys, wide fields, and dense forests. Kiefer's watercolour is a personal work, inspired by his own life and surroundings; yet, at the same time, given the backdrop of post-war Germany, it also speaks of the inextricably intertwined relationship of German landscapes with culture and history.

Kiefer's empty winter landscape recalls the paintings of Romantic movement artists, who captured the quiet, sublime encounters between men and the natural world, evident in works such as Caspar David Friedrich's *Winterlandschaft* (*Winter Landscape*; 1811; now in the collections of the Staatliches Museum Schwerin; above).[6] It is also reminiscent of the music of the Romantic period, such as the iconic lieder cycle *Winterreise* (*Winter Journey*; 1827) by Franz Schubert (1797–1828), in which the protagonist wanders isolated among snowy fields and streets, projecting his feelings onto the landscape. The Nazis abused the German's affinity to the landscape to support their patriotic ideologies and ideas of a fatherland; in their hands, the sublime landscape motif became a political instrument. Featuring a wide, empty snow field, Kiefer's quiet work contemplates this complex cultural memory of the German landscape.

Landschaft bei Buchen is typical of Kiefer's watercolours in that it is both literally and conceptually lighter in character than his paintings and installations. However, this does not make it any less powerful: the immediacy and intimacy of the size and medium serve only to show Kiefer's great skills to paint lyrical, subtly beautiful compositions that convey a sublime aura.

Lena Fritsch

6

WALD (FOREST), 1973–4

This watercolour of a forest is dominated by dark-brown and grey-toned tree trunks, which extend upwards, beyond the picture plane, and red-brown leaves covering the ground. The greys and transparent white elements on the leaves convey an impression of coldness, perhaps hinting

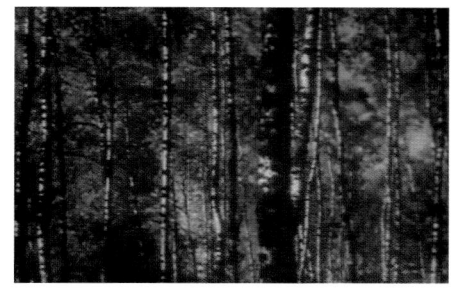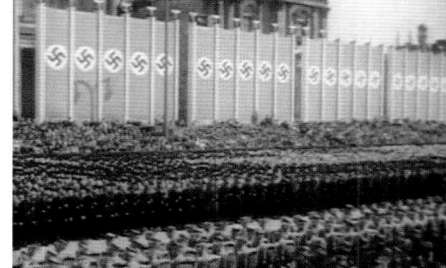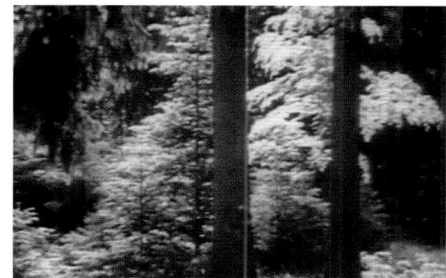

Film stills of *Ewiger Wald* (*Eternal Forest*), 1936
Directed by Hanns Springer and Rolf von Sonjevski-Jamrowski, produced by Albert Graf von Pestalozza

at snow and ice. The fact that the upper parts of the trees are not visible locates us deep within this dense forest scene. The vertical trunks contrast with the round shapes of the leaves, soil and snow on the ground, resulting in a compact, but well balanced, composition of the work.

Wald is one of many works in which Anselm Kiefer explores the motif of the forest. It was made while he lived in the mountainous region of the Odenwald, which is known for its natural beauty, as well as for its many folk tales and legends. In the heroic epic *Nibelungenlied* (*c.*1200), for example, the prince and dragon slayer Siegfried was killed while drinking from a spring in a wood thought to have been inspired by the Odenwald.

Kiefer and his first wife, Julia, moved to a small village in the Odenwald region in 1971. The village, Hornbach, was very close to forests, mountains, lush-green valleys, and raw quarries. It consisted of small houses and farms, many of which were built as early as the sixteenth and seventeenth centuries. Having grown up in Donaueschingen, a small town close to the Black Forest in south-western Germany, Kiefer was used to being surrounded by the woods. On a personal level, the calm *Wald* scene suggests an artist wandering around the Odenwald in solitude on a cold winter's day.

The forest has been a central part of German cultural history for centuries and is inextricably intertwined with German national identity.[7] In the fairy tales of the Brothers Grimm, Little Red Riding Hood meets the wolf in the forest; abandoned in the woods, Hansel and Gretel discover a witch's house; Snow White flees into the forest to find a small house in which seven dwarfs reside. The forest also became a particularly important topos in the context of the Romantic movement during the late eighteenth century, when people revolted against industrialisation. Paintings of forests by Caspar David Friedrich and Phillip Otto

Runge reflect a feeling of awe towards nature alongside a sense of spirituality and a pantheistic faith. There are countless German poems and novels by authors including Johann Wolfgang von Goethe (1749–1832), E.T.A. Hoffmann (1776–1822), and Heinrich Heine (1797–1856), that describe the forest in great detail, conveying a deeply romantic atmosphere. There is even a specific word in German that characterises the sublime and peaceful feelings that can come from being alone in the woods: '*Waldeinsamkeit*'.

In his philosophical key work *Masse und Macht* (*Crowds and Power*), written in the 1950s and first published in 1960, Elias Canetti (1905–1994) described the German forest culture:

> In no other modern country has the forest-feeling remained as alive as it has in Germany. The parallel rigidity of the upright trees and their density and number fill the heart of the German with a deep and mysterious delight. To this day he loves to go deep into the forest where his forefathers lived; he feels at one with the trees. Their orderly separation and the stress on the vertical distinguish this forest from the tropical kind where creepers grow in all directions.[8]

It is perhaps not surprising that Canetti also links the forest motif with the army – writing about a 'marching forest' – given that a few decades earlier the Nazis had exploited the German appreciation of forests, using them as a patriotic symbol promising German people strength and greatness. The forest became a metaphor for the father country, with strong 'roots' to one's ancestors. The 'German forest' was mobilised as a political instrument.

In the 1930s, paintings of forests by Walter Rose (1903–1964), among others, were published in the magazine *Die Kunst im Dritten Reich*, to create a feeling of national belonging or '*Volksgemeinschaft*'.[9] The

7

DIE ETSCH (*THE ADIGE*), MID-1970S

Watercolour, gouache and ink on paper
56 × 41 cm

Hall Collection

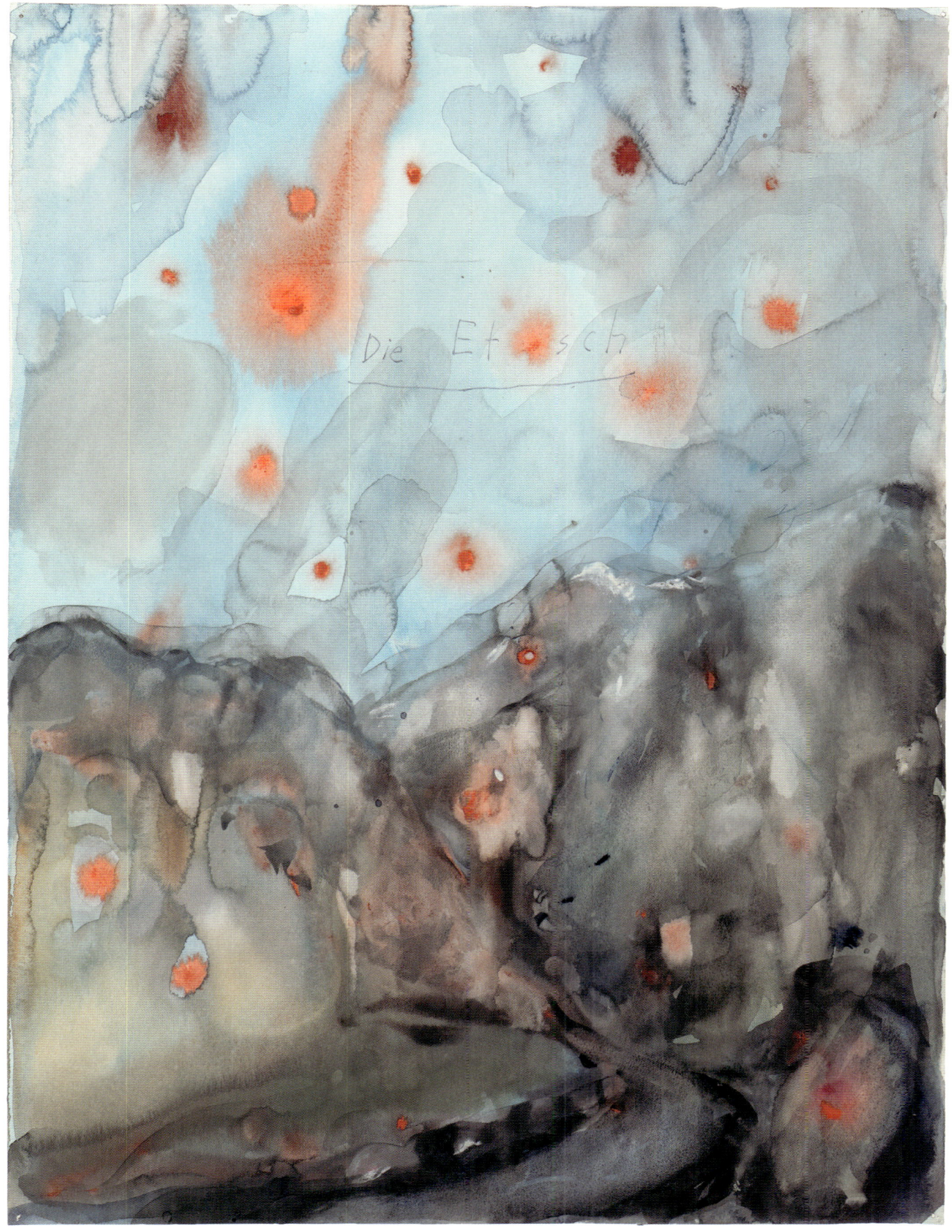

expensively produced (but commercially unpopular) feature-length propaganda film *Ewiger Wald* from 1936 portrayed the perfect symbiosis of an eternal forest with an eternal people rooted in it, propagating the 'blood and soil' ideology (p.43). In the film, the forest is used as a symbol for the good and bad times that the nation has experienced, such as the violence and defeat during the First World War. Faith in the power of the forest becomes a kind of religion to heal and succeed. The film ends with swastika flags, the German eagle, and a huge maypole surrounded by masses of uniformed people. The narrator proclaims confidently: 'The maypole blossoms like you and I. Under the maypole the Nation calls for you and me. Sing the new song of the time! Like the forest, the nation stands for eternity.'[10] Around the same time that *Ewiger Wald* was being produced, German professor of forestry, Franz Heske (1892–1963) wrote: 'German culture sprang from the forest. It is a forest culture. In holy groves the ancient Germans worshiped their gods.'[11] This forest culture culminated in enthusiastic followers of National Socialism planting 'German oaks' in honour of Adolf Hitler.

Kiefer painted *Wald* less than 30 years after the Nazis were defeated. Its balanced composition and the transparent watercolours convey a sense of lightness and intimacy that contrast with the heavy burden linked to the forest ideology espoused in Nazi propaganda. I agree with art historian Simon Schama, who, in his book *Landscape and Memory*, highlights Kiefer's great contributions to the recent history of landscape painting, describing him as a 'woodland exorcist, determined to track down the ogres of myth in their own lair'.[12] The academic Christian Weikop, who has explored Kiefer's work on forests, trees, and woods in depth, describes him aptly as a 'conceptual thinker possessed of a Romantic imagination, whose work demonstrates that he is a contemporary master of the sublime ... a true inheritor of Friedrich's legacy'.[13]

Wald is representative of Kiefer's relentless examination of Germany's complex cultural memory of the landscape, while also reflecting his deeply personal connection to it.
Lena Fritsch

7.

DIE ETSCH (THE ADIGE), MID-1970S

Running between transparent rock- and mountain-like structures, set before a light-blue background, a blue-black curve sweeps across the foreground of this painting, reminiscent of a river flowing through a rocky crevasse. Light-red spots cover the scene, enhancing its feeling of transparency and lightness. Dominated by blue, black, and red tones, the watercolour hues are blurred, creating a soft, watery composition. The work is indistinct and abstract, suggesting a picturesque landscape with a mountain valley and river. Thin letters in the upper-middle part of the composition reference the title of the work: *Die Etsch*. This title identifies the river depicted: the Adige.

Rising in the Italian province of South Tyrol, near the Italian border with Austria and Switzerland, the Adige flows 410 kilometres through most of north-eastern Italy to the Adriatic Sea. The Adige valley first divides the Alps from the Dolomites, and then, at its bottom, the Prealps and Lake Garda from the Venetian Prealps. Flowing through ancient cities, such as Verona, and some of the most picturesque valleys of Europe, with a backdrop of snow-capped mountains, the Adige is generally associated with beautiful views. Its German name 'die Etsch', however, also points to links with German history.

The first stanza of the national anthem that was sung between 1922 and 1945 references the river: '*Von der Maas bis an die Memel, von der Etsch bis an den Belt.*

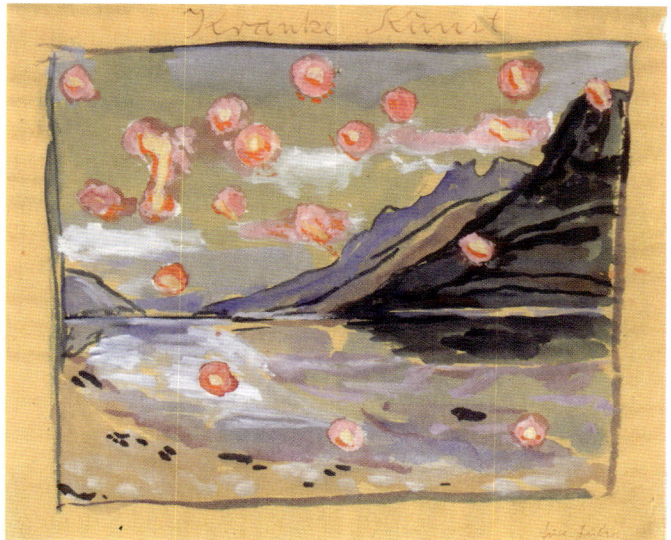

Anselm Kiefer
Kranke Kunst (*Sick Art*), 1974
Watercolour, gouache and ballpoint pen
on paper, 20 × 23.8 cm

Deutschland, Deutschland über alles, über alles in der Welt' ('from the Meuse River to the Nemen River, from the Adige to the Belt. Germany, Germany above all, above anything in the world'). The original text of the anthem was written in 1841 by August Heinrich Hoffmann von Fallersleben (1798–1874) on the island Helgoland, which, at the time, was British. At this time, Germany did not exist as a unified nation but was formed loosely of 39 individual states with different territorial interests. The main aim of Fallersleben's text was to encourage domestic German national unity above individual state interests. The rivers, including the Adige, referenced the borders of where the German language, with its different dialects, was spoken. During the Nazi regime, however, this first stanza was abused and sung to promote the greatness of Germany, which was viewed as superior to all other countries ('above all'). It was played at many public gatherings. Fallersleben's mentioning of the rivers and their borders became territorial claims, encouraging Nazi Germany's expansionist war aims. During the Third Reich, only the first stanza was sung, followed by the Nazi party's hymn, the *Horst-Wessel-Lied*. Fallersleben's second stanza, praising German women, wine, and music, must have sounded too much like a playful drinking song, and the third stanza, highlighting democratic 'unity and justice and freedom', did not fit with the ideologies of the National Socialists. After the fall of Nazi Germany, only the third stanza was used as the national anthem, since 1990 representing re-unified Germany.

When Kiefer painted his watercolour *Die Etsch* in the mid-1970s, the first stanza was strongly associated with the recent Nazi regime and their crimes. Against this historical context, the red spots covering the landscape are reminiscent of blood blotches. The innocent, picturesque, and perhaps mundane image of a landscape around the Adige appears to be covered with blood, representing Germany's fresh wounds and recent war memory. Similar blotches in a slightly lighter pink tone can be found on two of Kiefer's other watercolours from 1974 and 1975, both titled *Kranke Kunst* (*Sick Art*). Comparable with *Die Etsch*, the spots appear to be superimposed on the landscape, which features mountains and water. One of these works is in a private collection, while the other can be found in the collection of the Metropolitan Museum of Art, New York (above). In the summer of 1974, Kiefer travelled from his home in the Odenwald to the northernmost region of Norway, taking Polaroid photographs and collecting landscape postcards featuring fjords, rivers, and icebergs.[14] Over the years that followed he used these photographs, as well as images obtained during other travels, to create watercolours and artist books. It is therefore possible that *Die Etsch* is also based on a photographic image, although Kiefer himself does not clearly remember this today.[15]

Die Etsch is typical of Kiefer's practice of subtly linking the beauty of nature with difficult cultural memories by giving his paintings a specific title and/or including text within the image. The work oscillates between an exquisite abstract composition, featuring its gouache and watercolours in a beautifully transparent style, and a charged scene that reminds us how landscapes (and references to them) can be abused politically.

Lena Fritsch

8

VON OSKAR WILDE FÜR JULIA (FROM OSCAR WILDE FOR JULIA), 1973

'*Von Oskar Wilde für Julia*' is the enigmatic inscription on this work. Julia was Anselm Kiefer's wife in 1973, when he painted this watercolour of a rose as a present for her.

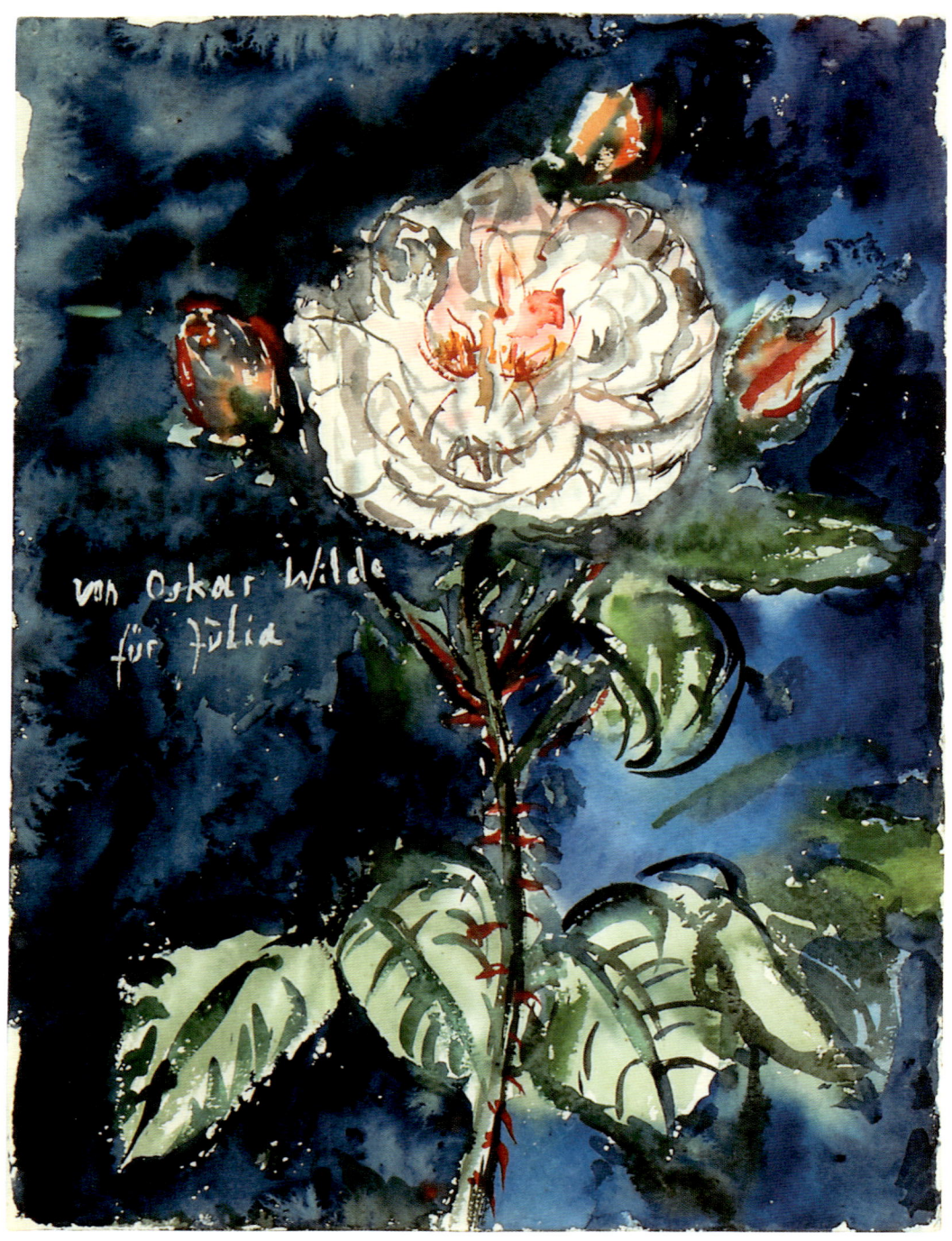

VON OSKAR WILDE FÜR JULIA
(FROM OSCAR WILDE FOR JULIA), 1973
Watercolour and gouache on paper
40 × 30 cm
Hall Collection

Another, very similarly painted rose, is in the collection of the Metropolitan Museum of Art, New York (p.51), and other versions also exist. The reference to the Irish poet and playwright Oscar Wilde (1854–1900) offers the viewer a raft of possible connections and meanings. The strokes of darker paint that outline the petals towards the lower half of the flower jostle together to suggest a skull-like grin. Two eyes appear to complement this visage within the blend of reds and yellows, while pinky-red buds bracket the main bloom. The anthropomorphic appearance is at once witty and sinister, perhaps conjuring up thoughts of the hidden face behind the eternal portrait of Dorian Gray.

Interestingly, Kiefer proffers a rose, and not a green carnation, as we might expect in connection to Wilde. On the opening night of his play, *Lady Windermere's Fan* in 1892, Wilde, aware of the potential symbolism of flowers, asked some friends to wear green carnations on their lapels, turning this gesture into a secret code for homosexual recognition. In contrast to the carnation (and possibly less effete) the rose is unisex, democratic, and ubiquitous as a symbol of love, and when faded, dried, and desiccated it turns into a lovelorn and fragile memento mori.

In 1888, Wilde wrote *The Nightingale and the Rose*, a story that considers the rose in relation to human desire and fickleness.[16] The tale is predicated on the necessity of finding a red rose for a student to give to the subject of his affections. A nightingale wants to help the besotted student in his seemingly hopeless quest for the symbolic red rose. Meanwhile, the rose trees chime with poetic descriptions but of 'wrong-coloured' roses: 'My roses are white ... as white as the foam of the sea, and whiter than the snow upon the mountain.' To create a red rose the nightingale is told she must 'stain it with [her] own heart's-blood'. The nightingale sings all night, her chest pressed up against the thorn of the rose tree, and she dies giving the rose its red colour with her blood. When the morning comes, the student finds the red rose and presents it to the girl, but she rejects it, for it does not match her dress. In anger, he throws the rose away callously, concluding:

> What a silly thing Love is ... It is not half as useful as Logic, for it does not prove anything, and it is always telling one of things that are not going to happen, and making one believe things that are not true.

Without the dedication, Kiefer's flower painting could remain quirky and lightweight. It does not relate to the wider realm of traditional flower painting but, as is often the case, it is self-reflexive with other Kiefer strands. However, the Wilde reference adds gravitas, allowing the work to become a springboard for our imagination. We can explore his story and segue into others. These other stories deepen his repetitious rose pictures, broadening out his theme. Because the rose is so universal, it recurs as a motif in many kinds of literary references applied to all types of situations, not only that of love. It is therefore interesting to expand on the theme as it appears in text and appreciate how this simple flower is in fact a very loaded bloom. The rose can be read as a mantra in the same way that Kiefer produces his repetitive repertoire of symbolic icons, be they rose or Valkyrie.

William Shakespeare (1564–1616) immediately comes to mind, and a different (from Wilde's) kind of tragedy with the star-crossed lovers in *Romeo and Juliet* (Act II, Scene II): 'What's in a name? That which we call a rose by any other name would smell as sweet; So Romeo would, were he not Romeo call'd.'

Gertrude Stein (1874–1946) wrote, 'A Rose is a rose is a rose is a rose' in her 1913 poem 'Sacred Emily'.[17] The first 'Rose' is the name of a person. The quotation became Stein's most famous, introducing the concept

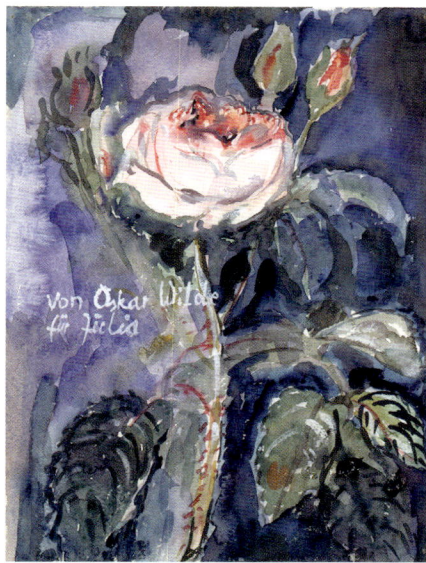

Anselm Kiefer
Von Oskar Wilde
(*From Oscar Wilde*), 1974
Watercolour and gouache
on paper, 40 × 29.8 cm

of the philosophy of the law of identity, 'things are what they are', the sentence expresses the fact that simply using the name of a thing already invokes the imagery and emotions associated with it. Kiefer's rose paintings are straightforward yet carefree depictions of the familiar form of that genus. It is his dedication that expands our thoughts and offers us further possibilities of interpretation.

Kiefer's rose is a pretty vehicle for the mind to wander around. We recognise its shape and smell, the thorns, and pinnate leaf format. Katherine Mansfield (1888–1923) employs a celestial garden rose to open the scene of another type of veiled tragedy in her short story, *The Garden Party* (1922), written 34 years after Wilde's *Nightingale*:

> As for the roses, you could not help feeling they understood that roses are the only flowers that impress people at garden-parties; the only flowers that everybody is certain of knowing. Hundreds, yes, literally hundreds had come out in a single night; the green bushes bowed down as though they had been visited by archangels ...[18]

Mansfield's opening lines clarify the ubiquitous status of the rose, but her comment about 'everybody' is ambiguous as this tale is about class consciousness (among other things) and perhaps only alludes to those (like Oscar Wilde?) who attend garden parties.[19]

A poem by Fabian Peake (b.1942) treats us to yet another perspective on role reversal and this versatile flower. It was written in response to a gift from his wife, the sculptor Phyllida Barlow (1944–2023):

> She brought me home a rose
> of welded metal,
> a slender stem with a head
> of tempered petals.

> I found a cut glass vase,
> blew away the dust,
> immersed the rod in water
> and watched the flower rust.[20]

Liz Rideal

THE DREAM KING, 1974

With Anselm Kiefer's proclivity for mythic characters, it is perhaps no surprise that he created portraits of Ludwig II von Bayern. This was a king known to favour extravagant artistic and architectural projects over the day-to-day business of state, and who commissioned Richard Wagner's *Ring Cycle*, a series of epic musical dramas that Kiefer also examined through his work (pp.121–4, 165–8, and 178–81).

This bust-length portrait shows Ludwig II, in three-quarter profile, his head turned slightly to the left towards the viewer. That head sits on top of his stiff white collar like a precarious egg balancing on a cup. Kiefer's 'dream king' suggests an insecure monarch whose military attire has never seen a battlefield. This is no Richard III (1452–1485). The inference here is that Ludwig's outfit is all puff and coded dress, make believe and fake protection. The high collar is rigid, the material is heavy, the sash of honour decorative.

Yet, if we view him in the company of other uniformed soldiers, he fits the brief. His solitary head and shoulders resonate with the 1812–14 portrait by Francisco de Goya (1746–1828) of Arthur Wellesley, 1st Duke of Wellington (1769–1852), a work now in the collection of the National Gallery, London (p.54). The eyes in that portrait also evoke a curious expression, perhaps a haunted look. But unlike Ludwig II, Wellington experienced battle, and Goya's

9

THE DREAM KING, 1974

Watercolour and gouache on paper

40 × 30 cm

Hall Collection

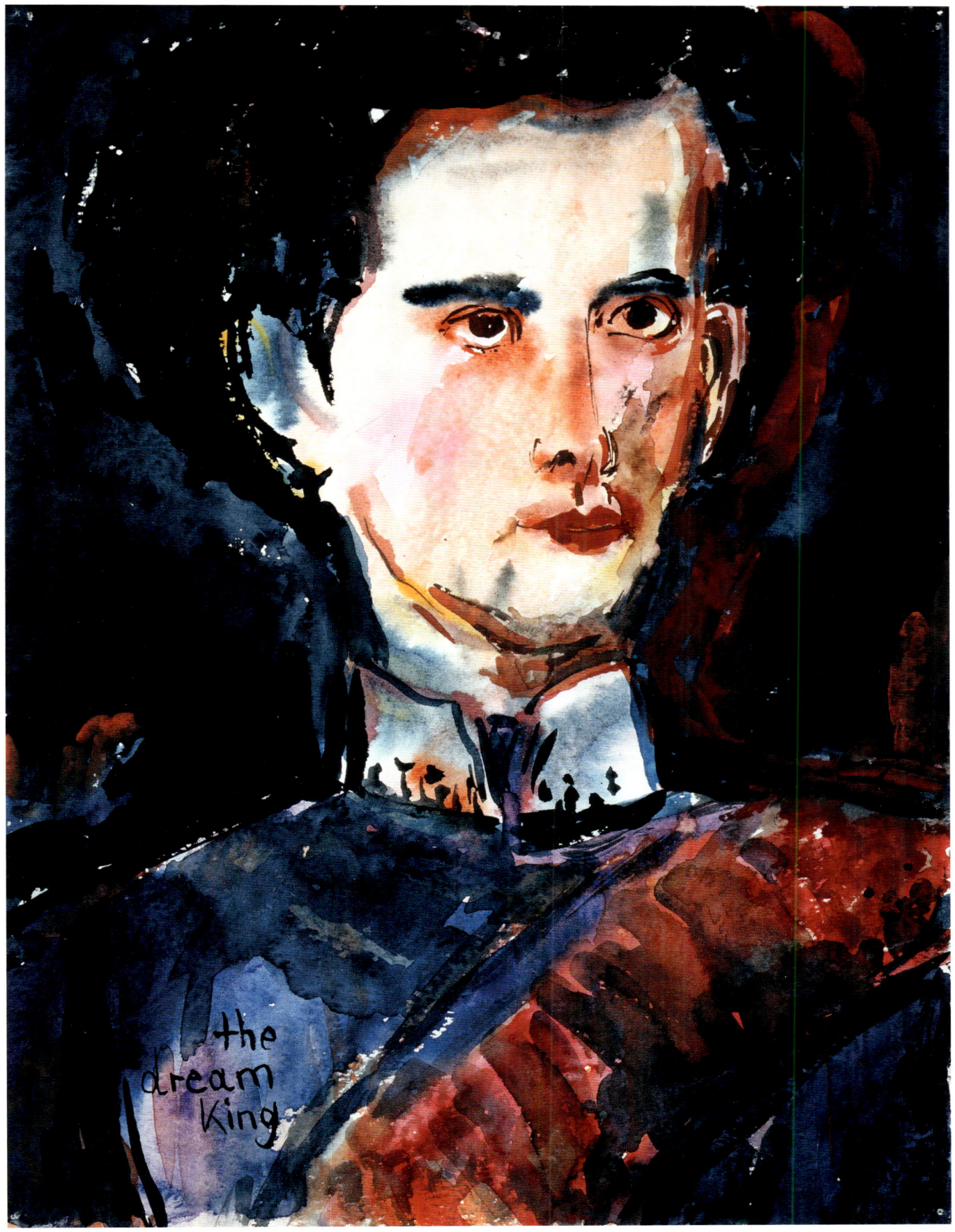

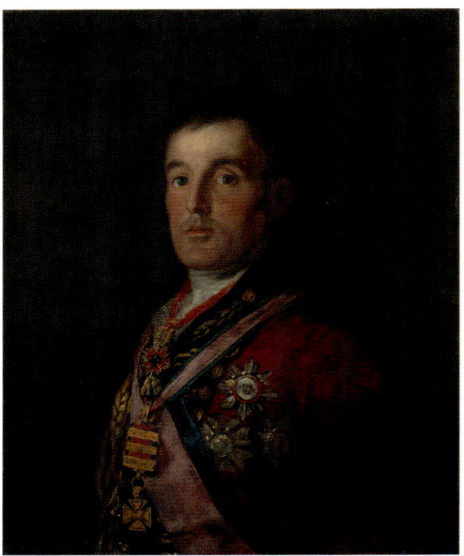

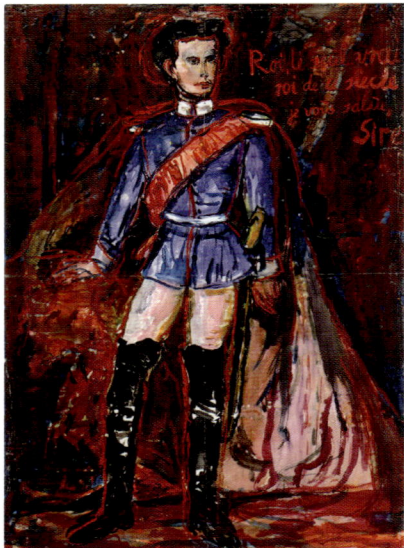

(left)
Francisco de Goya (1746–1828)
The Duke of Wellington, 1812–14
Oil on mahogany, 64.3 × 52.4 cm

(right)
Anselm Kiefer
Dream King (Ludwig II von Bayern), 1974
Gouache and watercolour on paper,
85 × 60 cm

painting records the honours he received when he arrived in Madrid after his triumphal defeat of Napoleon and the French at the Battle of Salamanca.

The *Dream King* is the focus and study for a full-length work in the Kröller-Müller Museum in the Netherlands (above). This work, also painted in 1974, shares the title 'Dream King'. It is also similarly annotated for context, in this case with the words: '*Roi, le seul vrais roi de ce siècle, je vous salue Sire*' ('King, the only real king of this century, I salute you Sire'). Both works use the vibrant blue contrasting with the white, and a powerful red sash for intense colour impact. These works appear to be based on Ludwig II's coronation portrait, painted by Ferdinand von Piloty (1828–1895), now in the collection of the Bayerische Staatsgemäldesammlungen, Munich (p.55). Yet while Kiefer's watercolours depict the Ludwig II known for his eccentricities – the builder of fantasy castles, king of Baroque interior decorations, and patron of Wagner – the Piloty state portrait shows him with more kingly attributes – a crown, ermine, and the Orders of the House of Wittelsbach, including the Order of St George and the Collar of the Order of St Hubert. Kiefer's portrait focuses on the *idea* of Ludwig: this is the key to approaching his revisualisation of iconic personalities.

In parallel to Goya's commander who looms out of the blackness is *Self-portrait with a Gunner's Helmet* by Otto Dix (1891–1969). Dix was initially keen to fight, but this enthusiasm faded once he understood the reality of brutal warfare. He paints himself in shiny helmet and polished buttons, 'in the fancy uniform of the Kaiser'. The work on the reverse of the paper, *Self-portrait as a Soldier* (1914) records an unflinching, aggressive, and manic persona; a visceral confrontation. The red used in this version is not about an attractive uniform but about bloody combat.

In contrast to the colourful paintings by Kiefer, Goya, and Dix is Gerhard Richter's *Onkel Rudi* (1965), who is depicted standing straight in front the viewer, smiling as if he is enjoying posing for a photograph (p.55).[21] The painting is a pattern of flat, grey colour, the uniformed figure and urban background almost merging as one entity; an embodiment of uniformity. The greatcoat and peaked appliquéd cap are recognisable as German military standard issue, sleekly fitted, full-length, with shiny buttons and a dark pointed collar that contrasts with that of Kiefer's *Dream King*. The manner by which Rudi seems to be assimilated into the permanent structure of the wall and modernist housing block beyond, attaches another kind of uniform functionality. He is at one with his context and yet the smile on his face undermines this immutable scenario.

All of these male sitters wear their uniform in different ways and for different purposes; the uniform is both decorative and functional. There is a sense whereby a uniform is instantly recognisable and imbued with status, rank, and meaning. Uniforms by their sameness and 'uniformity' preclude individuality, yet this concept is entirely at odds with the idea and purpose of a portrait. The portrait is meant as an identifier, and in former times was often an expensive way of recording one's achievements and status in life. The Goya portrait of Wellington succeeds in this respect, qualifying as a status portrait it survives as a monumental and enduring record of a great army commander. Dix's paintings bring to mind more than a young proud soldier off to war; it is also a record of the fragility of hope. It references (albeit unconsciously) hoards of cannon fodder, senseless deaths in the battlefield, and the dreams of young infantry men naively marching towards the unknown. Kiefer's *Dream King*, however, is just that. A rather fey, uncomfortable figure in kingly attire, who seems to suffer from imposter syndrome, but whose artistic legacy is tremendous. He is portrayed as a king full of imagination in a world of his own.

Liz Rideal

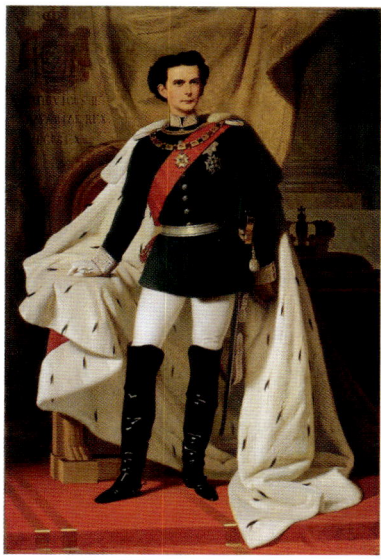
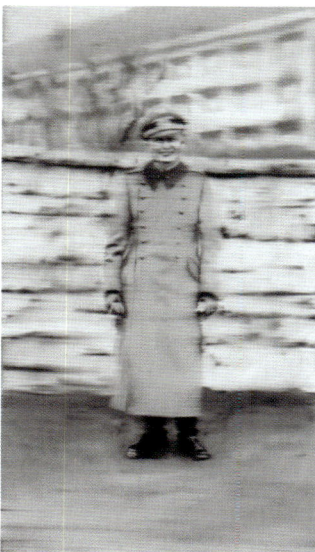

10

LANDSCHAFT MIT KOPF
(*LANDSCAPE WITH HEAD*), 1973

Landschaft mit Kopf is an assemblage-like composition of oil paint on an irregularly trimmed burlap ground, combined with a charcoal drawing on cardboard. It shows a dark seascape, perhaps announcing an approaching tempest. A merely suggested row of trees separates the troubled waters from an eerily glowing nocturnal sky. On the right, the work is immersed into deep blackness. The broad frame, with its illusory woodgrain, seems to disappear under an impasto layer of black distemper. On the left, the landscape has been extended by an edgy protrusion. It seems like the artist wanted to create more space for the portrait drawing of an androgynous-looking, half-length figure with a mask-like grim face. The sitter is looking to the right (seen from the viewer's perspective), in an almost mesmerised way. The sitter in question is Kiefer's grandmother – a remarkable exception in his oeuvre, since specific autobiographical references are rare in his work.[22] We only find personal hints in some watercolours and paintings of this very early phase, which reference his first wife, Julia, whom he married in 1971.

For a large part of his childhood Kiefer lived together with his grandmother in Donaueschingen. Here he used to play in the rubble of buildings destroyed during the war. As an adult, he remembers this time with pleasure. He had sketched his grandmother's portrait when he was a teenager, and this sketch helped him to project himself back into his youth.

The viewer sees the grandmother's head, ghostly pale, in profile, while she gazes at the sea as it is flooded by the black night. Kiefer has interpreted this right side of the painting as being open, as if the elderly figure is looking out into an uncertain future.[23] The landscape turns into a soulscape, as if it was an expression of internal processes and conditions. In this way, the composition is reminiscent of Romantic landscape paintings by artists including Caspar David Friedrich, one of the frequently cited artists in Kiefer's repertoire of Germany's cultural representatives (see also pp. 28 and 42).

Landschaft mit Kopf takes up its own particular place in Kiefer's early oeuvre. The work is unusual in ignoring the traditional rectangular frame. As early as the 1920s, Russian Constructivists had dared to leave the rectangular format behind. During the 1960s, in the context of Op Art, this departure from the standard format reappeared under the term 'shaped canvas', for instance in the works of Ellsworth Kelly (1923–2015) and Frank Stella (1936–2024). There, the irregular format was mostly based on geometric compositions, whereas in Kiefer's works the outer form is determined by the narrative content, for which the artist wanted to achieve the optimal 'frame'-work. During this early period, Kiefer created several paintings with irregularly formed borders, for instance *Resurrexit* (1973), where the ascending staircase expands upward towards heaven, conveying a religious aura.

Landschaft mit Kopf has a close temporal and formal connection with Kiefer's *Attic Series* (1973), where the artist enacted his critical analysis of the spiritual breeding grounds of fascism in heavy, wooden attic rooms. Its unusual frame of painted wood recalls Kiefer's own studio in the small village of Hornbach near Buchen, as if it was made out of its rough wooden planks. The illusory woodgrain seems to stare at the viewer like eyes; and, in fact, the subject of seeing and observing is predominant in this work. Two red lines, extending from the grandmother's eyes, mediate between the portrait and the seascape. They refer to ancient theories of 'rays of vision', when it was believed

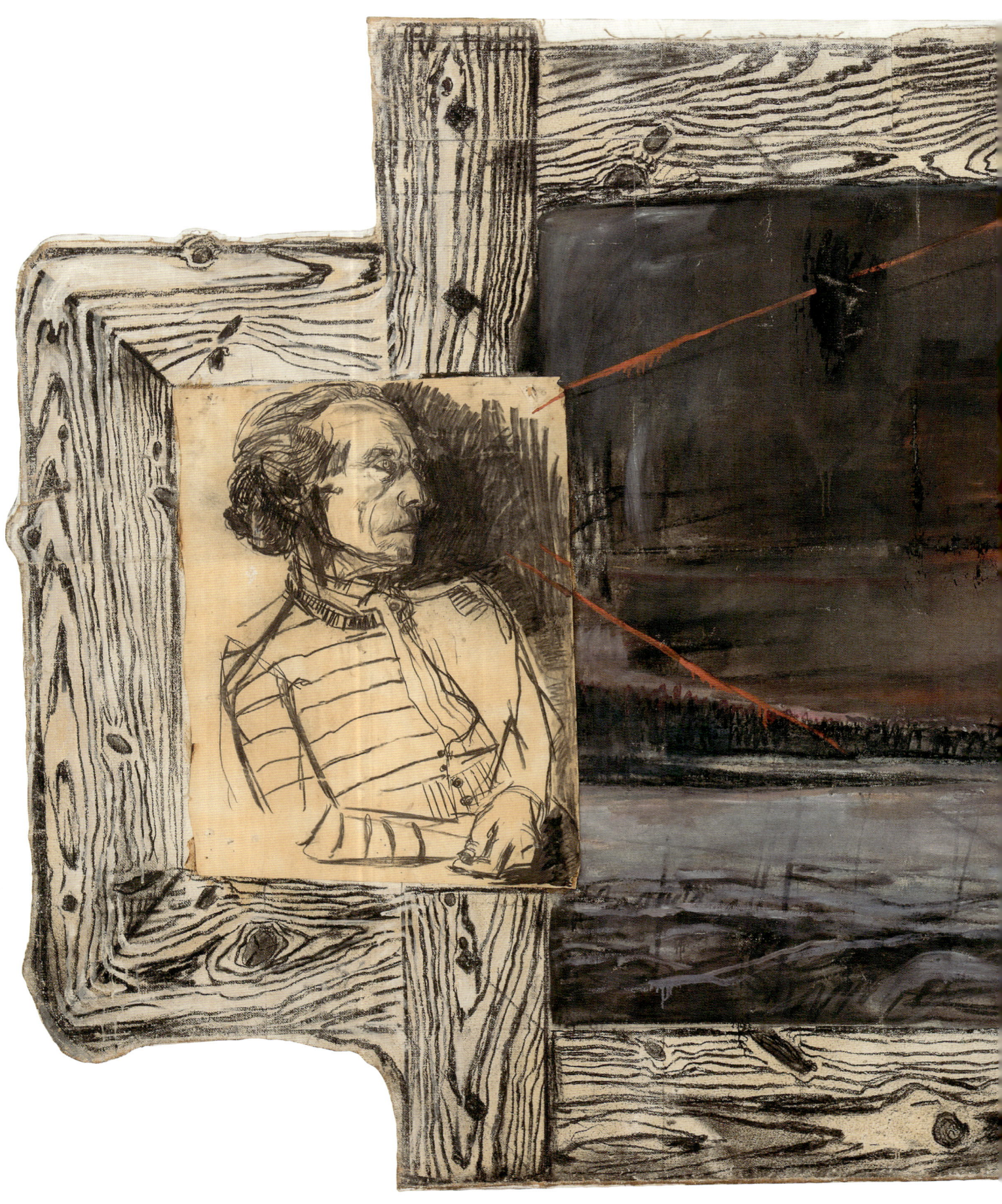

10

LANDSCHAFT MIT KOPF
(LANDSCAPE WITH HEAD), 1973
Oil, cardboard and charcoal on burlap
198 × 265.5 cm
Hall Collection

11

UNTITLED (U-BOAT), 1973

Oil on canvas

128 × 148 cm

Hall Collection

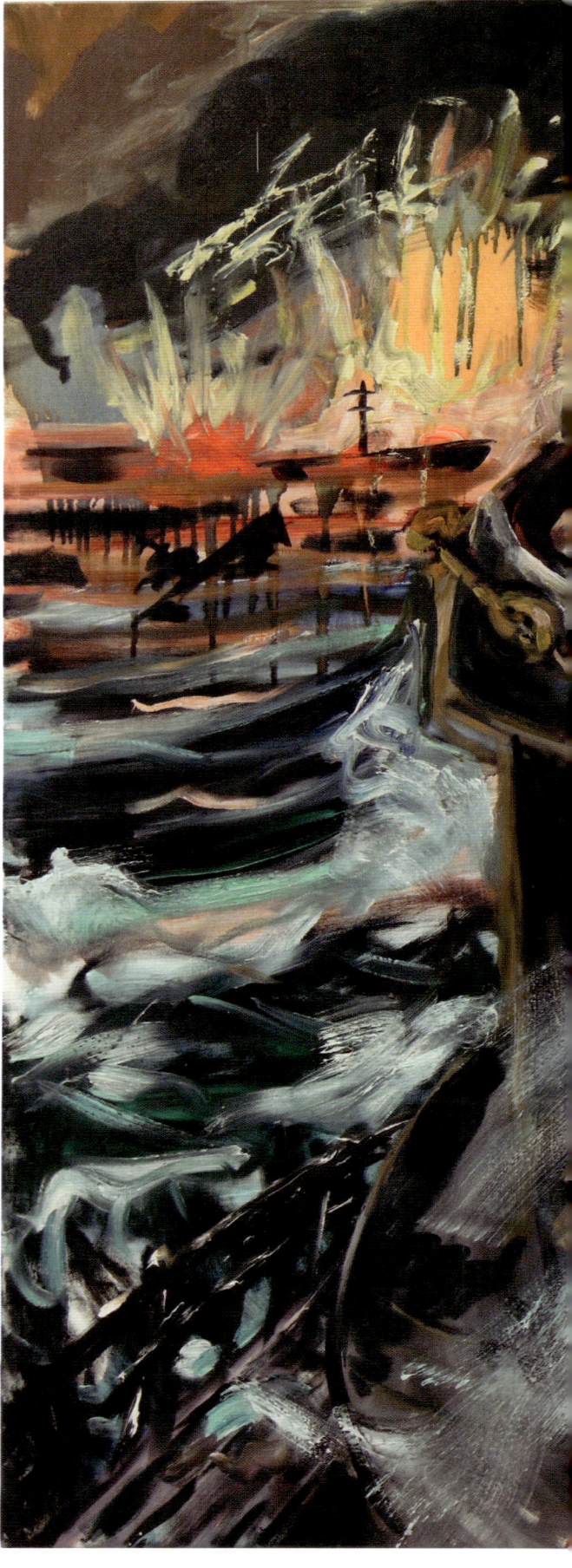

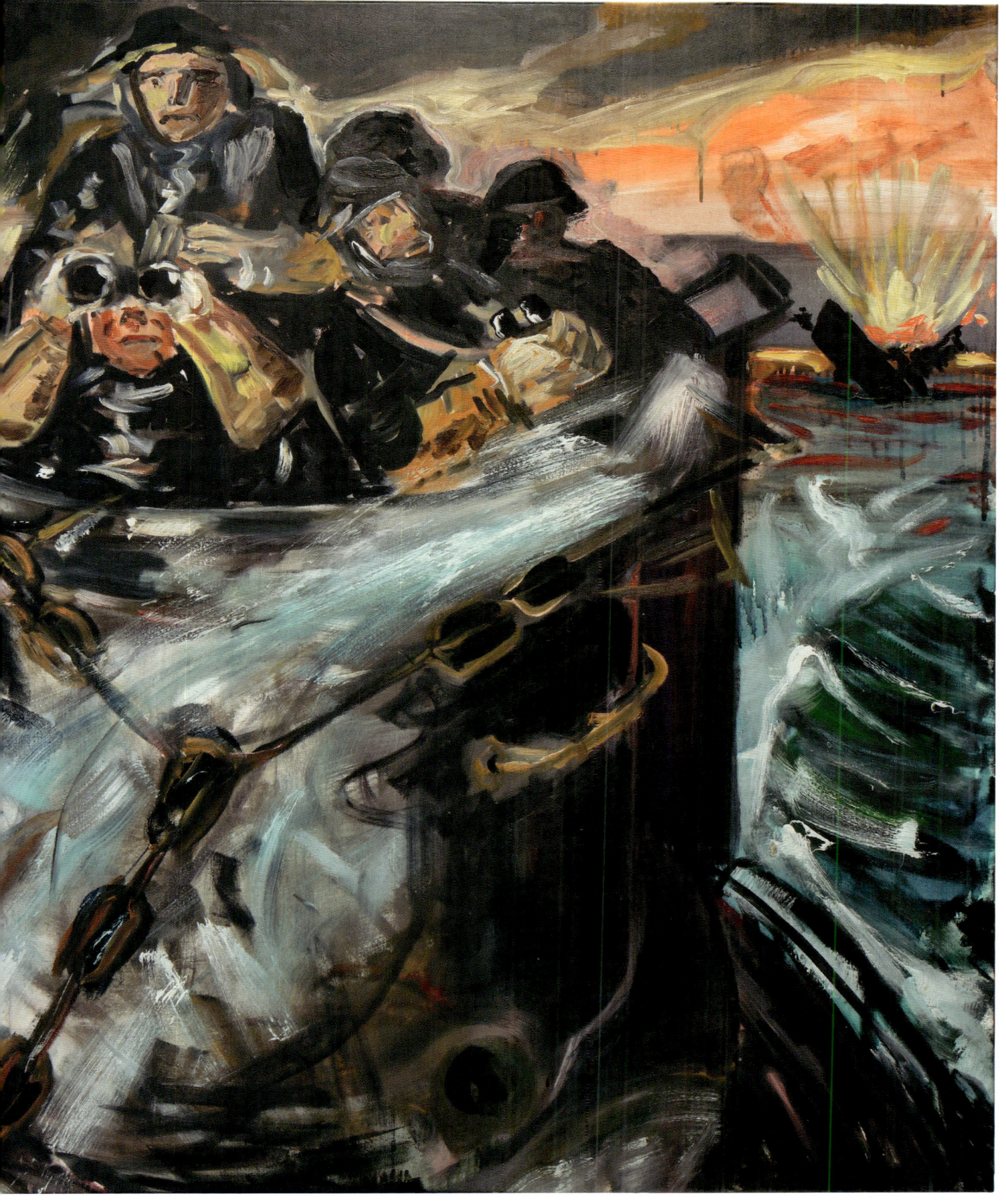

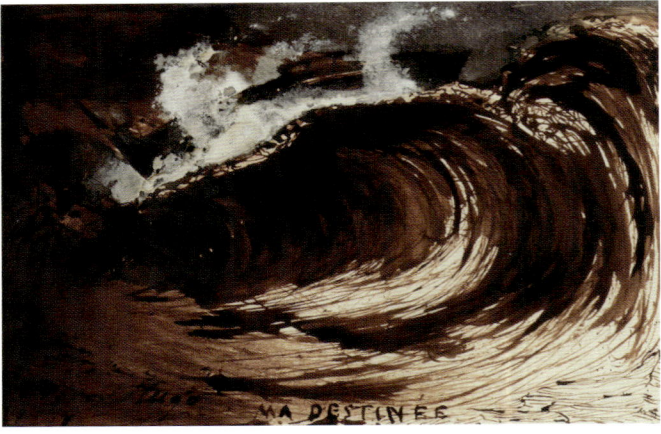

Victor Hugo (1802–1885)
Ma destinée (*My Destiny*), 1867
Brown ink and wash with white gouache
on paper, 17.2 × 26.4 cm

that light was emitted by the eyes to 'scan' objects. Later, it was assumed that the objects themselves were sending out rays of light. Isaac Newton (1643–1727) described tiny particles of light between object and eye, which he called 'emanation'. Newton's theory of light as consisting of tiny particles between object and eye has been referred to as a 'theory of emanation' and can be linked to his idea of a divine spatial extendedness of all existing beings.[24]

In 1857, the well-known French poet (and amateur painter) Victor Hugo (1802–1885) depicted a sombre, stormy sea with a tsunami-like wave that threatened to engulf everything: *Ma destinée* (*My Destiny*; above). In an essay about this gouache work, which somewhat resembles his own landscape, Kiefer quotes from Hugo's anthology of poems, *Les rayons et les ombres* (*Rays and Shadows*; 1840). In Kiefer's enigmatic interpretation, the ego, withdrawn into itself and confronted with the unnameable and incomprehensible, emanates 'rays into the free space that recall … its divine primordial form … The unnameable reminds the nameable of its emanation from the unnameable'.[25] In his exploration of the Shoah and Jewish mysticism, which Kiefer has pursued since the 1980s, the idea of 'emanation' represents an attempt to re-institute a supreme order in the world – 'the concept that the spiritual realm is a spiral going up and down'.[26]

Sabine Schütz

11

UNTITLED (U-BOAT), 1973

Painted in dynamic, expressive brush strokes in contrasting blue, orange-yellow, and brown tones, this vivid work features a small group of marine soldiers standing on a U-boat tower in midst of a wild sea. One man is looking out through

binoculars, which are directed towards the viewer, another is holding binoculars in his hands, staring concentratedly into the distance. The men are close together on the small command tower, while splashing water suggests strong movement. In the background, flashing lights and fire indicate explosions. The scene conveys an atmosphere of danger but also one of adventure and male camaraderie.

This untitled work is based on the 1943 painting, *Nach der Geleitzugschlacht* (*After the Convoy Attack*), by the artist Richard Schreiber (1904–1963; p.61). Schreiber's work was exhibited at the *Große Deutsche Kunstausstellung*, an exhibition organised by the Nazis in the Haus der Deutschen Kunst in Munich. The painting was reproduced in colour as well as in black and white on countless prints and postcards. Schreiber, who studied art history at Bonn University before becoming a painter, originally focused on landscapes, still life, and portrait painting. During the early 1930s he lived in Dusseldorf and then Paris, creating works in a modern, Expressionist style, and surrounding himself with other avant-garde artists. However, after joining the NSDAP in 1935 and becoming a member of its art association, Reichskammer der Bildenden Künste, which promoted a conservative, figurative painting language and only allowed subjects that fitted with Nazi ideology, Schreiber's artistic style changed. Based in La Baule-Escoublac, close to the sea in France, he was commissioned by Lieutenant Schwich in Munich to paint war images, creating a number of propaganda paintings that depict the marine and battle scenes at sea.[27] Schreiber's name can be found on the *Gottbegnadeten-Liste* (*List of the God-gifted*) in 1944, which included artists, writers, and composers whose works were considered crucial to National Socialist culture. The list was assembled by Joseph Goebbels (1897–1945), head of the Ministry of Public Enlightenment and Propaganda. After the war, Schreiber lived in Dusseldorf, presented his works in exhibitions in the Rhineland area,

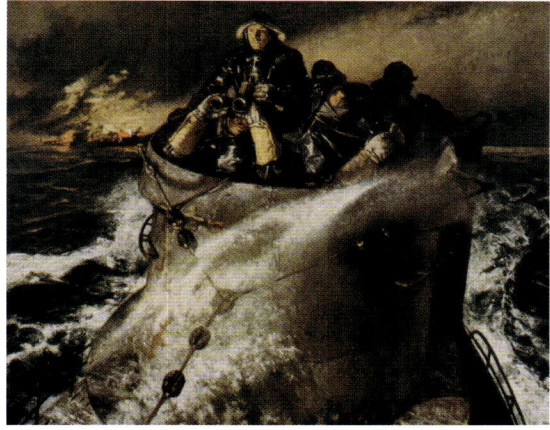

Richard Schreiber (1904–1963)
Nach der Geleitzugschlacht
(*After the Convoy Attack*), 1943
Oil on canvas

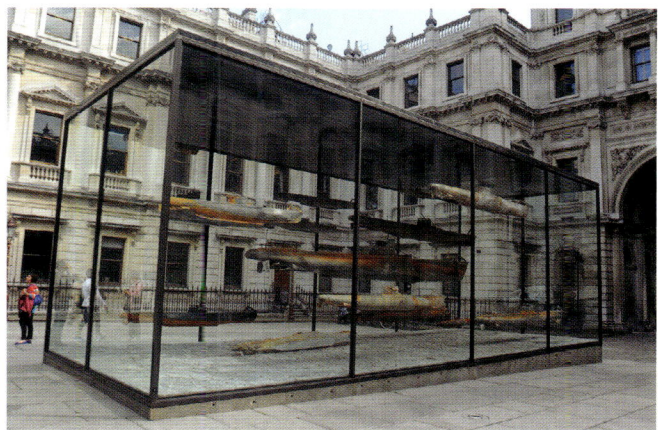

Anselm Kiefer exhibition in
forecourt of the Royal Academy of
Arts in Piccadilly, London, 2014

and taught painting at the prestigious Kunstakademie Dusseldorf. The fact that he was allowed to teach despite his Nazi past led to protests by colleagues and students, who told the German news magazine *Der Spiegel* in 1948 that he was a 'super-fascist', whereas Schreiber himself claimed that he had been ordered to paint the war propaganda images.[28]

German submarines, referred to as U-boats (an abbreviation of *Unterseeboot*), disrupted merchant traffic travelling towards the United Kingdom in both world wars. In the Second World War in particular, the submarine was considered to be an ultimate weapon of destruction. The title of Schreiber's painting references a specific event: what is referred to as the '*Geleitzug*', an allied convoy with numerous freighters slowly passing the Atlantic in March 1943 towards harbour cities in the east of England, such as Liverpool. German U-boats attacked them, using a wolfpack strategy, and within three days they successfully sank a number of British freighters. They did not experience any serious loss on the German side. Representing war success, it is not surprising that this attack was celebrated by the Nazis. Schreiber's propaganda painting from the same year presents the marine soldiers as war heroes, earnestly and passionately fighting naval battles for Nazi Germany.

Kiefer's work is painted in a more colourful, expressive, and gestural painting style than Schreiber's original, which appears darker and conveys a more conservative academic language, reminiscent of traditional history paintings. Kiefer also added more explosions in the background, enhancing the feeling of war adventure and emphasising the fictional, cinematic nature of the scene. Unlike Schreiber's propaganda painting, Kiefer's work openly presents itself as an attractive, and potentially seductive, momentary image of heroes, far from the true struggles of war.

Kiefer has been fascinated by the sea, boats, and submarines, and *Untitled* (*U-Boat*) was to become one of many works concerned with this subject. In recent installations, it is the U-boat itself rather than submarine soldiers that has been the main focus of Kiefer's work. An example of this is the almost 17-metre-long glass vitrine work *Velimir Khlebnikov: Fates of Nations: The New Theory of War. Time, Dimension of the World, Battles at Sea Occur Every 317 Years or Multiples Thereof, Namely 317 × 1, 2, 3, 4, 5, 6 . . . .* (2011–4). First exhibited in 2014, on the courtyard in front of at the Royal Academy of Arts, London (above), this monumental work emerged from Kiefer's exploration of the Russian avant-garde writer Velimir Khlebnikov (1885–1922), who argued that a major sea battle took place every 317 years, or multiples thereof. Kiefer's installation presents a mysterious and timeless scene, in which various rusty submarines appear to be floating in air, while the viewers – seeing each other and their own reflections in the glass – also became part of the work.
Lena Fritsch

12

SOL INVICTUS HELIOGABAL, 1974

Painted in dynamic brushstrokes, and with thick oil paint in grey, blue, purple, and beige tones, this work depicts a soldier's face and shoulders, as viewed from the side. He seems to be looking into the distance, facing something with a serious and tired facial expression. His steel helmet is reminiscent of the uniform that German Wehrmacht soldiers wore during the Second World War. Blue and red tones in the abstract dark background contrast with the pale grey face and body of the man.

The title of the work references the sun god of the late Roman Empire, Sol Invictus (from the Latin for 'invincible' or 'unconquered sun'), who first rose to prominence in Rome

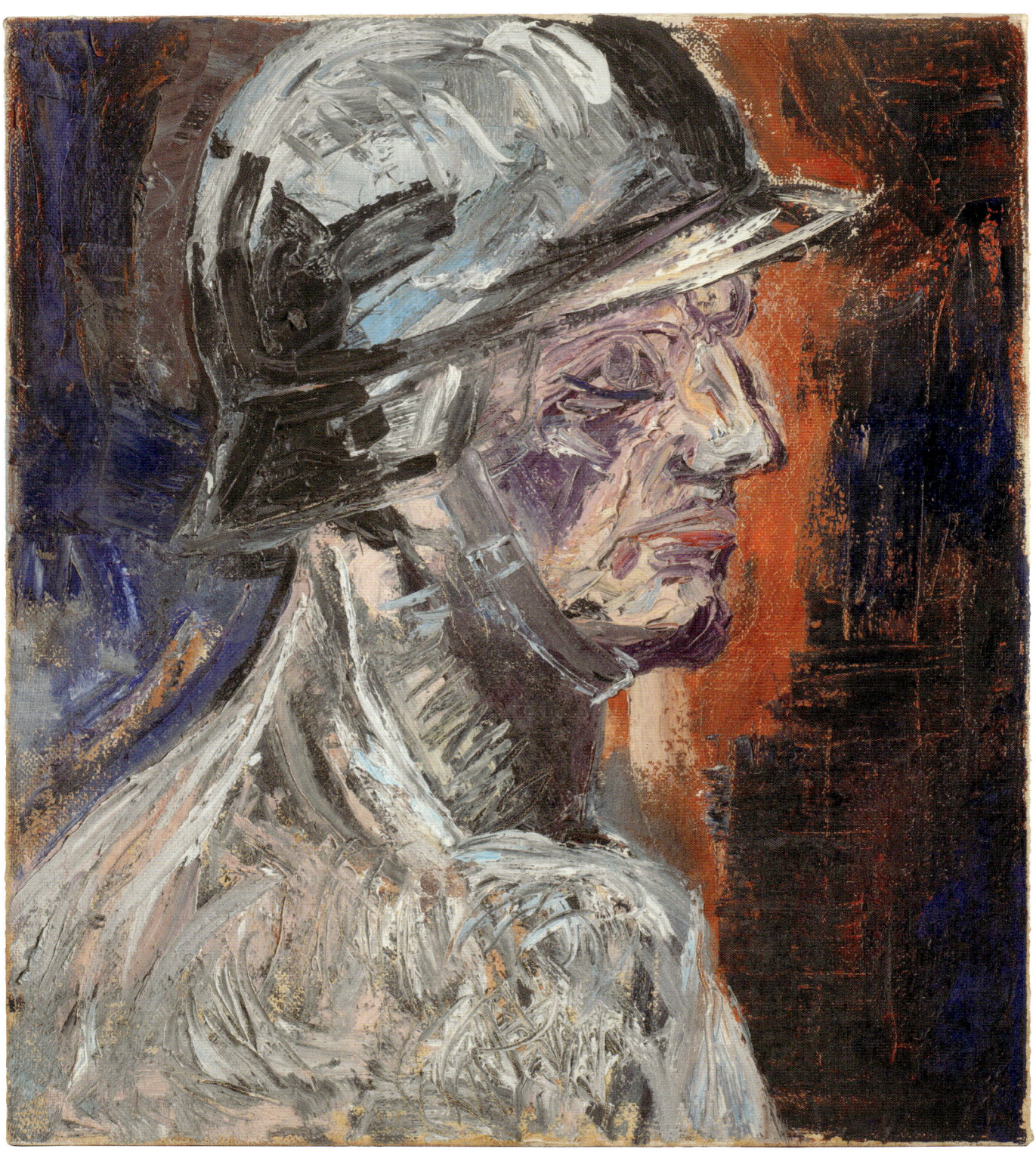

SOL INVICTUS HELIOGABAL, 1974
Oil on burlap
80 × 70.5 cm
Hall Collection

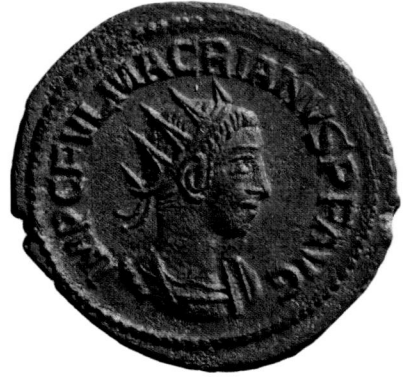
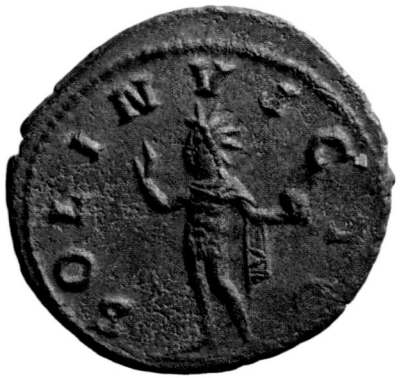

Roman Imperial coin depicting the
bust of Macrianus (d.261), *c.*260-61
Silver, 2.1 cm (diameter)

when teenager Marcus Aurelius Antoninus (*c.*204–222)
– better known as Heliogabalus or Elagabalus – was
emperor. Heliogabalus's short reign, from 218 to 222, was
notorious for religious controversy and sexual promiscuity.
Coming from a prominent Arab family in what is now Syria,
since his early youth Heliogabalus had served as head
priest of the sun god. It is said that he disregarded Rome's
traditional state deities and, controversially, replaced the
head of the Roman Pantheon, Jupiter, with the Syrian sun
deity, Heliogabalus (whose name he had adopted), forcing
leading members of the government to participate in rituals
celebrating the deity. Amid growing opposition to his rule,
he was assassinated in 222, at the age of eighteen, and
replaced by his cousin, Severus Alexander (208–235). Sol
Invictus continued to be celebrated, however, including
during the festival named after him on 25 December,
which featured chariot races at the Circus Maximus. As the
official deity of the Roman Empire, he became one of the
most important gods, symbolising victory and the defeat of
darkness. Sol Invictus was the patron of Roman soldiers and
was represented on coins.[29] In the Ashmolean Museum's
Roman coins collections alone, there are numerous
examples, such as a silver coin from *c.*260–61 that depicts
a bust of Macrianus (d.261) on the front, and on the reverse,
the sun deity majestically raising his right hand and holding
a globe, together with the inscription *Sol Invicto* (above).

During the Second World War, countless propaganda
paintings, prints, and postcards depicted soldiers with
steel helmets fighting for the German fatherland. In a
visual language similar to paintings supporting Joseph
Stalin's totalitarian government, or later Communism in
the GDR, Nazi soldiers were shown as idealised heroes
in action, passionately running on battlefields, crossing
rivers, or standing invincibly on U-boats after successful
attacks (pp.58–9). In contrast to Sol Invictus on Roman
coins, and to Nazi propaganda depictions of the army,

Kiefer's soldier appears wounded and battle weary. The
purple-grey paint around the eyes and cheeks suggests
bruises. The title mentions a strong emperor and invincible
deity but, ironically, the painting presents us with a
vulnerable human, tired of fighting.

In 1974, Kiefer made a number of works that reference
his interest in the controversial emperor Heliogabalus and
his destiny, for example the watercolour *Heliogabal*, also in
the Hall collection (pp.110–13).

Lena Fritsch

13/14

NASCITA DI PITTURA
(THE BIRTH OF PAINTING), 1974
UNTITLED, 1974

'The finished product must be pleasing to the eye.
Regardless of what you know to be right, composition and
creativity are the ultimate.'[30]
– Claretta White

These two paintings of a voluptuous woman dancing in
front of snow-capped mountains can be interpreted as
ironic references to the rebirth of figurative painting in
1970s Germany. Described as 'kitsch depictions' in the
catalogue accompanying the exhibition at Kunstmuseum
Schloss Derneburg (2022–3), the female subjects, who
both wear tight dresses and high heels, are painted in
expressive brush strokes and strong colours, suggesting
lively dance movements.[31] Their eyes and facial details are
left blank – their individualities are not important. With their
colourful dresses and black hair tied back in chignons, they
are reminiscent of Spanish flamenco dancers. On both

paintings, a large painter's palette is indicated in simple outlines, layered partly over the women's bodies, as if to draw attention to their painterly nature. The backgrounds suggest the picturesque mountain landscapes that can be found in Germany, Switzerland, or Austria in wintertime.

The dancing woman that Kiefer's *Untitled* is based on can be found in an American drawing and painting instruction manual titled *Dancers in Action: How To Draw #87* by Californian artist Claretta White (*c*.1915–2002), published by Walter T. Foster Publication in the mid-1960s (p.72). The manual shows how to paint a Spanish dancer named 'Millicent' in step-by-step lessons and with advice on technique and style, stating that the 'finished product must be pleasing to the eye'. Kiefer has copied the dancer's stance, while using much more expressive brush strokes and a less naturalistic style, changing her long dress into a tighter, shorter one, and leaving the detailed face almost blank.

When Kiefer painted *Nascita di pittura* and *Untitled* in 1974, the dominant trends of Conceptual and Minimalist art – often introverted and intellectualised abstract styles – were beginning to be challenged by artists in Germany and elsewhere. The arts in general, and works dealing with the Holocaust in particular, were questioned after the Second World War; as philosopher Theodor Adorno (1903–1969) famously wrote in his 1949 essay '*Kulturkritik und Gesellschaft*', 'writing poetry after Auschwitz is barbaric'.[32] Not only had art, culture, and cultural critique failed to prevent human barbarism, they had also been abused for Nazi propaganda. In the twenty to 30 years that followed the end of the Second World War, abstract art in Germany grew in response to the previous attack by the Nazis on subjective and modern art, which they had denounced as 'degenerate', while propagating figurative painting and sculpture in a classicist manner. As American art

histor an Bonnie Clearwater aptly put it in her 2016 exhibition catalogue, abstraction was viewed as a 'universal language' when Kiefer made these paintings, 'in contrast to the nationalistic figuration insisted upon by the Nazi regime and the Soviet Bloc'.[33] The 1970s began to see a gradual revival of painting in expressive, gestural, and experimental styles and with figurative motifs. An increasing number of artists viewed the dominance of abstract art as limiting and sought new ways of expressing themselves. This is particularly evident when looking at the works of Gerhard Richter, Georg Baselitz, A.R. Penck (1939–2017), and Jörg Immendorff (1945–2007), and also younger generations in Berlin, such as Rainer Fetting (b.1949), Elvira Bach (b.1951), and Salomé (b.1954). The movement of more gestural and free painting was soon to be described as Neo-Expressionism.

The palette motif appears frequently in Kiefer's work between 1974 and the early 1980s, and has also appeared occasionally since then. It can be found in small-scale watercolours as well as in oil and acrylic paintings, lead or earthenware objects, and large-sized installations.[34] Kiefer, who has used palettes in different sizes throughout his artistic career, has chosen it as a timeless leitmotif that references his art making in particular, as well as art making in general. It appears in paintings that appropriate Christian imagery, such as *Saint Eustace* (1974) or *Des Malers Schutzengel* (*The Painter's Guardian Angel*; 1975), as well as in works that deal with art containing an echo of Nazi crimes and imagery, such as *Herzleide* (1979) or *Unternehmen "Trappenfang"* (1976; pp.126–7). Against the background of the 1970s art world, and combined with dancing women from art manuals and unrelated picturesque landscapes, the palettes in *Nascita di pittura* and *Untitled* draw attention to the complexities around figurative painting in post-war Germany. The works remain ambiguous: with their strong expressive language, bright

***NASCITA DI PITTURA
(THE BIRTH OF PAINTING)*, 1974**

Oil on linen
180.5 × 129.5 cm

Hall Collection

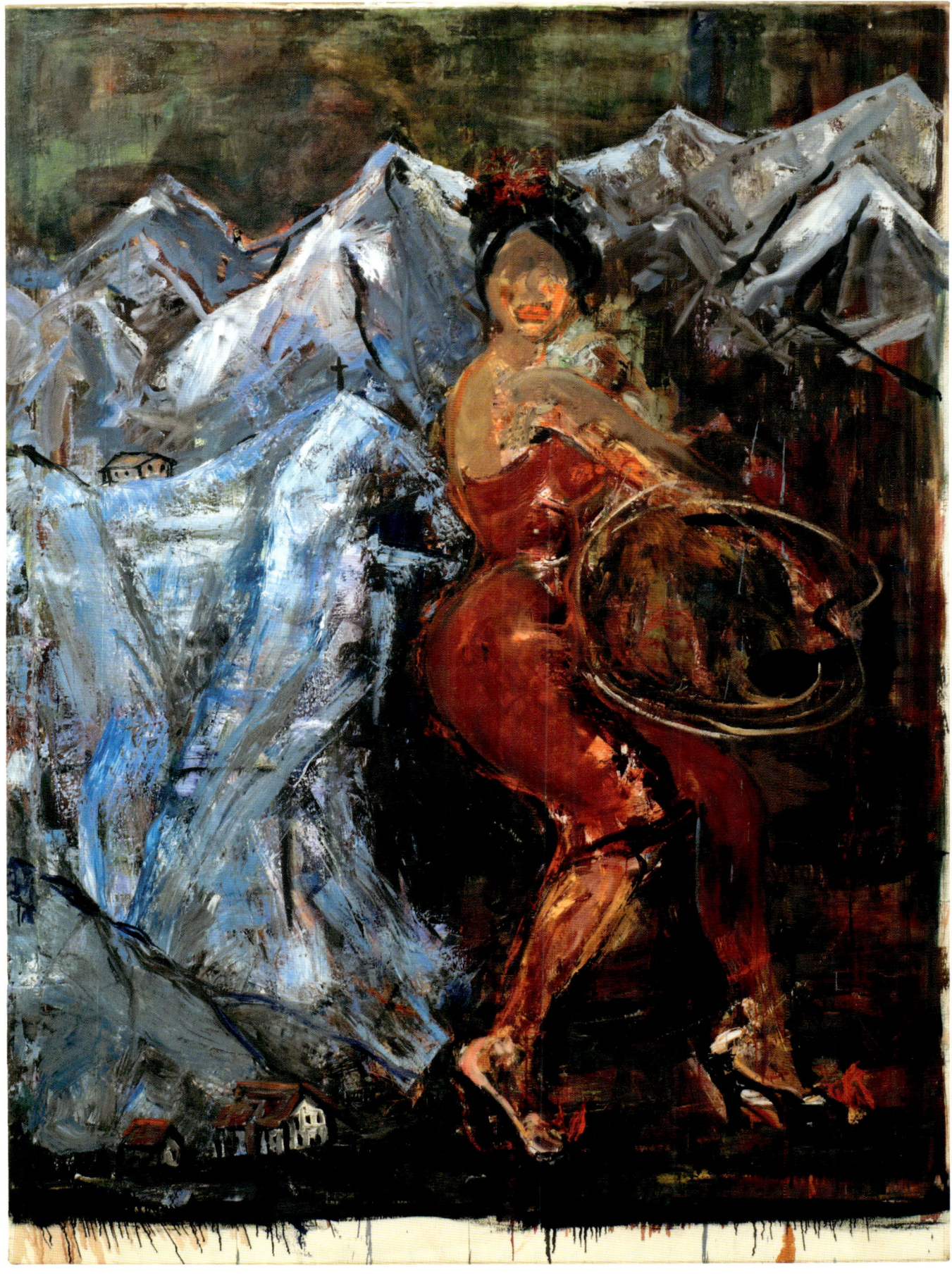

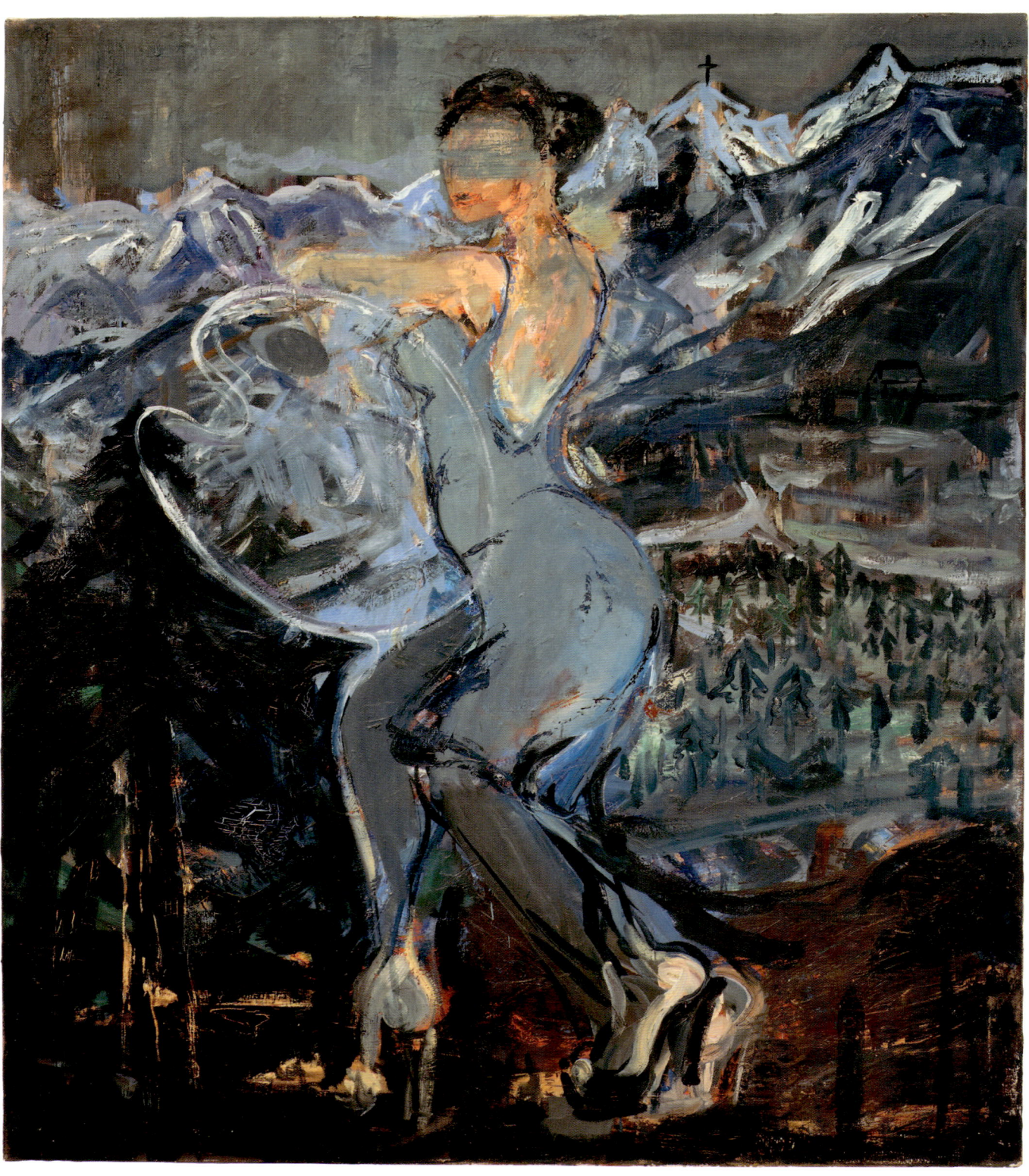

13
UNTITLED, 1974
Oil on linen
150 × 129.5 cm
Hall Collection

15

HOW TO PAINT NUDES, 1974

Oil on burlap

125 × 95 cm

Hall Collection

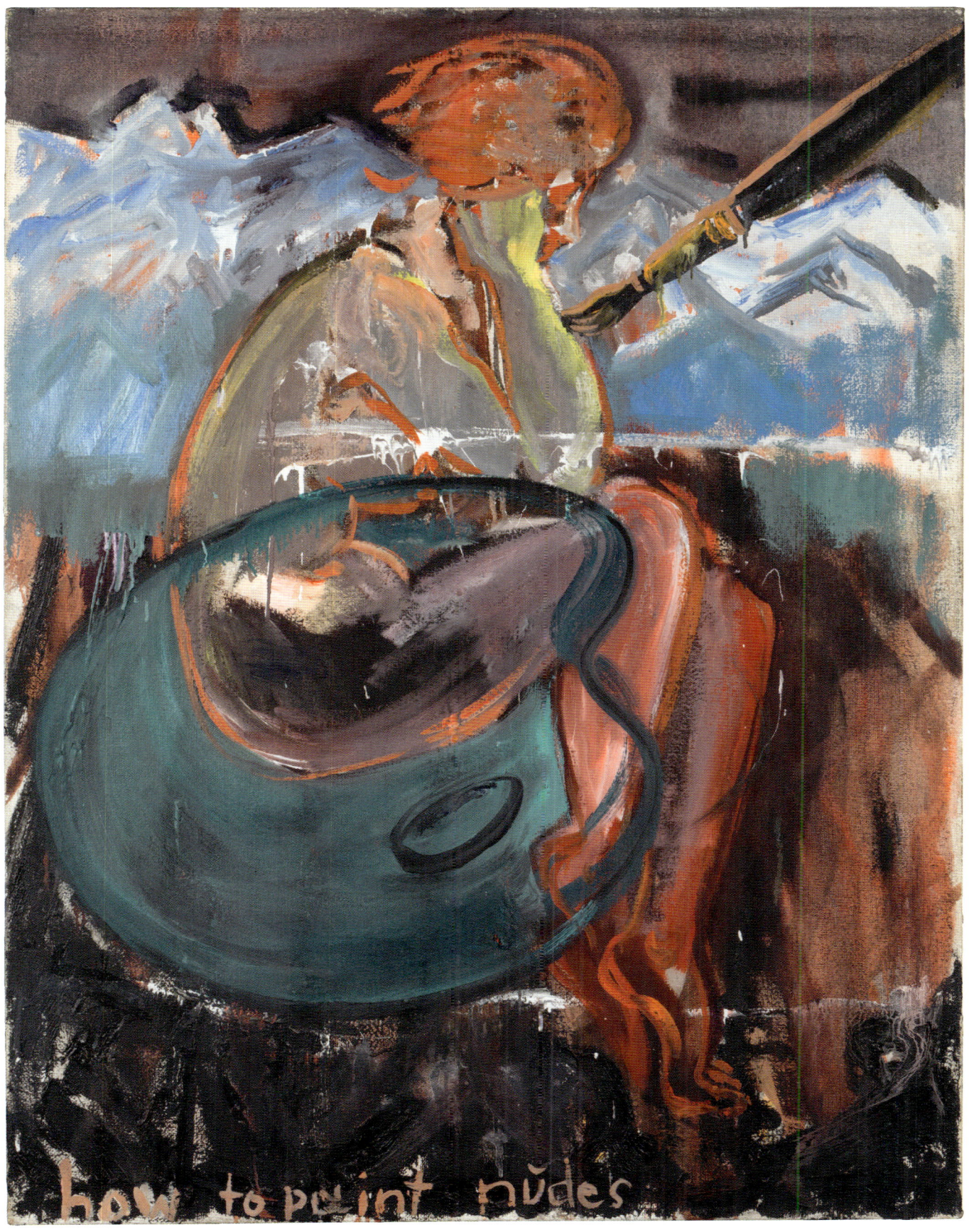

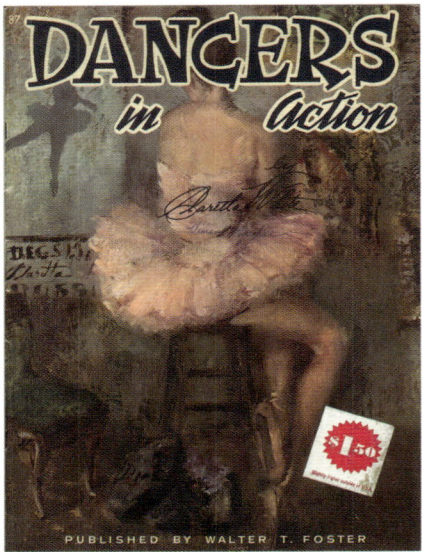

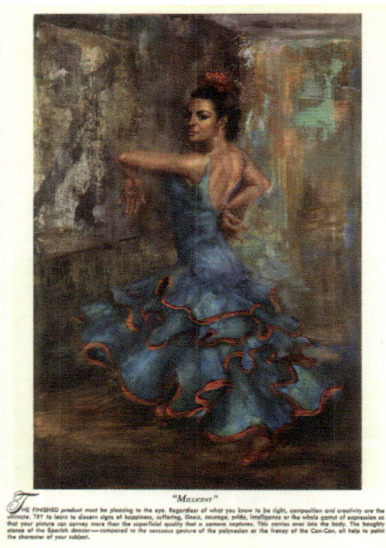

colours, and dynamic dance motifs, they can be viewed as celebrations of the art of painting, but they are also ironic comments on contemporary art trends as well as on banal stipulations in manuals deciding what 'good' and 'bad' painting is, and whether images are 'high' or 'low art'.
Lena Fritsch

HOW TO PAINT NUDES, 1974

Painted in energetic brush strokes, a naked woman sits on a rock-like structure, her face partly resting in her hand. Beyond her is a snow-capped mountainous landscape in blue-white tones. Superimposed on her body is a large turquoise painter's palette, which appears to be transparent as the woman's body shines through. On the top right-hand side of the painting a large brush approaches her arm, as if it were painting her. Her head and face are outlined expressively in orange, beige, red, and white tones, depicting the hair and features crudely and without detail. On the bottom of the painting the words read: 'how to paint nudes'.

Made in the same year as the paintings of dancing women and the work *Still Life is Exciting* (pp.74–5), *How to Paint Nudes* is similarly inspired by a Walter T. Foster art instruction periodical from the 1960s, while also referencing the complex cultural memory that impacted art making in post-war Germany. The woman's seated posture with crossed legs mirrors the illustration on the cover of *The Nude: How to Draw #96* by American artist Fritz Willis (1907–1979), an issue of the periodical that was dedicated to the female nude body (p.73). Fritz Willis was best known for his erotic pin-up illustrations, focusing on the female body and its form in intimate settings, mostly working in oil and pencil. The young woman on the cover of *The Nude* is painted in beige and brown tones in a soft, naturalistic style. She sits on a white cushion or bed and faces the viewer, covering her breasts and her behind with a brown fur-like piece of clothing, creating a seductive play of veiling and unveiling. A small tray with a rose, apples, and grapes sits in front of her on the floor, and a white candle in the background creates a casual bedroom impression. In contrast, Kiefer's figure, juxtaposed with mountains in the background and painted in more bright, non-naturalistic colours and dynamic brushstrokes, appears unconcerned about the viewer: she ignores him and does not cover her body. She has placed her face in her right hand and seems to look down pensively, reminiscent of *The Thinker* (1904; p.73) by Auguste Rodin (1840–1917).

The palette motif appears frequently in Kiefer's work across different artistic media, particularly between 1974 and the early 1980s. In *How to Paint Nudes*, the palette, together with the brush, functions as a symbol of painting, drawing attention to the complexities around (particularly figurative) art making in post-war Germany, after art had been abused by the Nazis for propaganda and failed to prevent the human barbarism of the Third Reich. Instead of creating an erotic scene that aims at female seduction for the male gaze, Kiefer's introspective figure is placed outside in nature. Through the presence of the brush within the image, the subject of the painting and the painter become one.
Lena Fritsch

STILL LIFE IS EXCITING, 1974

In this small painting, a round loaf of bread, a shiny apple, and a red-brown jug are set against a grey surface and a green-turquoise background. The viewer faces the

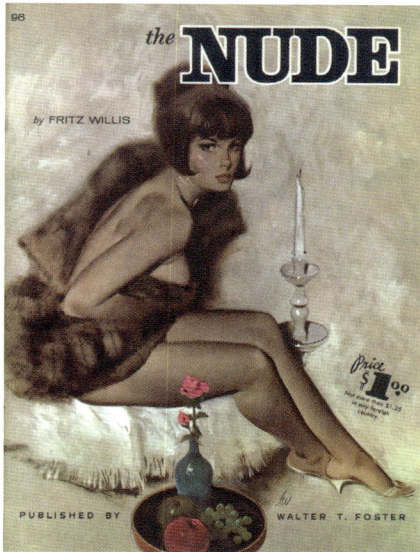

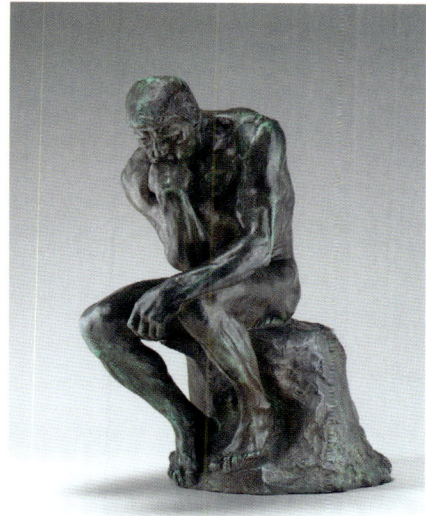

objects from slightly above; the composition conveys an impression of closeness and intimacy. White lines on the jug and yellow shadows under the apple create an illusion of light and three-dimensionality. In black letters at the top, the painting tells us that 'Still Life is Exciting'.

Made in the same year as the paintings that appropriate female subjects from Walter T. Foster art instruction periodicals, *Still Life is Exciting* is another work that comments ironically on the complex historical and cultural background of art making in post-war Germany. Having gained prominence in the Netherlands in the sixteenth century, and having remained relevant throughout modern art movements, the genre of still life depicts inanimate, everyday objects that not only represent life but also its fleetingness. Kiefer's painting seems to ask if, after the horrors of Auschwitz, it is still possible to create works of art depicting ordinary things that 'excite' us.[35] The humorous title references the Walter T. Foster art instruction periodical *Still Life is Exciting: How To #112* from the 1960s, in which American painter and art teacher Nan Greacen (1908–1999) teaches simple still-life paintings in step-by-step instructions, giving detailed advice on composition, light, and perspective, focusing on her own works (p.76). She also sets tasks for her readers, for example to paint the same objects in different colours.

Despite its ironic undertone, Kiefer's still life can also be viewed as a reminder of the beauty of mundane food and drink. Austrian journalist, editor, and food writer Christian Seiler wrote in a refreshing way about *Still Life is Exciting* for the Swiss newspaper magazine *Das Magazin* in 2022, linking the painting to our lives today:

> This small painting from 1974 ... directs my gaze to what makes life worth living, even under the dark omens of our present: the bread, the apple, the jug.

Sometimes these days I find it difficult to consider, in a cheerful tone, one or another way of preparing pasta or ratatouille. Like all of us, I think about the war that won't stop, the economic collateral damage that sooner or later we will feel in our own bodies, the pandemic that is preparing to change shape once again, the wretched people who persecute others with hatred from the darkness of their anonymity and make such beautiful facilities as Twitter or Instagram unusable for me because I don't feel like taking part in the competition of Know-It-Alls and belittling.

Of course, I know that Anselm Kiefer did not mean this context when he wrote the line 'Still Life is Exciting' above his painting. But I take the liberty to be comforted by this piece of bread, this apple, and this jug, because I discover the smallest dimension of a world that celebrates our life, with the bare necessities, with things without which we cannot live and whose beauty and ethics do not become corruptible or invalid at any moment.

I stood in front of Kiefer's picture for a long time. I saw the still untouched crust of the bread waiting for us to break and share it. I saw the apple with its seductive shine, and I thought to myself how I would like to give in to this seduction – like so many others – because it rewards me with sweetness and with freshness and with life. I looked at the jug, which holds the secret of whether it contains water or wine, and I understand Anselm Kiefer's picture as a completely out of character hint that it is worthwhile to look closely at the things that surround us, to see their beauty, to recognize their value and to derive from it the justification to hungrily love life, with which we sometimes struggle, and to enjoy it in its elementary particles.[36]

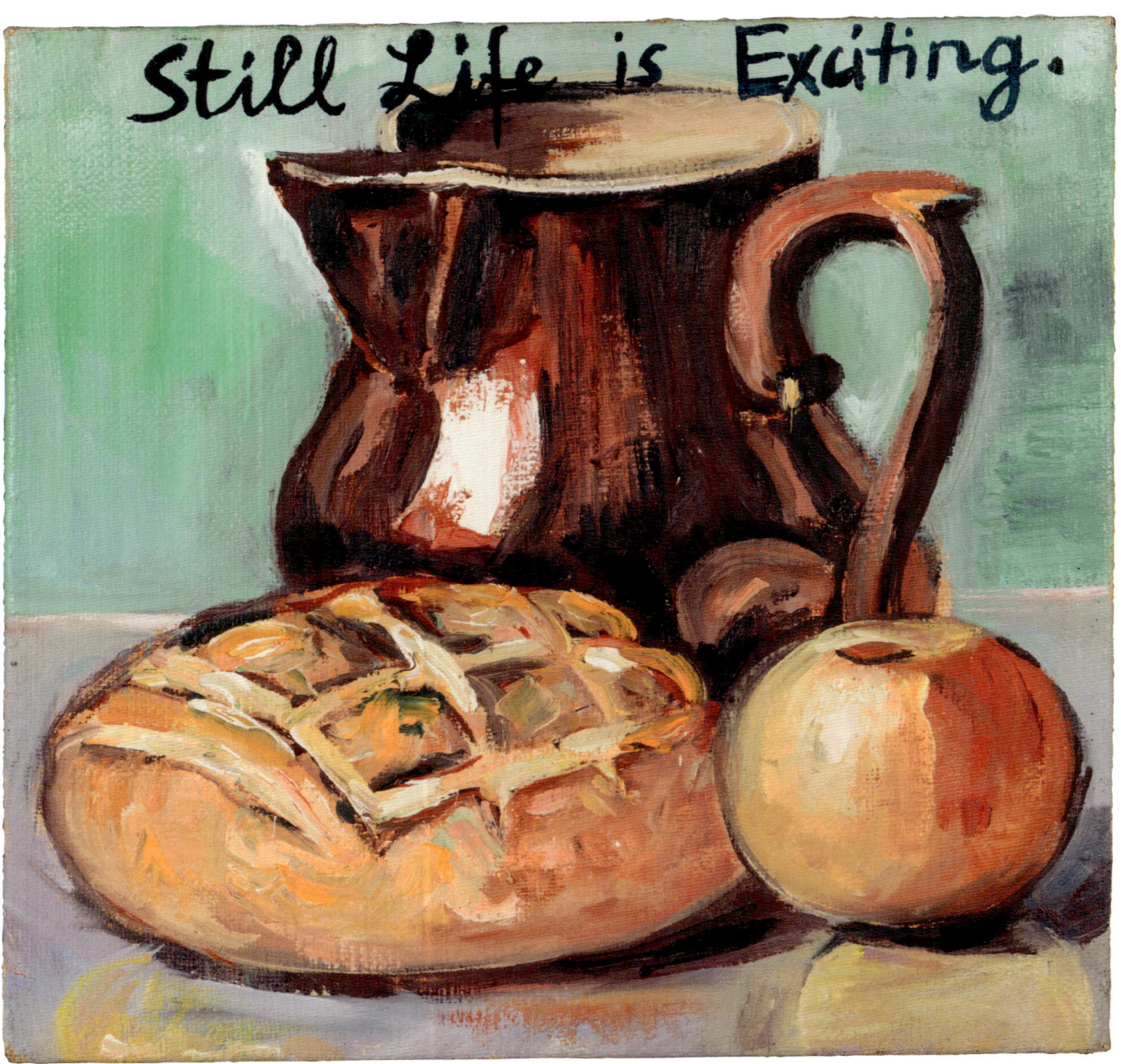

16

STILL LIFE IS EXCITING, 1974
Oil on burlap
51 × 51 cm
Hall Collection

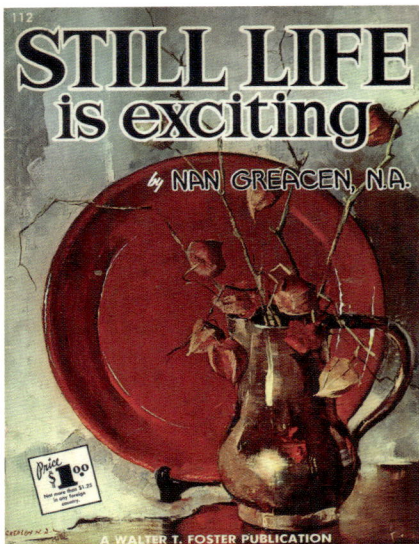

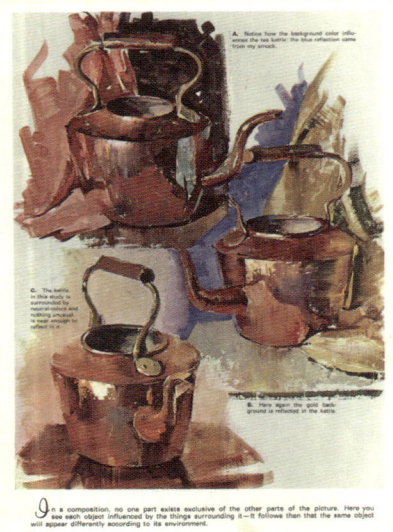

As Seiler's interpretation of Kiefer's unusual work suggests, a still life – regardless of the long art historical tradition of the genre and its popularity amongst amateur painters – can still move viewers today. A still life can, indeed, be exciting.

Lena Fritsch

17

DAS DEUTSCHE VOLKSGESICHT. KOHLE FÜR 2000 JAHRE (THE FACE OF THE GERMAN PEOPLE. COAL FOR 2000 YEARS), 1974

In 1932, a year before the National Socialists seized power in Germany, a small Berlin publishing company, Kulturelle Verlagsgesellschaft, published an elaborately designed photobook by German photographer Erna Lendvai-Dircksen (1883–1962) titled *Das deutsche Volksgesicht* (*The Face of the German People*). It consisted of 140 high-quality copper-plate prints in black and white, showing full-size portrait photographs. A folksy selection of short texts complements the images: citations, poetry lines, and comments by the artist herself. These portraits showed predominantly elderly residents of different rural regions of Germany, from North Frisia down to Upper Bavaria. The sitters remain anonymous; their attributes, costumes, and the titles assign them to certain regions and professions, such as 'peasant from the Altland' and 'Frisian Fisherman from the Wursten Marsh'.[37] Whereas the texts have been set in the old fashioned *Fraktur* – a font claimed to be typically German – the portrait photographs make use of a *Neue Sachlichkeit* (New Objectivity) modernist visual language, such as sharp black and white contrasts, clear lines, and closely observed details. Indeed, this book

belongs to a particular photographic genre, which had already become popular in the 1920s by *Neue Sachlichkeit* photographers like August Sander (1876–1964) with his 1929 photobook *Antlitz der Zeit* (*Face of the Time*), or with Helmar Lerski's *Köpfe des Alltags* (*Everyday Heads*; 1931), and other ideologically quite unsuspicious photographers, without any racial or nationalist motifs. Nevertheless, the collective 'Germanic' approach to portrait photography, as performed by Erna Lendvai-Dircksen and other contemporaries, was set to please the Nazis, as it complied perfectly with their project to inventory the anthropological and physiognomic traits of 'the German', in distinction to people of foreign origin or 'race'. After 1933, picture books like *Das deutsche Frauenantlitz* (*The German Woman's Countenance*) or *Das Gesicht des deutschen Arbeiters* (*The German Worker's Face*) spread rapidly. Their titles were kept in the singular in order to typify 'the German nature' and to suggest it as ethnically normative.

Lendvai-Dircksen often captured her 'German faces' close up. In their features, particularly in those marked by old age, the native landscape is almost metaphorically present: furrowed, gnarled, wrinkled, and creased. This is, above all, the result of a refined photographic staging that creates these effects. The face of the traditional rural population was, according to the photographer's basic concept, shaped by nature itself. Thus, its perfect form could only be found in the countenances of elderly rural people. Their continued existence was at risk, allegedly due to racial degeneration, which is why Lendvai-Dircksen considered it her task to create a photographic record of the German native people; out of their totality she created a collective 'face of the German race'. Her book, and even more so the subsequent volumes that she edited after 1935, confront the reader openly with their racist mindset. They fit seamlessly into the national socialists' propaganda machinery: 'Erna Lendvai-Dircksen understands the face

LENDVAI-DIRCKSEN

EIN DEUTSCHES MENSCHENBILD

Book cover of Erna Lendvai-Dircksen, *Ein deutsches Menschenbild* (*A German Image of Mankind*), 1961. Frankfurt a.M: Umschau Verlag

as a venue for ideological conflict.'[38] In the context of his artistic research on National Socialist ideologies and aesthetics, as well as the precarious role of the artist, in 1974 Anselm Kiefer dealt with this photobook intensively in a process of re-enactment and imaginative continuation.

Measuring 57 × 45 × 6 cm, Kiefer's *Volksgesicht* is unwieldy and much larger than Lendvai-Dircksen's 18 × 15 × 2 cm edition, and, with 182 pages, more voluminous than the original also. It is composed of two separate parts. First, Kiefer photocopied and enlarged a selection of Lendvai-Dircksen's photographs, which he put in his own order. Then, he mounted this 'photocopy-book' onto a larger book-like object, which protrudes over the side edges like a frame. Title and subtitle, written in Kiefer's typical schoolchild handwriting, are permanently visible when turning the pages: '*Das deutsche Volksgesicht. Kohle für 2000 Jahre*'. The second part of the title, *Kohle für 2000 Jahre* (*Coal for 2000 Years*), reflects, ironically, the Nazi's presumptuous idea of a 'thousand-year-long Reich', which fortunately, was to last for 'only' twelve years in the end. Anselm Kiefer has stated that:

> The coal, coming into existence over the course of millions of years from the left over of plants, represents the geological time, which will outlive the thousand-year-long Reich that humans were striving for, exposing it as insignificant and megalomaniacal.[39]

The larger book-object, made by Kiefer himself, consists of 50 sheets of thick woodchip wallpaper. It also has two separate sections: the beginning shows large charcoal drawings that remind us of rough Expressionist woodcuts; they are inserted transversely to the photocopies of the smaller book, which means that the reader has to rotate the object in order to recognise individual faces from the latter (pp.128–9). They have been graphically transformed, coarsened, and distorted. Kiefer reworked the sheets using a frottage technique, so that the contours and features gradually merge with the contrasting structure of the wooden elements – as the curator Mark Rosenthal wrote: 'Peasant's faces emerge from the linear patterns of woodcuts with the effect that their features are thoroughly one with the land.'[40] The second part of this wallpaper book shows a sequence of double pages, covered with undecipherable signs and geometrical patterns, which could be representing aerial views as well as pure painterly abstractions, in rhythmic alternation with double pages deeply blackened with tar and emulsion paint that extinguish everything underneath.

Kiefer was to return to the idea of lining up portrait heads in an 'ancestral gallery' only a few years later in his great cycle on the theme of *Hermannsschlacht*. Here, however, the archetypal German is no longer embodied by the rustic type, rather low in spirit, but by 'spiritual heroes', who, during the nineteenth century, had prepared the ground for the Nazi's racial thought-patterns. The praise of the rural life with its soil – the so called '*Blut und Boden*' ideology – belonged, just like the worship of the spiritual leader – the cult of the Führer – to the great Nazi founding myths; their impact extended well into the 1950s and 1960s, as a glance at German school books from Kiefer's schooldays proves.

In 1961 a new edition of Lendvai-Dircksen's *Das deutsche Volksgesicht* was published, although under the softened title *Ein deutsches Menschenbild* (*A German Image of Mankind*; above). In 2003, it was once again re-edited; this time a young girl's face adorned the cover.

Time and again, Anselm Kiefer has carried out profound artistic research on the ideologically burdened ways of German thinking and creating; at an early stage, he already dared to track down and denounce their return – and to extinguish them.

Sabine Schütz

17

DAS DEUTSCHE VOLKSGESICHT.
KOHLE FÜR 2000 JAHRE
(THE FACE OF THE GERMAN PEOPLE.
COAL FOR 2000 YEARS), 1974

Bound original photographs, emulsion,
coal, linseed oil and ferric oxide on
woodchip paper (184 pages)
57 × 45 × 6 cm

Hall Collection

Das deutsche Volksgesicht

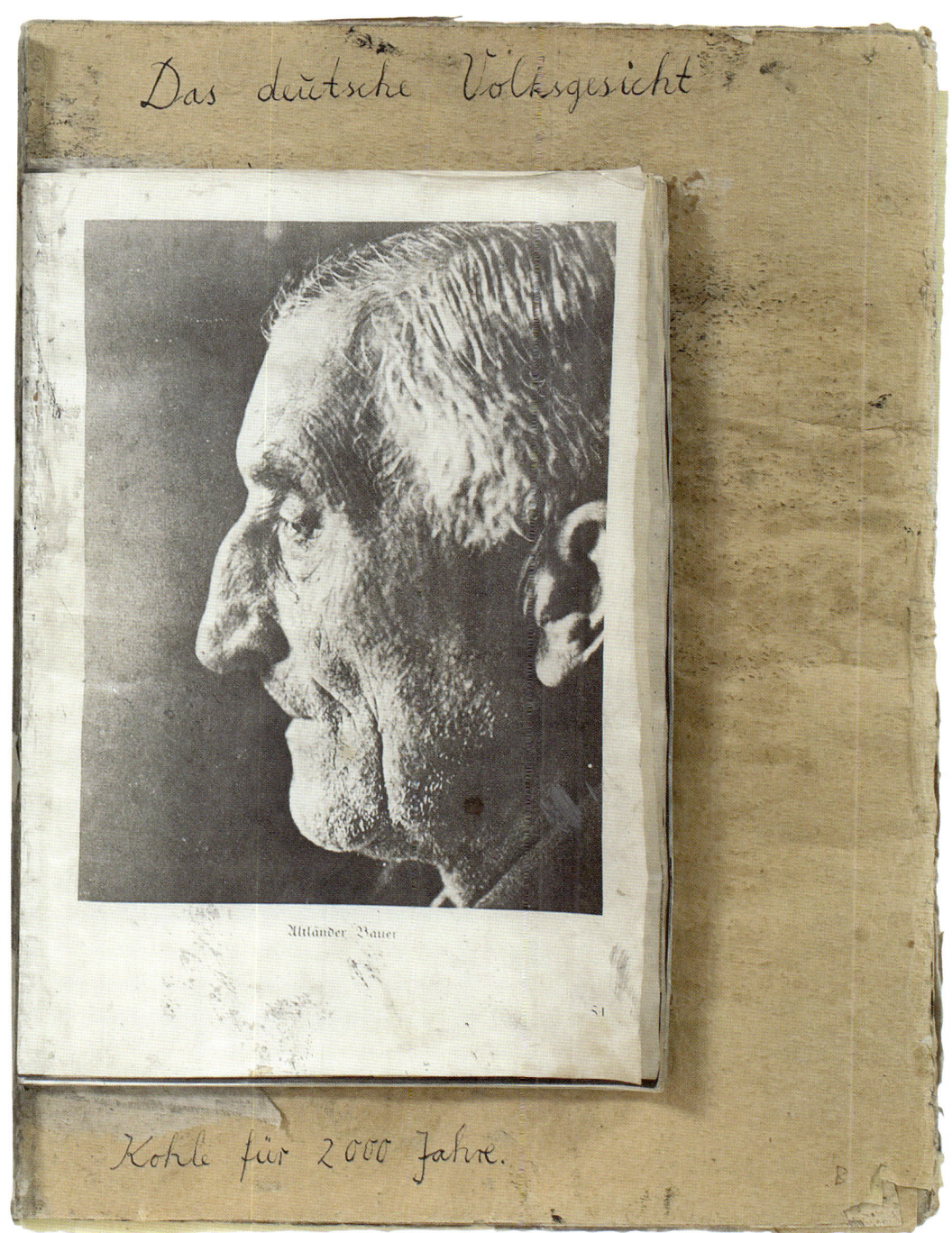

Altländer Bauer

Kohle für 2000 Jahre.

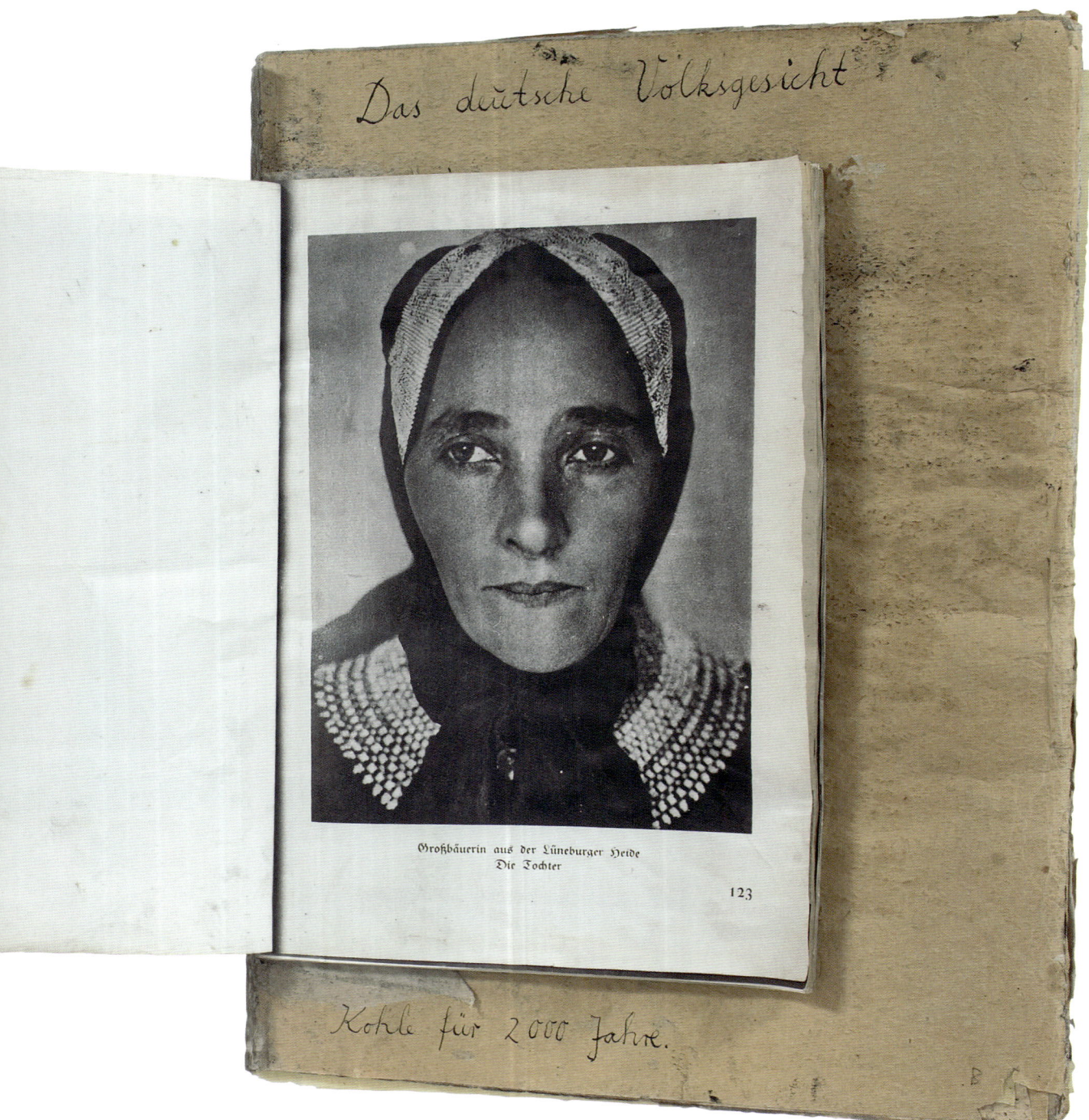

Großbäuerin aus der Lüneburger Heide
Die Tochter

123

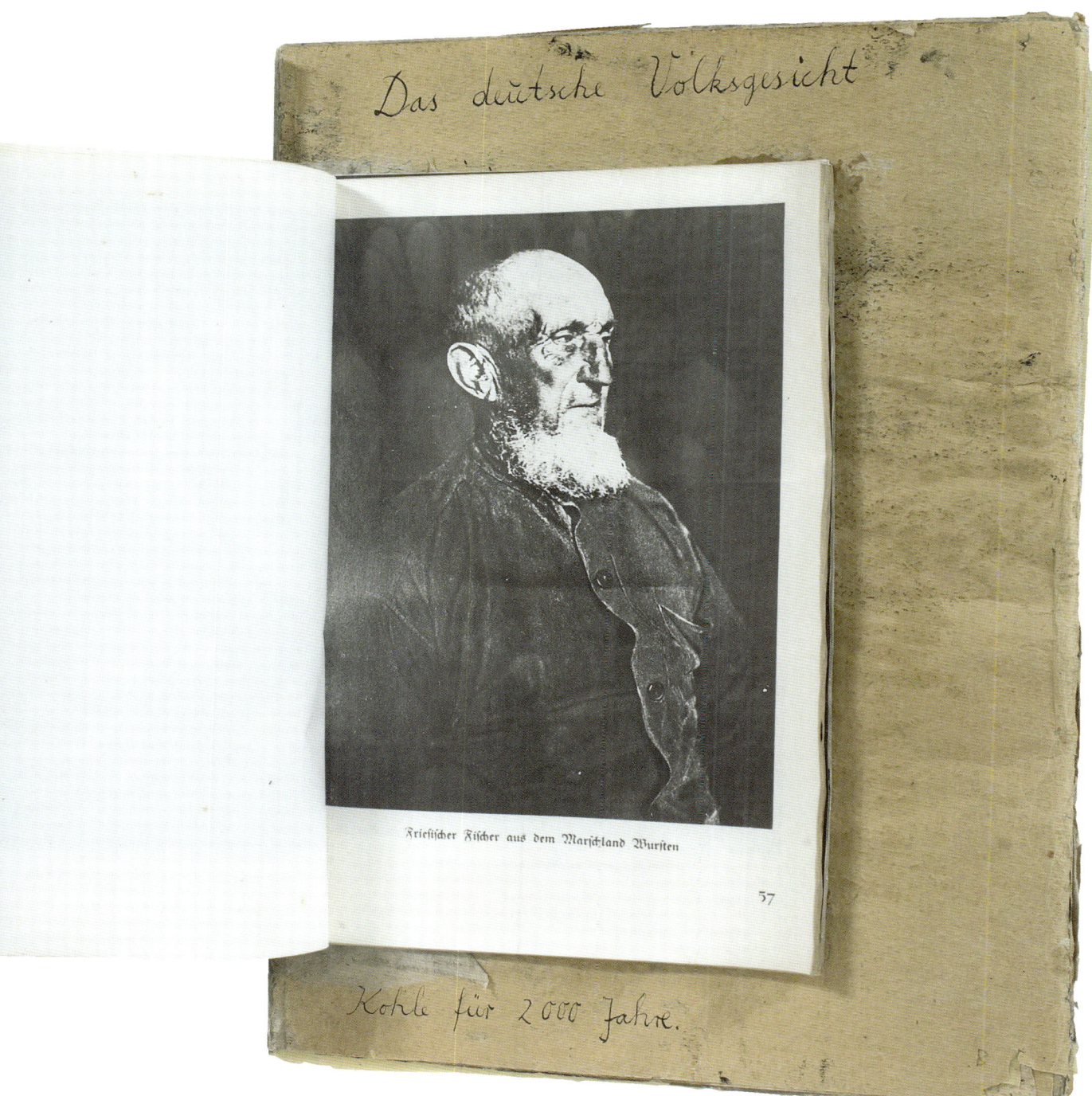

Friesischer Fischer aus dem Marschland Wursten

57

Kohle für 2000 Jahre.

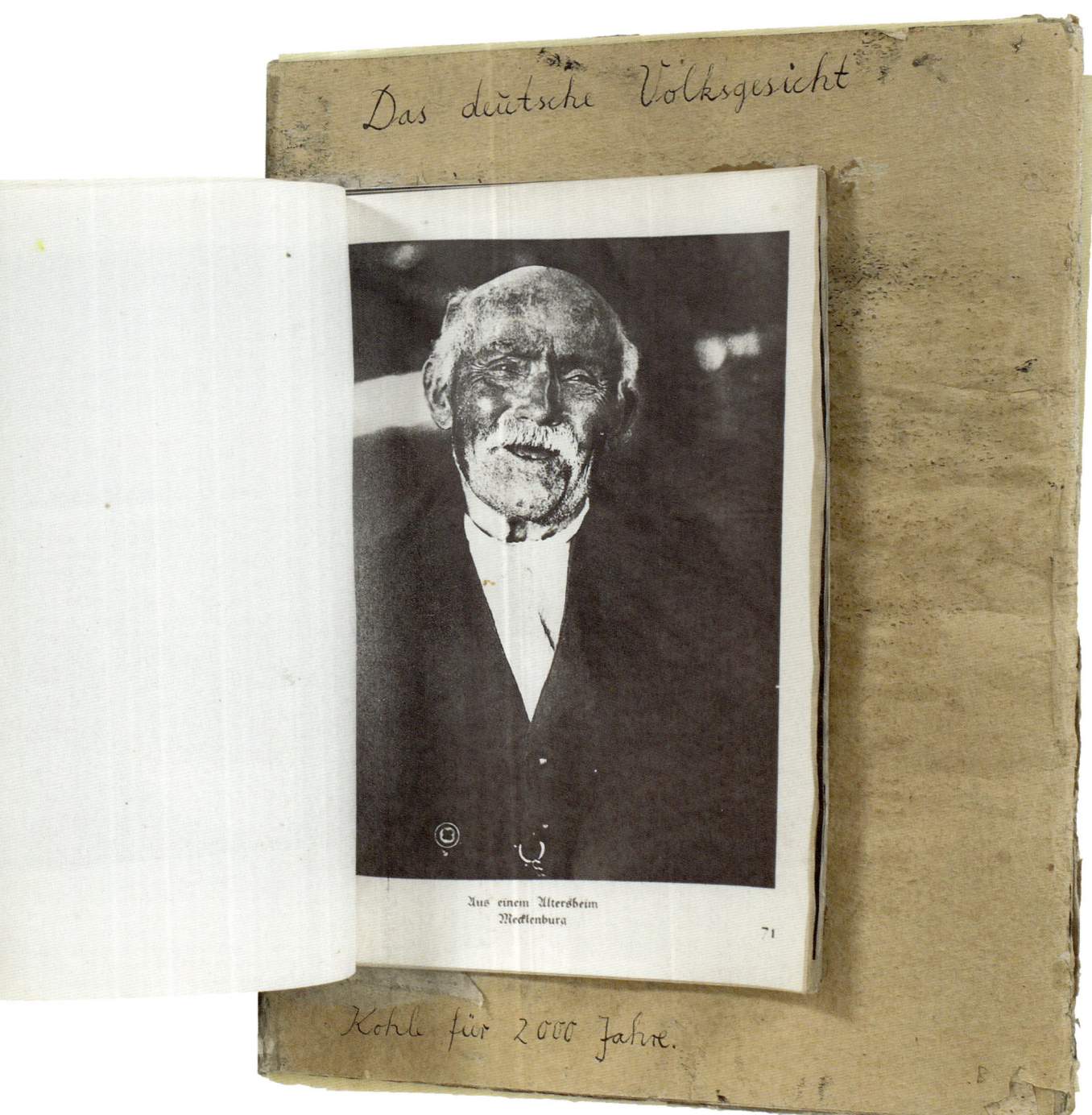

Das deutsche Volksgesicht

Aus einem Altersheim
Mecklenburg

71

Kohle für 2000 Jahre.

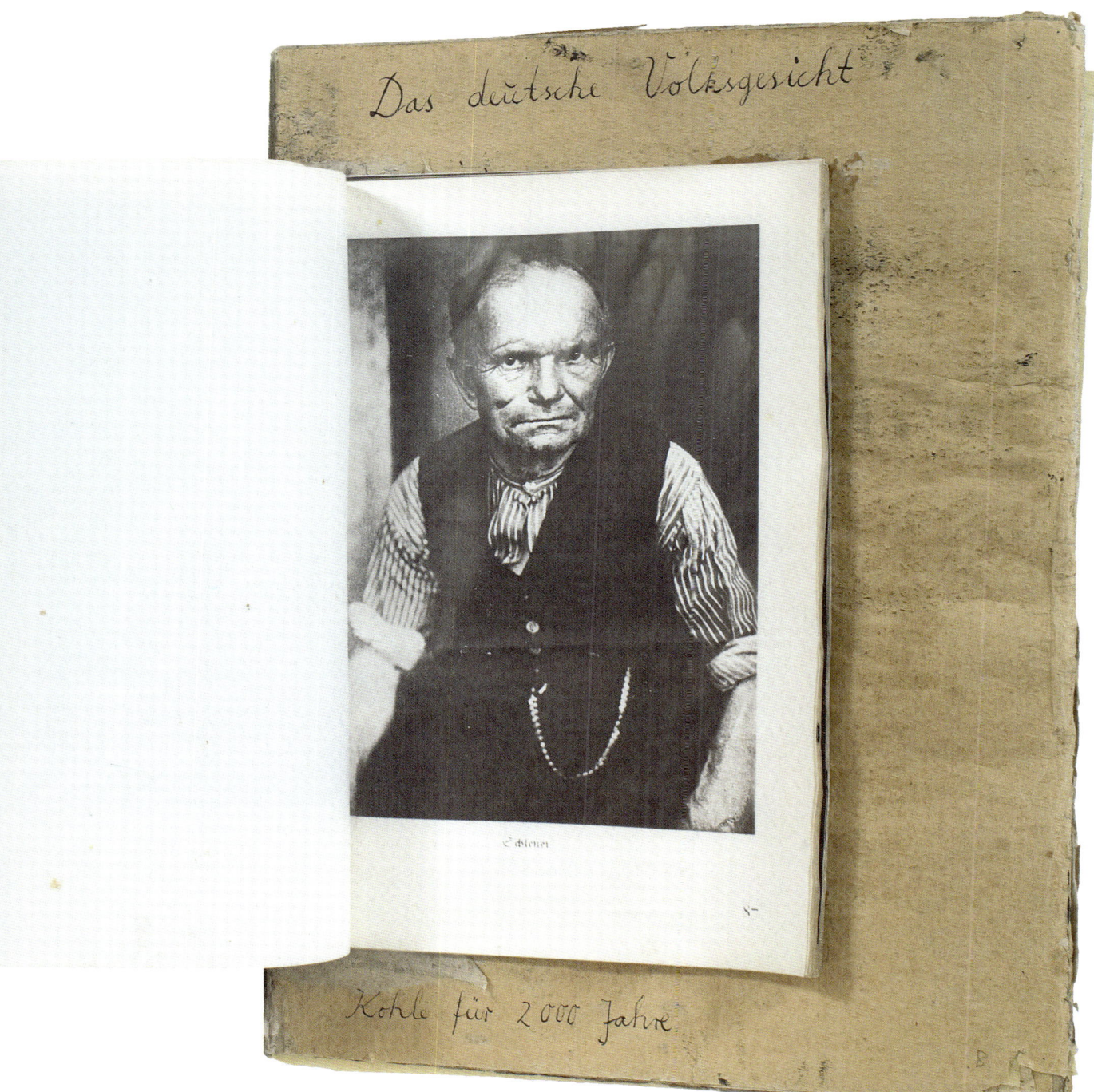

Das deutsche Volksgesicht

Schlesier

Kohle für 2000 Jahre

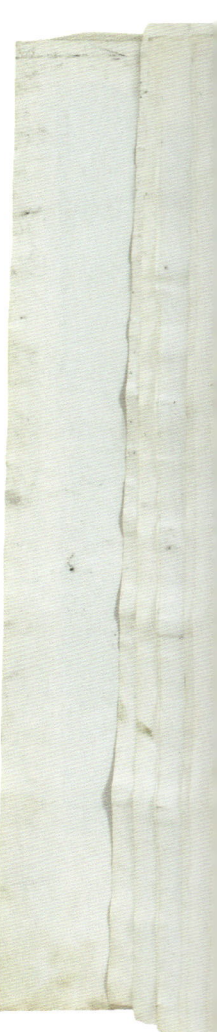

Das deutsche Volksgesicht

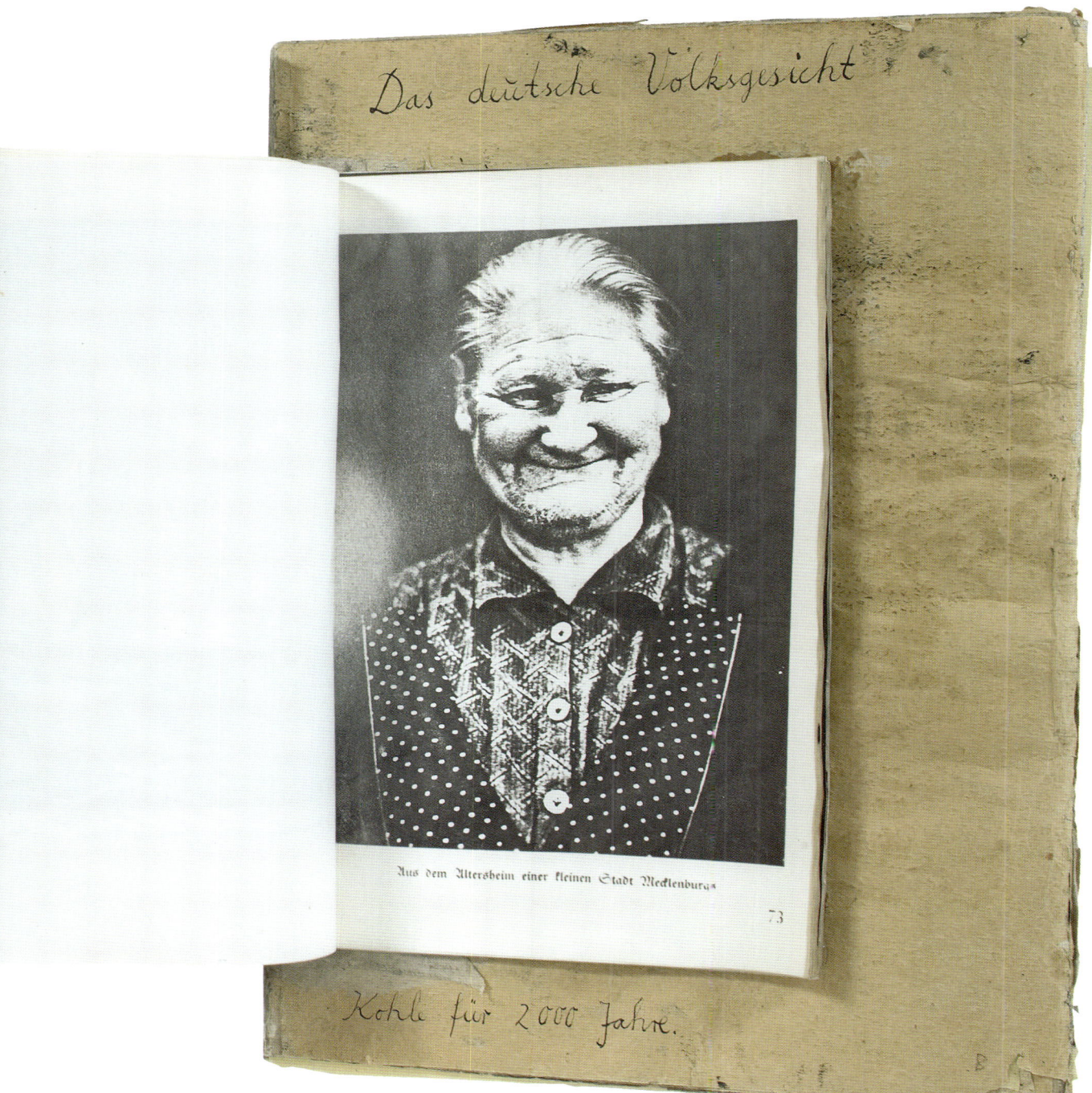

Aus dem Altersheim einer kleinen Stadt Mecklenburgs

73

Kohle für 2000 Jahre.

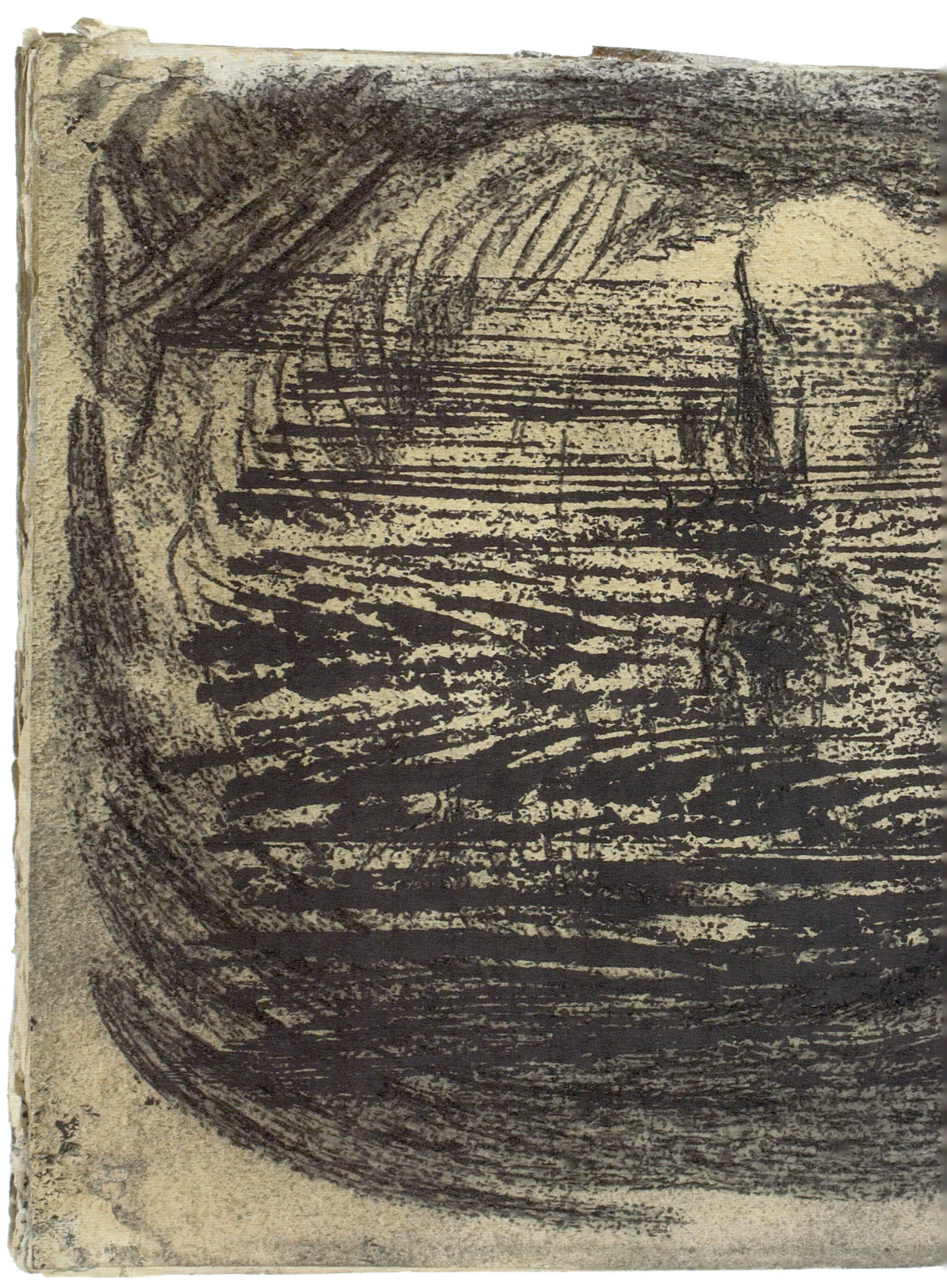

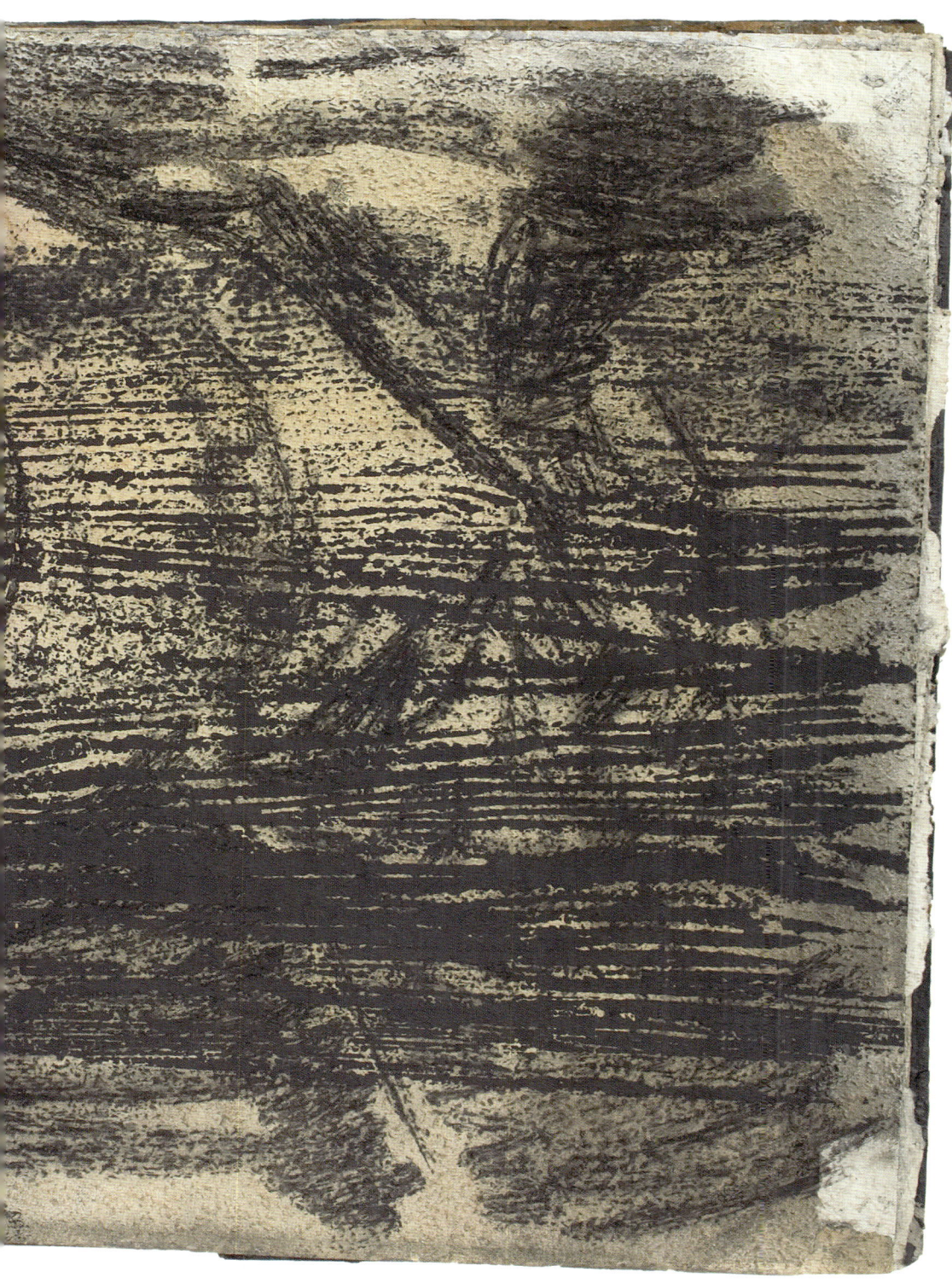

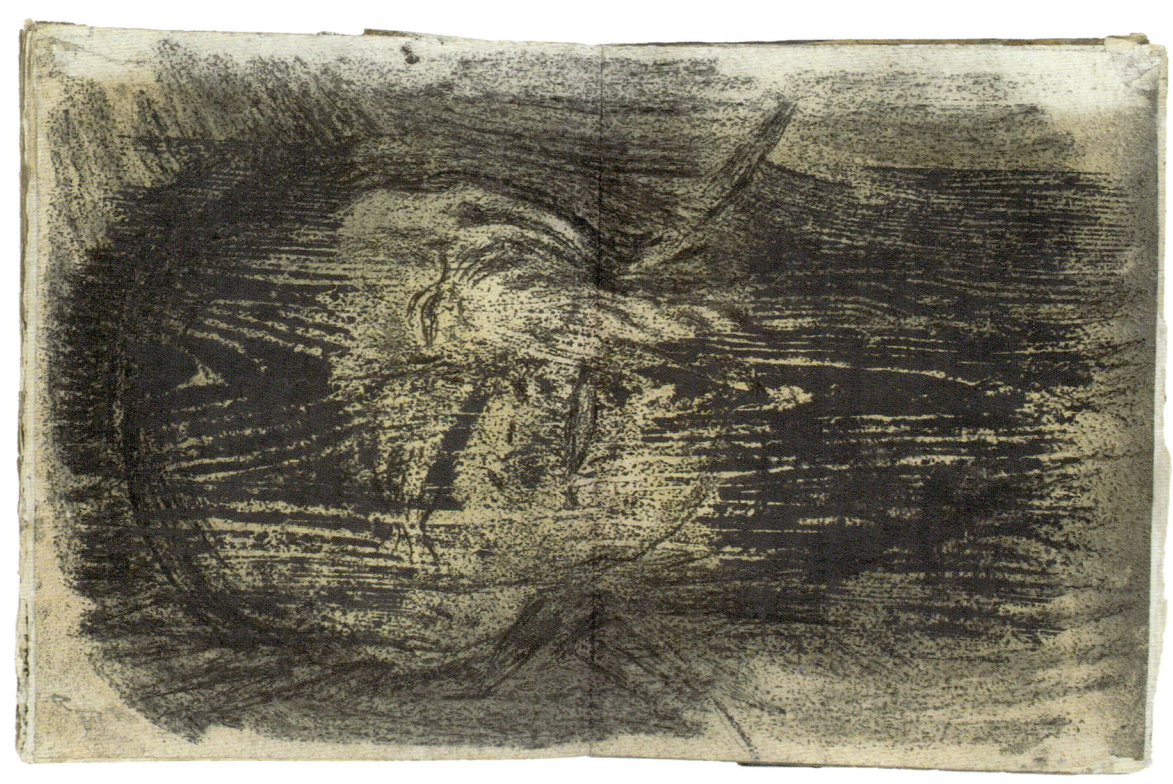

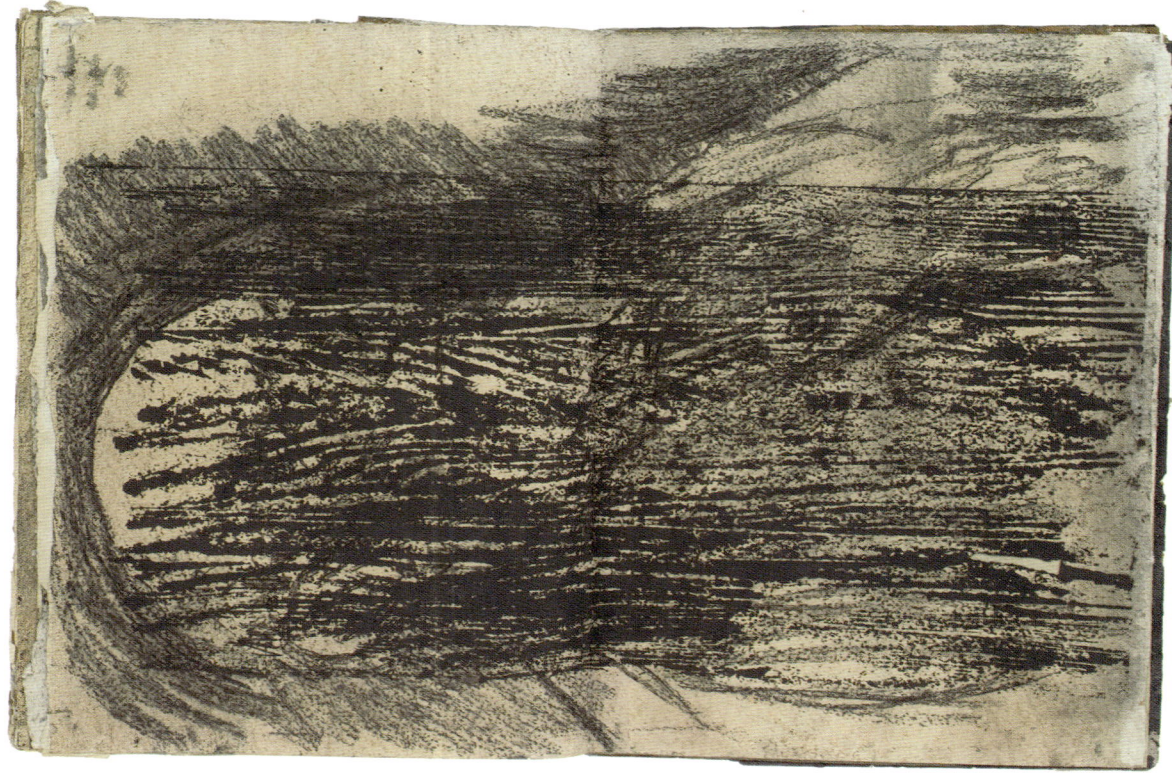

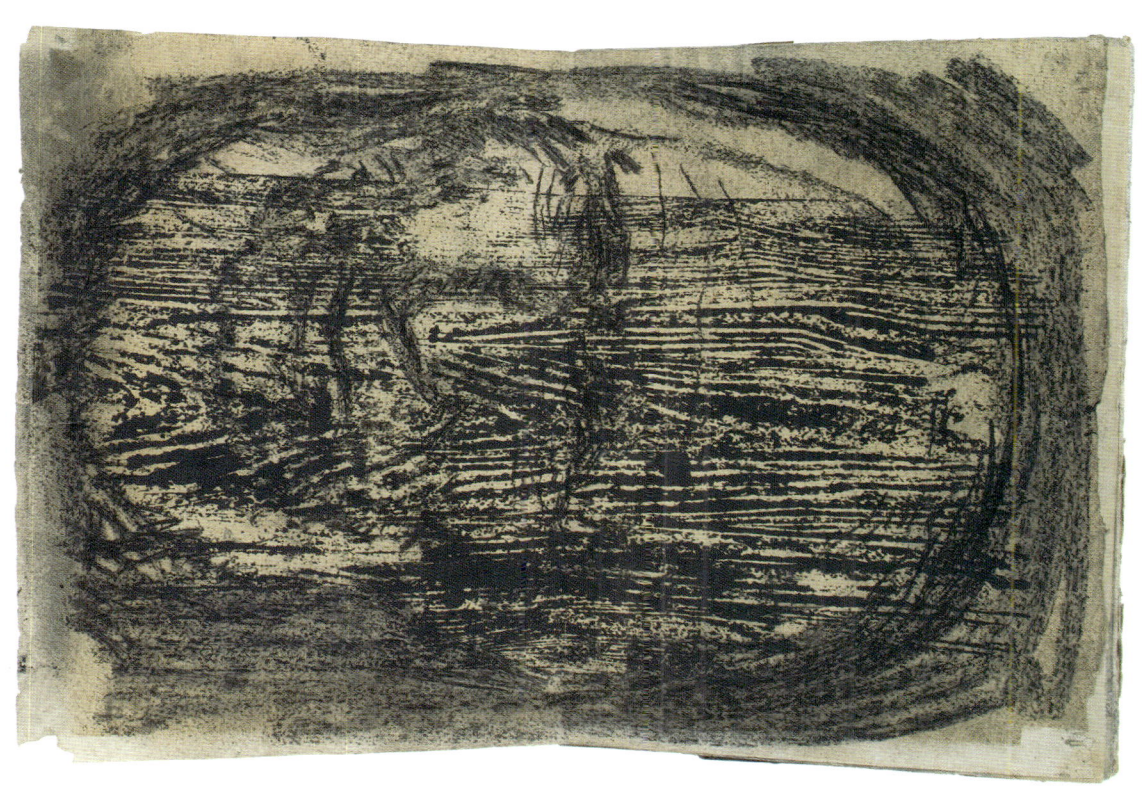

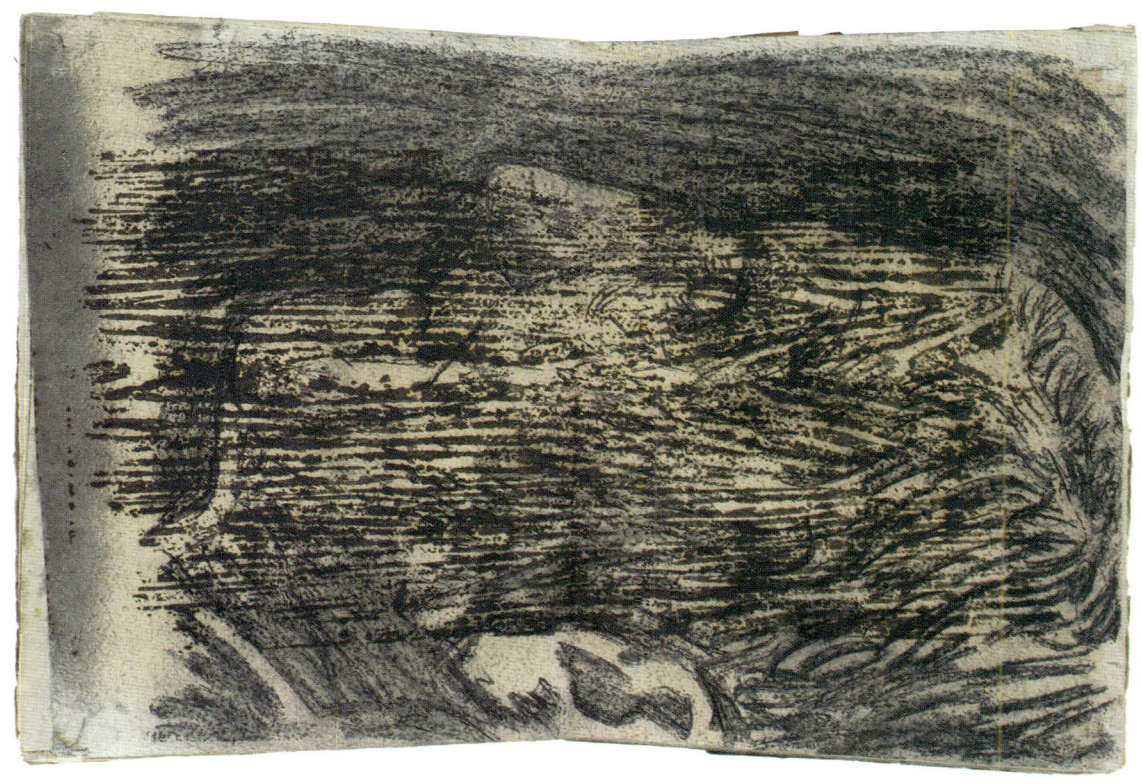

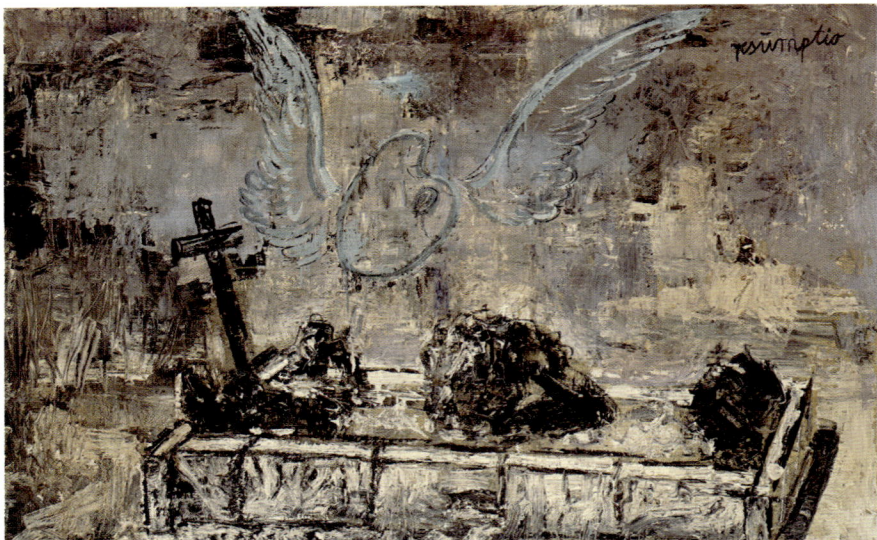

Anselm Kiefer
Resumptio, 1974
Oil, emulsion and shellac
on burlap, 115 × 180 cm

18

UNTITLED, 1974

A white nebulous glow in a turquoise-grey opaque sky; outlines of wings and small white spots that twinkle in darkness; a dark-red painter's palette with white wings floating towards us as if in flight. This dark mixed-media painting presents us with a mysterious scene. Are the wings in the nebula indicating an angel? Why is there a winged palette flying in obscure celestial realms? Is this a fantastical night scene inspired by Christian religion? In small subtle letters it reads on the palette: *'für Elke Baselitz'* – the only concrete information we have is that this painting was dedicated to the wife of the artist Georg Baselitz.

Not only the painter's palette, but also the winged painter's palette, is a frequent and powerful motif in Kiefer's oeuvre. It can be found in a number of his small watercolours from the 1970s as well as in monumental paintings and sculptures made of materials such as lead, steel, and tin from the 1980s. Considering the principal question that Kiefer's work was addressing at this time – how can an artist make work in the tradition of German culture after the Nazi regime and Auschwitz? – the winged palette in *Untitled* (1974) can be interpreted as a symbol for artistic aspirations. The palette appears to be reaching for the stars and the light, spreading its wings and flying freely into the sky. The white glow with the outlines of wings, as well as some thin vertical lines, suggest the presence of a winged figure, such as an angel, appearing fleetingly, as if in a vision. Many of Kiefer's paintings from the 1970s combine the motif of a palette with Christian iconography, for example *Resumptio* (1974; above), *Des Malers Schutzengel* (1975), and *Engel mit Palette* (1977–8; pp.152–3).

Linking the palette motif with wings and angels, it is elevated to an icon, conveying a divine impression. The winged palette here suggests a free artistic spirit that is looking for ideas and creative inspiration, effortlessly moving through celestial space.

Kiefer's wings, flying towards a source of light, are also reminiscent of the ancient Greek story of Icarus. Icarus, the son of skilful artist and inventor Daedalus, manages to escape Crete by flying with wings formed from feathers and wax, made by his father. Ignoring his father's warnings, Icarus flies higher and higher, until he is too close to the sun. The wax melts, and he falls.

Against the background of Christian iconography, mythical tales of men with wings, and the historical context of 1970s Germany, the winged palette in this work can be viewed as a self-referential symbol of Kiefer's own artistic spirit. Like an alter ego of Kiefer, the palette is flying higher and higher without restrictions, reaching for a divine glow in an obscure, but beautiful, celestial space. Transcending gravity, it suggests freedom and elegance, while also conveying an aura of risk: flying too high can lead to a long fall.

Georg Baselitz and his wife Elke, who had been introduced to Kiefer's work the year before *Untitled* was painted, became Kiefer's first major collectors. They became friends and Kiefer sometimes bought clothes for his wife in Elke Baselitz's shop, Modemädchen.[41] He has noted that he found Baselitz's early interest in his work 'extremely encouraging'.[42]

Lena Fritsch

Anselm Kiefer
Ausbrennen des Landreises Buchen
(*Burning of the Rural District of Buchen*), 1974
Bound original photographs, ferric oxide and linseed
oil on woodchip paper (210 pages), 62 × 45 × 3 cm
Hall Collection

AUSBRENNEN DES LANDKREISES BUCHEN (BURNING OF THE RURAL DISTRICT OF BUCHEN), 1974

This artist book, consisting of 210 pages, contains a series of black and white photographs of the countryside of Buchen in Odenwald – where Kiefer's studio at the time was located – and carbonised sections of former finished paintings. The photographs, taken in a 'straight' documentary style, are devoid of people. Initially, they focus on wide fields, farmland, and a few empty streets with village houses, conveying a monotonous feel. Similar landscape views run from page to page with location names handwritten in the upper section of the photograph. However, these images slowly make space for staged photographs of dramatic explosions, covering the landscapes in thick smoke. On some images, large cans are visible next to the smoke- and fire-engulfed landscape. The final pages continue the motif of fire and smoke, presenting burnt paper with small parts of painted landscapes still visible. These black, charcoal-encrusted pages are thick and opaque, conveying a sense of physical weight that contrasts with the photographs earlier in the book.

In a typical Kiefer manner, this multi-layered work offers various references and makes different readings possible, not least through its title. Against the contemporary post-war context of the 1970s, Kiefer's representation of the region as unpopulated mirrors the economic decline of the *Landkreis* (district) of Buchen, which had been dissolved as an administrative subdivision in 1973 and absorbed into a neighbouring district. At the same time, the photographs of explosions also reference the presence of the German armed forces, the *Bundeswehr*, in the region. As of 1958,

a barrack called Nibelungenkaserne had housed hundreds of soldiers and stored large quantities of highly flammable petroleum. In 1974, work on new buildings to expand the barracks had begun. Kiefer's book presents a landscape soaked with oil, showing how the district of Buchen could easily explode, burn, and become cauterised. Fire as a tool of destruction as well as of (re)creation, and the theme of burning, can be found in many other works by Kiefer, including the paintings *Urd, Werdandi, Skuld (Die Nornen)* (1981; pp.182–3) and *Margarethe – Sulamit* (1981; pp.184–5.).

Considering its three artistic media – book, photography, and painting – *Ausbrennen des Landkreises Buchen* can also be read in a more conceptual and medium-specific way, as dealing with different forms of artistic representation. Traditionally associated with ideas of truth and authenticity, photography here is used to 'document' both actual landscapes, to which Kiefer added location inscriptions, and artistically staged fire scenes. The burnt paintings at the end present the actual effect of fire in an indexical sense. How much truth is revealed by photography and by text, and how revelatory is landscape painting, reduced to abstract blackness as a result of fire? The photographs, arranged in a series, not only suggest a narrative component that points at the district of Buchen turning to ashes, but they also reference Kiefer's creative process of making the book, which includes the use of fire. As such, photography and painting combined with the medium of the book create a unique history of their own. Progressive degradation is a repeated motif within Kiefer's books, mirroring his interest in the transformative nature of materials. The carbonised paper will continue to change and evolve over time.

Ausbrennen des Landkreises Buchen combines Kiefer's interest in the German landscape with his fascination with fire, while raising questions about art and representation. The name of Buchen is reminiscent of the German word

18

UNTITLED, 1974

Mixed media on paper

62.5 × 44 cm

Hall Collection

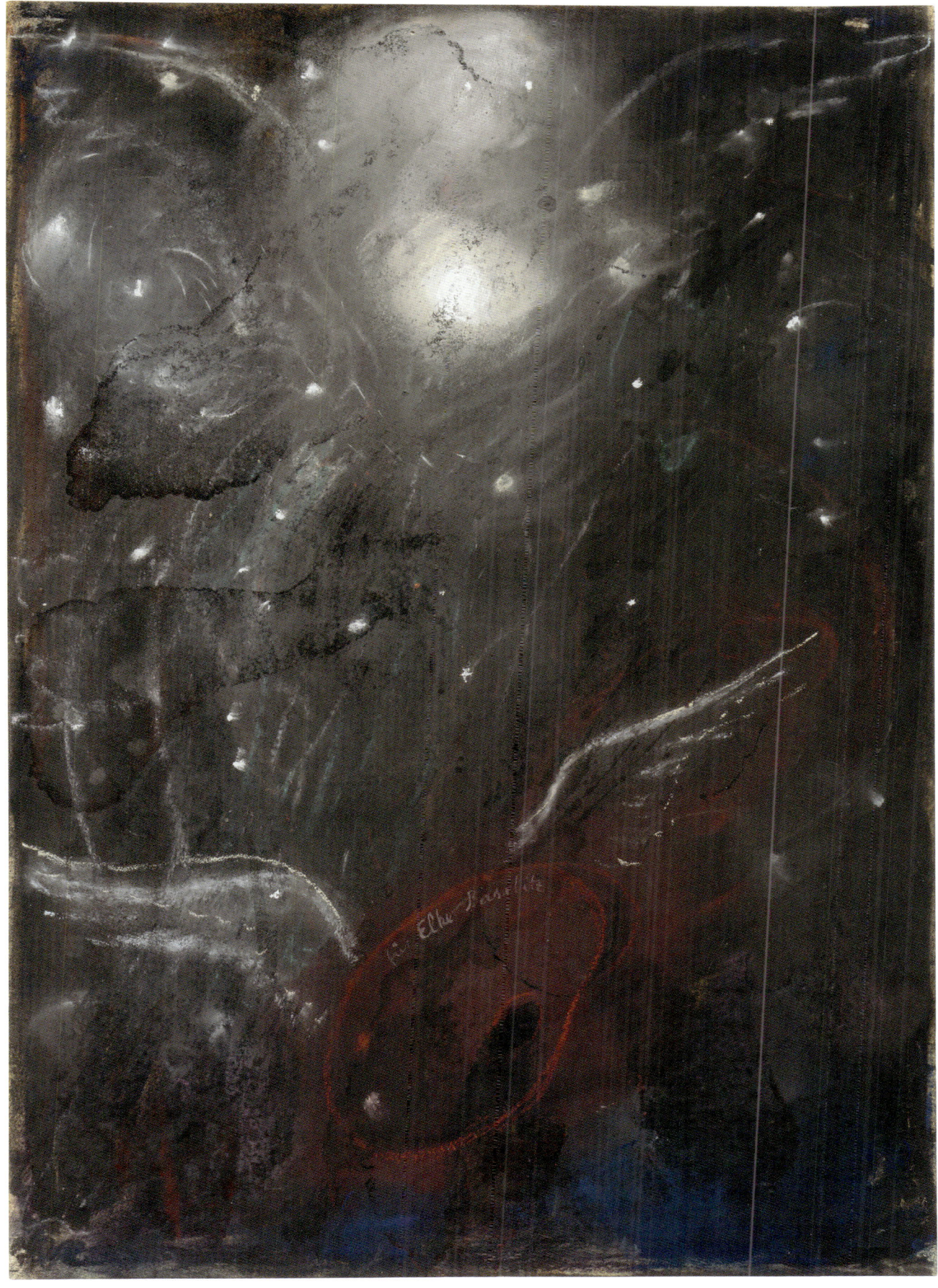

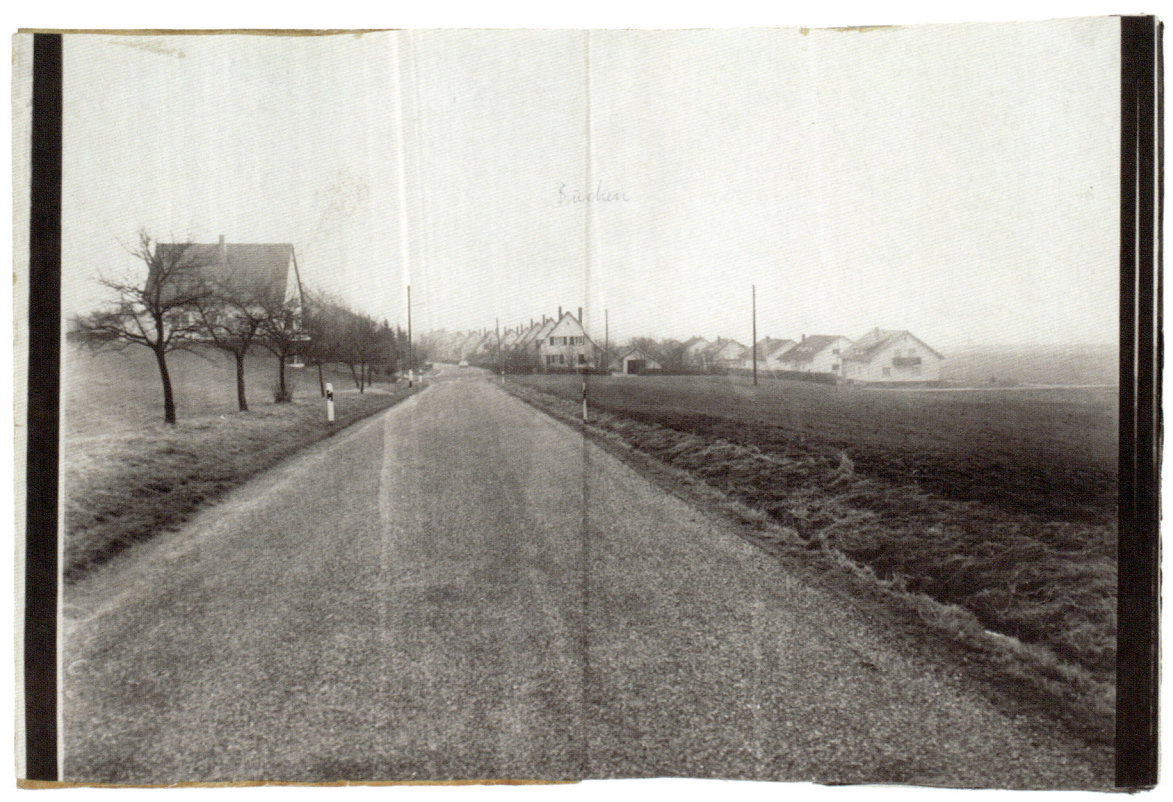

19

***AUSBRENNEN DES
LANDKREISES BUCHEN
(BURNING OF THE RURAL
DISTRICT OF BUCHEN), 1974***

Bound original photographs, ferric oxide and
linseed oil on woodchip paper (210 pages)
62 × 45 × 3 cm
Hall Collection

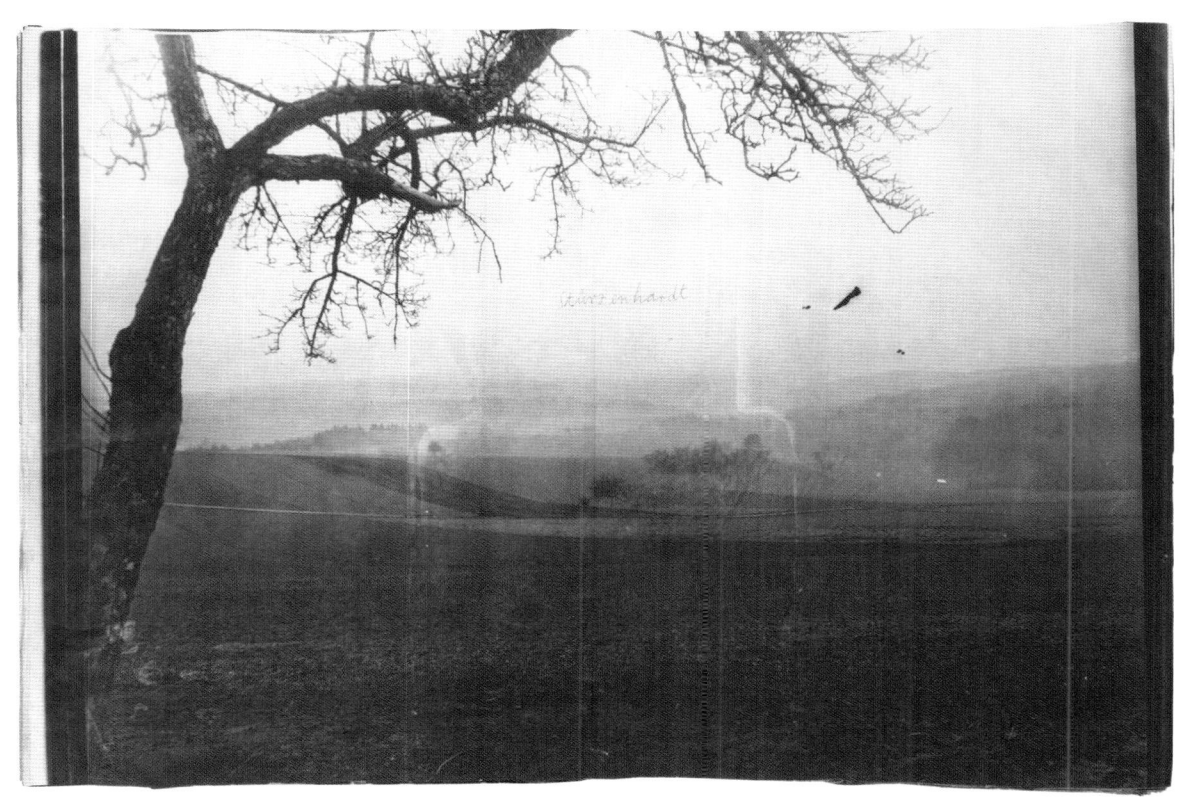

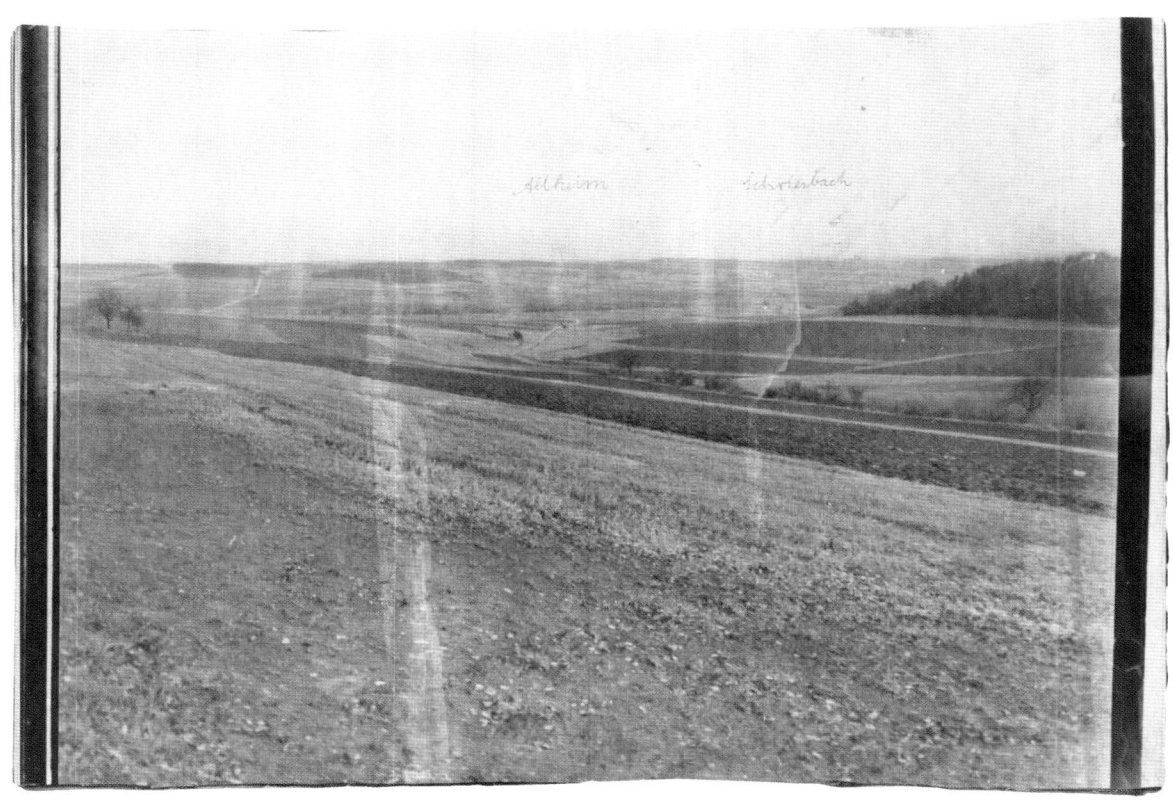

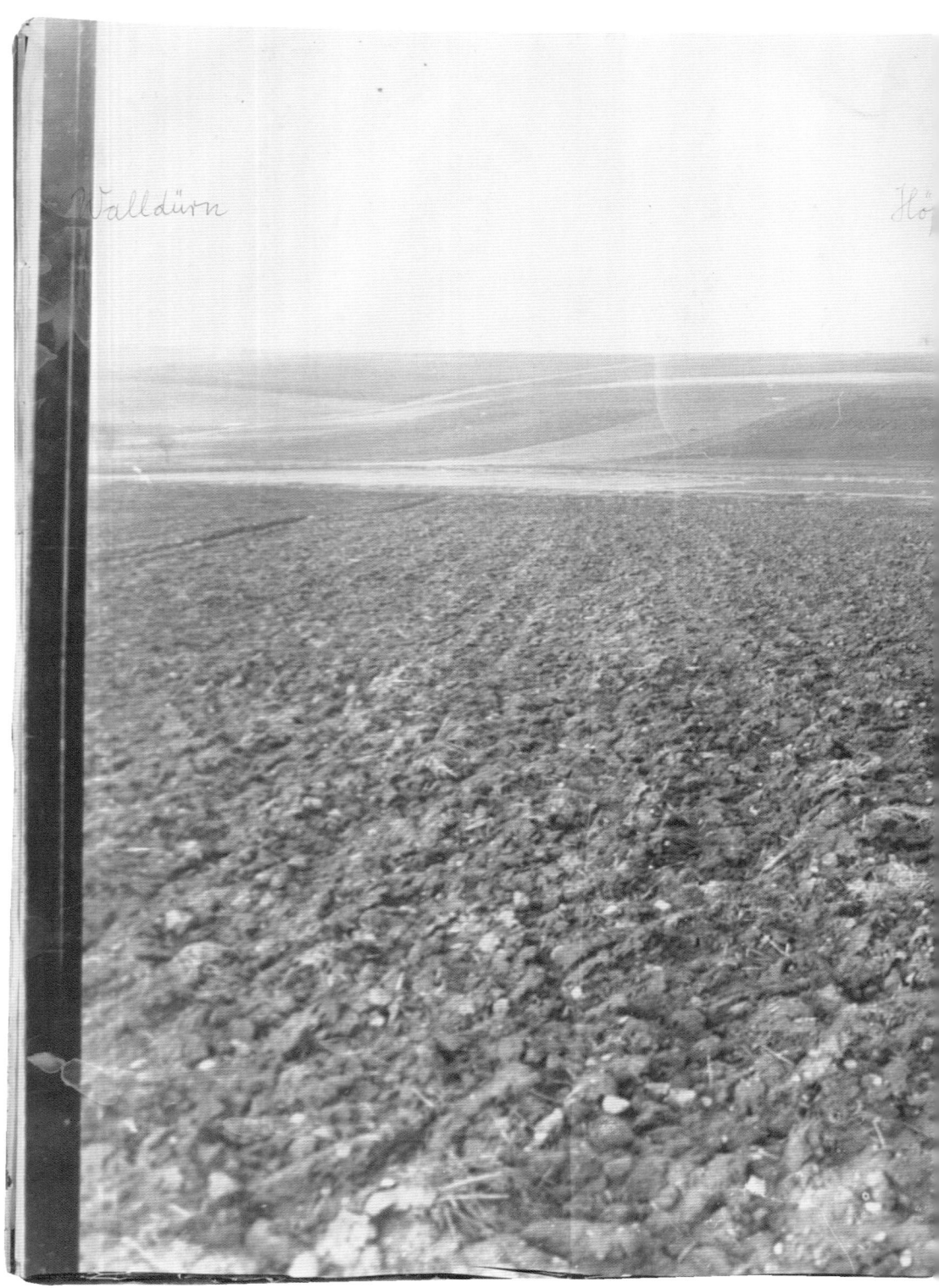

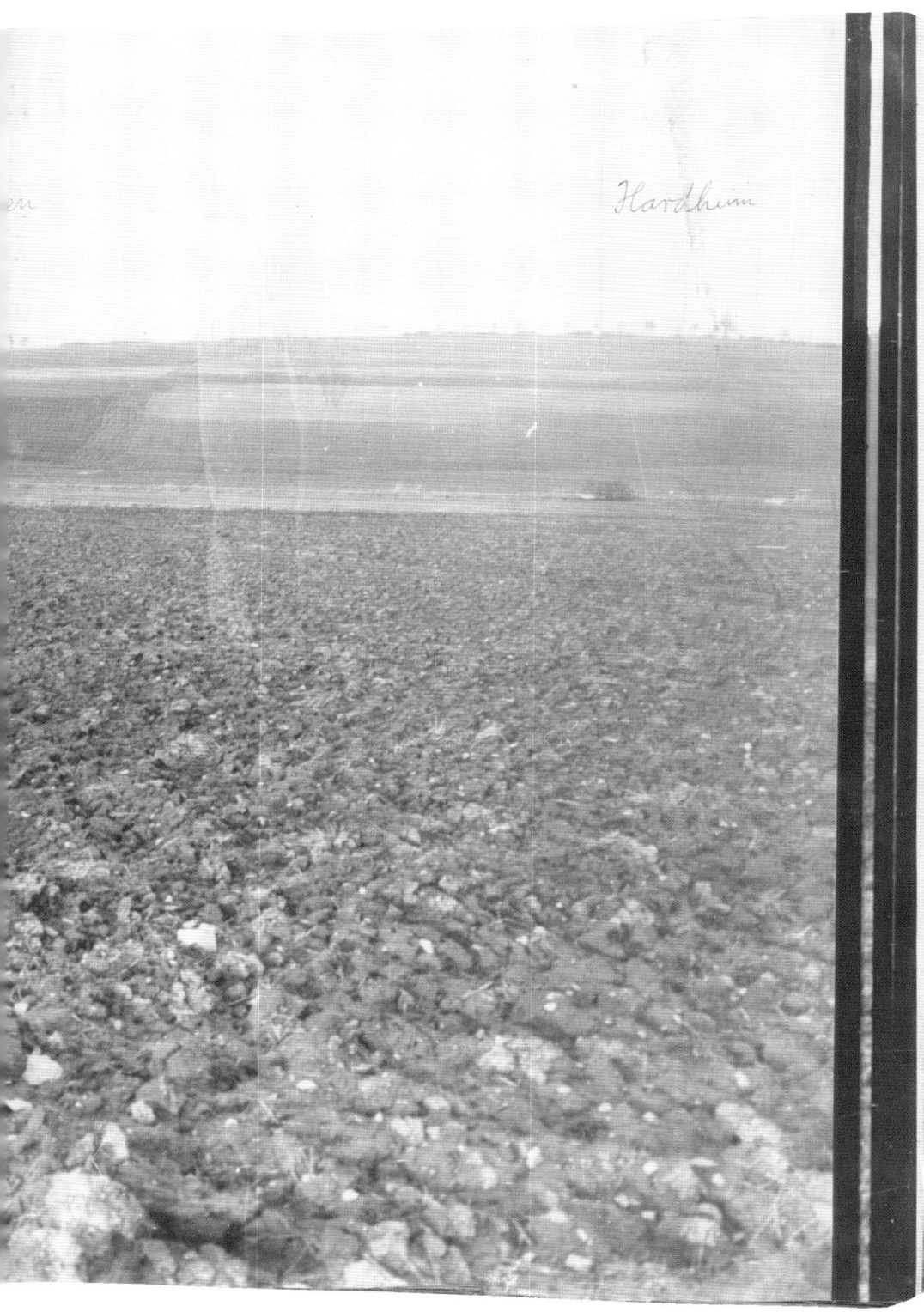

Hardheim

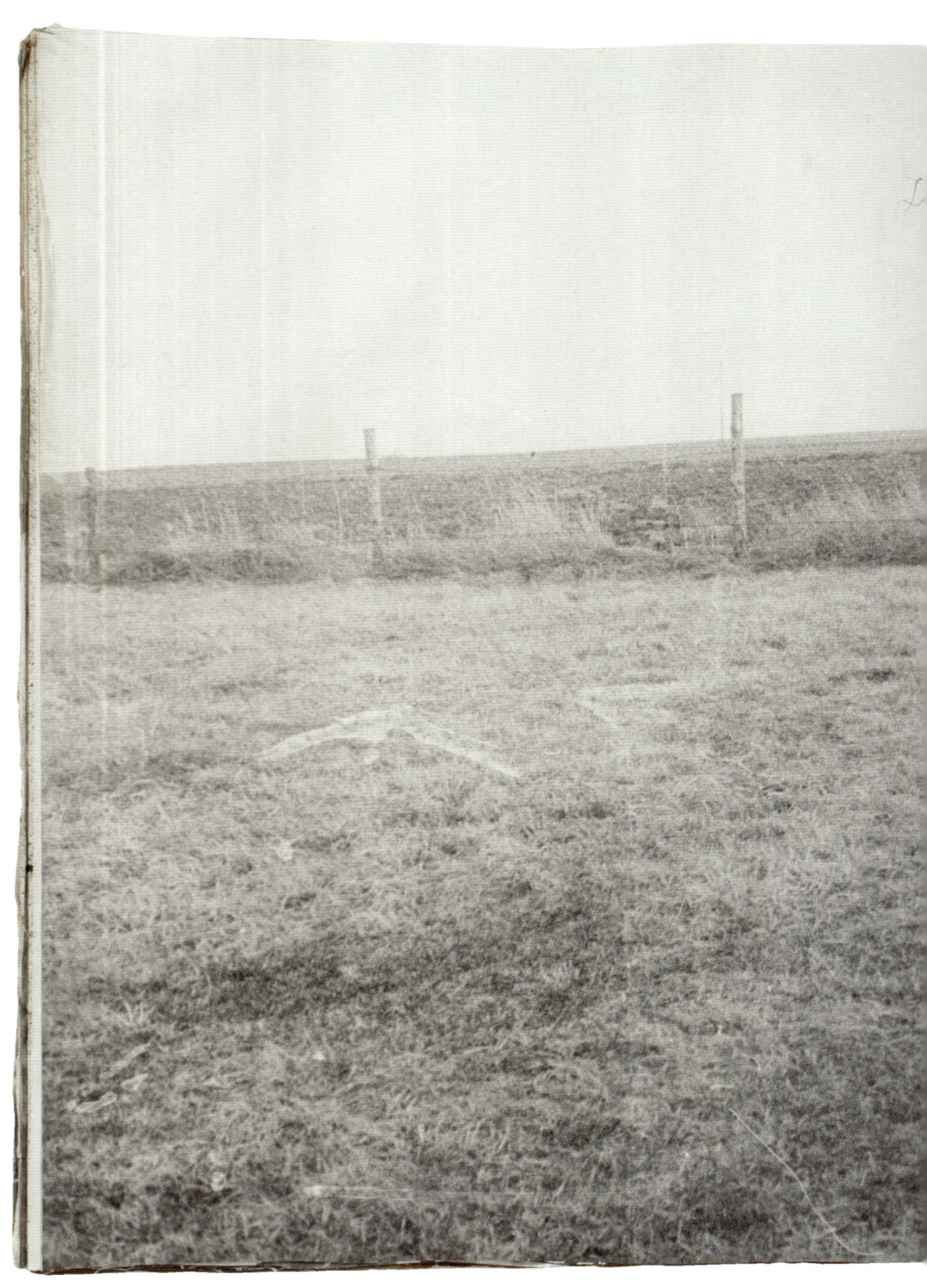

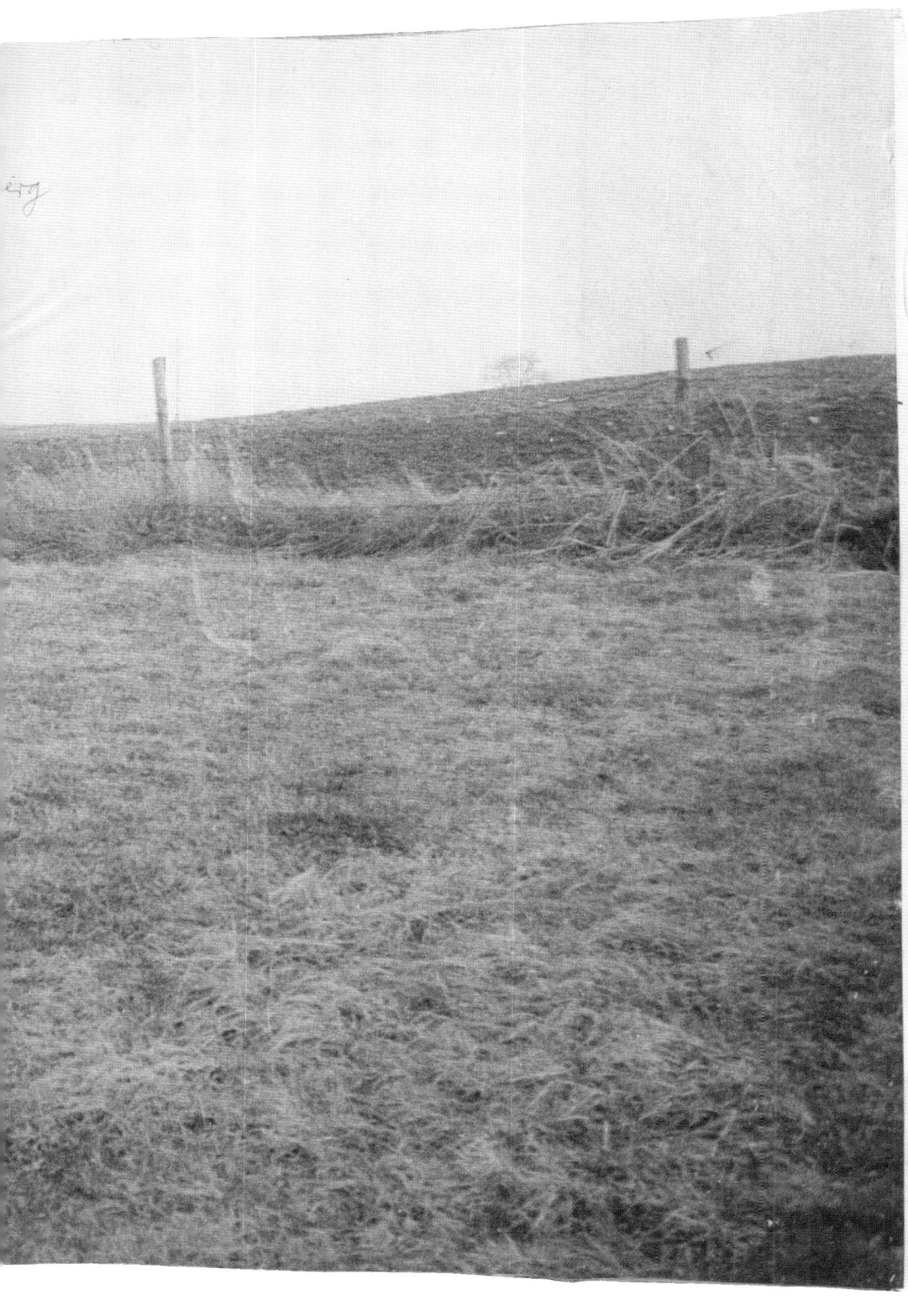

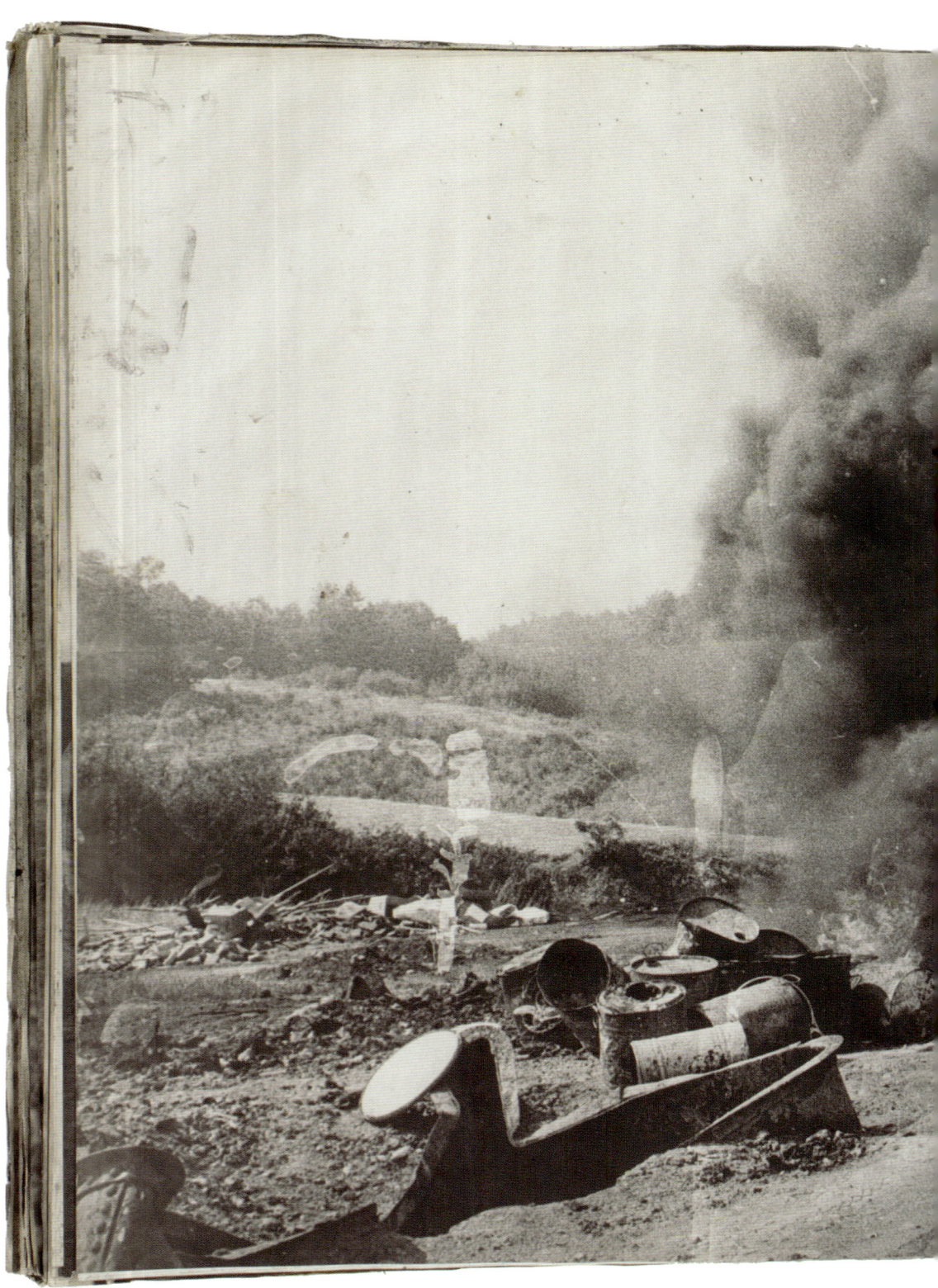

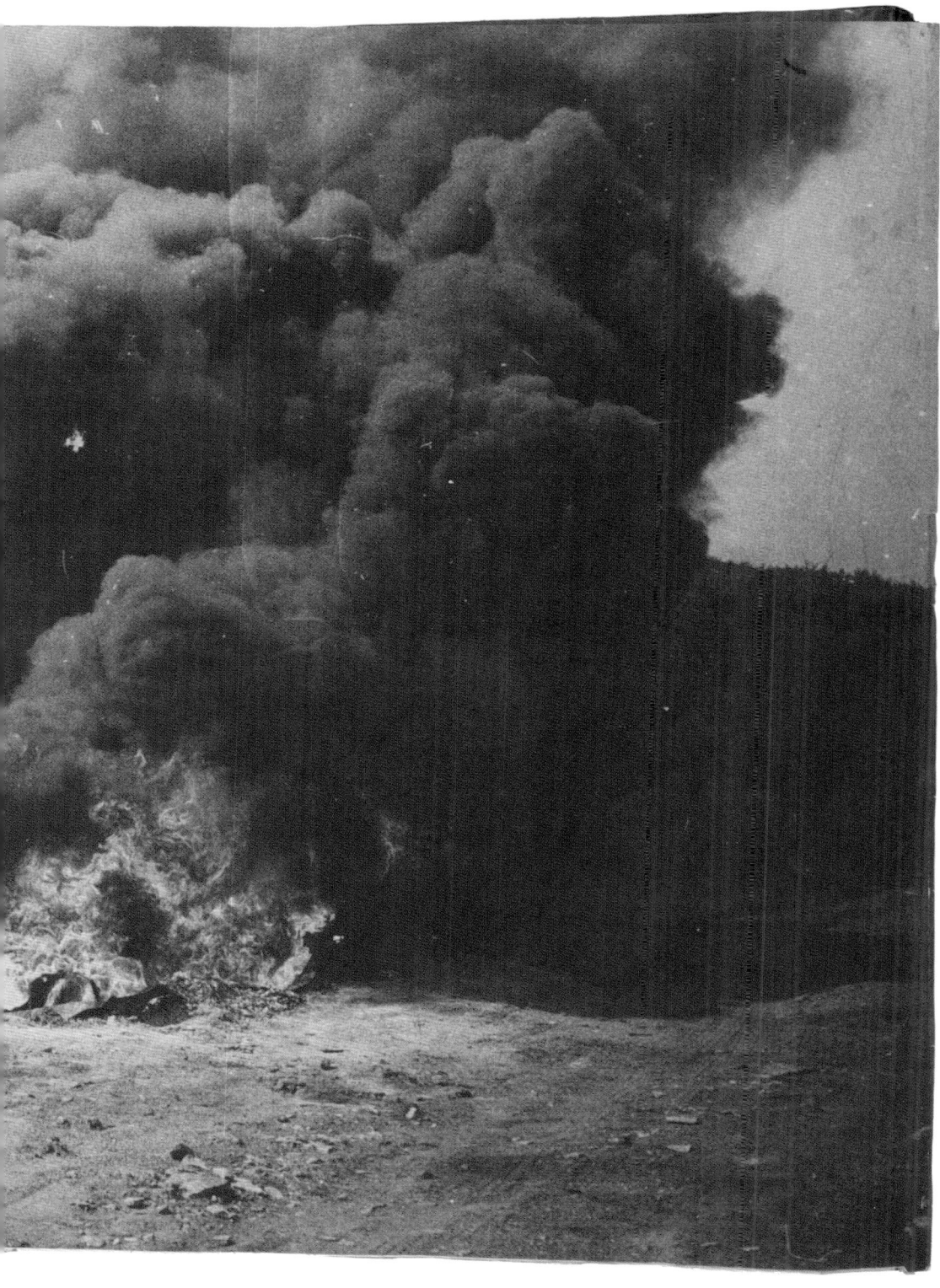

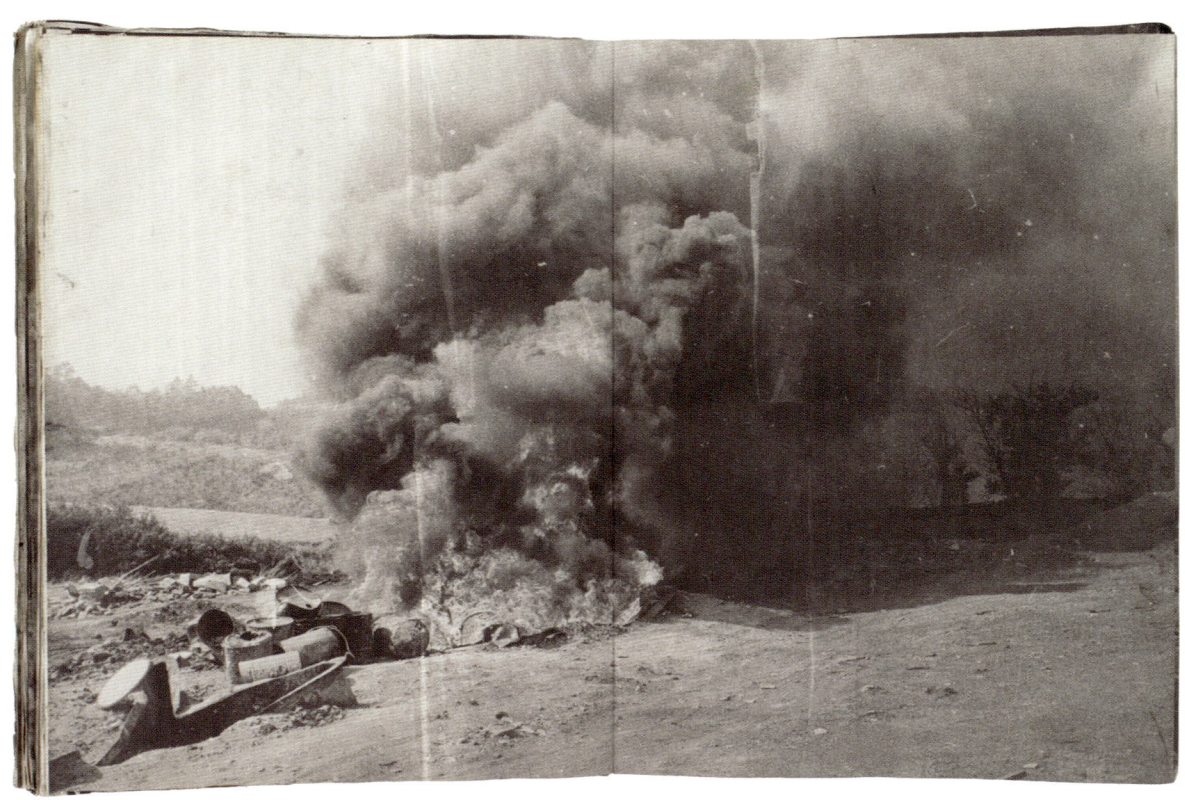

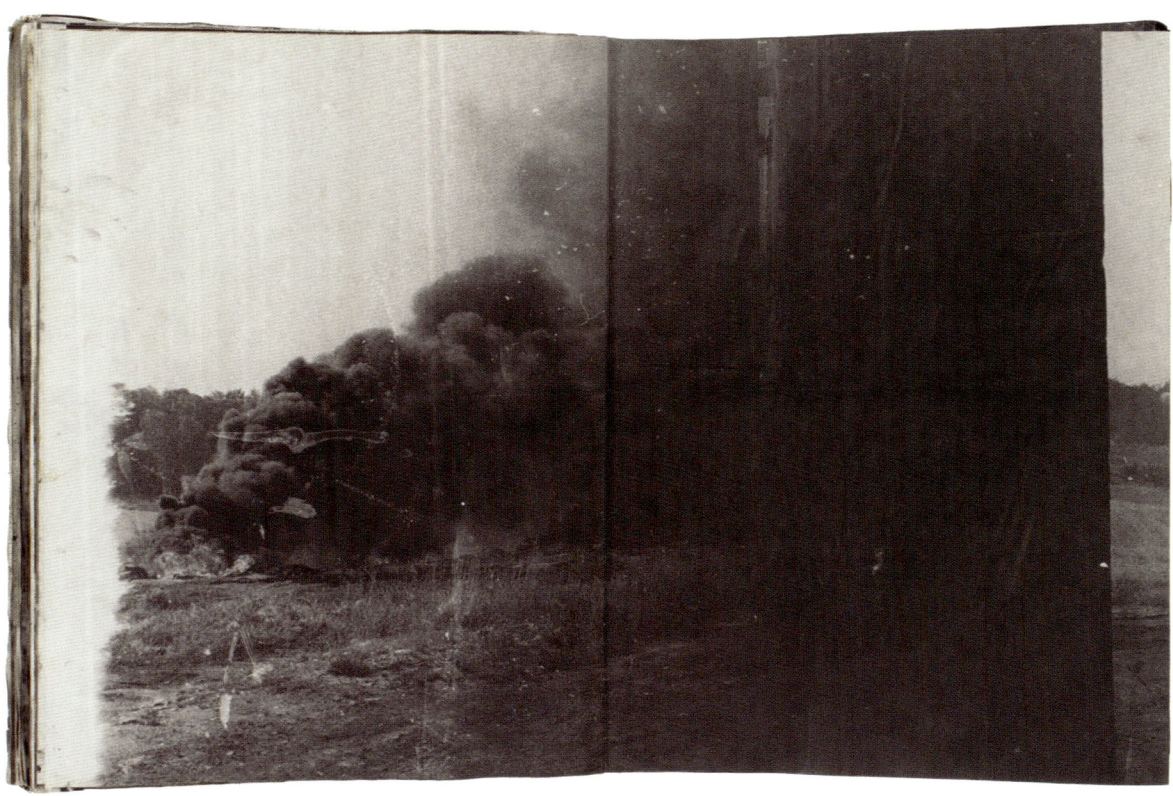

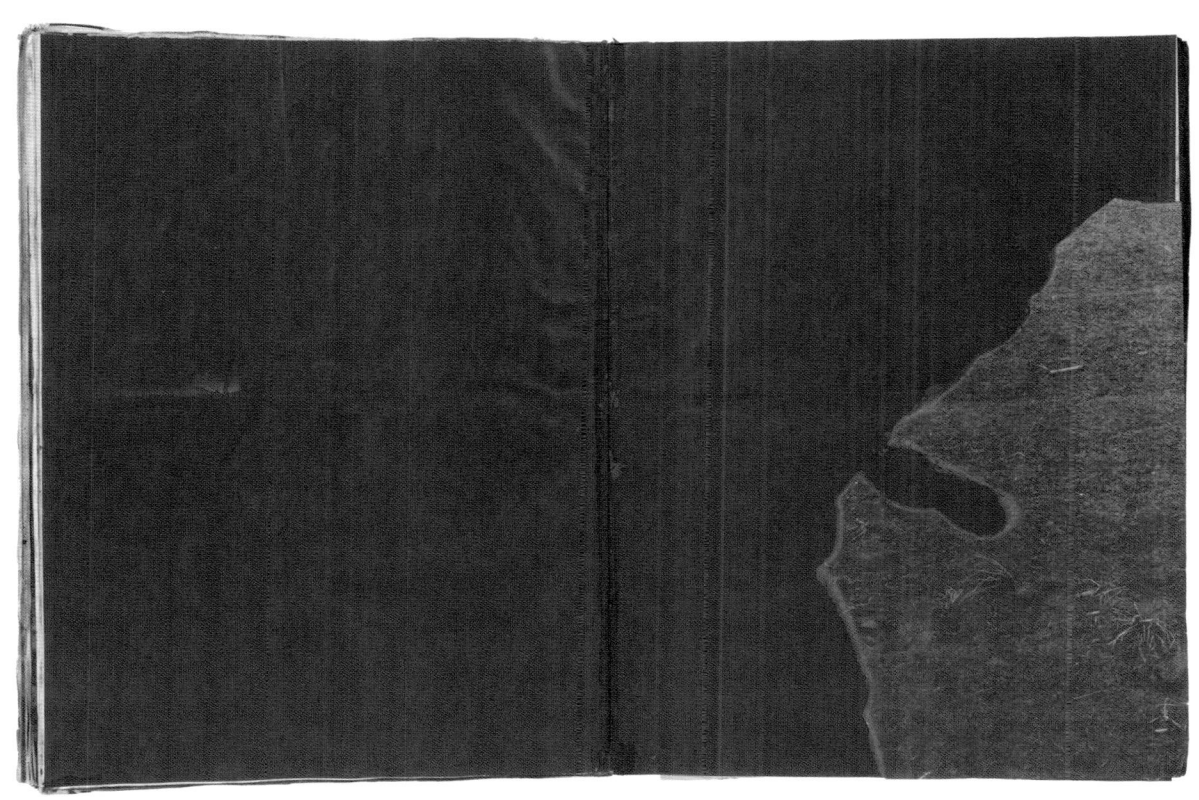

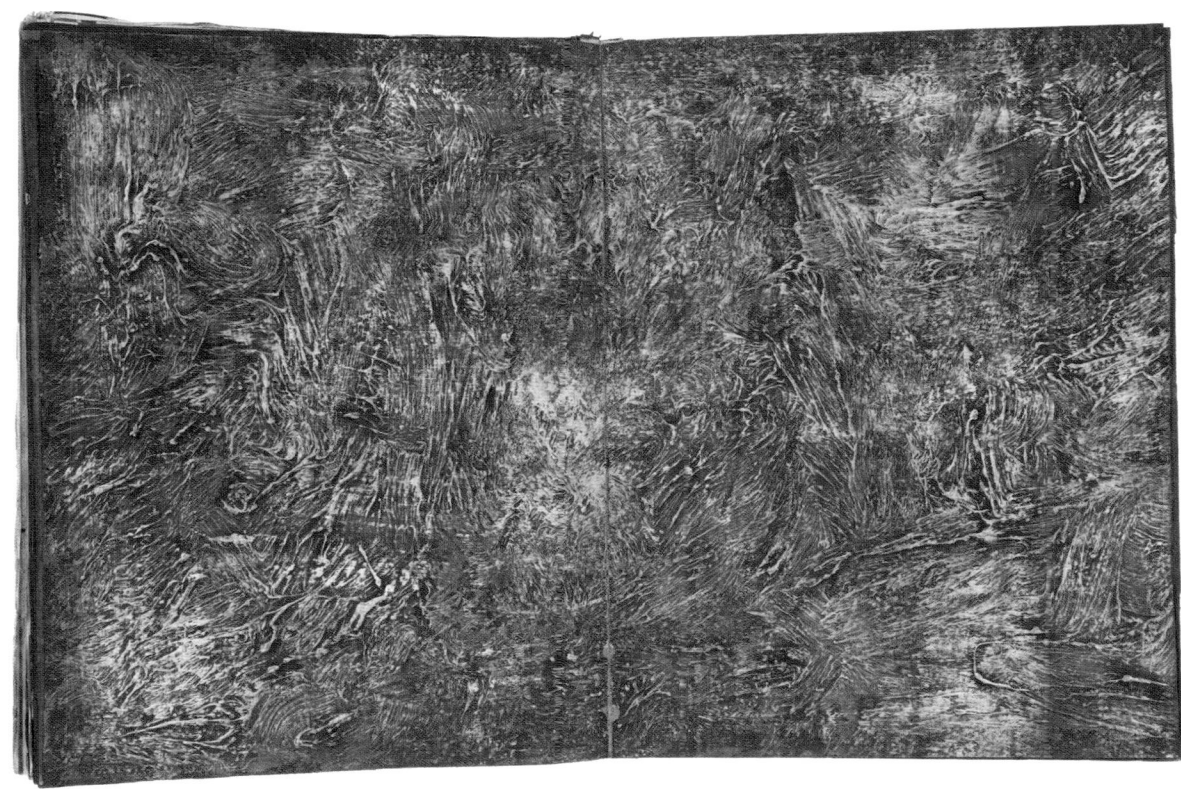

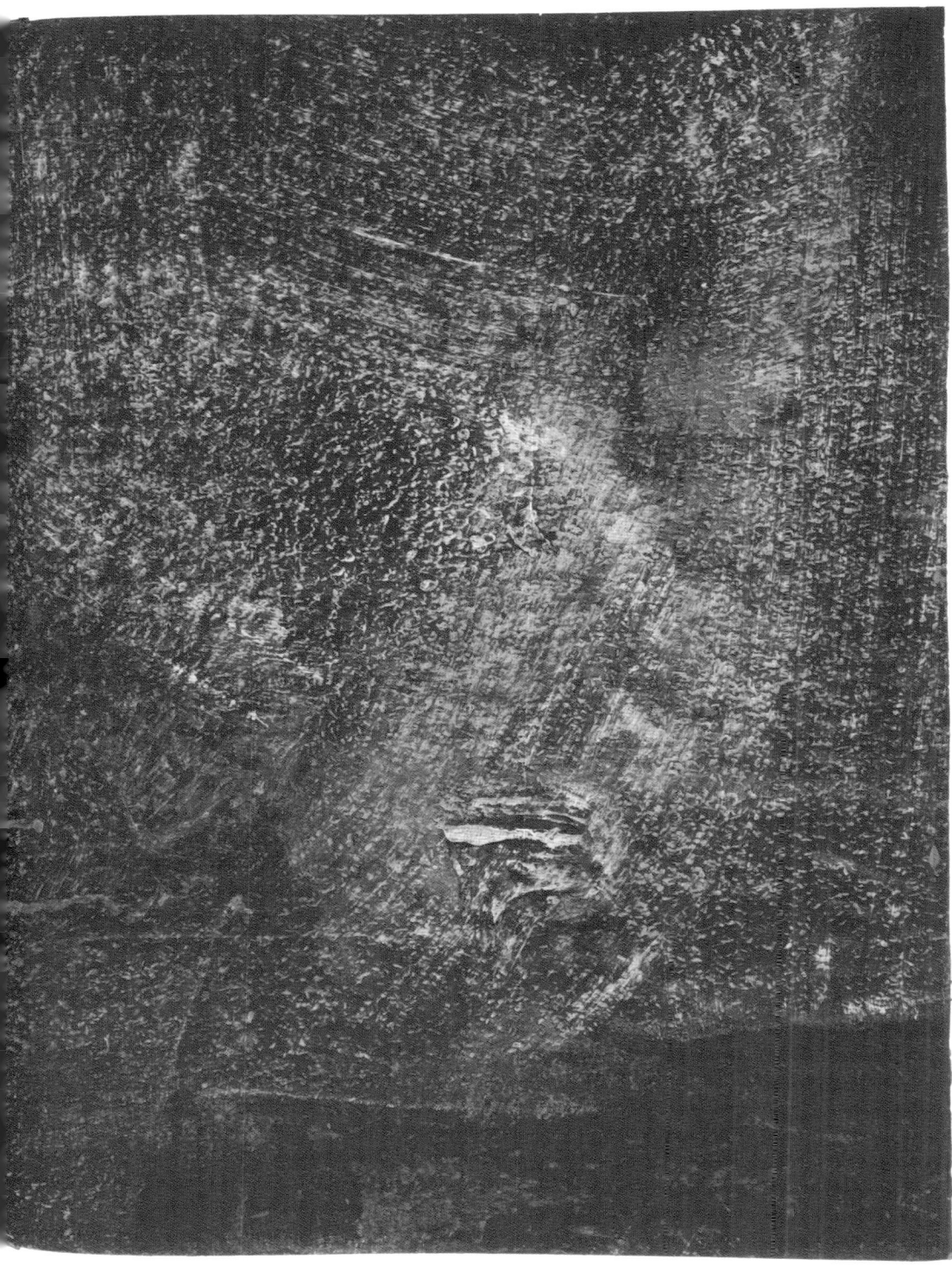

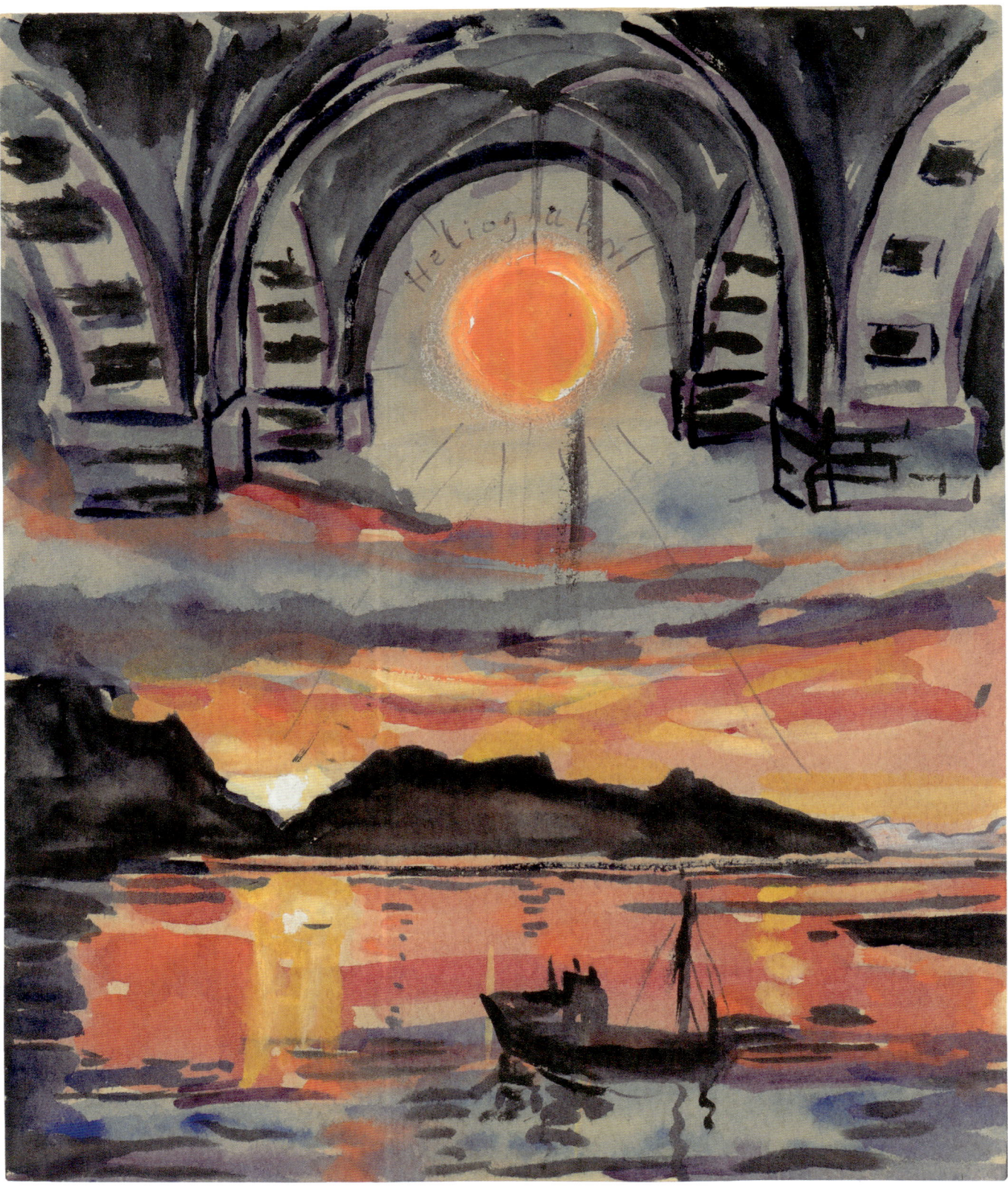

HELIOGABAL
(_HELIOGABALUS_), 1974–5
Watercolour, gouache and ink on paper
24 × 20 cm
Hall Collection

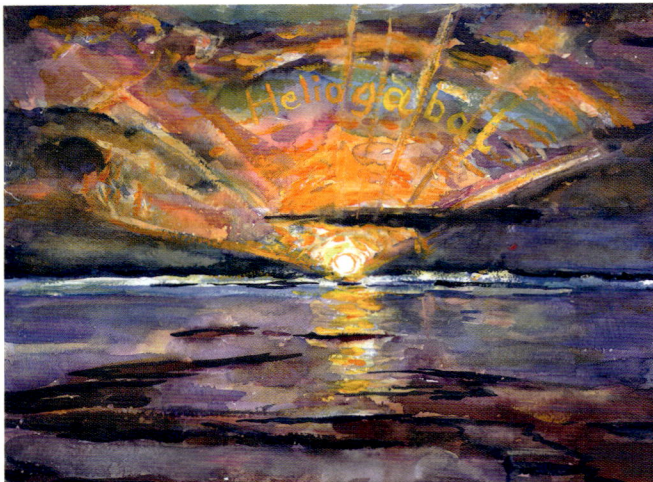

Anselm Kiefer
Heliogabal (*Heligobalus*), 1974
Watercolour and oil on paper,
29.8 × 39.5 cm

for book, *buch*. As such, there is a humorous link between the work's title and the artistic medium. The work is an example of Kiefer's deep concern not only with photography but also with the book, which started his artistic career and has remained central to his work: as inspiration, artistic object, and, since the mid-1980s, as a motif in countless paintings, installations, and sculptures, and in an extensive range of materials.

Lena Fritsch

HELIOGABAL (*HELIOGABALUS*), 1974–5

The sun, glowing in warm yellow and orange hues, dominates this luminescent watercolour painting. It is reflected on the water of a river or lake, glittering in blue, purple, and red tones. A small boat in the right foreground seems to be swaying on the water. In the background, the colourful evening sky is contrasted with dark, grey mountains. In the top part of the painting, stone pillars, indicated effortlessly in grey and purple gouache strokes, suggest an ancient bridge. The peaceful landscape conveys an impression of warmth and perfect beauty, reminiscent of images seen in postcards.

The title of the work, written in thin ink letters above the sun, references the Roman teenage emperor Marcus Aurelius Antoninus, better known by his nicknames Heliogabalus and Elagabalus. Heliogabalus's short reign, from 218 to 222, was notorious for religious controversy, political wrangling, and the emperor's decadent lifestyle and sexual promiscuity. Coming from a prominent Arab family, in his early youth he had served as head priest of the sun god Heliogabal. He was raised to the principate aged just fourteen following an army revolt instigated by

his grandmother, Julia Maesa (*c*.160–*c*.224) against the emperor, Marcus Opellius Macrinus (*c*.165–218).

Heliogabalus disregarded Rome's traditional state deities. He controversially replaced the head of the Roman Pantheon, Jupiter, with the sun deity from his homeland, and forced leading members of the government to participate in rituals celebrating the sun god. He threw extravagant dinner parties for lower-class friends. He married numerous times, and historians have debated his gender and sexual orientation; rumours abounded that he also prostituted himself. Amidst growing opposition, Heliogabalus and his mother were assassinated in 222 by mutinying soldiers, who were most likely incited by his grandmother. It is said that their bodies were thrown into the River Tiber in Rome. Heliogabalus was then replaced by his fifteen-year-old cousin, Severus Alexander.

Heliogabalus's reign was described by historian John Stuart Hay in 1911, in the first modern biography of the ruler, as one of 'enormous wealth and excessive prodigality, luxury and aestheticism, carried to their ultimate extreme'.[43] More recently, historian Adrian Goldsworthy has described him as 'an incompetent, probably the least able emperor Rome had ever had', and Harry Sidebottom titled his biography of the ruler *The Mad Emperor*.[44] An inextricably intertwined web of historical truth and mythology surrounds Heliogabalus's life, and while many have condemned him, his reign did bring with it a degree of religious innovation, while his lifestyle caused much upheaval amongst the senators.

Kiefer's calm scene of the colourful sunset above what is probably the River Tiber contrasts with the spectacular stories around Heliogabalus's short but eventful life, and his brutal assassination. The pillars could be a reference to one of Rome's ancient bridges on the Tiber, such as the Pons Aelius (Ponte Sant'Angelo) or Pons Mulvius (Ponte Milvio). The fact that Kiefer chose to depict a sunset not only alludes to Heliogabalus's name and the latter's

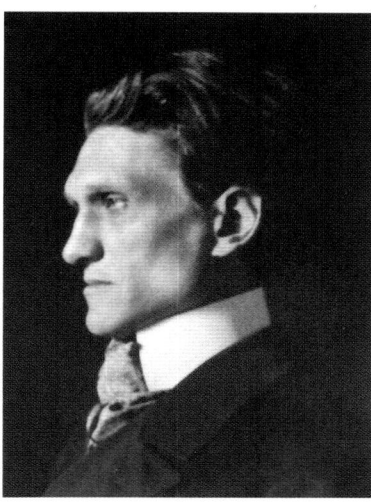

admiration of the sun deity, but it also symbolises the young emperor's murder and the dousing of his religious revolution. In a wider sense, the timeless water scene also indicates the fleeting authority of rulers, ranging from emperors in ancient Rome to political leaders today.

In 1974 Kiefer made a number of works that showed his fascination with Heliogabalus and the myths surrounding him, for example a gouache and watercolour work on paper also titled *Heliogabal*, which can be found in the Kröller-Müller Museum in Otterlo, in the Netherlands, and a watercolour and oil painting of a sunset with the same title in the Saint Louis Art Museum, Missouri (p.112). The oil painting, *Sol Invictus Heliogabal*, also in the Hall Collection (pp.62–3), portrays a German soldier, ironically linking the myth of an invincible deity with a vulnerable human. Kiefer has also come back to Heliogabalus in more recent larger works, such as *Antonin Artaud Heliogabalus* (2010–11), referencing Antonin Artaud's 1933 novelised biography of the emperor.

Lena Fritsch

21/22

STEFAN!, 1975
STEFAN II, 1975

The two small watercolours *Stefan!* and *Stefan II* show the face of a serious-looking man in profile, emerging from the mountains in an almost Surrealist style. Both works combine the portrait of the man with a picturesque landscape scene: *Stefan!* features a glowing orange sunset, reflected on a lake in front of mountains, while *Stefan II* shows blue-white mountains and water together with a small house on a wide green field in daylight.

Stefan! is accompanied by text: not only is the title of the work written in small letters between blue lines that indicate the mountainous outlines, but it also says '*aller Tage Abend, aller Abende Tag*' ('the end of days, the day of all end') on the top left-hand side of the painting.

The paintings reference Stefan Anton George (1868–1933), who was a German poet, originally inspired by French Symbolism and Aestheticism, and a skilled translator of works by Dante Alighieri (1265–1321), William Shakespeare, and Charles Baudelaire (1821–1867) into German. In 1892 he co-founded the literary magazine *Blätter für die Kunst* (*Journal for the Arts*) in Berlin and became the leader of the influential (and, due to homosexual encounters with many younger followers, controversial) literary circle the George-Kreis.[45] George and his disciples represented a literary revolt against the realism trends in German literature in the early twentieth century. George's later works, including the poems published in *Das neue Reich* (*The New Empire*) in 1928, criticise the absence of heroism and irrational forces, and condemn what he perceived to be the evils of contemporary life. Despite his Nietzschean interest in the will to power, George was critical of National Socialism and warned about the Nazi party. In 1933 he died in self-imposed exile in Minusio, Switzerland. Perhaps unsurprisingly when considering his interest in historical German literature, the title of his publication *The New Empire*, and his strong influence on contemporary intellectuals, George was embraced by the Nazis as a national literary hero – an example of their abuse of a cultural figure for their own ideology.

Kiefer's watercolour paintings present the poet's head on the mountain as if it was a pillow. There are strong similarities to an often-reproduced studio portrait of George taken by photographer Jacob Hilsdorf (1872–1916) in 1910 (above), but in Kiefer's work, George appears to be sleeping or resting on his death bed. The picturesque mountainous

21
STEFAN!, 1975
Watercolour, gouache and
ballpoint pen on paper
20.5 × 28.5 cm
Hall Collection

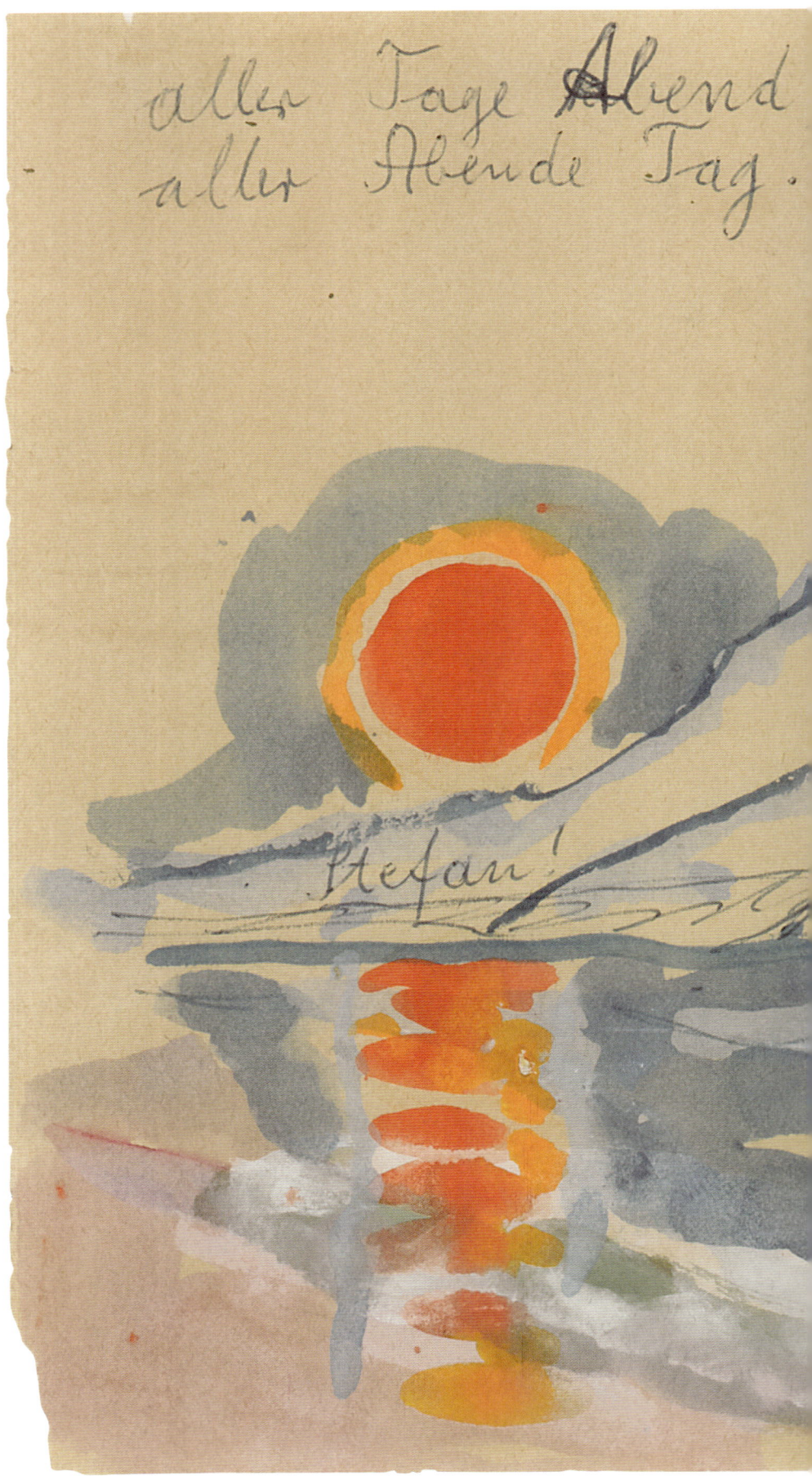

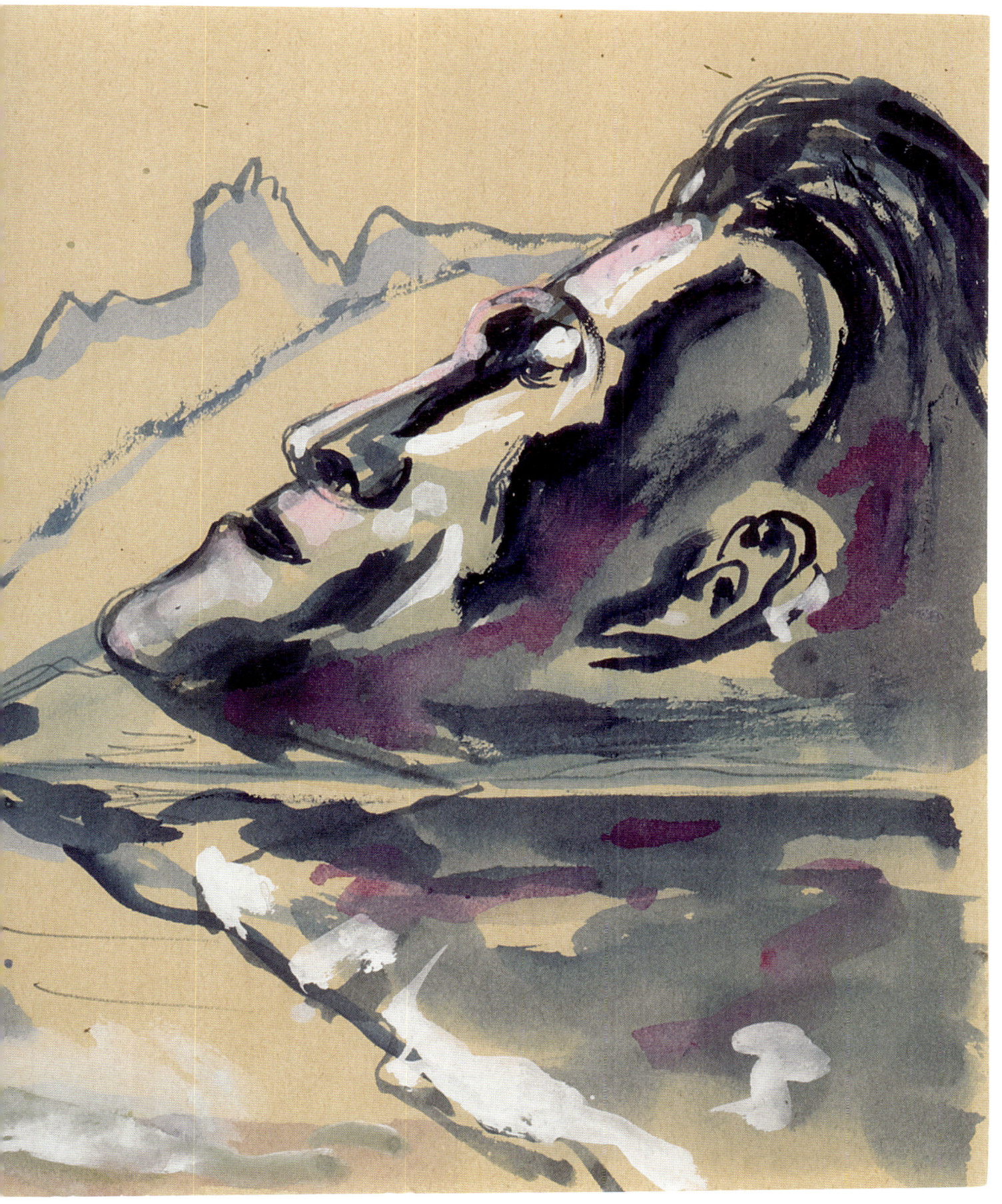

22

STEFAN II, 1975

Watercolour and gouache on paper
20.6 × 28.5 cm
Hall Collection

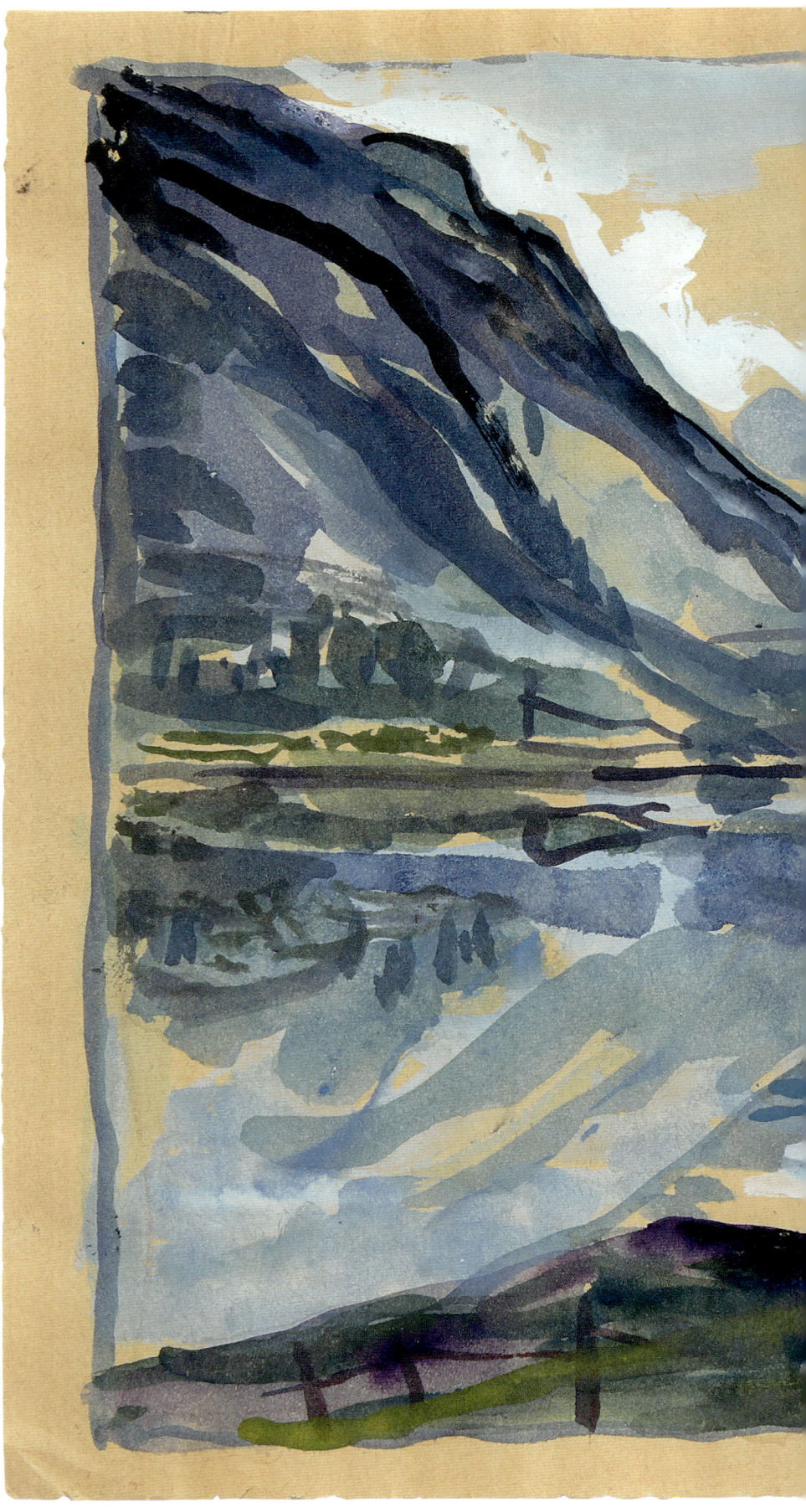

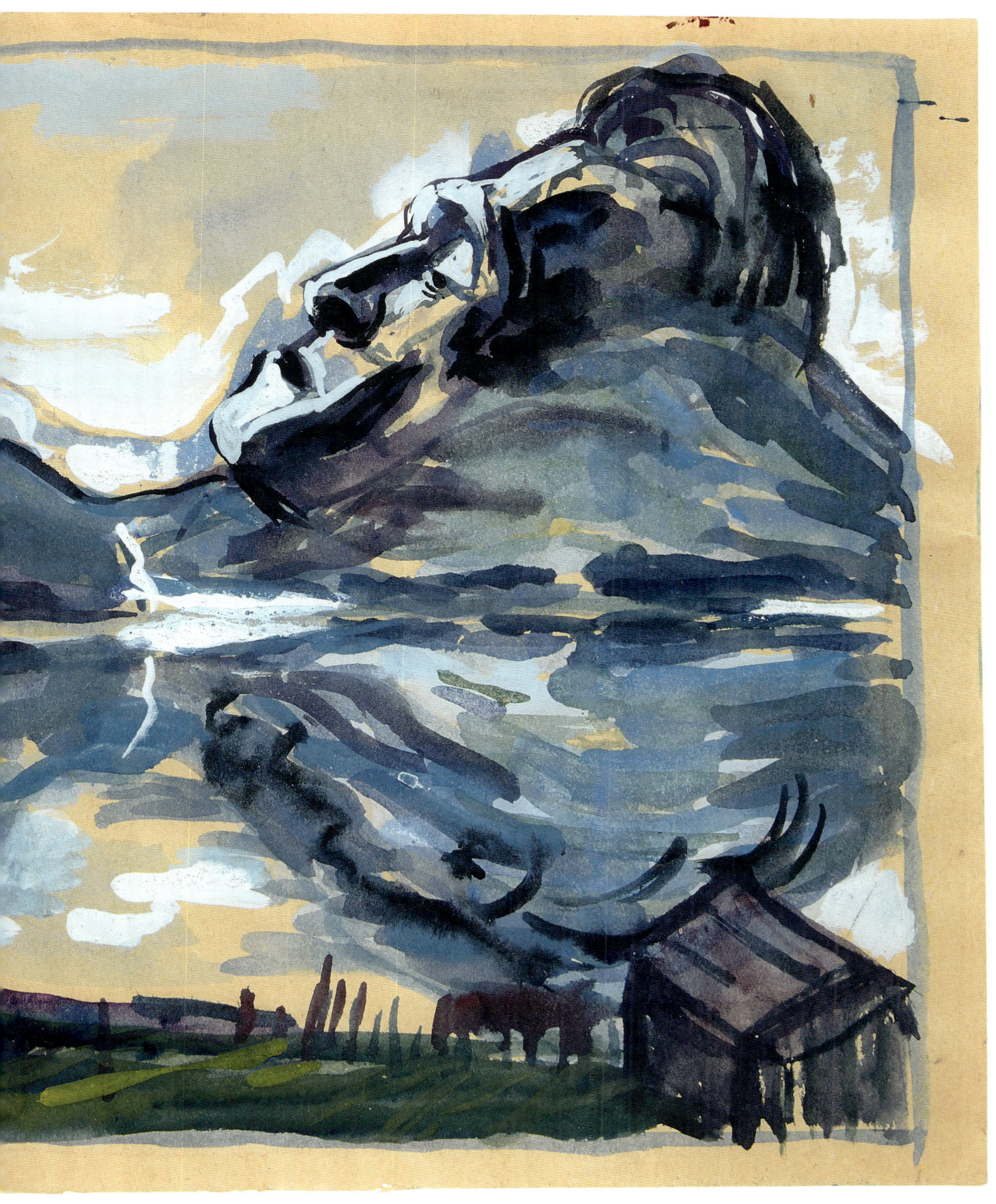

23

DIE KUNST GEHT KNAPP NICHT UNTER (ART WILL SURVIVE ITS RUINS), 1975

Watercolour and ink on paper

24 × 20 cm

Hall Collection

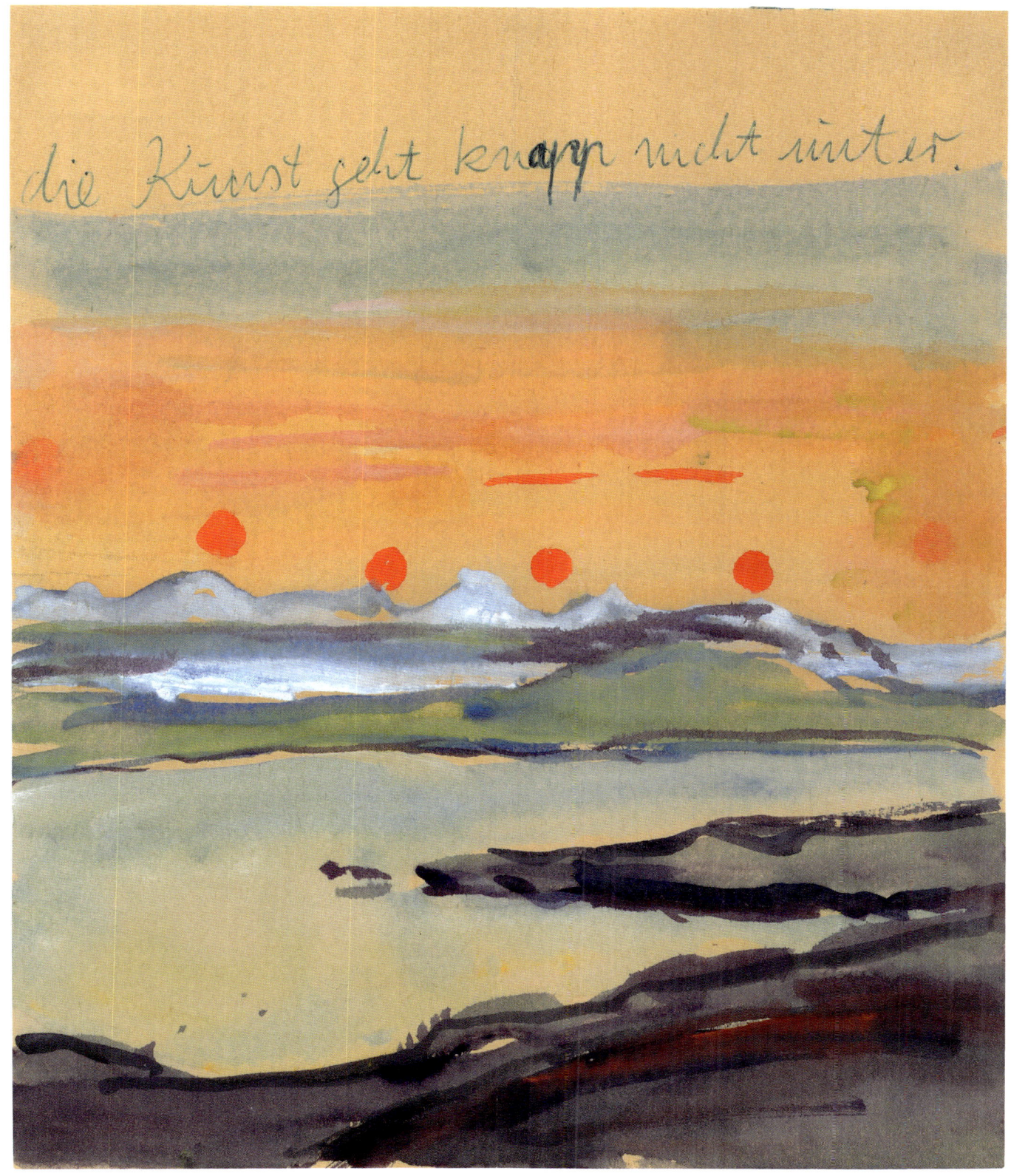

die Kunst geht knapp nicht unter.

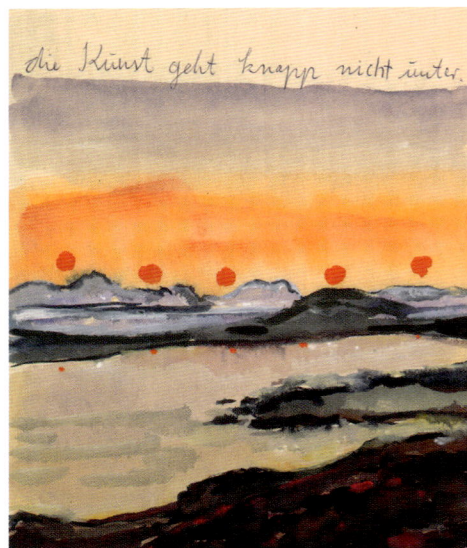

Anselm Kiefer
Nordkap, 1975
Watercolour and ink on paper,
23.8 × 19.8 cm

landscape with the lake is reminiscent of Minusio with Lake Maggiore, where George passed away in Ticino, Switzerland. In *Stefan!* Kiefer's reference to the poet's death is made particularly obvious: the sunset and the quotation '*aller Tage Abend*' point to the end of George's life, and to the end of all life. *Stefan!* and *Stefan II* also allude to the charged complexities of German cultural heritage since the Nazi regime. The paintings can be interpreted as an attempt to redeem George from the disgrace of political exploitation and the controversies surrounding his life and persona.

Kiefer made a similar watercolour and pencil work in the previous year, also titled *Stefan!,* now in the collections of the Metropolitan Museum of Art, New York. The quotation '*aller Tage Abend, aller Abende Tag*' can be found in numerous other watercolours by the artist, including the watercolour paintings titled *Aller Tage Abend, aller Abende Tag* from 2014. The line can be read as a reference to philosopher Ernst Bloch (1885–1977) and his *Principle of Hope* (1954–9), in which Bloch uses the term 'militant optimism' to encourage positive social change. Bloch suggests a theory of 'concrete utopia' within real possibilities: 'understood as one in which it is definitely not yet the end of days, but, equally, also not the day of all end'.[46] Directed towards the not-yet become, hope is staked on possibility and uncertainty: a better future is not impossible.

Lena Fritsch

<hr>

23

DIE KUNST GEHT KNAPP NICHT UNTER (ART WILL SURVIVE ITS RUINS), 1975

The sky, shimmering in ice-blue, yellow, and orange hues, features six red circles reminiscent of suns; mountains glittering with blue-white snow accompany light-blue water and dark-blue land. In this small painting, curved lines, round forms, and soft contours, arranged horizontally, create a harmonious composition that conveys a calm and organic feel. Painted in light watercolours, the surreal landscape presents itself with a luminescent atmosphere. Above the light-blue section of the sky at the top of the painting, it reads in thin ink letters: '*Die Kunst geht knapp nicht unter*' (which is difficult to translate literally into English: it means that art almost drowns but just survives. It has been translated loosely as 'art will survive its ruins').

In summer 1974, Kiefer travelled to Northern Norway. He took countless photographs and purchased postcards of the breathtaking landscapes of the outermost reach of Europe, which he later repurposed in his studio to create work. This painting is inspired by the Arctic Ocean and the North Cape, where, in summer, sunlight is never-ending.

The North Cape is not only associated with natural beauty but also with a naval battle that occurred in December 1943: the Battle of the North Cape. The German battlecruiser *Scharnhorst*, on an operation to attack Arctic convoys of war materiel from the western Allies to the Soviet Union, was brought to battle and sunk by a British battleship. Over 1,900 crew members drowned. There is a watercolour from the same year titled *Nordkap (North Cape)* that looks almost identical (above): this work, which can be found in a private collection in New York, was included in Kiefer's major solo exhibition touring US museums, such as the Art Institute of Chicago and the Museum of Modern Art, New York, between 1987 and 1989.

The statement '*die Kunst geht knapp nicht unter*' can be interpreted in different ways. In the context of 1975, it points at the post-war discourse in Germany: not only had German culture been censored and denunciated, it had also been misappropriated by the Nazis to propagate

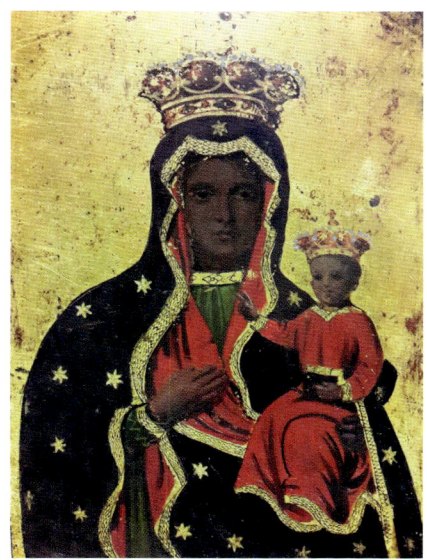

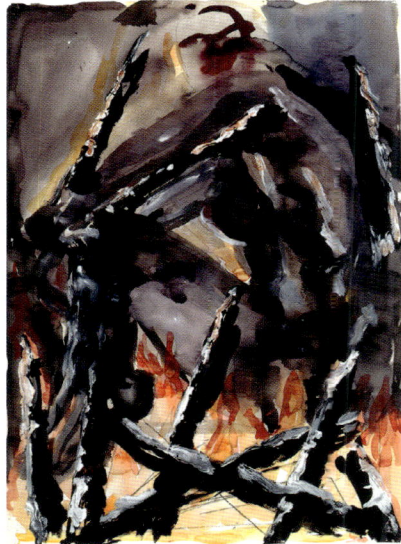

their ideologies. Art had almost drowned. As Theodor Adorno's much-quoted 1949 statement – 'writing poetry after Auschwitz is barbaric'[47] – indicates, written and visual culture dealing with the Holocaust and war trauma was viewed in post-war Germany with scepticism. Descriptive and figurative art in general was largely avoided for a long time. As the English version of the painting's title in the future tense corroborates, Kiefer, however, optimistically claims that art will survive.

The title of the work can also be read in a more general, timeless sense. Depicting six suns at once, the painting illustrates the phenomenon of the Northern Norwegian 'midnight sun', where above the Arctic Circle, summer days are unending as the sun can be seen crossing the sky throughout the night. Showing this phenomenon, Kiefer's painting not only emphasises the picturesque, postcard aesthetic of the landscape, but it also suggests infinity and a non-chronological sense of time. The long geological history of the North Cape, shaped through several ice ages, reminds us of the endlessness of nature and the extreme shortness of human existence – perhaps, art will endure and survive humankind.

Lena Fritsch

24

BRÜNHILDES TOD (BRUNHILD'S DEATH), 1976

Brünhilde is a recurring character within Kiefer's set of themes and iconographies. Titles can offer us a convenient method of interpreting and analysing the art we are viewing. They can be a guide, and therefore useful, but they can also narrow the gaze and render our interpretations more prescriptive.

Kiefer started this series of interpretations of Brünhilde in 1975. As a mythic figure, Brünhilde springs from the world of Norse mythology, evoking thoughts of Wagnerian operas and storybook images of Amazonian war women. If we consider Brünhilde beside another icon, for instance *The Black Madonna of Częstochowa* (1655, above), in the Jasna Góra Monastery in Poland, we can appreciate the clever use of contrast in both images: dark vibrates against glowing yellows and reds of shimmering golden bands and outlines. The recognition of the icon is essential in terms of fashioning our response to this work. We can approach the standardised image in the way that we might recognise a monarch's head on a coin. However, Kiefer does not allow us to rest upon this singular 'type'; we encounter his icons in a myriad of different guises as he uses these visual mantras to broaden his experimental approach to the medium of watercolour. For this purpose, titles are essential. His series focusing on Brünhilde expands in all directions. *Brünhilde Sleeps* (1980) in the collection of the Metropolitan Museum of Art, New York, is based on a photograph of Catherine Deneuve (b.1943) in the 1969 film *Mississippi Mermaid* by François Truffaut (1932–1984), whereas a 1976 version in the Kröller-Müller Museum (above) is more akin to the image here, as it describes her ultimate immolation on a funeral pyre.

Richard Wagner's epic opera *Der Ring des Nibelungen* (*The Ring of the Nibelung*) was first performed in Bayreuth on 16 August 1876. The story was adapted from the thirteenth century *Poetic Edda* that told of the 'shield maidens' of Norse mythology, otherwise known as Valkyries, who led warriors after glorious death to eternity in the hall of Valhalla. Brünhilde is pivotal to the story, and her part in it offers Kiefer multiple opportunities for diverse compositions. Wagner's four operas are

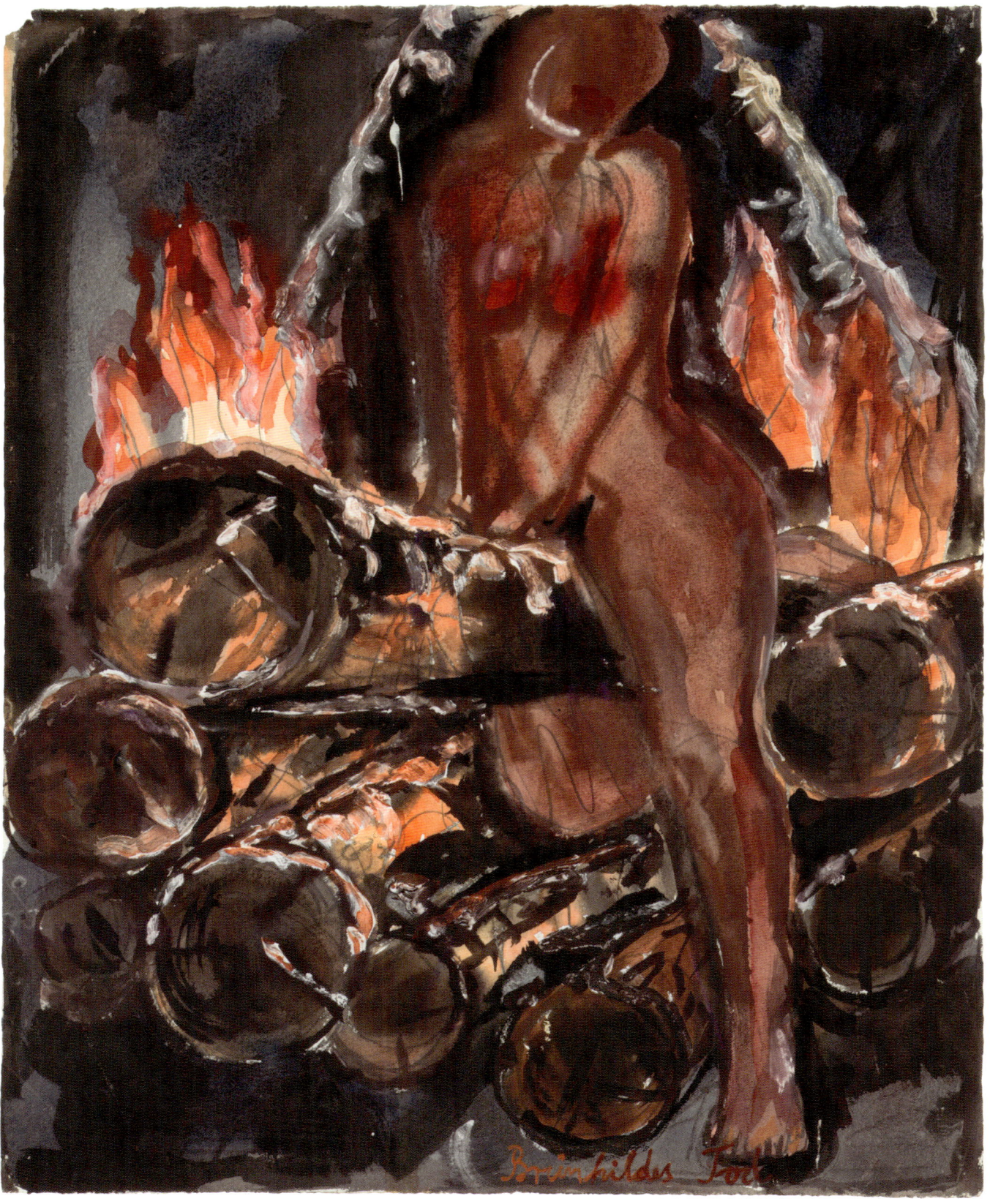

**BRÜNHILDES TOD
(BRUNHILD'S DEATH), 1976**

Pencil and watercolour on paper
70 × 56 cm

Hall Collection

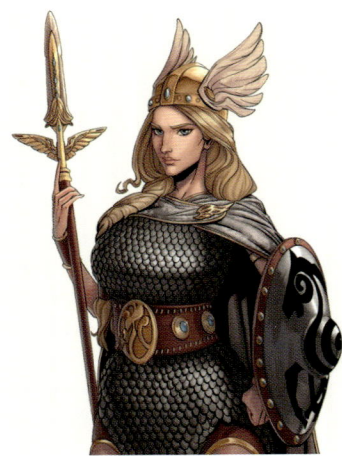

Brunhilde gaming character, *King's Throne: Game of Lust*

interlinked by the magical ring that is lost, found, stolen, and coveted. Its supernatural powers are imparted to all who wear it. The complicated story recounts that Brünhilde, having disobeyed Wotan, fell into an enchanted sleep within a magical circle of fire. Her lover, Siegfried, found her and broke the spell. Eventually, however (after many twists and turns of fate and deception), she dies when she joins Siegfried in self-sacrifice on his funeral pyre, riding her horse Grane (pp.166–7) into the flames at the close of Wagner's last part of the opera cycle, *Götterdämmerung* (*Twilight of the Gods*).

In the present image, Kiefer depicts Brünhilde astride the flaming funeral pyre, a tree trunk between her legs in a passive but provocative manner. It is a strange image with what seems to be a halo of hair cascading down around her as she becomes engulfed in flames, topped by scattered white pinpricks of light, with no horse visible. Kiefer pictures the Valkyrie Brünhilde as a powerful, sexual being, an icon of a type recently made familiar via powerful women characters in the dramatic series *Game of Thrones*, or in computer games such as *King's Throne: Game of Lust* (above). With a circle of burning flames glowing beneath her, she is incandescent with red hot cinders, their circular forms reflecting a quivering, white-tipped canopy above. Her left foot is firmly planted on the ground while flames lick the black night behind. She is faceless, her bosoms highlighted in red, the space she occupies is tight and claustrophobic. Brünhilde is locked into her fate and the story, which is one of death and revenge.

Watercolour is often associated with the realm of the gentle and delicate, however, in this instance the brush is loaded and the palette restricted to dark colours, only alleviated by orange-red flames and dotted spots of white. Kiefer suggests a Brünhilde who, in the vein of war-warrior Boudicca, is astride no ordinary tree trunks.

Her pyre has morphed into a cannon, the dark browns and blacks anchor the sparkling barrels as the embers quiver and pile up beneath her. She dominates the luminous scene, an embodiment of determination, literally seeming to be firing on all cylinders, while evoking the Indian Hindu tradition of Sati.[48]

Liz Rideal

UNTERNEHMEN "TRAPPENFANG" (OPERATION "TRAPPENFANG"), 1976

'*Unternehmen "Trappenfang"*', inscribed in the artist's signature script, the words – a somewhat idiosyncratic rendering of a German Second World War military code name, *Unternehmen Trappenjagd* (Operation Bustard Hunt) – serve at once as a title for, and portal to, the painting that lies beneath. Rendered in the same white pigment that is layered atop the canvas's thickly encrusted surface to create the impression of lingering patches of snow, the words summon a scenario of devastation, a landscape furrowed, not by the tracks of ploughs and threshers, but by the treads of troop movements and tanks. Indeed, in early May of 1942, German bombs rained down on the easternmost tip of Crimea, the Kerch Peninsula, amplifying the destructive force of the assault unleashed by its artillery and panzer divisions. In a matter of days, the combined military offensive ravaged the Soviet army and allowed Germany to concentrate its forces on the Siege of Sevastopol. Looming above the scene is not, however, the bustard – the largest bird of the steppes that gave the operation its name – but instead, a massive palette, also rendered in white. An emblem of artistic identity, it is also, in this instance, an apparition, as if its contours are

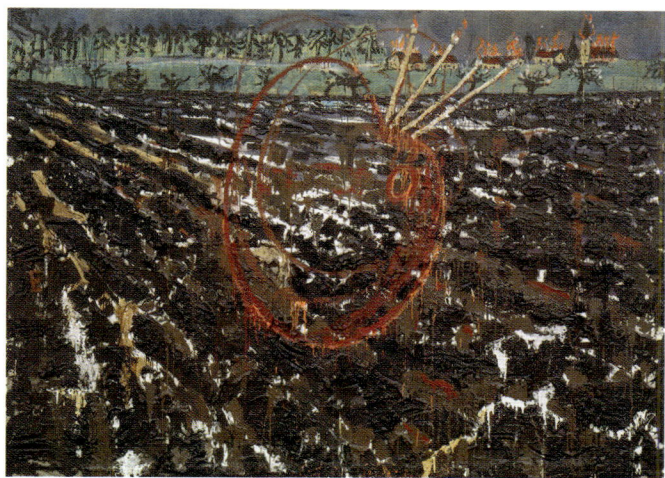

Anselm Kiefer
Nero malt (*Nero Paints*), 1974
Oil on canvas, 220 × 300 cm

consolidating from the contrails of German war planes that laid waste to the landscape below.

No subject has exerted a more enduring hold on Kiefer's artistic imagination than German history. Although Kiefer's work has come, in its later decades, to embrace a global, even cosmic worldview, adding to his arsenal of emblems the numbered stars and nebulae of an ever-expanding understanding of the universe, it has never wholly strayed from its grounding concern with the legacy of Germany's Nazi past, its responsibility for perpetrating the genocidal destruction of European Jewry, and starting what remains the deadliest war in world history. Whether one looks to the earliest works, where a form of performative masquerade, captured photographically or rendered pictorially, finds Kiefer occupying the tainted subject position of the Nazi soldier, or one turns to the early paintings, where forests and fields, attics and other architectural interiors serve as the backdrop for his explorations of German national identity, military history emerges as one of his most persistent subjects.

As if to begin at the beginning, in 1976, Kiefer created *Varus*, a painting now in the collection of the Van Abbemuseum, Eindhoven, that commemorates, or, at the very least represents and reimagines, the founding historical battle of the German nation, waged between the troops of the Germanic leader Arminius (Hermann) (18 BCE–19 CE) and the Roman soldier Quinctilius Varus (46 BCE–9 CE), the snowy floor of the Teutoburg Forest stained by blood. Two years earlier, he had already painted *Nero malt* (*Nero Paints*; 1974), a work now in the Pinakothek der Moderne in Munich (above): a palette, armed with flaming brushes and inscribed across a precipitously pitched landscape, ignites the little Russian village hovering on the high horizon of the painting, its darkened, almost cauterised surface evoking the scorched earth campaigns of Nazi soldiers in the East, even as the

palette pulls the painting deeper into history, summoning the last in the line of Julio-Claudian emperors to create an emblem at once militaristic and artistic. And there is *Icarus – March Sand* (1981), in the collections of the Museum of Contemporary Art Tokyo, a canvas that conjures at once delusional ambition and its defeat. Its winged palette, something of a figure for the artist, even perhaps a kind of oblique and evacuated self-portrait, looms above the Prussian landscape of the Brandenburg Heath, doomed not by a mythical sun above, but by the historical fires beneath, the weight of that tainted inheritance and moral responsibility exerting an almost gravitational pull. That those winged palettes will find themselves returning reimagined in the many leaden planes of the years and decades to follow, in museum galleries turned hangars for a mothballed fleet, suggests the endurance across Kiefer's oeuvre of these military motifs.

All that said, if *Unternehmen "Trappenfang"* shares a landscape setting and military subject with so many of Kiefer's other paintings – perhaps none more so than the contemporaneous *Unternehmen Barbarossa* (1975), a painting so close in its treatment that it might be considered a companion piece, its evocation of the aftermath of military battle also haunted by ghostly trace of a palette – *Unternehmen "Trappenfang"* remains distinct. Assembled into what, in an earlier era of pictorial practice, might be considered a collage of fragments – landscape, language, things – *Unternehmen "Trappenfang"* displays a method of making that will come to define Kiefer's recombinative practice of affixing objects to the surfaces of his canvases or gathering them together as sculptural tableaux, all encased in massive vitrines.

A furrowed field, scorched and covered in snow, the inscription of the code name of a Nazi battleplan, the spectral trace of a palette, all of these pictorial elements can be identified to signal the subject, or subjects, of

25

UNTERNEHMEN "TRAPPENFANG"
(OPERATION "TRAPPENFANG"), 1976
Oil on linen
120 × 150 cm
Hall Collection

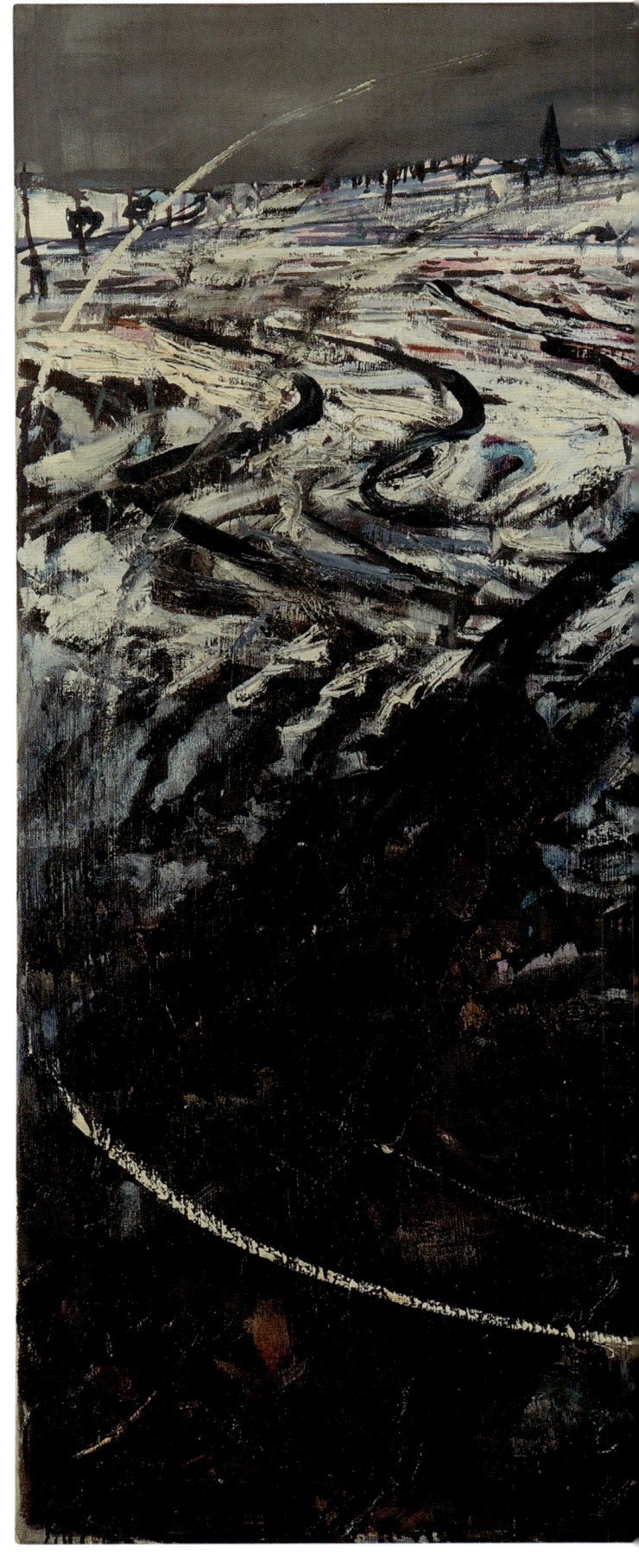

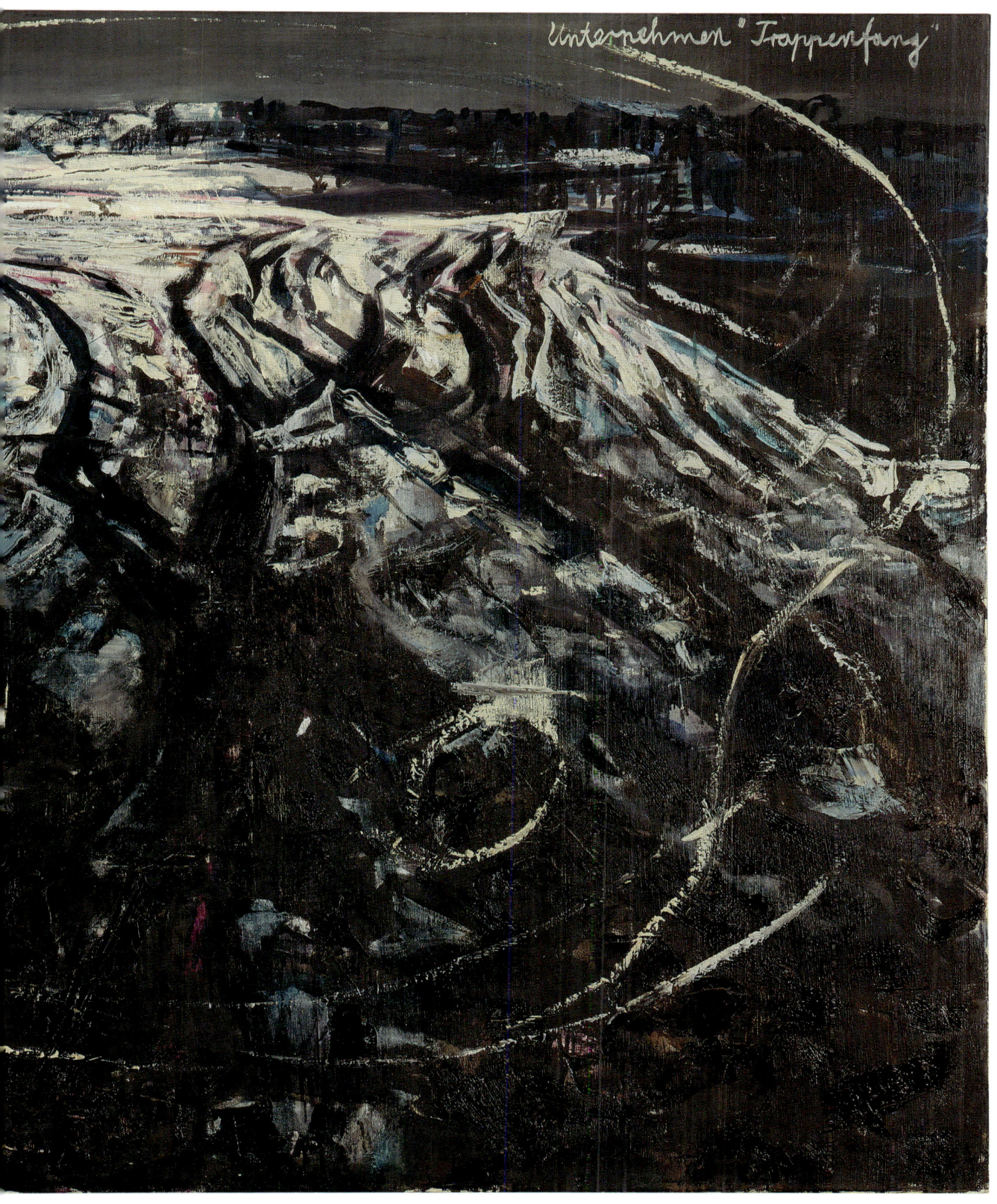

Unternehmen "Trapperfang"

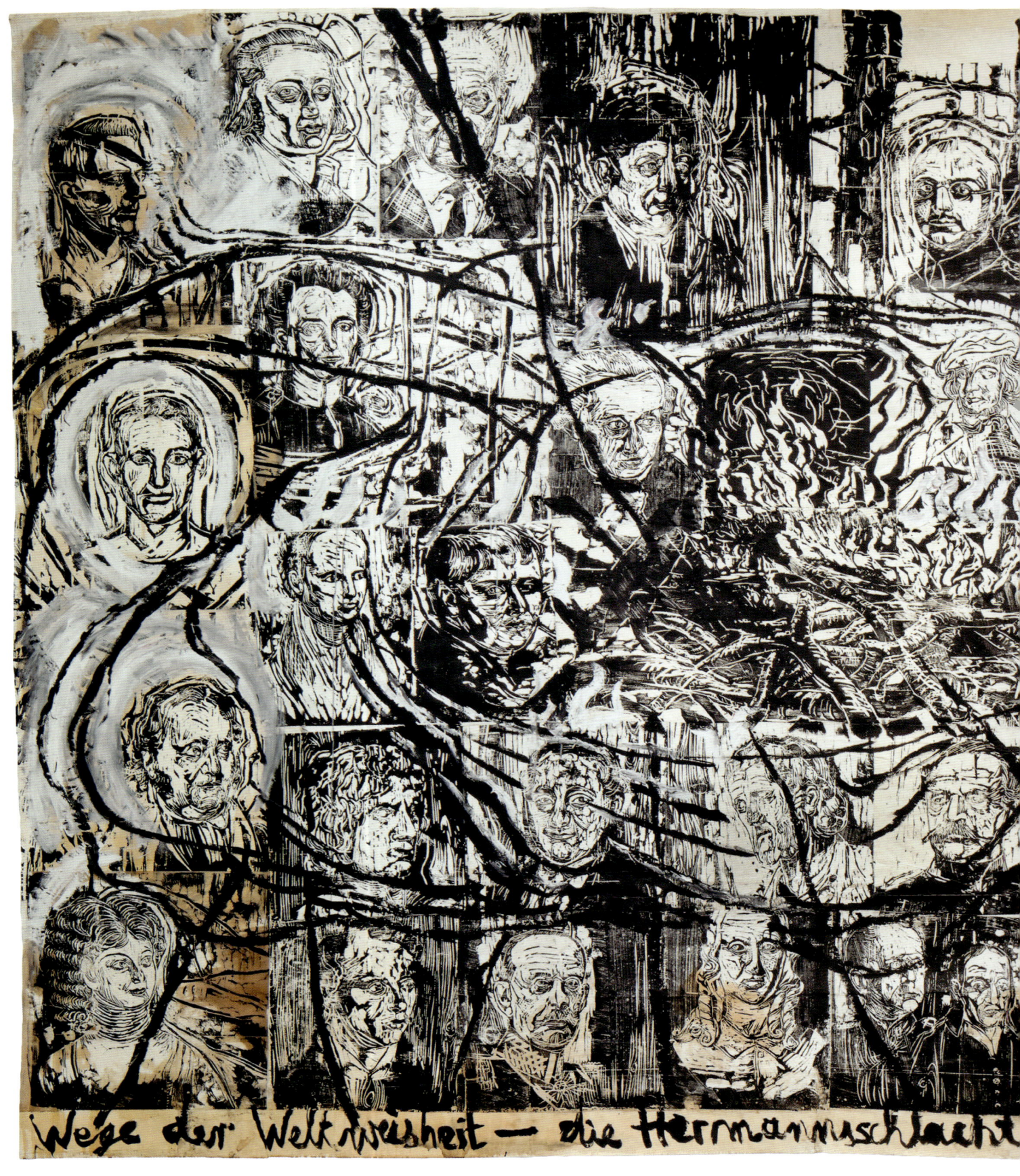

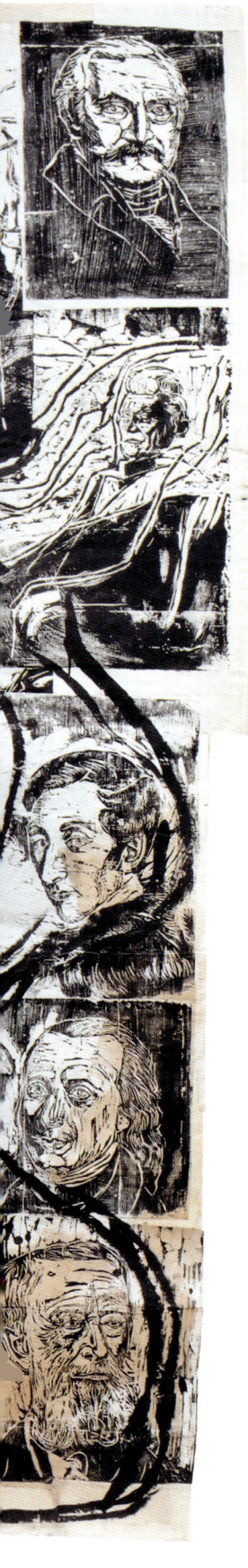

**WEGE DER WELTWEISHEIT –
DIE HERMANNSSCHLACHT
(WAYS OF WORLDLY WISDOM –
THE BATTLE OF HERMANN), 1977**
Collage of woodcuts on paper with
acrylic and shellac, mounted on fabric
305 × 321 cm
Hall Collection

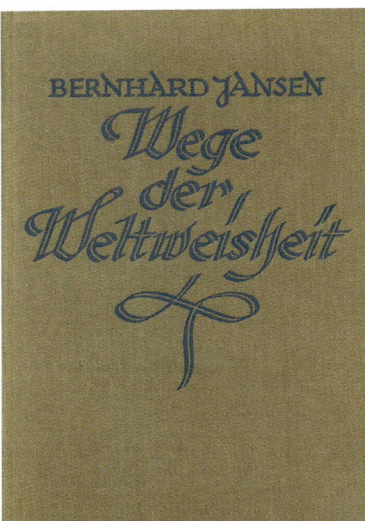

Book cover of Bernhard Jansen,
Wege der Weltweisheit, 1924
Freiburg: Herder

Kiefer's painting. But the question of meaning remains. An artist's palette haunting the ravaged landscape of the East? An artist haunted by his nation's history? A critique of the wages of war?

Occupied and annexed by the Russians in 2015, the Crimean Peninsula is yet again the site of military actions and aggression, of populations displaced, of fertile lands left fallow, of death and destruction. In turn, even as Kiefer's painting may be said to bear belated witness to the aftermath of an ever-more distant war, it also augurs those wars that continue to play out on contested lands in a future that, in the case of the Crimea, is now our collective present.

Lisa Saltzman

WEGE DER WELTWEISHEIT – DIE HERMANNSSCHLACHT (WAYS OF WORLDLY WISDOM – THE BATTLE OF HERMANN), 1977

'The more people see the image and think about it, the wider its meaning becomes. That is how the spiritual space develops.'[49]
– Anselm Kiefer

With the title, *Wege der Weltweisheit – die Hermannsschlacht*, Anselm Kiefer references a history book from 1924 by Jesuit Father Bernhard Jansen (1877–1942; above), who tried to rationalise Catholic religion through multiple philosophical systems. Kiefer's title stands for a major group of works of mostly large collages of woodcuts. The Hermannsschlacht (literally 'the battle

of Hermann') took place in 9 CE. In the Teutoburg Forest, Roman legions led by Quinctilius Varus encountered Arminius-led Germanic tribes, who came out of the battle victoriously. Historians later called Arminius 'Hermann', and he became one of the most important heroes of Germany. In the nineteenth century in particular, the Battle of Hermann developed into a symbol of national freedom, and the Teutoburg Forest was viewed as the place where German history was founded. Many historic and mythological events are located here, not only the Battle of Hermann but also the heroic epic poem the *Nibelungenlied*.

The portrait heads of representatives of German culture and history, cut into wood, are taken from historical publications from the National Socialist era. The images show writers, such as Heinrich von Kleist (1777–1811), philosophers like Immanuel Kant (1724–1804), important figures of German history, including Otto von Bismarck (1815–1898), and propaganda heroes, such as Horst Wessel (1907–1930), the latter stylised by the Nazis as a National Socialist martyr. In doing so, Kiefer unmasks the National Socialist appropriation of historical figures as propaganda deformation.

In Kiefer's woodcuts the relationship between the wood and humans, and the ageing of both, plays a role. The meaning of the woodcut for Kiefer is also connotated with Renaissance art in Germany, when the medium reached a high with works by Albrecht Dürer (1471–1528), before peaking again in the twentieth century in the hands of German Expressionists. During the Third Reich, Old Master woodcuts were often adored, whereas Expressionist pieces and their makers were humiliated as *entartet* ('degenerate'). In principle, Kiefer, with his exploration of German history, seeks to re-establish memory, by depicting content that has been historically and culturally covered, suppressed, or captured. In doing so, he makes people aware and enables a new way of dealing with a subject – without moralising or accusing.

Together with paper, glue, and paint, the woodcut prints are the materials and devices of new pictures, built from an understanding about all these contradictions and with the option of creating – in a new and free way – visual worlds, without considering any traditional reference systems of time and space. As Kiefer has said:

> As an artist, you always hope that under the surface of what you see, there is something that means more at a later date than it does today. This is the veil. Looking at important works of art, for example by Fra Angelico or Michelangelo, in every Century you can always discover something new.[50]

At the centre of this composition there is a fireplace, around which snakes and concentric circles are placed. The black lines link and, at the same time, cut the portrayed figures apart, dynamically breaking the static of the image through the flickering fire. Fire in general plays an important role in Kiefer's work. He uses it during the artistic process of creating images, for example burning painting surfaces or melting lead. It also appears as a key motif in many of his works. Fire is a symbol of transformation: it turns wood into ashes, it warms and glows, it destroys and purifies, it creates room for something new. For Kiefer, however, this symbol, which is important and multi-layered with regards to content, also leads to rituals during National Socialism:

> For the Nazis, fire worshipping was also going backwards. They wanted to extinguish Christianity. They thought that Christianity was the wrong way – Germanic identity was earlier and therefore the right thing. The Nazis had this idea that the Germanic tribes, the Aryans were still left from Atlantis and that their roots had been covered and withered by Christianity. Important words for the Nazis were also purity, the purgatory, cleansing through fire.[51]

Fire is an energy source and at the same time destroyer; it bears both sides and links these contradictory qualities. Materials that come into contact with fire change fundamentally. Its glowing to warming to heating energy contrasts with the cold silence after it has been extinguished. Yet even from these quiet ashes something new can develop. This endless process of change also happens in Kiefer's works: the continuously changing colours due to light, temperature, and humidity, for example. Within complex transformation processes there occurs a cyclical process of birth and death, corroborating Kiefer in his statement that every end is also a beginning. Kiefer compares this explosion and, at the same time, implosion of transcending material and matter through fire with his artistic work, viewing his art creating as a kind of speeding up process up to the point of just being visible: 'I work on this border that is between the trace of almost nothing and nothing.'[52] For Kiefer, the artist becomes a symbol of the connection between the visible and invisible, integrated deeply in the process of creation and decay. He sees his work as coming from and going towards an omnipresent intelligence:

> A secret is something veiled. With my work I do not unveil the secret. I create the secret. Matter also keeps a secret. I don't think that the secret is on top and matter is at the bottom, and that it is only the idea that gives the thing a life. I believe that the idea is part of the thing. The secret is already inherent in things.[53]

He continues: 'I secretize, as Novalis says, the matter, by undressing it.'[54]

Antonia Hoerschelmann
Translated from the German by Lena Fritsch

27

WEGE DER WELTWEISHEIT: GOTTFRIED KELLER (WAYS OF WORLDLY WISDOM: GOTTFRIED KELLER), 1977

Woodcuts on Japanese paper on cardboard
and bound with canvas strips (66 pages)
70 × 50 × 15 cm

Hall Collection

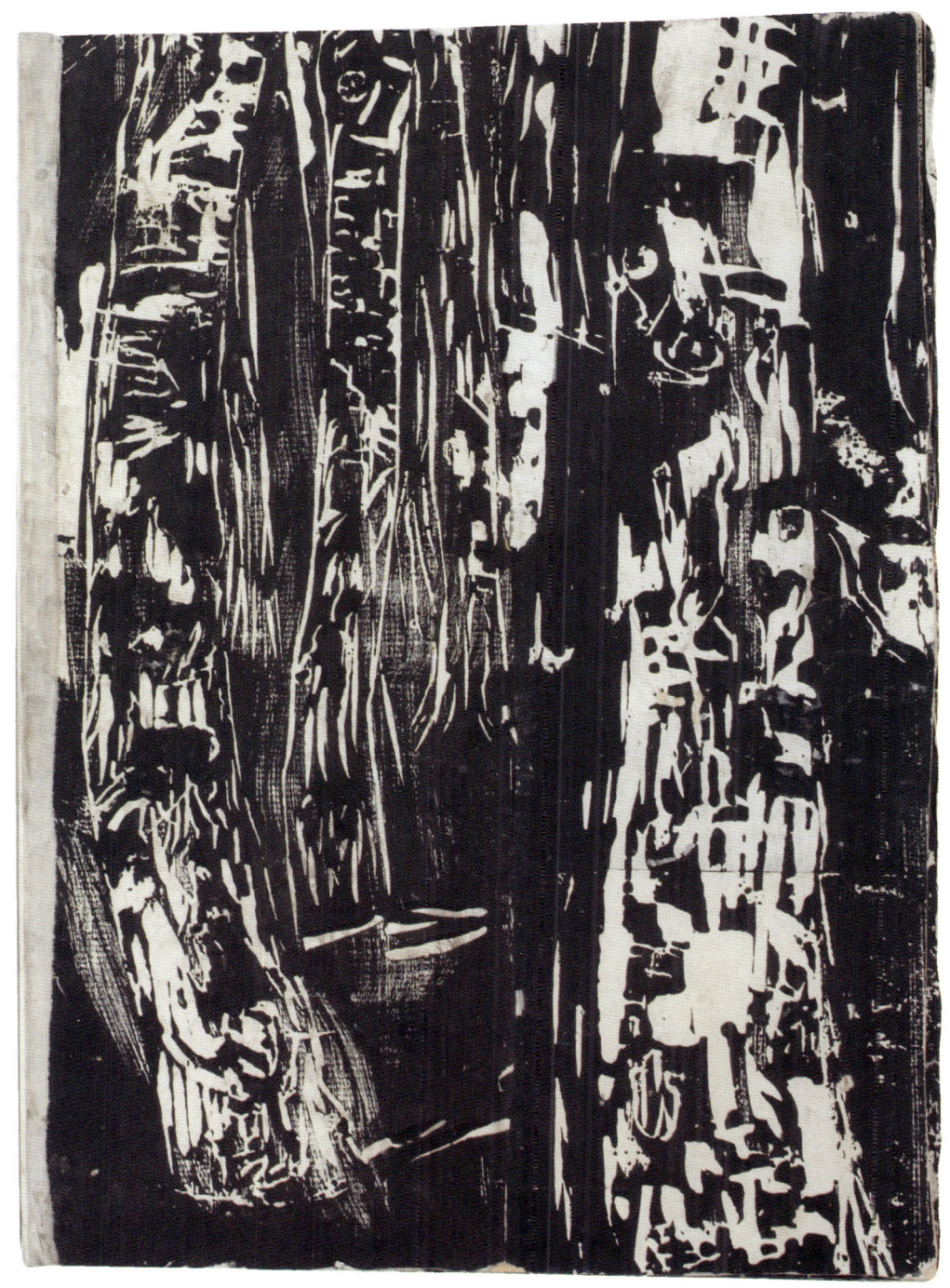

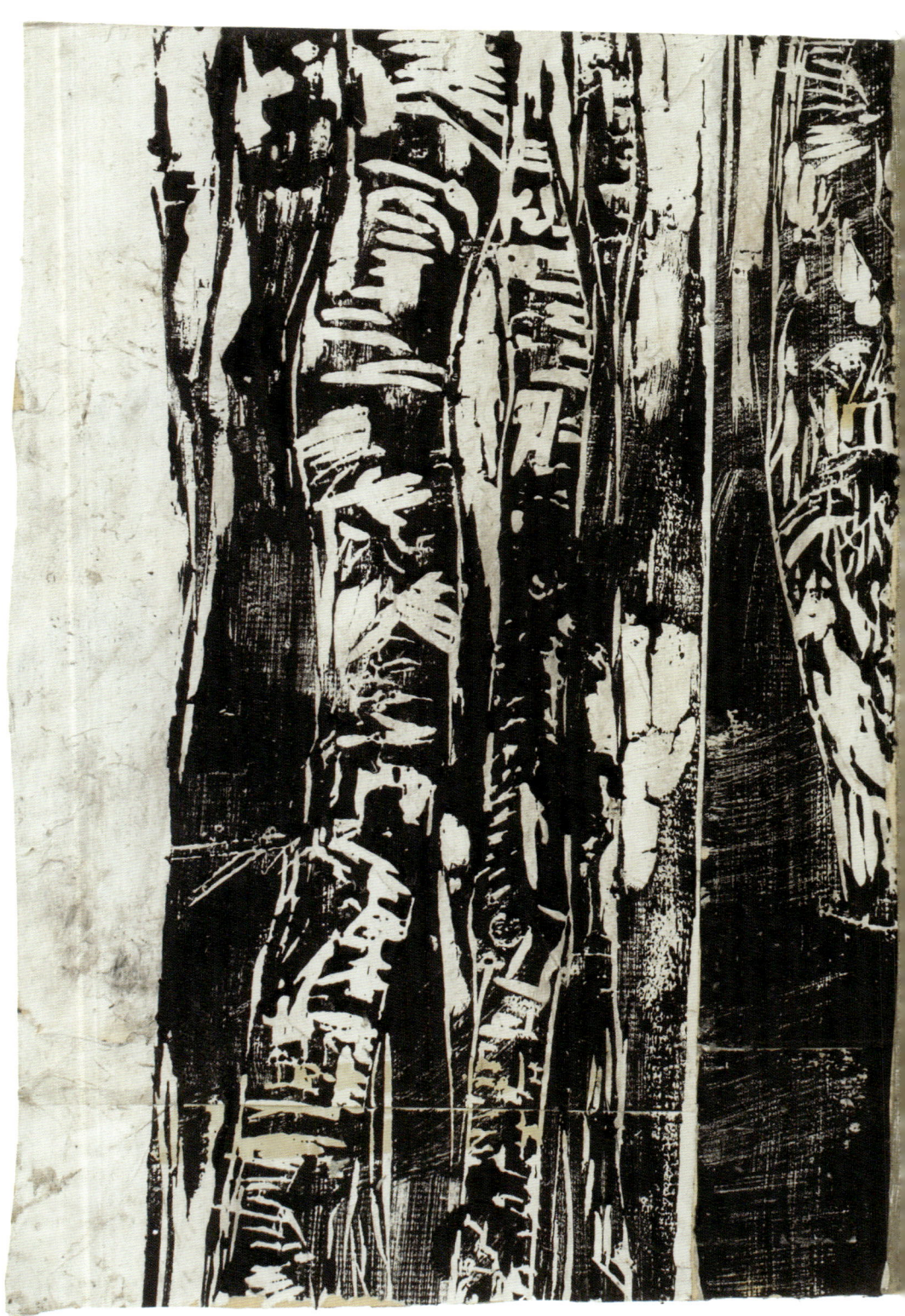

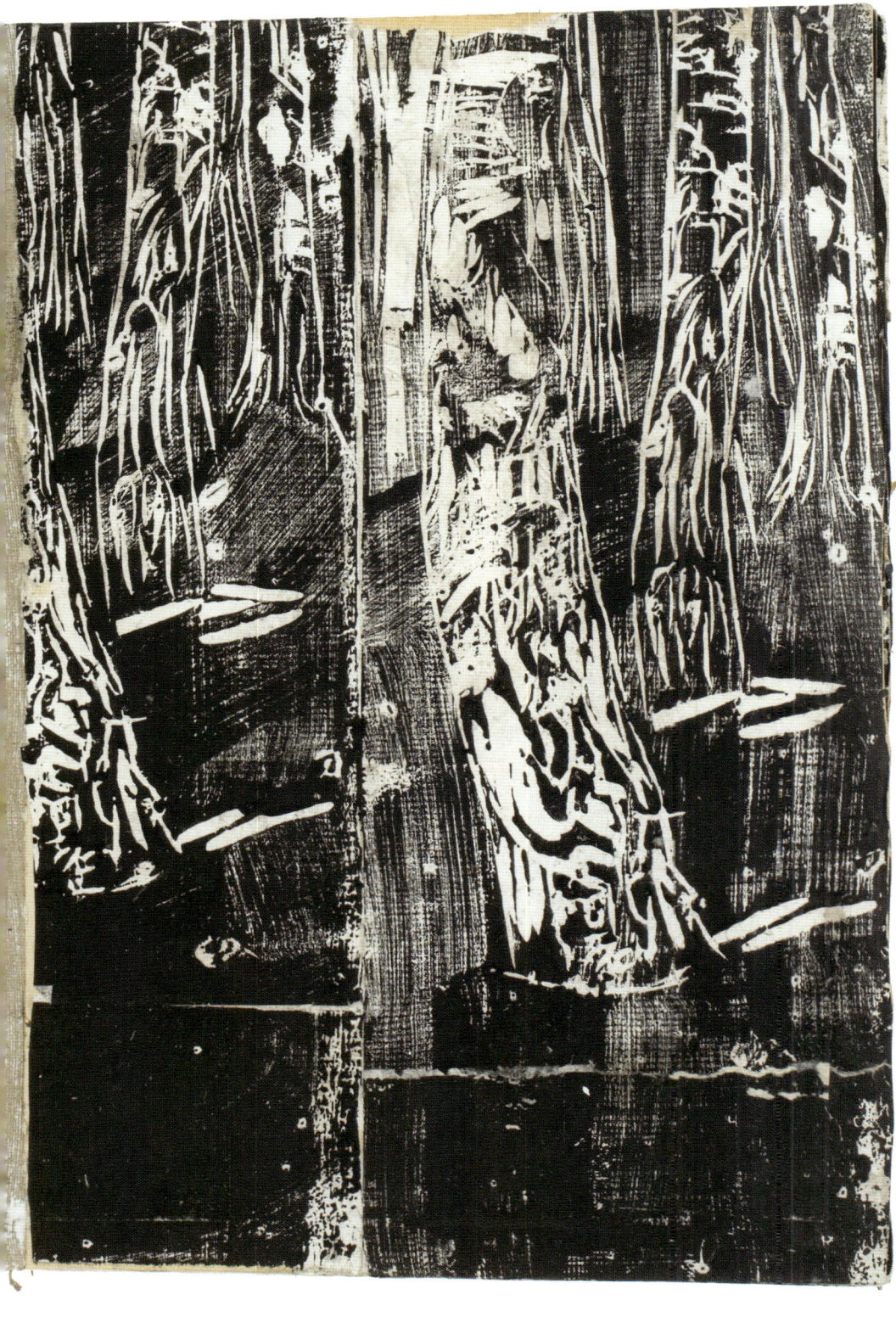

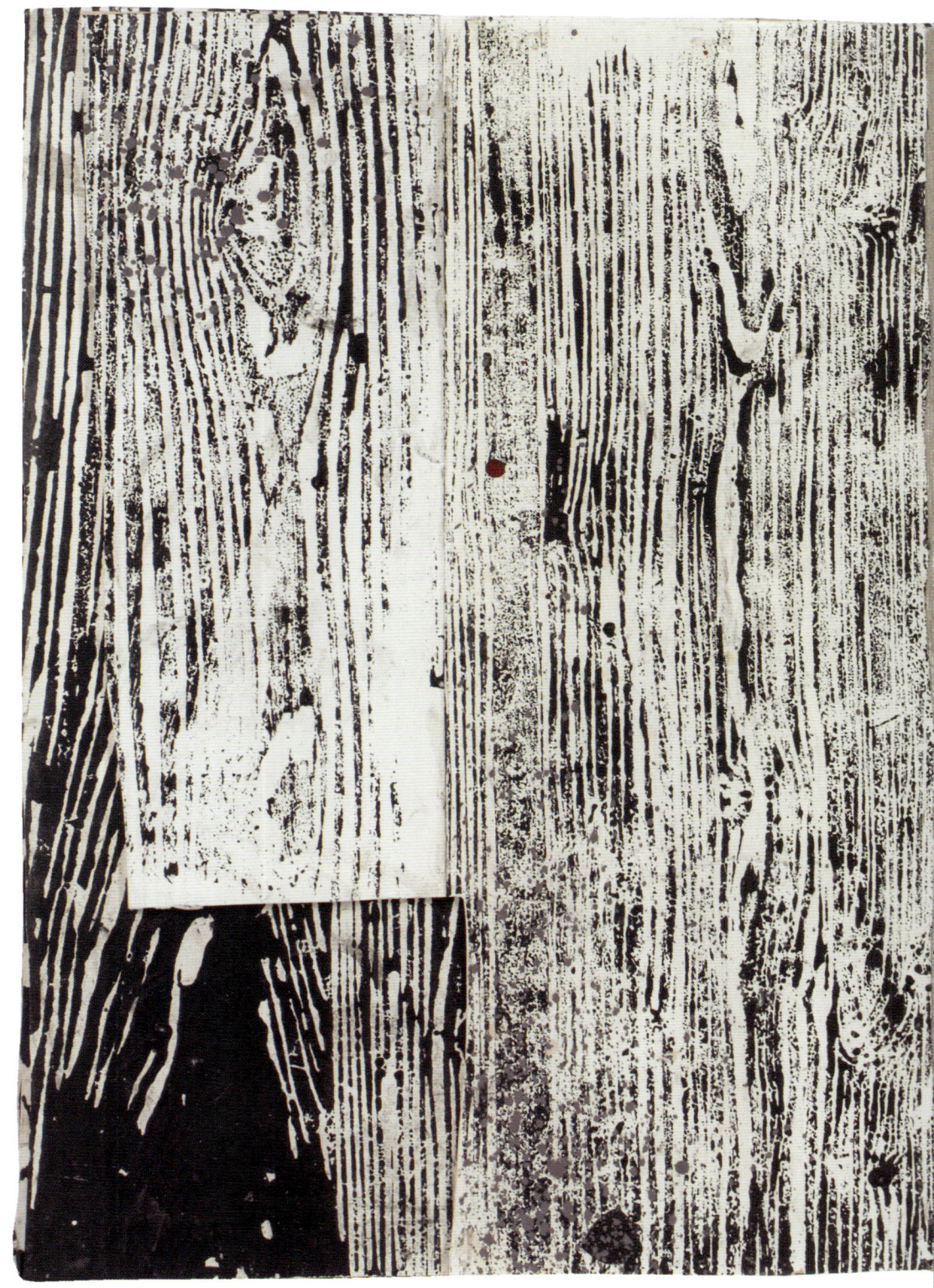

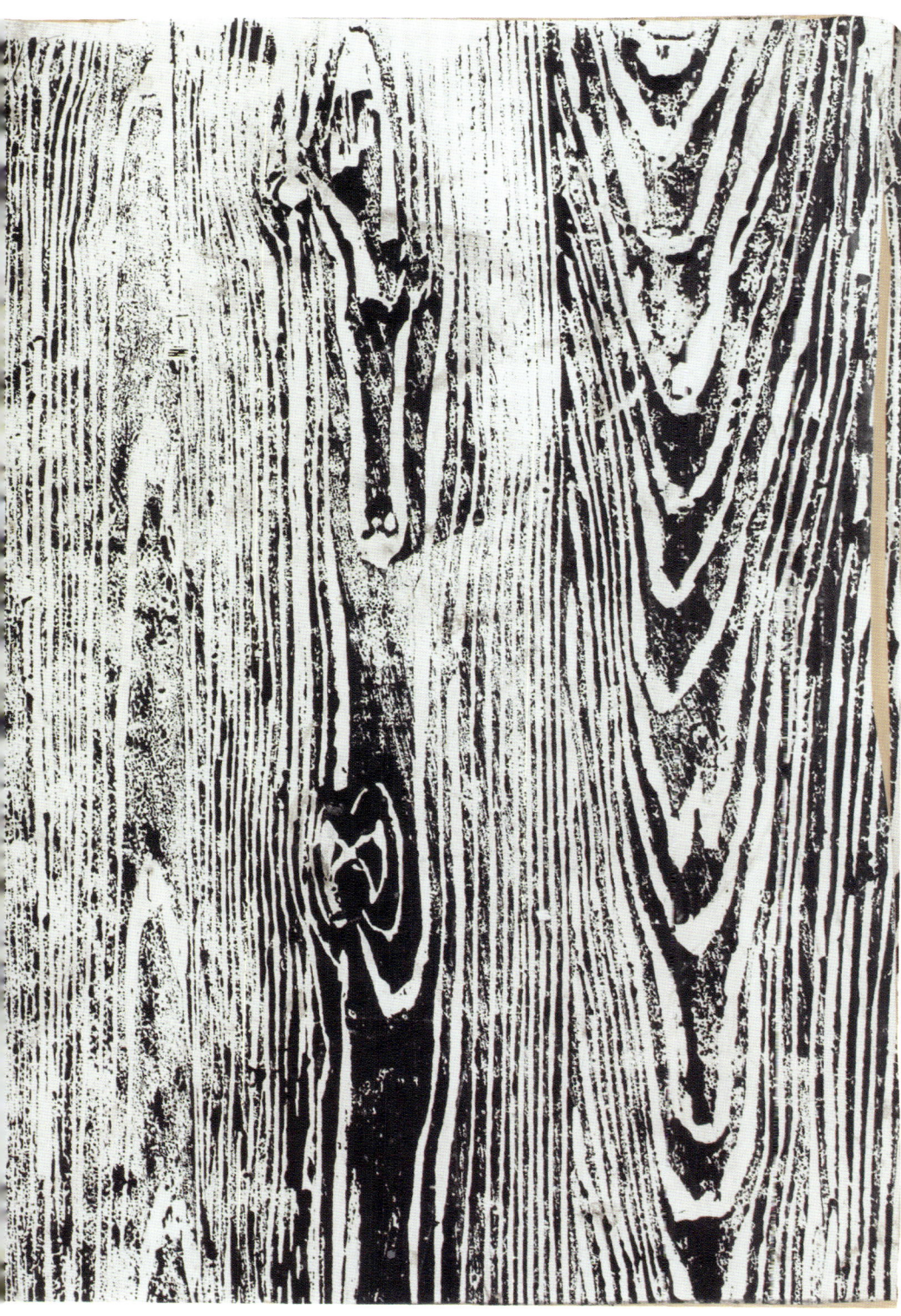

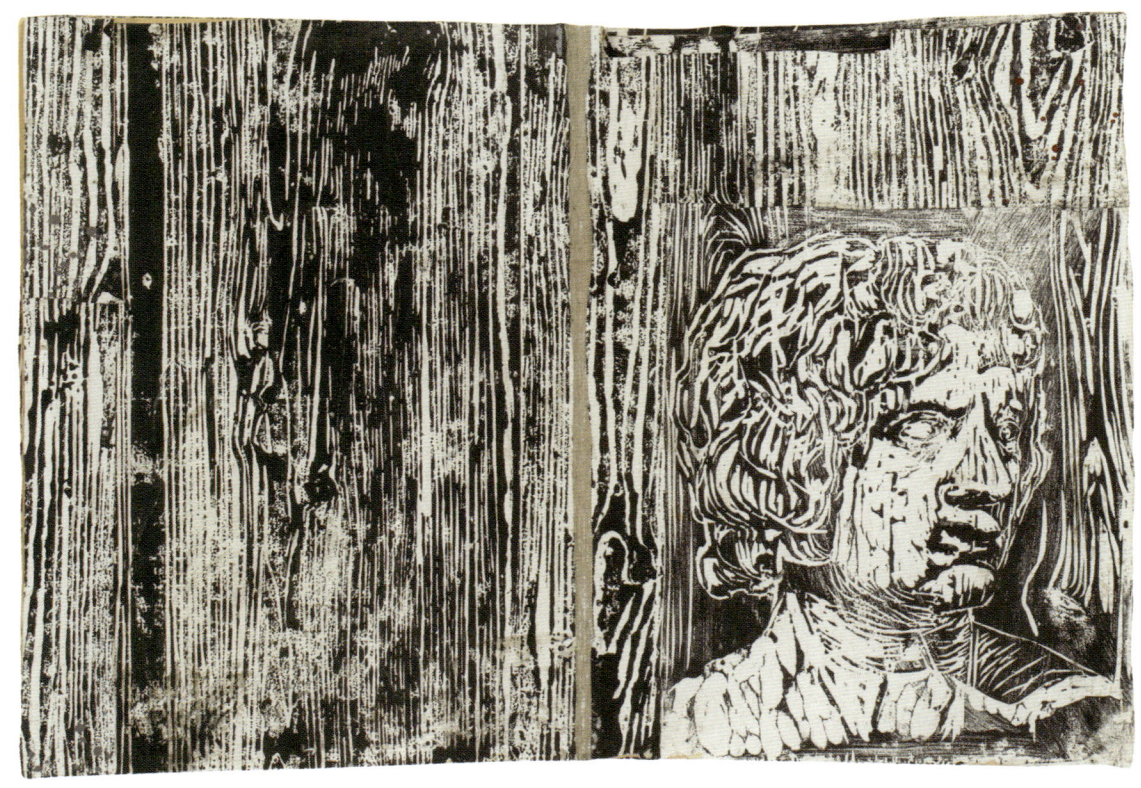

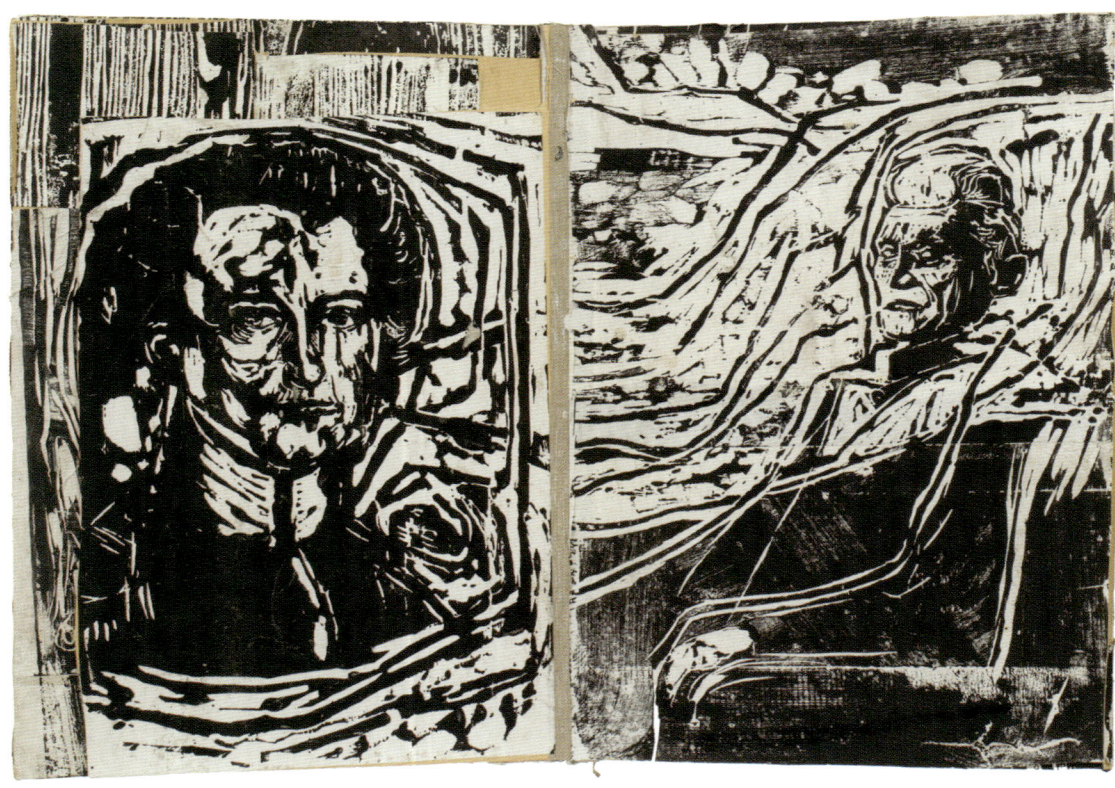

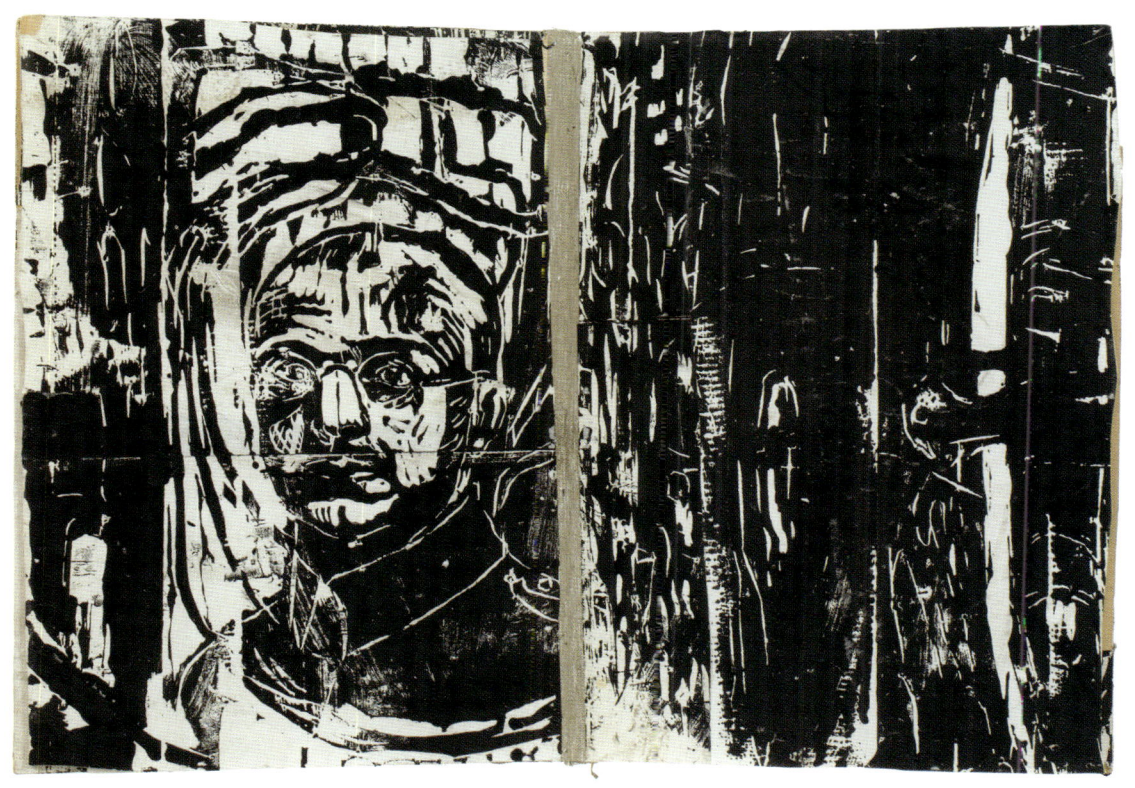

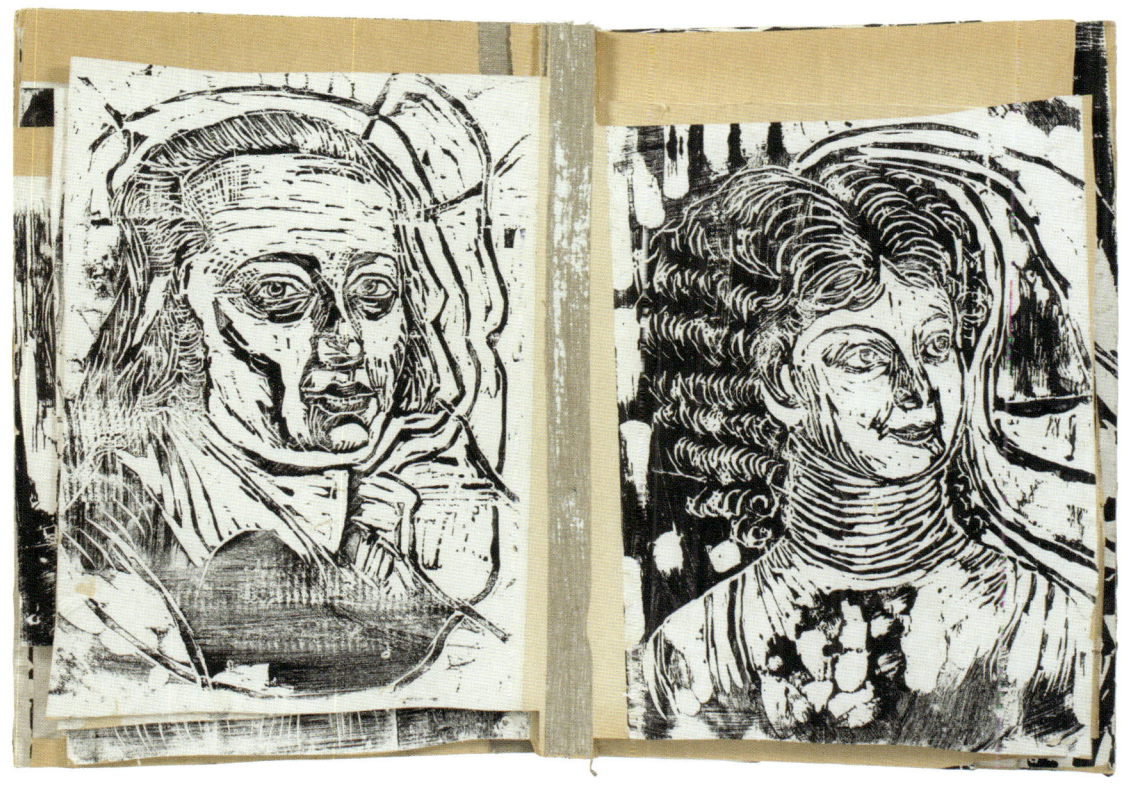

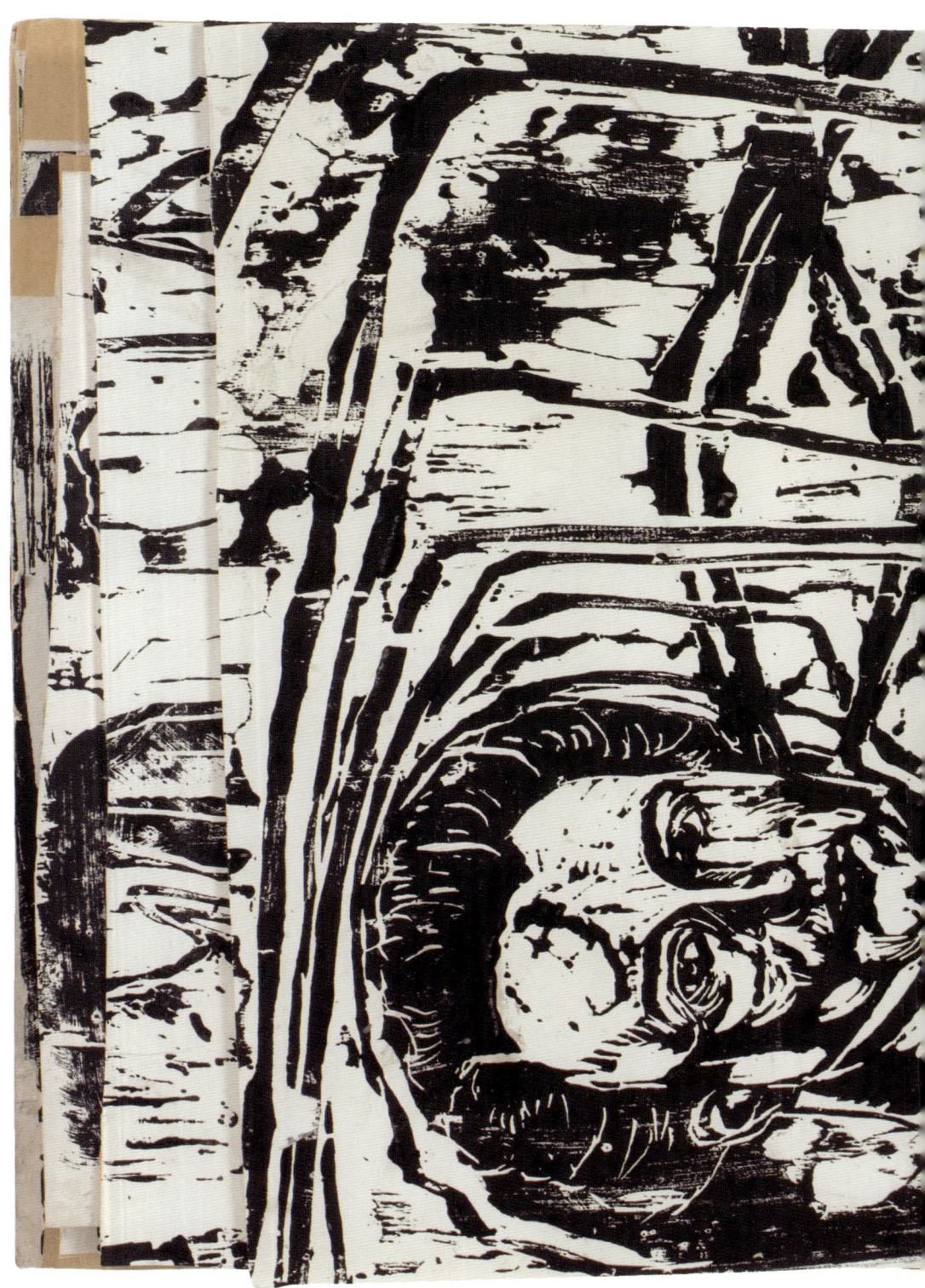

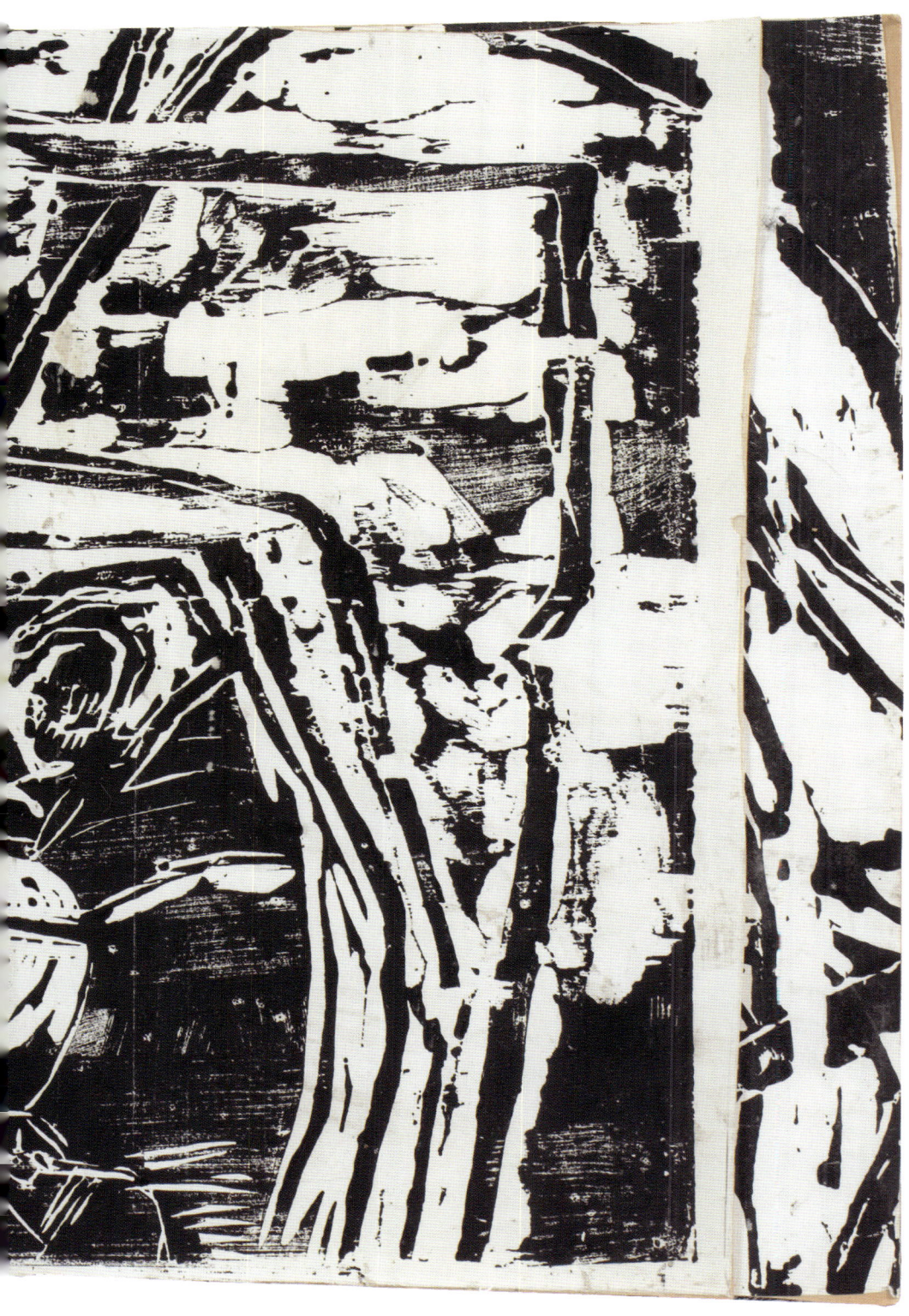

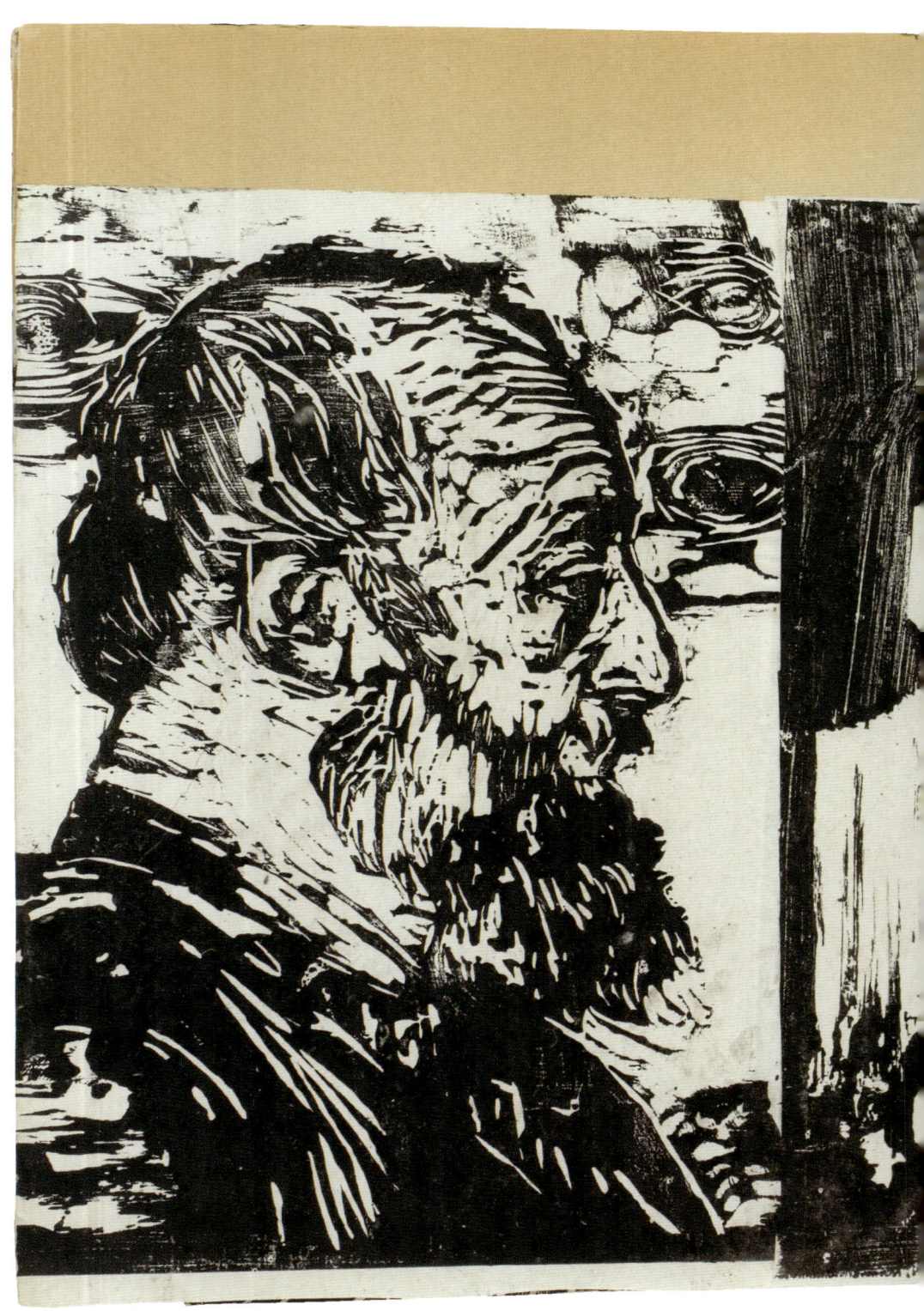

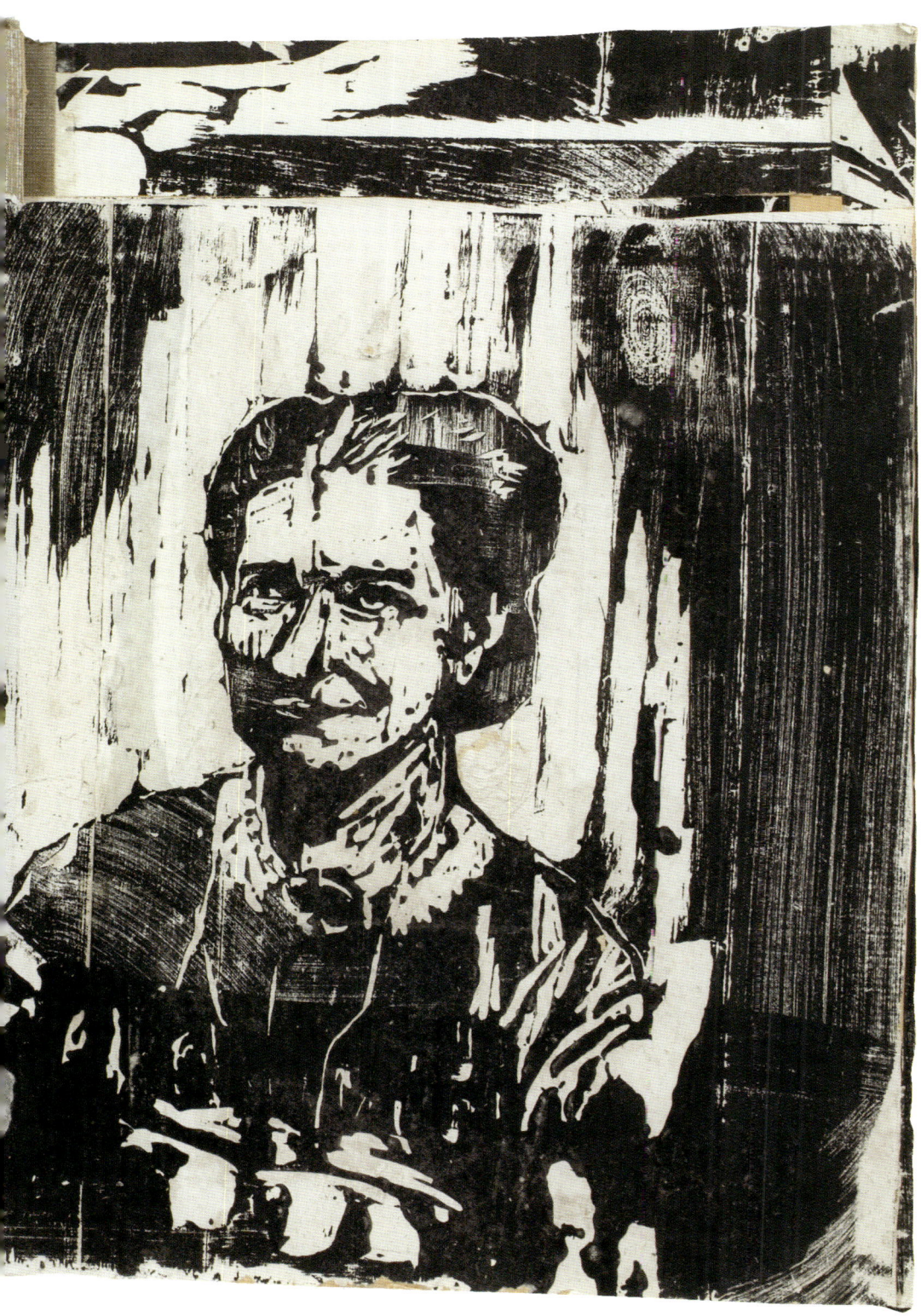

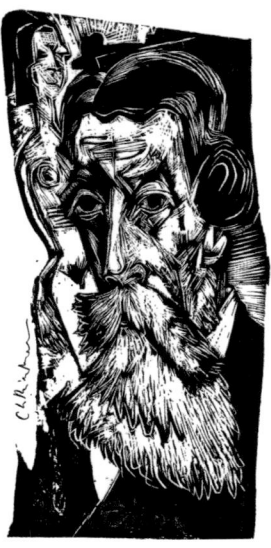

Ernst Ludwig Kirchner (1880–1938)
Portrait of Ludwig Schames, 1917–8
Woodcut on paper, 56.5 × 27.3 cm

27

WEGE DER WELTWEISHEIT: GOTTFRIED KELLER (WAYS OF WORLDLY WISDOM: GOTTFRIED KELLER), 1977

Wege der Weltweisheit: Gottfried Keller is an artist book containing 66 woodcuts, ranging from abstract printings of an unworked wooden plank (which can be considered the purest form of woodcut), to single and double portraits, cleverly combining portraits of now largely forgotten men and women. The portrait woodcuts were printed on different sizes of Japanese paper, which have been pasted on cardboard and bound as a book with canvas strips. Portraits range from the Germanic chieftain Arminius (*c.*18 BCE–19 CE; copied from the marble head at the Capitoline Museums in Rome) to Louise of Mecklenburg-Strelitz, Queen of Prussia (1776–1810; after a 1799 painting by William Böttner), the German poet and composer Annette von Droste-Hülshoff (1797–1848; after a sculpted bust at Meersburg Castle) to the Prussian Minister of War Albrecht von Roon (1803–1879; after a photograph). For more information on the portrait series, see also pp.145–55.

Anselm Kiefer started making woodcuts in the 1970s, embracing a printmaking technique that has been prolifically used by German artists for centuries.[55] Woodcuts are created using relief printing. This means that the lines of the composition to be printed are left standing raised (in relief) on the printing block, which is usually made of pear or boxwood.[56] These fine-grained woods can be easily worked by the woodcutter using pointed knives and chisels.[57] Once the design is complete, the raised lines are covered in ink, either with dabbers (soft leather balls) or rollers, ready to be printed. This could be done either on a book-printer's press or by hand, placing a sheet of paper on top and rubbing the surface. The printed result is, logically, a reverse image of the original design cut into the woodblock, a process the woodcutter must always take into account.

Kiefer stands in a long tradition of woodcut art in Germany, starting from its European origins in the fifteenth century, although it had been previously invented in Asia.[58] As the oldest printing process, woodcut was initially practised by anonymous craftsmen or artisans working in religious contexts such as convents, often incorporating images into religious texts. From the 1450s woodcuts appear as single-sheet prints (called *Einblattholzschnitte* in German) for devotional or votive use, as well as illustrations in secular texts. These early examples appear rather linear and rough and, because of their mostly ephemeral nature, have rarely survived. From the last quarter of the fifteenth century, woodcuts entered the artistic realm with established artists often providing a design drawing to pass on to a professional block-cutter. This resulted in delicately carved designs that were eagerly collected by connoisseurs as precious masterpieces. From around 1500 German artists like Albrecht Dürer, Lucas Cranach (1472–1553), Hans Burgkmair (1471–1531), and Hans Sebald Beham (1500–1550) highly rated printmaking. Prints could be produced relatively quickly and printed in multiples, meaning that they were more widely distributed than, for instance, paintings. Alternative printmaking techniques became popular in Germany from the seventeenth century onwards, with finer wood-engraving dominating in the nineteenth century for newspaper- and book-illustrations. However, the 1910s and 1920s saw a revival of the woodcut technique by German Expressionists like Emil Nolde (1867–1956), Ernst Ludwig Kirchner (1880–1938; above), Karl Schmidt-Rottluff (1884–1976), Erich Heckel

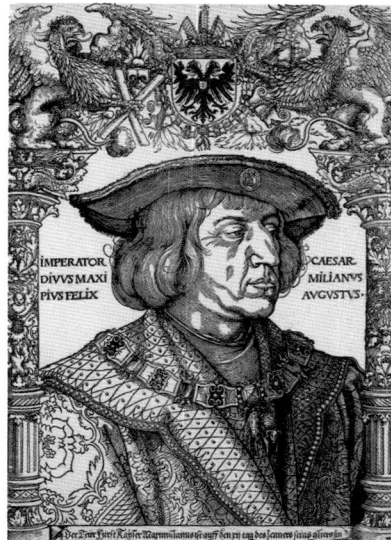

Albrecht Dürer (1471–1528)
Kaiser Maximilian I (*Holy Roman Emperor
Maximilian I*), 1519
Woodcut on laid paper, 38.2 × 54.2 cm

(1883–1970), as well as Käthe Kollwitz (1867–1945).
After the Second World War, artists like Kiefer's teacher
Joseph Beuys made woodcuts in the 1960s and 1970s,
just before Kiefer's own first efforts.[59]

The woodcut has always been considered an
inherently German artform, connected to a national feeling
of Germanness. Within the wider context of Kiefer's
work and its intricate references to German history, his
forays into woodcuts are therefore entirely logical. Kiefer
started printmaking around 1973–4, exclusively working
in woodcut. His personal connection with wood stems
from his childhood, when the German forest represented
refuge and safety for Kiefer.[60] His grandfather was a
carpenter, whose tools he inherited and used on rough
planks of linden (lime) wood, incorporating their grain
structure and imperfections such as knots. As art historian
James Hyman has noted, 'it is the wood as wood and
the woodcut as a general signifier of Germanness that
concerns Kiefer above all'.[61]

Instead of employing a printing press, Kiefer prints all his
woodcuts himself by laying a sheet of paper on the inked
woodblock and rubbing the back of the paper by hand.
In the early years, Kiefer carved one large portrait a day,
without a specific project in mind.[62] They are roughly, but
skilfully, carved, often with the tool marks and the grain of
the woodblock framing the sitter. These prints are unique
works and were not numbered or published in editions.
Some of the early woodcut portraits were kept in Kiefer's
studio for many years to be later reused in other works. For
instance, from the end of the 1970s up until 1993, Kiefer
produced several works titled *Wege der Weltweisheit*,
subtitled *Gottfried Keller* or *Die Hermannsschlacht* (see
also pp.128–31). They all contain a varying number of his
early portrait woodcuts, whether in monumental collages,
artist's books or smaller print series.[63]

An Van Camp

WEGE DER WELTWEISHEIT: GOTTFRIED KELLER (WAYS OF WORLDLY WISDOM: GOTTFRIED KELLER), 1977

Wege der Weltweisheit: Gottfried Keller consists of six
woodcuts showing individual portraits, as opposed to
the more elaborate artist book also created in 1977
(pp.132–43). The first and largest portrait provides the
series with its title: Gottfried Keller (1819–1890) was a
Swiss political poet and is shown in profile to the right.[64]
The other portraits include Swiss poet Conrad Ferdinand
Meyer (1825–1898); Gottfried Keller again, but this
time portrayed from the front; political author Ludmilla
Assing (1821–1880); German poet and revolutionary
Ferdinand Freiligrath (1810–1876); and German political
poet Georg Herwegh (1817–1875). This combination
of nineteenth-century male and female writers seems
random at first. Interestingly, Kiefer annotated the first
portrait with a ten-line handwritten note to his good
friend Johannes 'Jonny' Gachnang (1939–2005), the
influential curator and director of the Kunsthalle Bern
from 1974 to 1982. In the letter, Kiefer explains that he is
sending Gachnang a few woodcuts. This was probably
written in 1977, when he was working on *Wege der
Weltweisheit: Gottfried Keller*, in anticipation of one of
Kiefer's earliest exhibitions to be held in Switzerland,
which would take place in 1978.[65] He refers to the two
portraits of Keller, one in profile and one frontal ('*einmal
von der Seite und einmal von vorne*') and two further
portraits of women called 'Ludmilla' and 'Betty'.[66] It is
possible that this series of six woodcuts was therefore
carefully selected by Kiefer and sent as a package to
Gachnang as a taster for the rest of the show.

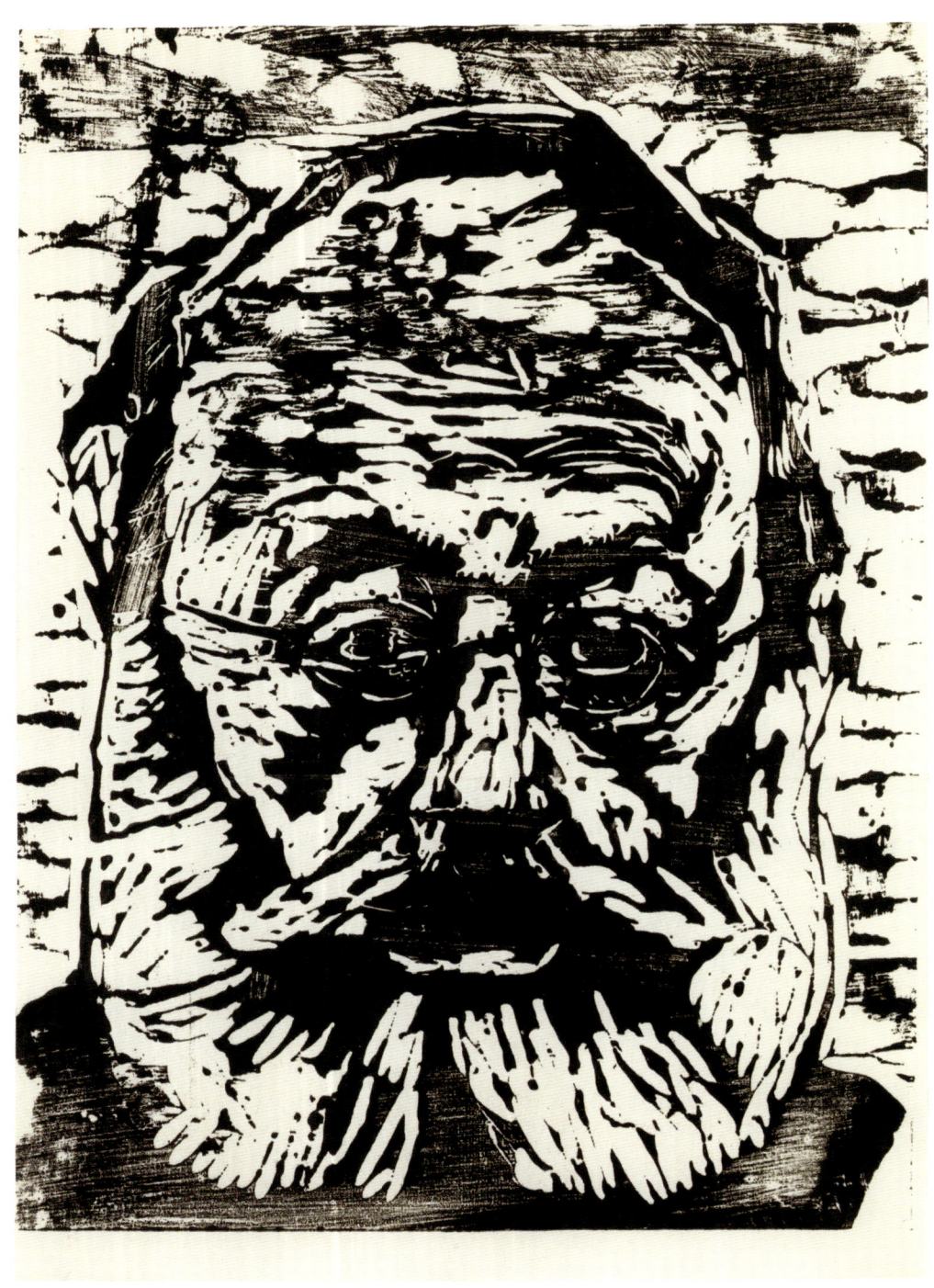

28
WEGE DER WELTWEISHEIT: GOTTFRIED KELLER
(WAYS OF WORLDLY WISDOM: GOTTFRIED KELLER), 1977
Six woodcuts on paper
Approximately 74 × 43 cm each. Paper sizes differ
Hall Collection

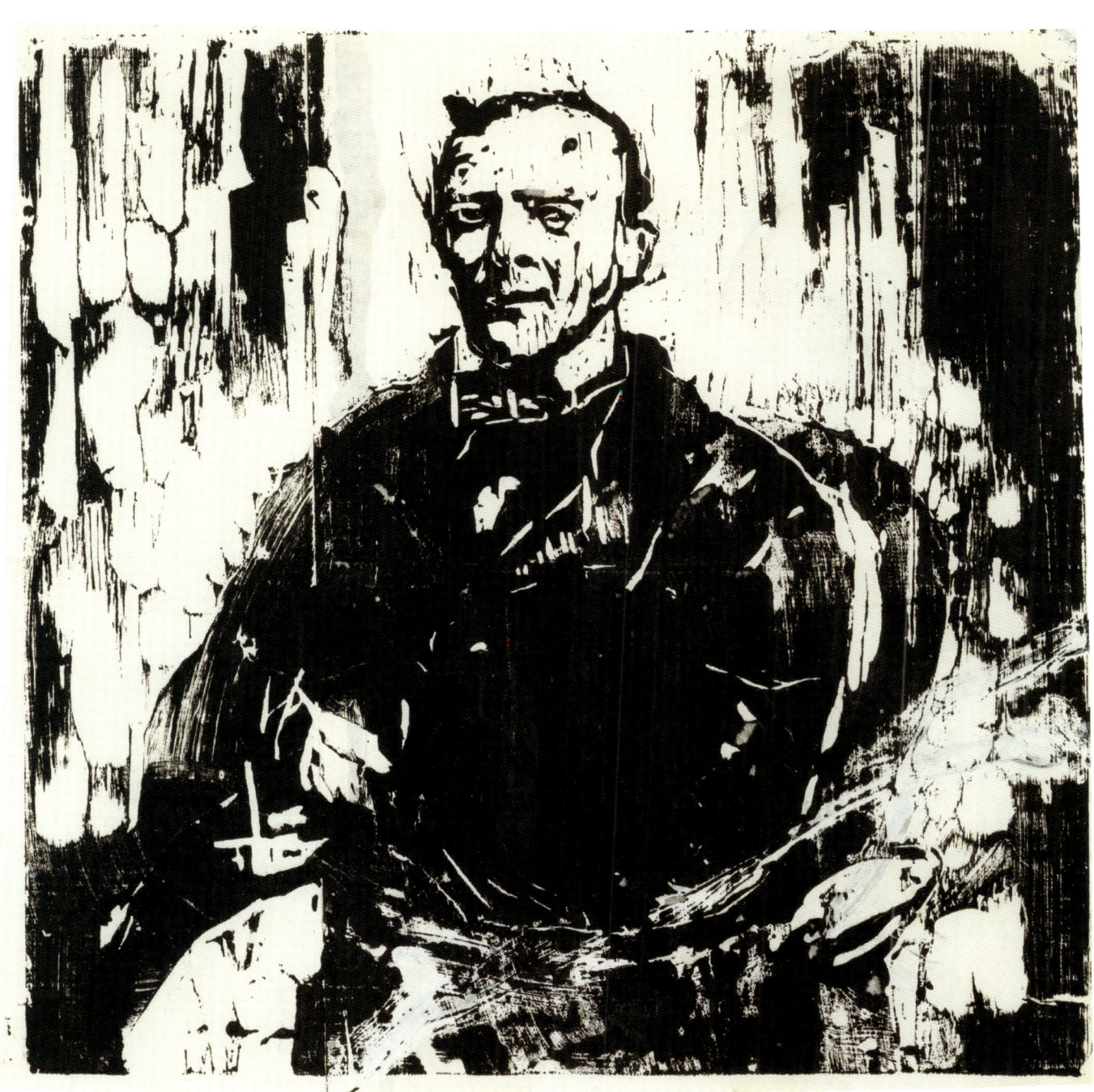

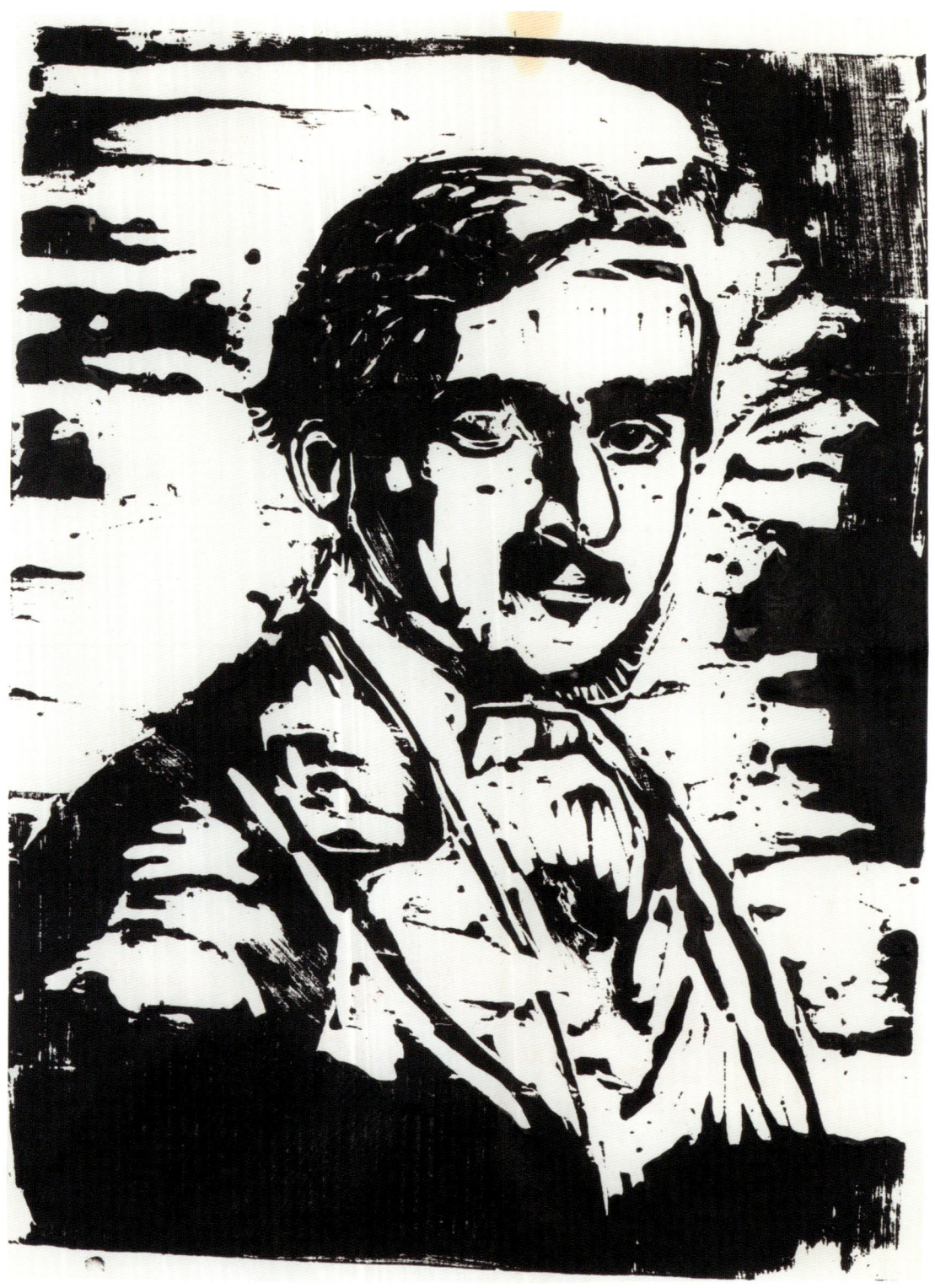

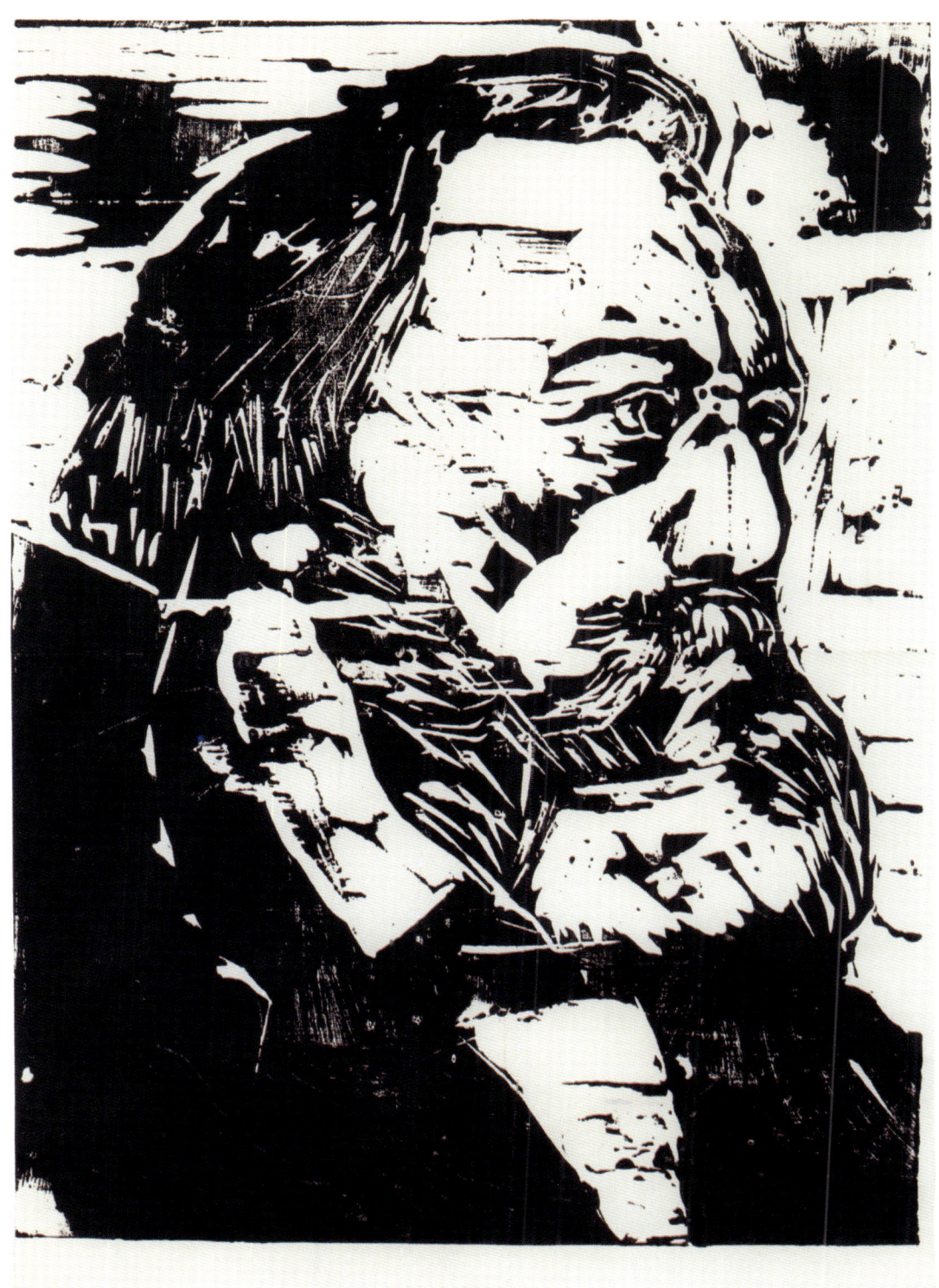

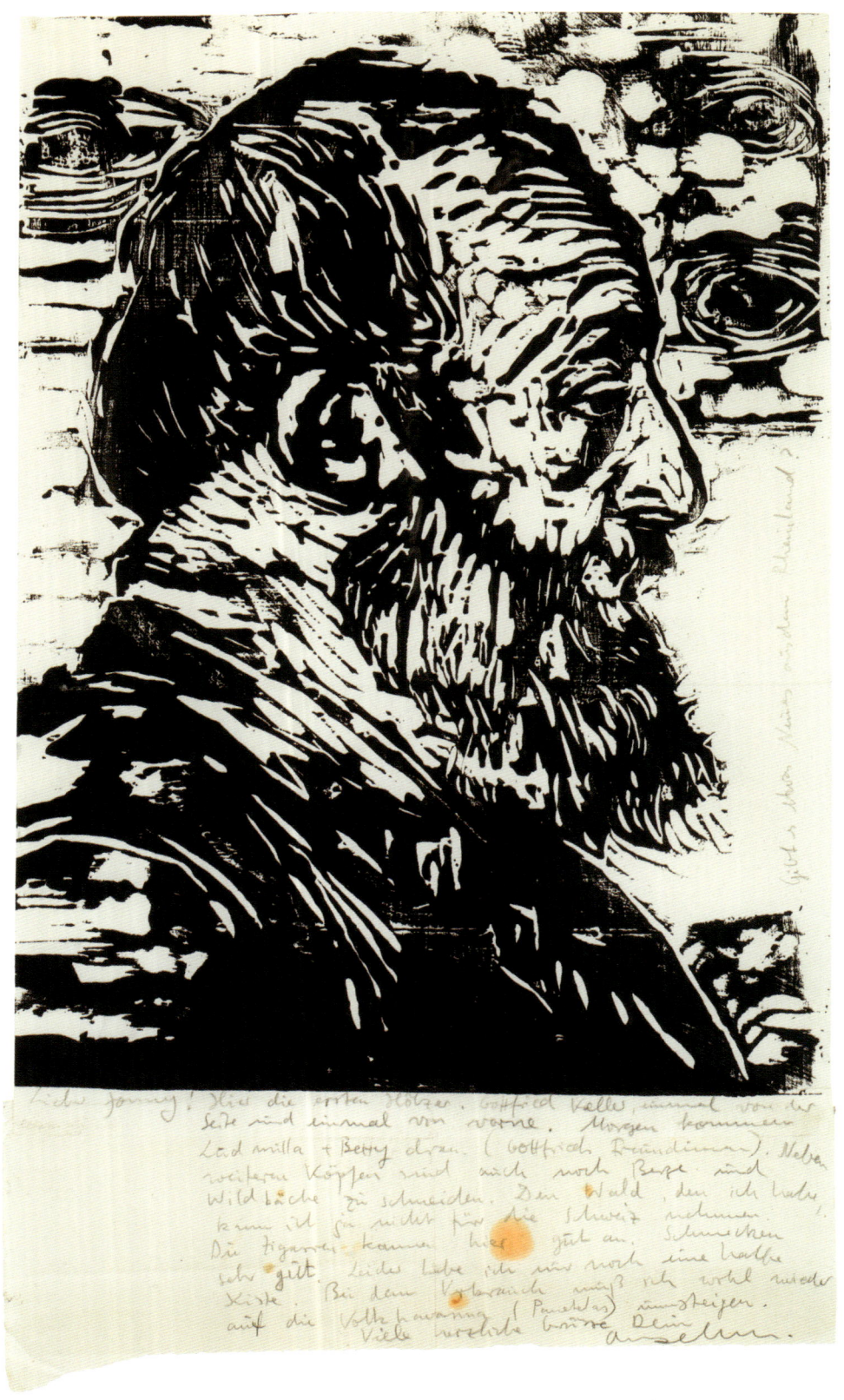

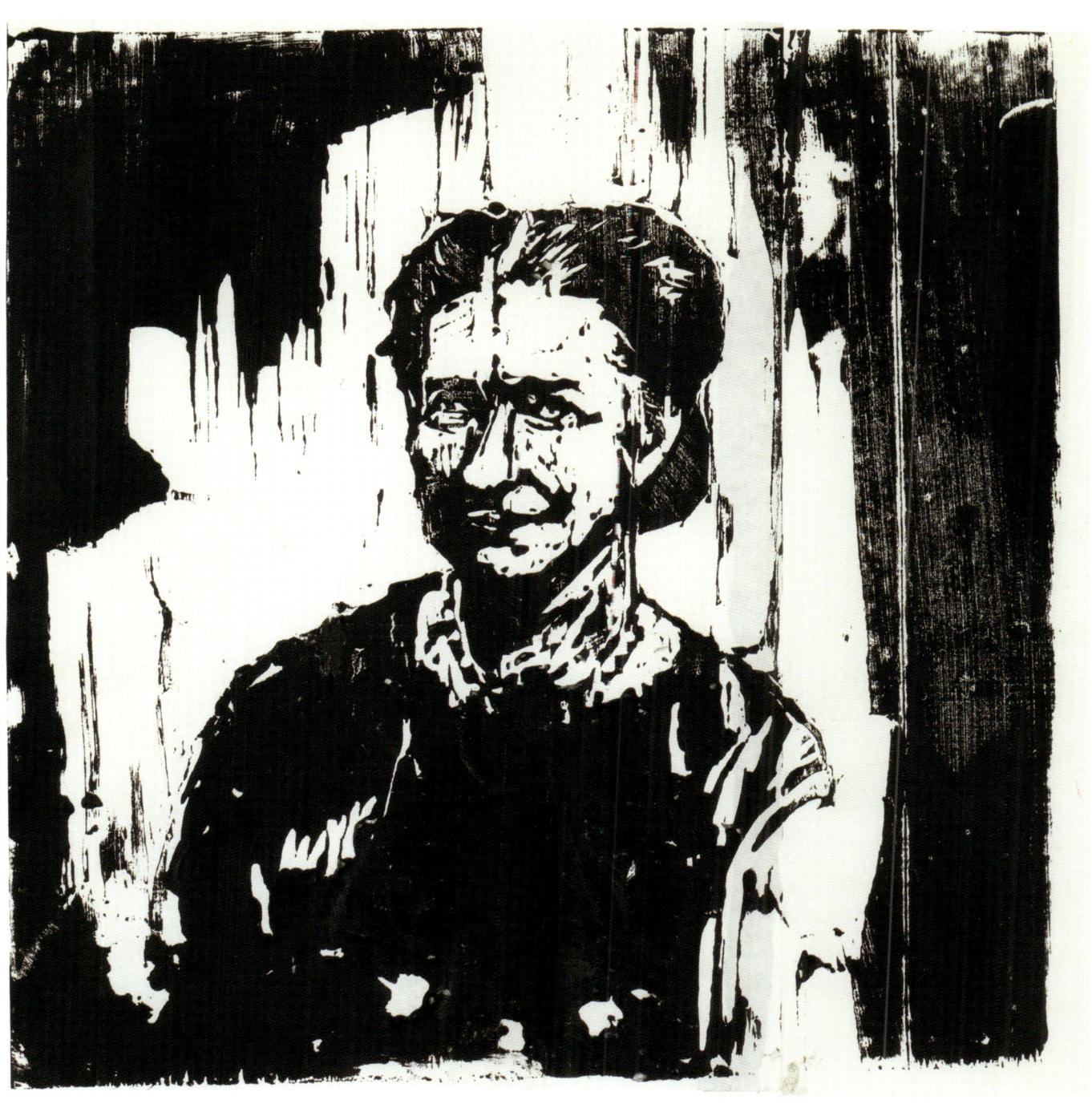

29

ENGEL MIT PALETTE
(ANGEL WITH PALETTE), 1977–8

Oil, emulsion and shellac on canvas
160 × 139 cm

Hall Collection

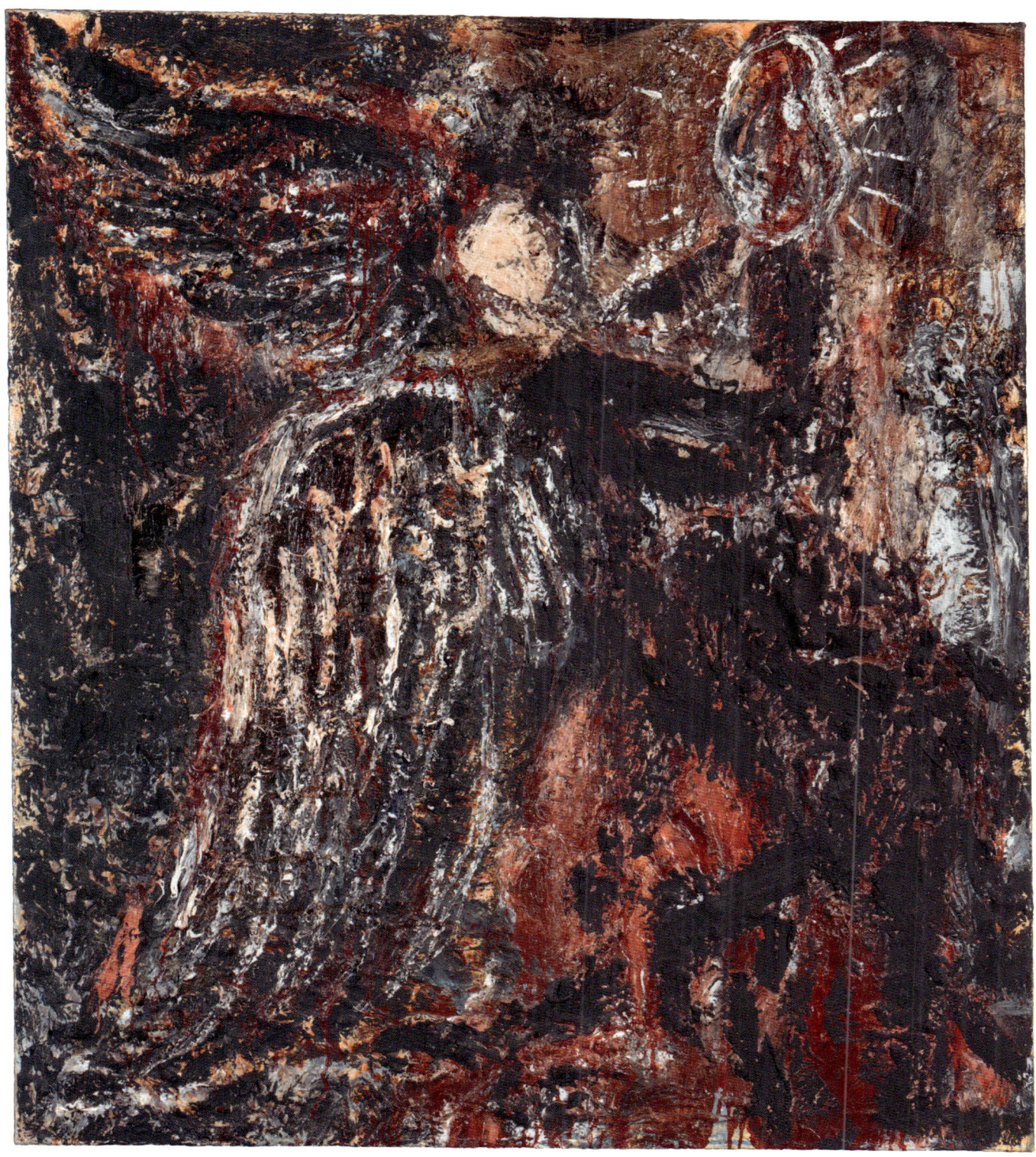

Kiefer's inspiration for these portraits of now mostly unknown or forgotten people can be found in a book: the 1935 publication by Karl Richard Ganzer (1909–1943), *Das deutsche Führergesicht* (*Face of the German Leader*).[67] It features a pantheon of historical and contemporary figures – political rulers, commanders, artists, poets, musicians, etc. – connecting them through history in order to legitimise National Socialism. From Arminius, the Germanic commander who destroyed three Roman legions, over the Holy Roman Emperor Charles V (1500–1558), Albrecht Dürer, Ludwig van Beethoven (1770–1827), Arthur Schopenhauer (1788–1860), and Friedrich Nietzsche (1844–1900), to Adolf Hitler. The accompanying portraits consist of reproductions of paintings, prints, or statues of the historical figures, and photographs of the more contemporary figures. Kiefer based some of his woodcuts on these portraits, investigating the connections between German history and how it led to the popularity of Nazism. Kiefer was most interested in portraits of nineteenth-century intellectuals, poets, novelists, politicians, and industrialists. Fascinatingly, the two portraits he made of Gottfried Keller – after whom he named (at least) two artworks – do not correspond to the photo illustrated in Ganzer's book.[68] The title of the series, *Wege der Weltweisheit*, usually translated as *Ways of Worldly Wisdom*, is borrowed by Kiefer from the 1924 writings by the Jesuit Bernhard Jansen, who tried to rationalise the Catholic religion through multiple philosophical systems (see also p.130).

When Anselm Kiefer started making woodcuts in the 1970s he was following in the footsteps of numerous illustrious German artists, many of whom specialised in portraiture and/or woodcuts. Albrecht Dürer was a pioneer in printmaking and by far the most influential German artist whose portraits were already collected during his lifetime. His popularity in Germany rose again in the late nineteenth century, boosting German nationalism.[69] Dürer was subsequently eagerly adopted as a hero of Germanness by the Nazi regime, and his work became synonymous with their visual language, which preferred the blackness of line. Since then, Germany has attempted to dissociate Dürer's name from National Socialism. Born in 1471, Dürer's quincentenary was celebrated in Nuremberg in 1971 under the anti-Fascist slogan '*Dürer anstatt Führer*' ('Dürer instead of Führer'). Many direct references to Dürer's prints can be found in Kiefer's work. The most obvious is the recurring motif of a polyhedron from the 1980s onwards, taken from Dürer's *Melencolia I* engraving from 1514 (p.155). Kiefer often incorporates the three-dimensional shape in his paintings and woodcut collages.[70]

At first sight, Kiefer's woodcut portraits are a far cry from Dürer's smaller and more delicately carved designs. However, the length of the portraits (bust or half-length), the positioning of the sitters (mostly in profile or slightly turned), in addition to the sitter almost filling the entire woodblock surface, were all innovative features that rendered Dürer's portraits so popular. Surprisingly, Dürer only made two portrait prints in woodcut, one of which became the most iconic image of its time.[71] Around 1518–9, Dürer made a painted and a printed portrait of the Holy Roman Emperor Maximilian I (1459–1519). Maximilian, as one of the most powerful rulers of his time, recognised how prints could further enhance the establishment of his power, since they could be distributed on a mass scale. In fact, the image became so popular that the woodblocks had to be replaced at least four times, including posthumous printings to commemorate the emperor after his death in January 1519 (p.145). Maximilian is shown turned to the right (in an almost identical pose as Kiefer's portrait of Freiligrath), wearing a wide-brimmed cap and his collar of the Golden Fleece.

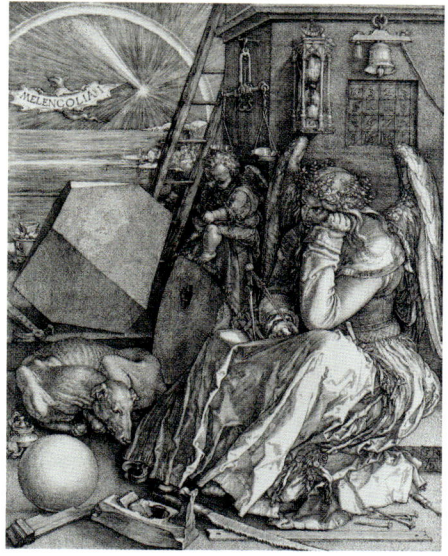
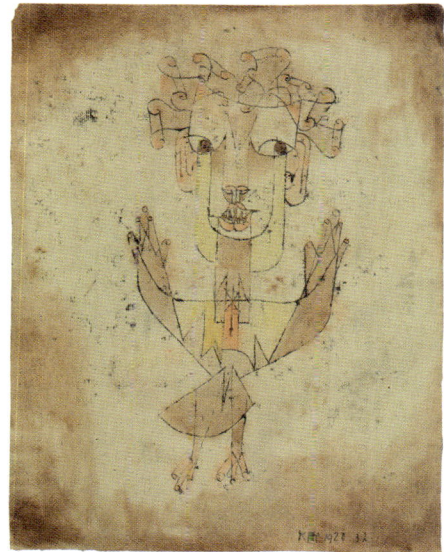

(left)
Albrecht Dürer (1471–1528)
Melencolia I, 1514
Engraving on laid paper,
24.1 × 18.8 cm

(right)
Paul Klee (1879–1940)
Angelus Novus, 1920
Oil transfer and watercolour on paper,
31.8 × 24.2 cm

Interestingly, in Ganzer's *Das deutsche Führergesicht*, the portrait illustrating Maximilian is Dürer's portrait painting from 1519.[72] On a side note, while Kiefer never copied Maximilian's portrait in woodcut, the original Dürer painting was executed on linden wood, which was Kiefer's preferred source for his woodblocks.

Technically, Kiefer's woodcut portraits do not at all resemble those made by Dürer or other Renaissance counterparts. Rather than the minutely rendered examples by his predecessors, Kiefer's works are larger (around 70 centimetres high) and more roughly carved, almost hewn, often exposing the grain of the wood. While these are visibly inspired by the German Expressionists woodcuts created in the 1910s and 1920s, it is evident that Kiefer's sources go back for many more centuries.

An Van Camp

29

ENGEL MIT PALETTE (ANGEL WITH PALETTE), 1977–8

Fallen angels animate the surfaces of two monumental canvases in Kiefer's eponymous 2024 installation at the Palazzo Strozzi in Florence. Their depiction, particularly the leaden airplane wing in *Luzifer* (2012–23), are at once an iconographic return and departure. For of all the ethereal beings that animate Kiefer's imagistic repertoire, the angel appears only rarely in his archive of archetypes. If there is a celestial presence hovering atop the surface of his canvases, it is more often than not the Seraphim or Cherubim of the Hebrew Bible. These visions of prophets are named, not depicted. Instead, it is Jacob's ladder that is rendered upon or affixed to their surfaces, ascending to the unrepresentable fire throne of God.

Elements of the Hebrew Bible routinely inspire the iconographic programs of Kiefer's first decades of painting (e.g. *Aaron*, *Departure from Egypt*, and *The Red Sea*, all 1984–5). But in time, his interests expand to Kabbalah, those esoteric teachings of Judaism that entered secular circles and German culture principally through the writings of the dear friend and dedicated correspondent of Walter Benjamin (1892–1940), Gershom Scholem (1897–1982). These texts would ultimately allow Kiefer to plumb the depths of that once celebrated, now sundered, German–Jewish symbiosis.

The philosophical doctrines, lore, and vocabulary of Kabbalah are virtually catalogued in the work by Kiefer that draws on such materials. These are divided between those dedicated to the figure of the destructive mythic demoness Lilith – counter-figure to Eve, dark side of Shulamith – for example, *Lilith* (1987–9), *Daughters of Lilith* (1986), and *Lilith at the Red Sea* (1990), and those inspired by mystical accounts of creation through destruction – *Emanation* (1984), *Zim Zum* (1990), *Breaking of the Vessels* (1990), *Sefiroth* (2000), and *Merkabah* (2002), to name but a few. A recurrent figure in Kiefer's work from that point on, Lilith first emerges as a tress of long black hair. Later, she is figured only by way of her progeny, Lilith's daughters, dispersed across the surfaces of his paintings, a retinue of so many soot-sullied, smock-like white dresses, not angels, but ashen remainders and reminders of all that was extinguished in the camps. There is almost an uncanny affinity between Kiefer's strategies of making and the mystical processes described in Kabbalah – his use of lead, his interest in alchemy and transformation, his insistent reliance on language, on the word. But, even more, it is the relationship of Kabbalah to historical trauma –

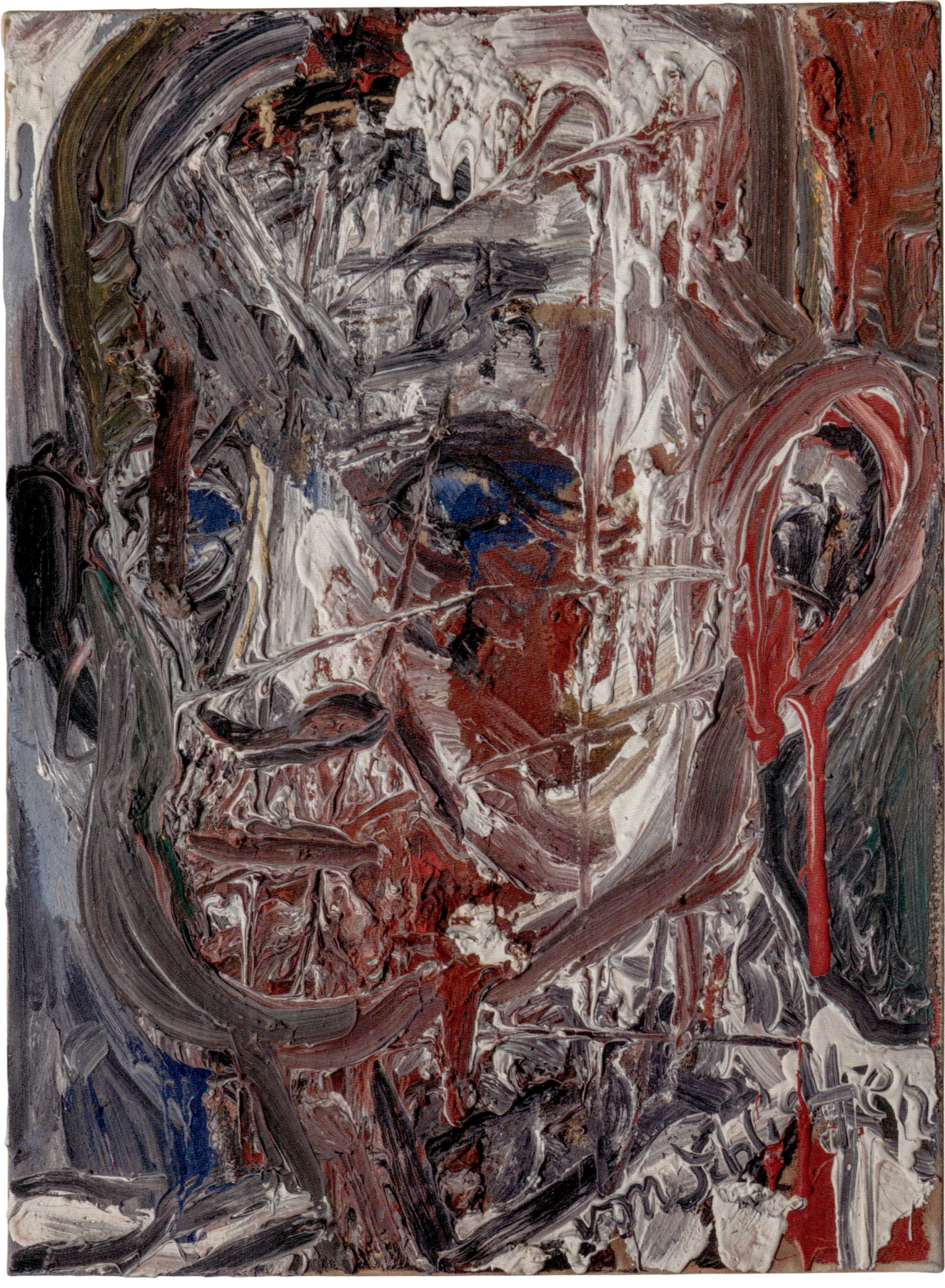

VON SCHLIEFFEN, 1977
Oil on canvas
70 × 50 cm
Hall Collection

31
FÜR JULIA (FOR JULIA), 1977–8
Oil on burlap
70 × 50 cm
Hall Collection

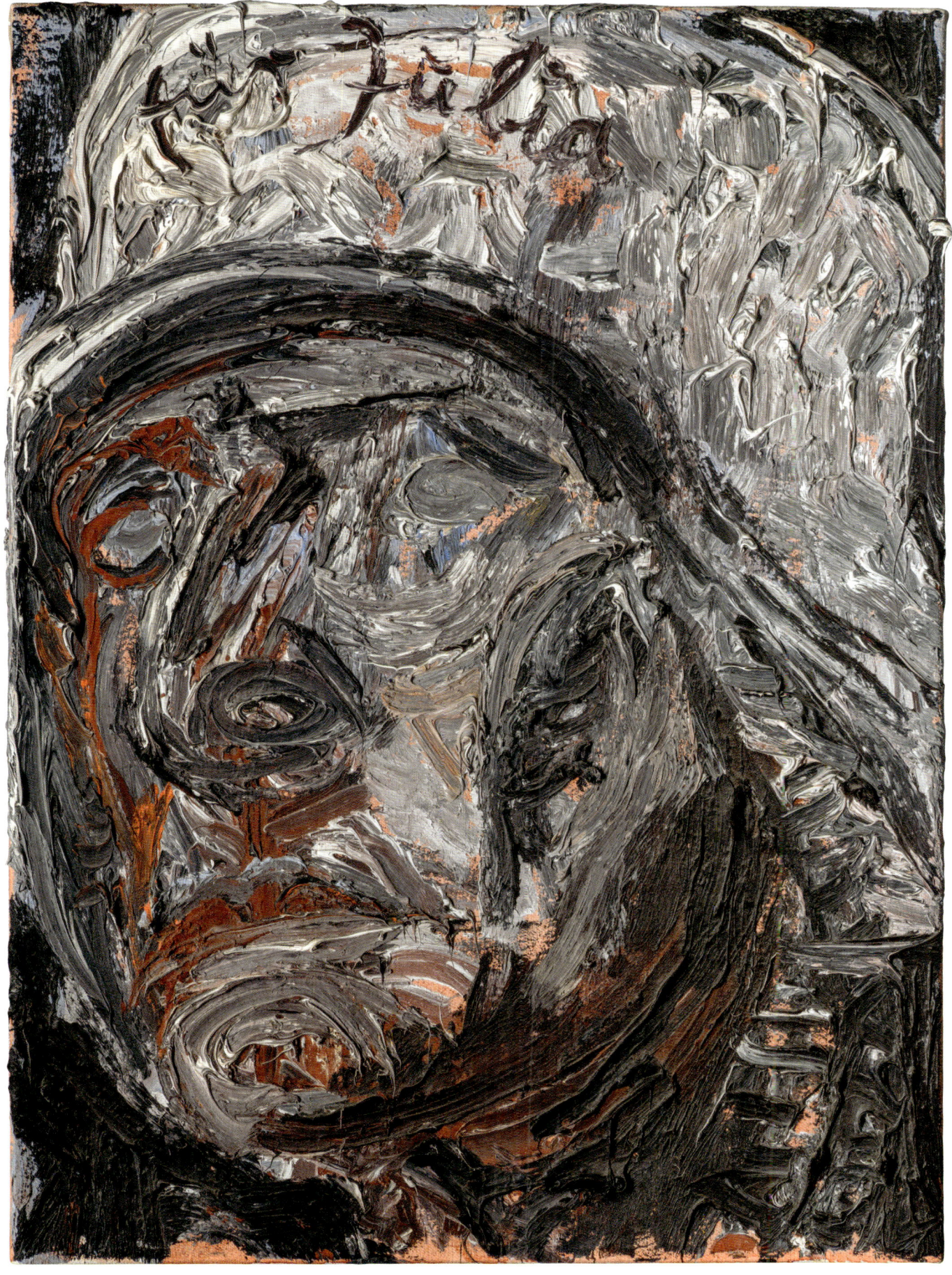

from the destruction of the Second Temple in the first century of the Common Era, to the expulsion of the Jews from Spain in 1492, to the destruction of European Jewry in the twentieth century – that makes Kiefer's invocation and evocation of its tenets so significant, nowhere more so than when modern Lurianic Kabbalah transposed historical trauma into mythic trauma, a cosmic catastrophe as the original moment of creation, the shattering of the mystical vessels. That logic gives to Kiefer's massive sculptural installation, *Breaking of the Vessels* (1990), a certain historical force, its surround of shards a vivid reminder of the cataclysmic night of rampaging destruction that was Kristallnacht, the night of broken glass, an irredeemable shattering of all that had accrued to Germany's Jewish population over a long history of emancipation and assimilation.

What then to make of this painting of a winged figure; an angel whose tiny blank face beholds a radiant, if schematic palette, raised up as if in triumph or veneration? An amalgam of art historical antecedents, Kiefer's *Angel with Palette* reprises and reimagines something of Albrecht Dürer's 1514 *Melencolia I* (p.155) and *Angelus Novus* from 1920 by Paul Klee (1879–1940; p.155), translating and transforming those iconic images of winged figures into a painterly portrait for the post-war present. Absent the enigmatic attributes that surround Dürer's Saturnine subject, Kiefer's angel possesses nothing more than one tiny artist's palette. Earthbound from the weight of its outsized wings, which pull the figure back (into the past) even as its little legs propel it forward (into the future), Kiefer's angel would seem to enact something of the temporal standstill that Benjamin saw on the surface of his most cherished possession, that little Klee transfer drawing that was ultimately transfigured by his last philosophical writings into the 'angel of history'.[73]

Save the almost fleshy tones of the angel's visage, the dark and thickly encrusted surface is built up from layers and skeins of black, red, and white pigment, which churn around the blackened intimation of the angel's body and roil the white-topped surface of its massive, feathered wings. If this painting is a vision, it offers a glimpse not of the holy, atop his throne of fire, but instead, in its elevation of the artist's palette to that position of veneration, held aloft, haloed, hallowed, it proffers the painter as divine presence. And for an artist who will go on to enshrine that symbol of painterly identity in his signature depictions of Nazi architectural interiors, elevated as if in tribute to and commemoration of an 'unknown soldier', this early iteration of the motif, held aloft by an angel, testifies at once to the vainglorious self-fashioning of a young artist who had yet to debut on the world stage and, more broadly, bespeaks the aura of the sacred that emanates from Kiefer's work even when anchored by the secular subject of history.

Lisa Saltzman

30

VON SCHLIEFFEN, 1977

Dominated by grey, red, white, and blue, applied heavily and energetically in irregular impasto oil paint, a close-up portrait presents us with a serious-looking, bold man. Reminiscent of blood, red paint is dripping from his ears and at the chin, while lines scratched into the thick paint suggest wrinkles and scars. The rough, gestural painting style conveys an aggressive impression. In small letters on the right bottom corner, scratched into white paint in grey, it reads 'von Schlieffen'.

Alfred von Schlieffen (1833–1913) was a major Prussian military strategist and chief of the Großer

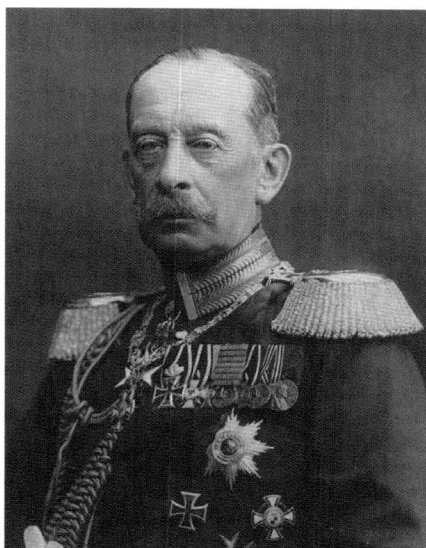

Generalstab (Great General Staff) from 1891 to 1906. In 1905 and 1906 he devised an army deployment plan for an offensive against France: German forces were to invade the country through the Netherlands and Belgium rather than across the common border. His strategic plans, now mostly lost, were famously named the 'Schlieffen-Plan' after his death, and use by Schlieffen's successor, Helmuth Johannes Ludwig von Moltke (1848–1916), led to the outbreak of the First World War in 1914. Moltke made changes to the plan, but still tried to invade France through the Netherlands and Belgium in August, expecting to defeat them quickly. The German army was initially successful and overran a large area of northern France and Belgium. However, within a month, the Franco-British forces had outnumbered the Germans, and in a decisive counteroffensive – the First Battle of the Marne – forced them to retreat. The German retreat marked the end not only of the Schlieffen-Plan but also of the German dream of winning the war quickly. Moltke had to resign.

The posture and features of the face in Kiefer's painting are reminiscent of a (sometimes coloured) black and white portrait photograph of Schlieffen from 1906 (above), often reproduced in encyclopaedias, war literature, and history school books. The strategist presents himself as an inscrutable and confident officer, leading the German army with dedication. In contrast to the photograph, however, the painting does not feature Schlieffen's many military badges, focusing on his face only. His thick moustache has disappeared. The dripping paint, Kiefer's scratching into the wet paint, and his crude, gestural painting style all convey an aura of violence and gruesome fighting. The red hues suggest human flesh and blood. *Von Schlieffen* presents us with a vulnerable and broken man, evoking the image of an injured soldier returning from war. The tired and wounded face could be interpreted as personifying Germany's loss of the First World War, strongly contrasting with the blueprint victory expectations once associated with the Schlieffen-Plan.

Lena Fritsch

31

FÜR JULIA (FOR JULIA), 1977–8

In the same gestural, expressive style, and at the same size as *Von Schlieffen*, this work presents us with a close-up portrait of a man with a military helmet, reminiscent of the German Second World War uniforms (see poster on p.164). Dominated by grey, red, white, and a few light-blue hues, applied heavily in impasto oil paint that the artist has partly scratched into, the face conveys a tense and serious expression. With empty eyes the soldier seems to look out into the far distance. The rough, animated painting style conveys a violent feeling comparable with the atmosphere in *Von Schlieffen*. On the helmet, Kiefer has written in black letters a dedication to his wife at the time: '*für Julia*'.

During the Second World War, German soldiers were shown as idealised heroes in propaganda images. Often portrayed 'in action', they appeared strong, ambitious, and passionate about their fatherland. In contrast to these romanticised Nazi depictions, the unknown person in Kiefer's *Für Julia* appears battle weary and disillusioned, comparable to the subjects of *Von Schlieffen* (pp.156–7) and *Sol Invictus Heliogabal* (pp.62–3). The experience of war has left heavy marks on the soldier's face. It expresses a feeling of disillusionment and human sorrow, representing the brutal truths of the Second World War and, more widely, the struggles of human existence.

**PALETTE MIT FLÜGELN
(PALETTE WITH WINGS)**, 1978
Oil, acrylic and shellac on burlap
116 × 145.6 cm

Hall Collection

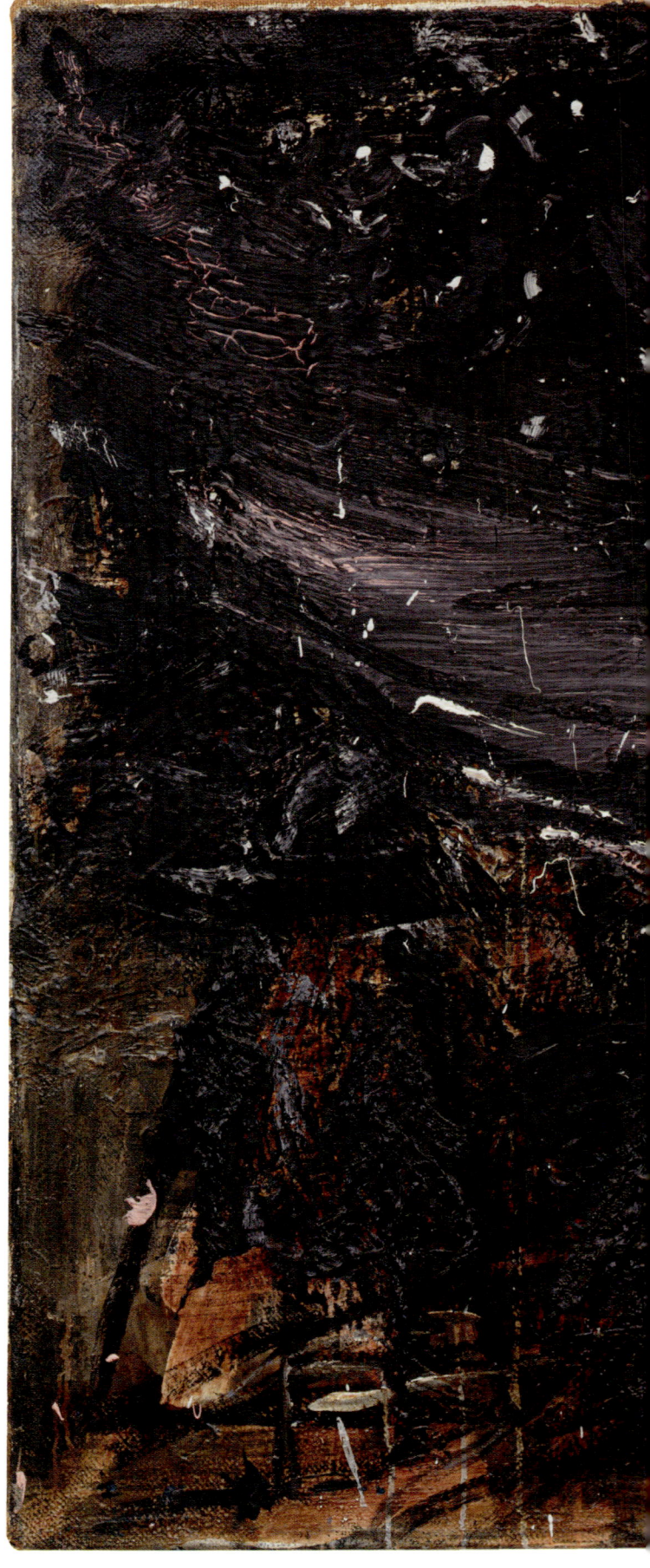

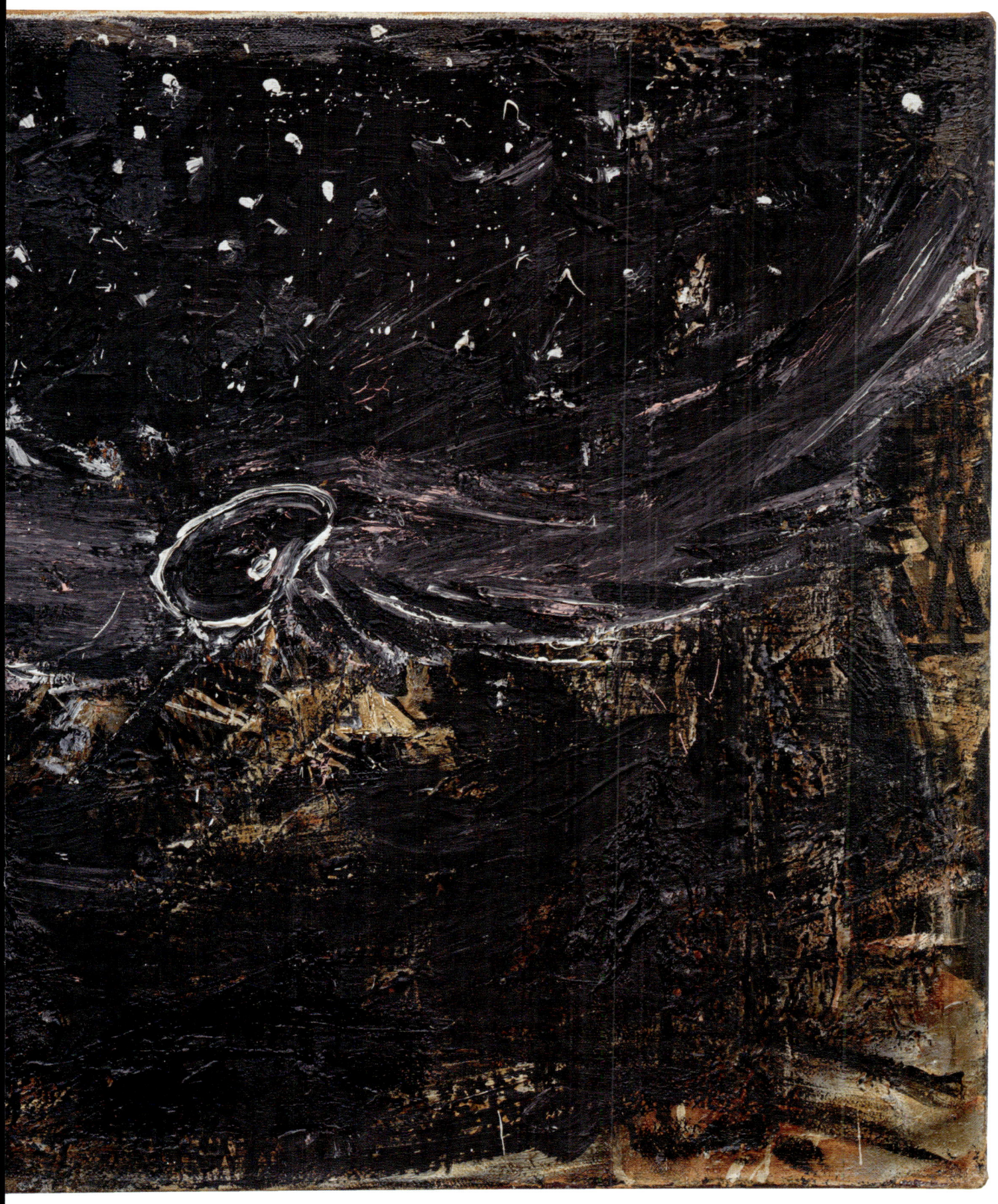

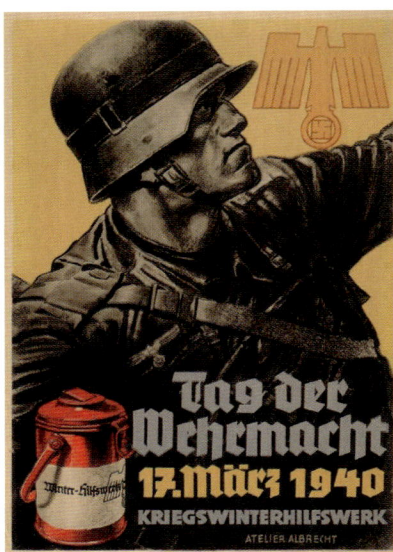

Atelier Albrecht
Tag der Wehrmacht, 1940
Poster

Kiefer inscribed many of his paintings to Julia, who he married in 1971, but considering its subject, this painting is perhaps a rather surprising gift for a loved one.

Lena Fritsch

32

PALETTE MIT FLÜGELN (PALETTE WITH WINGS), 1978

This poetical painting, made nearly half a century ago, shows one of Anselm Kiefer's most important symbols: a painter's palette. The central motif appears to be flying with its two widely spread wings over a nocturnal forest. The landscape format of the work underlines the landscape theme, despite large areas of the painting appearing to be quite abstract. In the upper part, a few white dots are scattered across the dark, almost black, sky that might be interpreted as stars. Meanwhile, in the lower section of the image, the viewer can identify a dark, deserted forest. Here, the trees almost completely conceal the village beyond, though the red roofs of the houses are just discernible. It seems as if the thumbhole of the palette in the centre of the painting is looking down onto the landscape below like a large eye.

The palette is a motif that has repeatedly appeared in the artist's oeuvre, from 1974 to the present day. Initially in painted form, and usually outlined in black or white, it floats or flies over landscapes, winged or wingless. From 1977 onwards, Kiefer developed the lead palette, which was the first three-dimensional object to be applied to his paintings. In 1985, the palette was also the subject of the artist's first free-standing sculpture – *Palette mit Flügeln* (*Palette with Wings*, in the collections of Städel Museum,

Frankfurt am Main, p.165) – where the palette crowns a thin lead rod. In the present painting from 1978, the painted palette dominates the dark, poetic landscape. Considering other paintings, such as *Engel mit Palette* (*Angel with Palette*; pp.152–3), or *Noch ist Polen nicht verloren* (*Poland is Not Yet Lost*), both also executed in 1978, in which the palette plays an important pictorial role, the palette can be understood as a clear symbol of painting itself. On another level, it becomes a motif through which Kiefer questions his work as a German post-war artist.

In the present image, the palette appears as a neutrally observing subject, which lets the black – burnt? – landscape pass beneath. The association with scorched earth brings to mind Kiefer's 1974 painting, *Malen = Verbrennen* (*Painting = Burning*), in which a huge, white-contoured palette hovers above a scorched black rural landscape. Compared to this depiction of the palette and the one in *Engel mit Palette*, in which the palette is held aloft like a cross by a black angel against a golden background, our landscape takes on a more dramatic aspect. The dark, deserted forest becomes the typical representation of the German earth familiar in Kiefer's works of this period. In combining the German earth with the artist's tool, an important struggle, between the artist's work and the history of his homeland, becomes apparent. The artist himself commented once on the palette in his work:

> The palette is the painting; everything else that can be seen in the picture, such as the landscape, is cancelled out by the palette as natural beauty. You can see it like this: the palette wants to cancel out the beauty of nature. It's all very complicated because it's not actually cancelled out completely. It's about the problem of art in general; the kind of imitation or cancellation of it.[74]

Kiefer deals with questions that painters have addressed for centuries: to what extent is art an imitation or

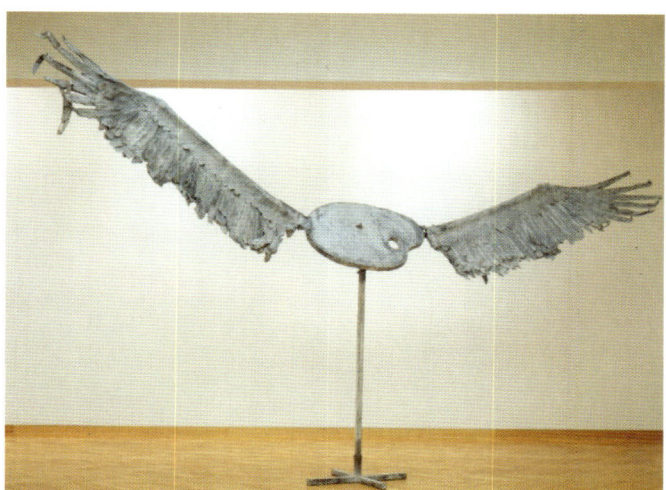

Anselm Kiefer
Palette mit Flügeln (*Palette with Wings*), 1985
Lead, steel and tin, 250 × 700 × 140 cm

annihilation of nature? He concentrates on this fundamental relationship between art and nature by scrutinising himself locally and temporally as a German post-war artist. This kind of self-reflection appears throughout his oeuvre up to the present day – particularly in the form of the palette, but also in the form of his own body in his self-portraits.

Harriet Häußler

33

BRÜNHILDE GRANE (BRUNHILD GRANE), 1978

Shown from the side, a large skeletal horse stands in a burning pyre; black and white woodcut grains are contrasted with transparent brown-orange shellac dripping down the canvas and white acrylic paint. Dynamic, flame-like lines and the T-shaped composition of the work emphasise the verticality of the scene. In large white acrylic letters it reads: 'Brünhilde Grane'. This large woodcut collage belongs to a series of mixed-media paintings and artist books inspired by the epic poem *Nibelungenlied* (*Song of the Nibelungs*) and the Nibelung saga, which are linked to oral Germanic and Old Norse sources, such as the *Poetic Edda*.

The *Nibelungenlied* was written around 1200 as the first heroic epic put into writing in Germany. Together with Norse sources, elements of the *Nibelungenlied* were adapted into Richard Wagner's legendary operatic cycle *Der Ring des Nibelungen* (*The Ring of the Nibelung*), written and composed between 1848 and 1874. The total playing time of the *Ring* cycle's monumental, richly textured music and drama is around

fifteen hours. It is divided into four nights at the opera: *Das Rheingold* (*The Rhinegold*), *Die Walküre* (*Valkyrie*), *Siegfried*, and *Götterdämmerung* (*Twilight of the Gods*). They tell about the loves of heroes, gods, and mythical creatures and their struggles over the eponymous magic ring that grants domination over the entire world. The complex drama continues through three generations of protagonists, until the dramatic end of *Götterdämmerung*.

Warrior queen Brünhilde is a major character in the *Nibelungenlied* and of Wagner's opera, in which she is introduced as 'a queen who resided over the sea, whose like no one knew of anywhere. She was exceedingly beautiful and great in physical strength. She shot the shaft with bold knights – love was the prize'.[75] Brünhilde is instrumental in bringing about the death of her lover, the hero Siegfried, after he deceives her into marrying the Burgundian king, Gunther. In this piece by Kiefer, Brünhilde is not represented visually but only by her name and her loyal horse Grane, who is the main protagonist of the picture. Grane transports Brünhilde from battlefields to Valhalla and beyond. Near the end of *Götterdämmerung* (and the entire *Ring* cycle), Grane is ridden by Brünhilde into the flames of a large funeral pyre, which Brünhilde erected close to the River Rhine in Siegfried's honour, to join her beloved dramatically in death and to restore peace to the world. The libretto quoted on p.168 is from this scene, which is usually referred to as 'Brünhilde's immolation scene'. Wagner's original 1876 performance at Bayreuth featured the black stallion Cocotte, a prized horse loaned for the purpose of playing Grane by King Ludwig II of Bavaria (p.168).

Much of the expressive energy of *Brünhilde Grane* derives from Kiefer's bold use of the woodcut medium; the jagged edges of the white areas mirror his forceful cutting of the woodblock. The prints were carved from

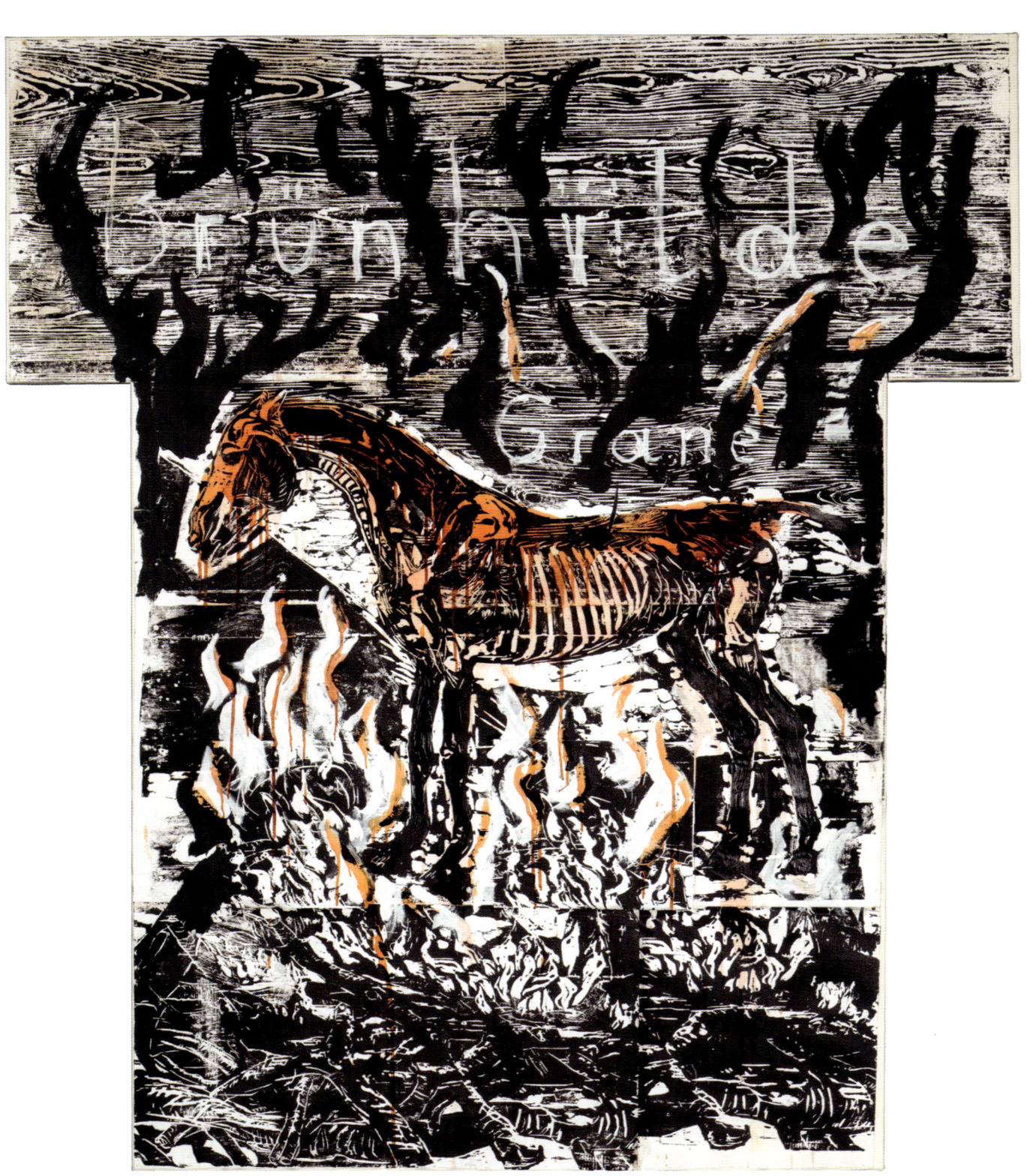

33
BRÜNHILDE GRANE (BRUNHILD GRANE), 1978
Collage of woodcuts on paper with acrylic
and shellac, mounted on canvas
250 × 213 cm
Hall Collection

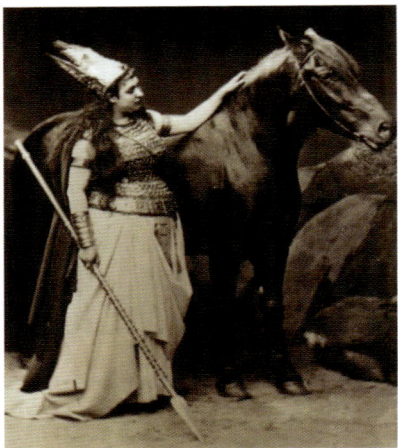

Soprano Amalie Materna as Brünhilde with horse Cocotte as Grane, 1876

Götterdämmerung
Richard Wagner, 1848

Grane, my steed, I greet thee, friend!
Know'st thou now to whom
and whither I lead thee?
In fire radiant, lies there thy lord,
Siegfried, my hero blest.
To follow thy master, joyfully neigh'st thou?
Lures thee to him the light with its laughter?
Feel, too, my bosom, how it doth burn;
glowing flames now lay hold on my heart:
fast to enfold him, embraced by his arms,
in might of our loving with him aye made one!
Heiajaho! Grane! Give him thy greeting!
Siegfried! Siegfried! See!
It is your bride who greets you! [94]

at least eight individual planks of wood, and in the final work the seams of the construction are still visible.[76] Working with woodcut has had a long tradition in Germany with works ranging from incunabula, made in the earliest stages of printing in the mid-fifteenth century, to Old Master prints by Albrecht Dürer, to Expressionist prints by modern artist groups like Die Brücke (see also pp.144–5). The medium of the work as a signifier of Germanness thus fits with the traditional Germanic topic. There are at least eighteen variations of *Brünhilde Grane* and *Grane*, made between 1977 and 1993, in many of which Kiefer used the same woodblocks, partly combining the prints with acrylic and shellac paint, sometimes highlighting the flames, always experimenting with both the woodcut medium and the motifs.[77]

Adolf Hitler was captivated by the music of Richard Wagner, who expressed anti-Semitic views in an essay on 'Jewishness in Music' in 1850. However, Wagner died 50 years before Hitler came to power in 1933 and was not involved in any National Socialist politics. Wagner's music was often performed during the Third Reich, and specific attempts were made to present his works as an expression of 'typically German' strong music, exemplifying the regime's propaganda intentions of 'Nazifying' existing culture. It is said that the Berlin Philharmonic Orchestra's last performance before their evacuation from Berlin at the end of the Second World War was, ironically, of Brünhilde's immolation scene at the end of *Götterdämmerung*. Controversial because of the Nazi's misappropriation of his music as well as his anti-Semitic text, Wagner is an example of an artist whose genius and undoubtedly revolutionary compositions on the one hand, and his personal opinions on the other, should best be viewed separately.

In *Brünhilde Grane*, Kiefer does not directly reference the Nazi's misappropriation of the *Nibelungenlied* and Wagner's theatrical music. Instead, he reduces Brünhilde to an animal, her horse, combined with the natural elements of wood and fire. The skeletal horse positioned over flames, the grainy woodblock texture and the tombstone-like format of the composition all allude to death. In the *Ring*, the leitmotif fire provides the climatic end of the operatic cycle: the gods are consumed in flames, peace and love are restored, and then the curtain falls. Containing references to Germany's traditional myths and recent historical past but also serving as a metaphor for universal pain, sacrifice, and destruction, *Brünhilde Grane* is representative of Kiefer's multifaceted art. It also shows his distinctive use of the woodcut medium to create epic composite images that convey a unique powerful aesthetic.

Lena Fritsch

34

YGGDRASIL, 1978

The painting *Yggdrasil* appears to be a rather atypical work by Anselm Kiefer, firstly, in its use of the colour pink in large parts of the painting, and secondly, in covering nearly the complete surface of the work with animal figurations. Furthermore, the animals are shown in a kind of whirl, which seems to capture the total composition.

Despite its atypical style, this painting is part of a series in which Kiefer deals with the Nordic myth of the world tree Yggdrasil. In this series, tree stumps and animal heads and bodies with corresponding inscriptions appear again and again. In the present work from 1978, four pink stags dominate the depiction of the tree, which is barely recognisable in the background. A majestic yellow eagle sits in the centre of the

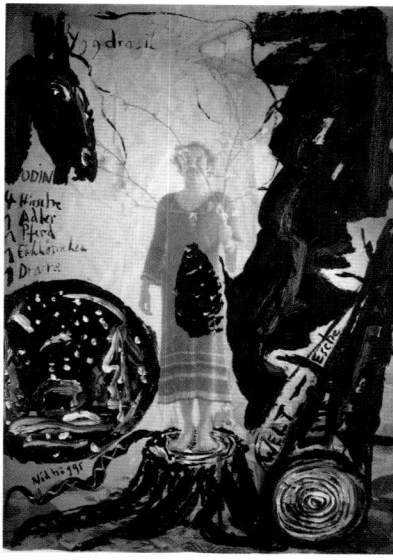

Anselm Kiefer
Yggdrasil, 1978–80
Gouache and acrylic on photograph,
82.6 × 59.1 cm

composition – this appears to be the only 'calm' part of the painting. A black horse's head, outlined in white, is depicted in the upper right-hand area. A white squirrel touches the title inscription. The viewer is presented with a list-like enumeration: '1 horse, 1 eagle, 4 stags'. Yet this complex work can be read in the context of the other paintings from this series.

In Norse mythology, Yggdrasil is considered as the first tree to grow; the largest and most magnificent tree in the world. The tree embodies life itself and the cycle of growth and decay. Forest animals feed on its life force, and it will never die. In the Norse saga the *Prose Edda*, the tree is also referred to as the 'measuring tree', as it can be used to measure the world. The size and length of its branches and roots define the scale and boundaries of our world. The tree connects the three realms of the world: its top supports the sky, its trunk nourishes living beings, and its roots have penetrated deep into the earth. The *Edda* explicitly mentions the names of the animals, as depicted by Kiefer: the eagle without a name, the squirrel Ratatöskr, the four stags Dain, Dwalin, Dunneir, and Durathror. The black horse, in turn, appears to be directly related to the title of the painting. In Old Norse, Yggdrasill is composed of '*yggr*', meaning fear, and '*drasill*', meaning horse. The title can therefore also be translated as 'Horse of the Terrible', equating it with Odin's horse.

Kiefer's painting shows clearly how deeply rooted his examination of Nordic-Germanic mythology is. Throughout his entire oeuvre, he repeatedly explores this primal myth of human history. Kiefer is not only interested in aesthetically exploring and transforming animal and landscape paintings into the twentieth and twenty-first centuries, but he is also asking about man's place in the universe: where do we come from? Where do we stand? Where are we going to? The extent

to which these questions can also be understood in a self-reflective way can be seen in other works from the series, such as the work on paper *Yggdrasil* from 1978–80, in which a photograph of Kiefer shows himself standing on a tree stump, holding a branch in his hands (above). The words 'World – Ash' can be read next to him. In the drawing, the black horse's head with the titular 'Yggdrasil' is complemented by the name of the god 'Odin', which corroborates the interpretation that Kiefer also refers to Odin's horse in our painting. Odin, the highest god in the Germanic religion, is described as the god of wisdom, death, and war as well as of magic and poetry. Accordingly, the Nordic god combines seemingly contradictory characteristics: he is regarded as angry, furious, and possessed, but at the same time as inspiring, prophesying, and poetic. Germanic mythology imagines him as a strong, powerful god, constantly riding and travelling. This idea may also have fascinated Kiefer because he sees himself as an artist constantly in search of his place in the universe. He looks for a cosmic explanation of his own artistic being in the world.

Our first observations that he used the atypical colour pink, and that the animals are shown in a huge whirl, underlie our interpretation that Kiefer refers to the powerful Nordic god Odin. Pink and black are both powerful and contrasting colours, which might go with Odin's complex character, while the whirl might express his restlessness. The painting *Yggdrasil* can be viewed as a quintessential work, in which Kiefer is once again concerned with the fundamental questions of mankind: what do life and death mean? What possibilities does an artist have to capture and depict the world? This work also offers another example of Kiefer taking a cultural theme that had been misappropriated and abused by the National Socialists and reclaiming it within his own art works.

Harriet Häußler

34

YGGDRASIL, 1978

Oil on canvas
146 × 118 cm
Hall Collection

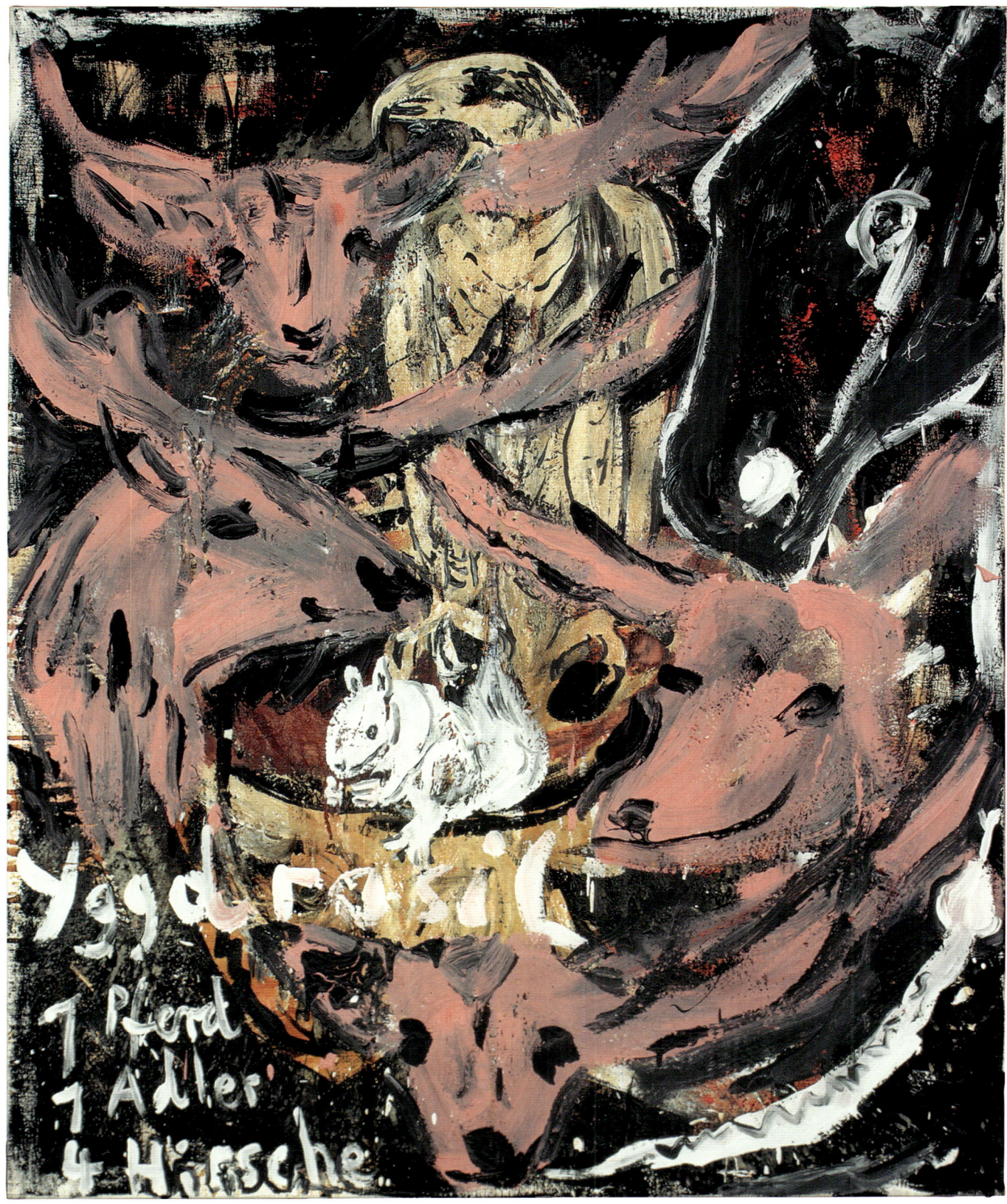

35

RITT AN DIE WEICHSEL
(*RIDE TO THE VISTULA*), 1980–1

Oil, sand, wood shavings
and charcoal on canvas
130 × 160 cm

Hall Collection

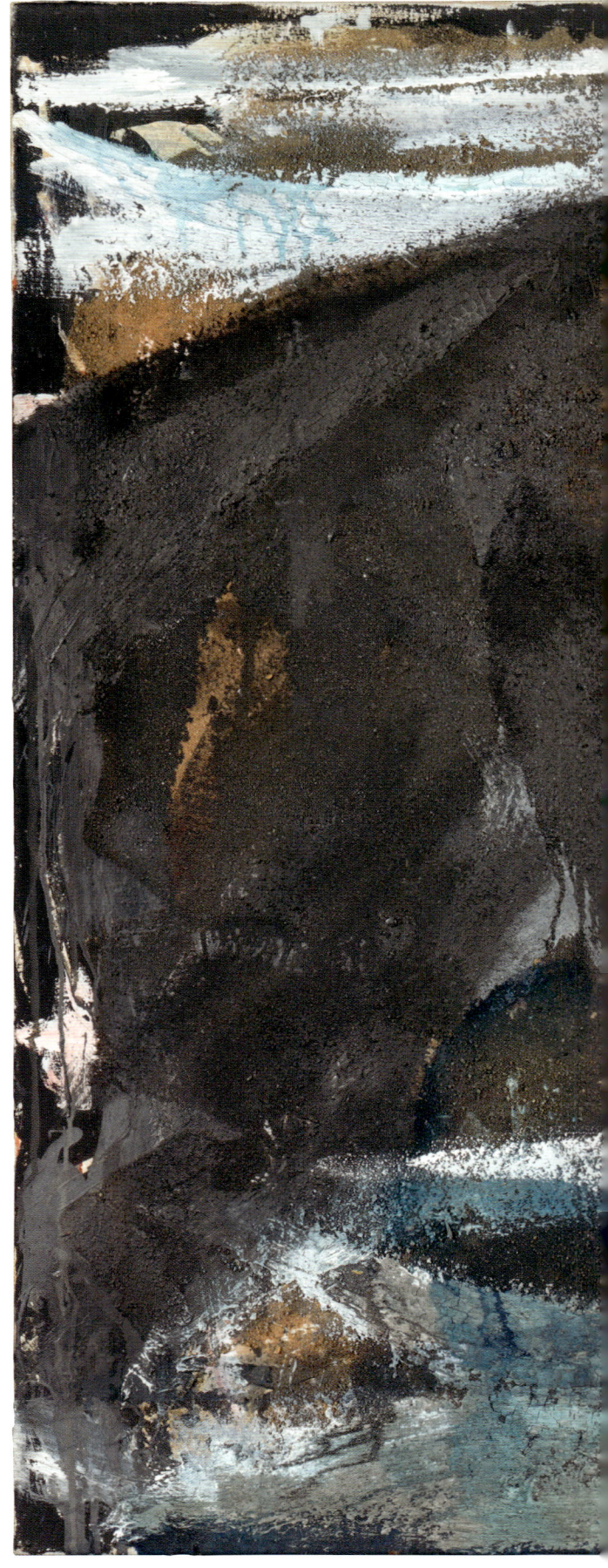

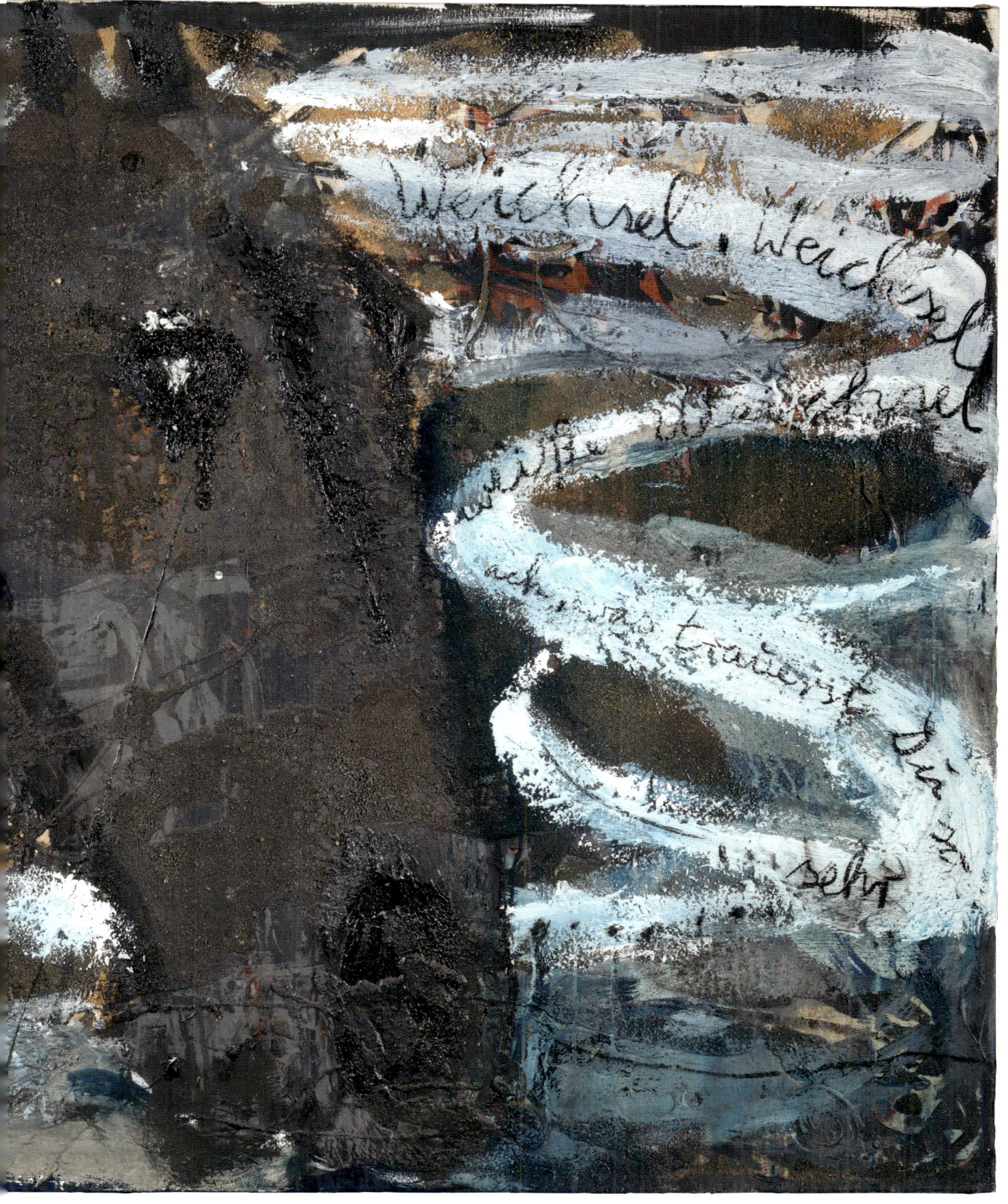

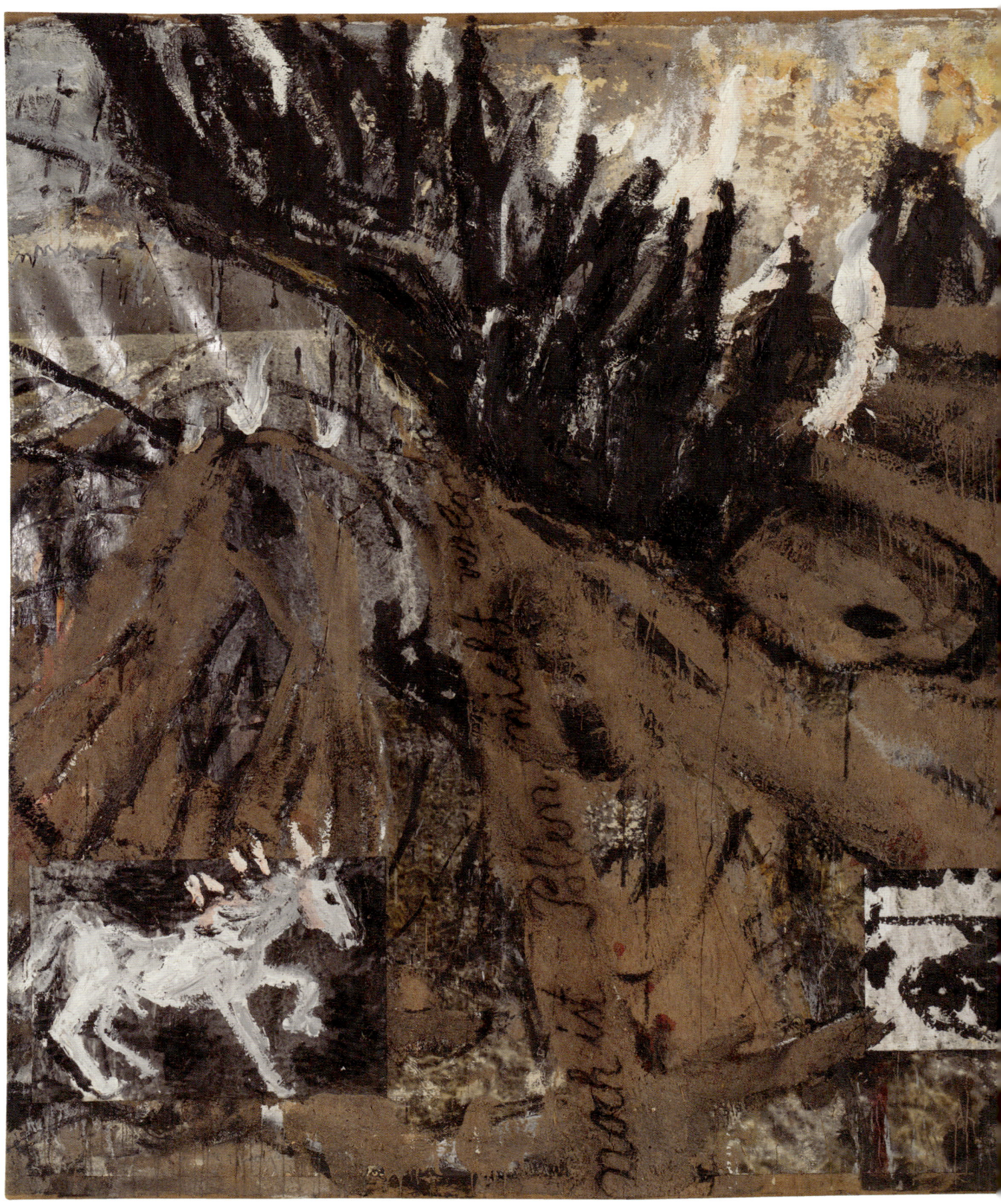

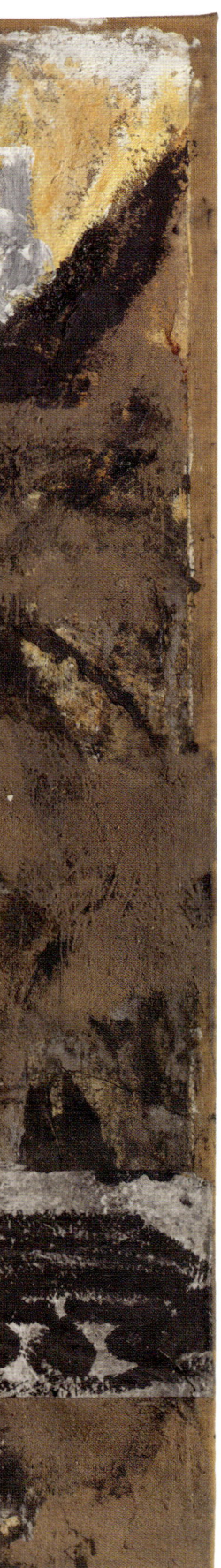

**NOCH IST POLEN NICHT VERLOREN
(POLAND IS NOT YET LOST)**, 1981
Oil, acrylic, emulsion, straw, photograph,
sand and charcoal on canvas
292 x 289.5 cm
Hall Collection

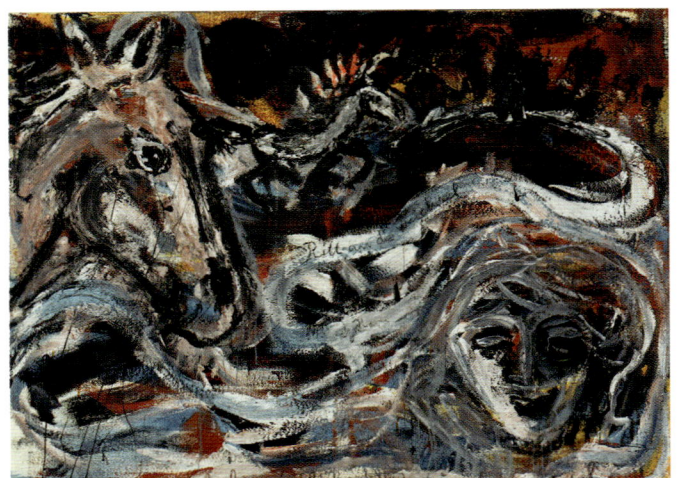

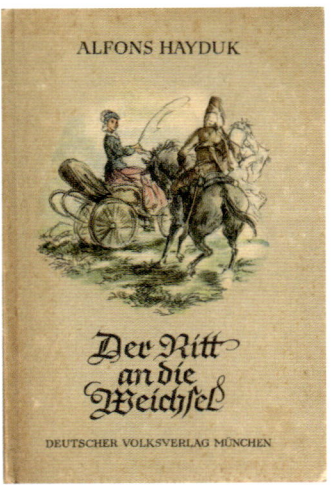

(left)
Anselm Kiefer
Ride to the Vistula, 1980
Oil, emulsion and shellac
on canvas, 130 × 170 cm

(right)
Book cover of Alfons Hayduk,
Der Ritt an die Weichsel, 1941
Munich: Deutscher Volksverlag

35

RITT AN DIE WEICHSEL (RIDE TO THE VISTULA), 1980–1

A large, dark-brown horse head, portrayed from the side, dominates this painting. White and light-blue curves, dynamically rendered behind and next to the horse, indicate a foaming river. Sand and wood shavings, mixed into the oil paint, create deep and rough structures and add a sense of three-dimensionality to the work. On the right side of the painting it reads in thin charcoal letters on top of the white water: '*Weichsel, Weichsel, weiße Weichsel, ach, was trauerst Du so sehr*' ('Vistula, Vistula, white Vistula, oh why are you grieving so much').

The Weichsel or Vistula is the longest river in Poland. It rises at Barania Góra in the south of Poland, where it begins with the White Little Vistula and the Black Little Vistula. Flowing through cities such as Kraków, Warsaw, and Gdańsk, it empties into the Vistula Lagoon and the Baltic Sea. The Vistula plays an important role not only in Polish but also in Prussian-German history and culture, due to Germans settling in, what became known after the 1863 Polish rebellion as, the Vistula territory, which encompassed most of the Vistula watershed of central Poland up to the east of Toruń. The Vistula Germans, most of whom were Lutheran protestants, retained Germanic cultural traditions and dialects. In September 1939, Nazi troops crossed the Vistula and marched into Poland. This played a key role in the invasion of Poland and started the Second World War. Poland's only defence was its cavalry, which forced the Polish army to withdraw to the southern bank of the Vistula and then even further to the south-east.

Ritt an die Weichsel shares its title with a novel by Alfons Hayduk (1900–1972), a Silesian teacher, historian, and writer of the Vistula region. Based on historical facts, it describes the carefully organised, spectacular escape in 1770, from Poland to Silesia, of over 300 German Lutherans, who had been discriminated against by the Catholic majority. Guarded by a large group of Prussian hussars who had entered the Polish-Lithuanian state illegally, the refugees walked and rode along the Vistula towards Prussian Silesia, where they found a new home, approximately 50 kilometres north of their original village. The new settlement remained a German 'island' religiously and linguistically until 1945, since most people in the surrounding villages were Catholic and spoke a different, Slavic Silesian, dialect. Hayduk's *Der Ritt an die Weichsel* (above) was published in 1941 by the Deutscher Volksverlag, a publishing house in Munich best known for its antisemitic monthly journals, such as *Der Weltkampf*, and other anti-Jewish publications. Excerpts from the book were also included in the Nazi party newspaper *Der oberschlesische Wanderer* in 1943. Hayduk was not only a member of the Nazi party but also Head of the Reichsschrifttumskammer (Reich Chamber of Literature) of the Gau Silesia region. A subdivision of the Reichskulturkammer (Reich Chamber of Culture), the Reich Chamber of Literature sought to gain control over all publications in Germany by creating and promoting Aryan texts consistent with Nazi ideals. Mirroring his National Socialist views, *Der Ritt an die Weichsel*, as well as all of Hayduk's other writings, were included in the West German *Verzeichnis der auszusondernden Literatur* list of 1945–6, ordered by Georgy Konstantinovich Zhukov (1896–1974), Marshal of the Soviet Union. The aim of this list was 'the quick extinction of the Nazi idea and militarism', by banning relevant books, authors, and publishing houses.[78]

Focusing on a horse and river, Kiefer's painting is a subtle reminder, not only of the 1770 trek and the complex history and national identity of the Vistula German people, but also of Hitler's aggressive invasion of Poland and the

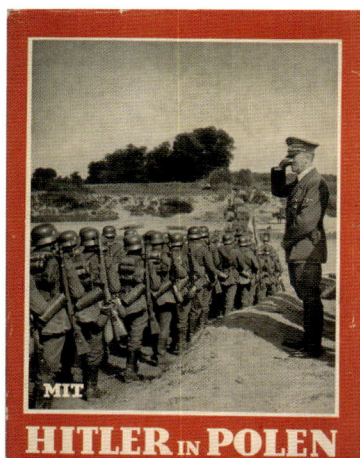

trauma this caused to the Polish population. At the same time, the painting protests against the approach of simply banning cultural material linked to the Nazis to extinct their ideals. Instead of banning and forgetting, Kiefer's work has always suggested that we need to look and explore the uncomfortable past to try and understand the different mechanisms by which the Nazis mobilised and abused German history and culture to successfully promote their Aryan ideologies. The written exclamation, '*Weichsel, Weichsel, weiße Weichsel, ach, was trauerst Du so sehr*', personifies the Vistula, mourning the harm and suffering that she has seen over the centuries. Typical of Kiefer's approach, it is the animal and landscape combined with text, rather than any human figure, that serve to reflect the complexities of the region's cultural memory.

Working through the Vistula theme, Kiefer made a number of paintings and works on paper with the same title, most notably a comparable 1980 oil painting with horses, water, and a female face (p.176), and a 1980 watercolour and acrylic on paper of a galloping horse, both in the Metropolitan Museum of Art, New York. The invasion of Poland at the beginning of the Second World War is also dealt with in paintings like *Noch ist Polen nicht verloren* (1981; pp.174–5).

Lena Fritsch

36

NOCH IST POLEN NICHT VERLOREN (POLAND IS NOT YET LOST), 1981

Dominated by brown, ochre, black, and white tones, and executed in dynamic brush strokes, this square-shaped painting presents us with an abstracted landscape featuring a small white horse in the left foreground and a small black tank on the right. The horse seems to be galloping towards the vehicle with its mane flying high in the wind, while energetic black and white lines in the background suggest explosions or fires. The horse directly faces the tank, which is aiming its main gun towards the animal, conveying an impression of confident confrontation on both sides. In the middle of the painting, handwritten in thin black letters from the bottom upwards, it reads: '*noch ist Polen nicht verloren*' ('Poland is not yet lost').

This painting invokes the epoch-defining invasion of Poland by Nazi Germany, the Slovak Republic, and the Soviet Union in autumn 1939, which marked the beginning of the Second World War. The German invasion of Poland, known as *Polenfeldzug*, began on 1 September 1939, with German troops entering the country aggressively from the north, south, and west with a significant quantity of modern artillery. The campaign ended on 6 October, with German and Soviet forces gaining full control over the country, dividing and annexing it under the terms of the German–Soviet Frontier Treaty. Hitler visited occupied Poland in October and presented himself, together with his Wehrmacht soldiers, in the field, propagating an image of their supposedly 'clean' fighting in the German press. Photographer Heinrich Hoffmann (1885–1957), one of Hitler's trusted confidants, portrayed the visit in a propaganda photobook (above).

The image of a German tank on the right side of Kiefer's painting and that of a horse on the left symbolises the legendary battle of Krojanty on 1 September 1939. A Polish cavalry charge near the Pomeranian village of Krojanty attacked a group of German infantrymen in a clearing of the Tuchola Forest. This took the German soldiers by surprise, dispersing them. German motorised vehicles soon appeared and confronted the Polish units with heavy machine-gun fire. However, the Polish cavalry charge had successfully caused a delay in the offensive

37

BRÜNHILDE (BRUNHILD), 1981

Oil and woodcut on paper, mounted on burlap
170 × 189.5 cm
Hall Collection

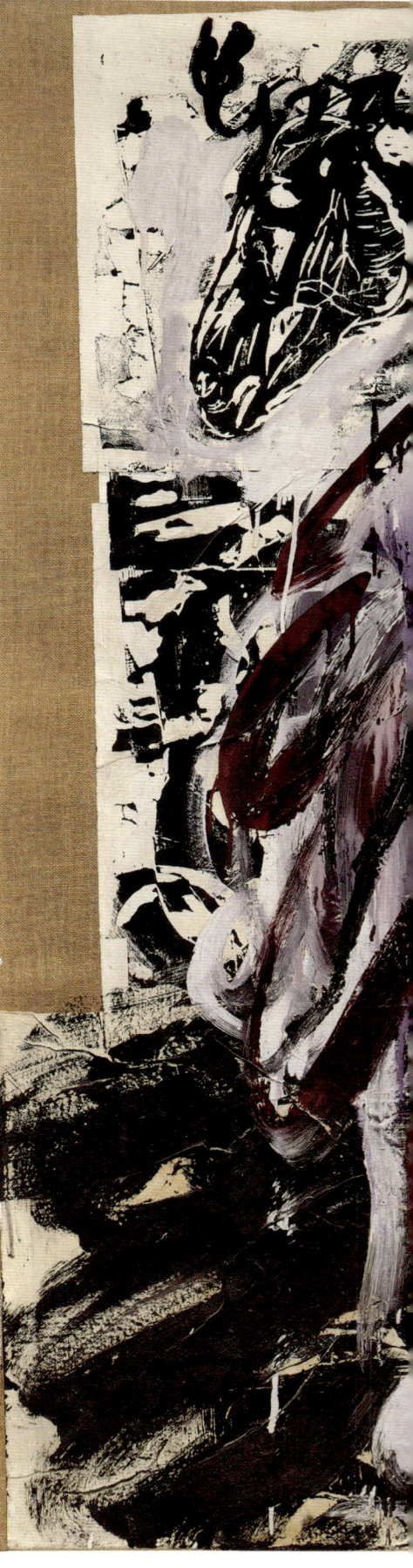

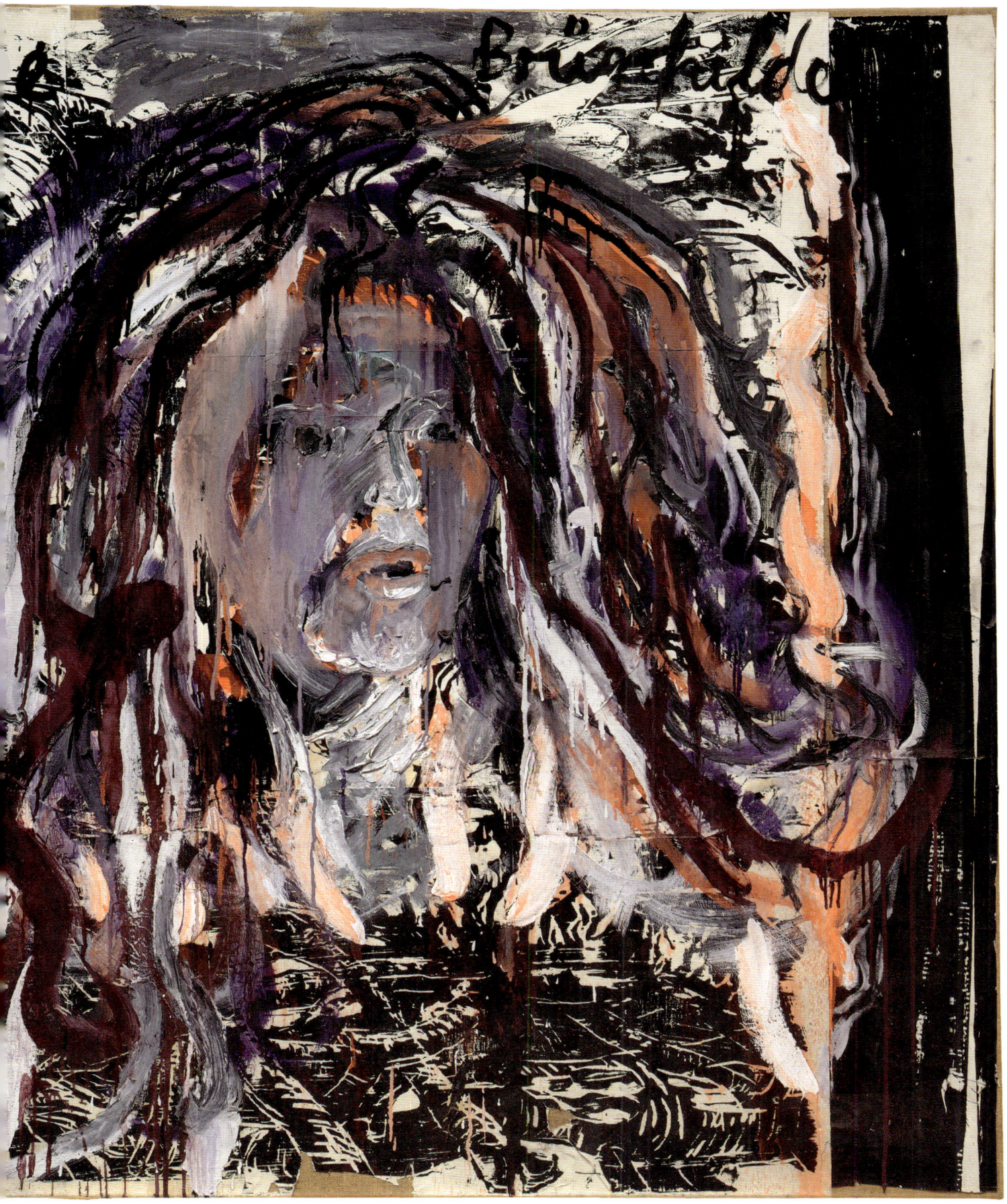

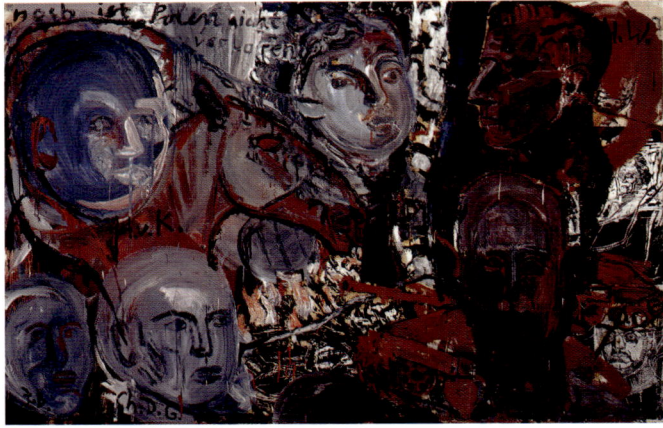

Anselm Kiefer
Noch ist Polen nicht verloren V
(*Poland is not yet lost V*), 1978
Oil on canvas, 195 × 285 cm

of the Nazis and stopped their pursuit for the day, enabling Polish soldiers to withdraw, unopposed, to the south. The contrasting image of horses versus modern tanks not only strongly visualised the military power difference between the two countries – which German war propaganda used to create a myth about the naïve Poles gravely underestimating German weapons – but it also represented the last great charge of the famous Polish Cavalry. The battle at Krojanty has also been seen as an event that symbolised the brave spirit of the Polish people, putting into unfortunate but glorious action the words of the *Dąbrowski Mazurka*, which has been the official national anthem of Poland since 1918: 'Poland is not yet lost, so long as we still live. What the alien power has seized from us, we shall recapture with a sabre.' The original lyrics were written by nobleman and poet Józef Wybicki (1747–1822) in 1797 to express the idea that Poland, despite at the time lacking an independent state of their own, had not yet perished as long as the Polish people lived and fought in its name.

The fact that there are a number of paintings with the same title as the present work shows Kiefer's deep concern with the legendary Second World War battle. Some works, for example a 1978 painting at the Kröller Müller Museum (above), feature humans and horses, some include the spiralling forms of a circular current. The contrast of the horse as a strong but vulnerable animal and the man-made, much more powerful metallic tank in the present work represents the mythological character of the combat that has become a romantic 'David and Goliath' story. Citing the Polish national anthem, Kiefer's paintings draw attention to the Polish side of this story, and the trauma that Hitler's invasion of Poland caused to its people. Typical of Kiefer's approach, and comparable to his painting *Ritt an die Weichsel* (1980–81; pp.172–3), it is an animal and landscape combined with text, rather than any human

figure, that serve to reflect the complexities of cultural memory, in a powerful and resonant timeless image.

Noch ist Polen nicht verloren was included in the MoMA P.S.1 exhibition *Expressions: New Art from Germany* in 1983. It entered the private collections of art dealer Ileana Sonnabend (1914–2007), who gave Kiefer his first exhibition in New York. Coming from Sonnabend's estate, the painting was purchased by the Hall Collection in 2024.

In 1989, Kiefer also created a film titled *Noch ist Polen nicht verloren*, produced by Filmbüro Walter Smerling. In this film, slow-moving images of Warsaw, the Vistula River, Warsaw's deep underground stations, train stations, and other architectural buildings are combined with Kiefer's voiceover, sharing his views on Warsaw in the 1980s, when he visited the city. He talks about its socio-political present, history, ideas about time and space, and his own art historical and personal associations with Poland.

Lena Fritsch

37

BRÜNHILDE (BRUNHILD), 1981

Painted in energetic and rough brush strokes in oil paint, this work presents us with a female face shown slightly from the side. Curvy lines in purple, grey, and light-orange tones surround the face, suggesting long and thick hair. In the black and white background, we see a horse and, at the bottom, pieces of wood, piled up like a pyre. The creamy and partly thickly applied oil paint of the women's portrait contrasts with the woodcut background, creating an unusual interplay between the artistic genre of oil painting and woodblock printing. In black handwritten letters two names identify the woman and her horse:

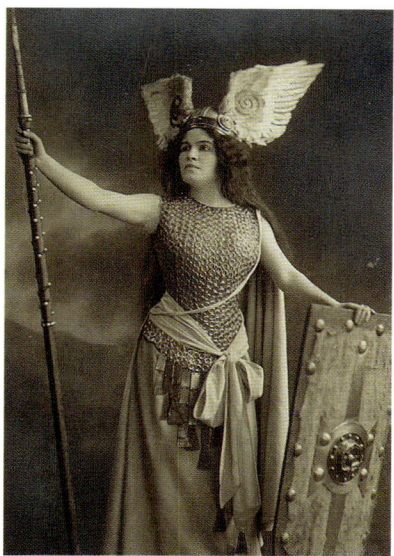

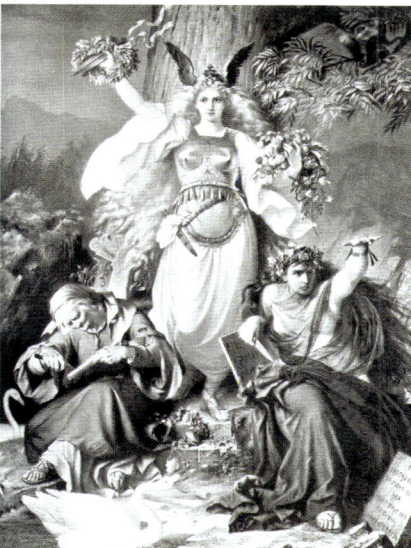

'Grane Brünhilde'. This woodcut was based on the same plate as the collage *Brünhilde Grane* (1978; pp.166–7).

The warrior queen Brünhilde is a recurring motif in Kiefer's work (pp.122–3 and 166–7). She is a major character in the epic *Nibelungenlied* (written around 1200) and in Richard Wagner's monumental fifteen-hour operatic cycle *Der Ring des Nibelungen.* Near the end of Wagner's *Ring* cycle, Brünhilde rides her horse, Grane, into the flames of a large funeral pyre, erected by the River Rhine in Siegfried's honour, to join her beloved in death. The Gods are consumed by fire, and the ring's gold is returned to the Rhine and the Rhine maidens. The fourth opera, *Götterdämmerung*, ends with this highly dramatic, masterly composed scene, known as 'Brünhilde's immolation scene', which then finally restores peace to the world.

In contrast to *Brünhilde Grane*, this work from three years later features Brünhilde herself, painted dominantly and expressively in oils on top of the woodcut of her horse. Brünhilde's slightly open mouth and determined gaze into the distance evoke the image of opera stars, such as Madame Charles Cahier (1870–1951; above), Martha Mödl (1912–2001), Leonie Rysanek (1926–1998), or Birgit Nilsson (1918–2005), delivering a brilliant Brünhilde performance in the *Ring* finale. Wagner's theatrical music was often performed during the Third Reich, and specific attempts were made by the Nazis to present his works as an expression of 'typically German' authentic music, exemplifying the regime's propaganda intentions of 'Nazifying' existing culture. When Kiefer made *Brünhilde* in 1981, Wagner's opera was still strongly associated with the bitter taste of Germany's Nazi past. This has not changed: Wagner's music is still rarely performed in Israel, and, in Germany, the composer's proximity to antisemitic movements is still discussed regularly in cultural and academic discourse. Kiefer's work dares to feature the Germanic warrior Brünhilde as a mythic hero as well as a Wagnerian opera star, while also critically alluding to the allure that fascism and associated culture can convey.

The meandering lines and curves around Brünhilde's face are ambiguous: they seem to resemble both hair and the flames that engulf her face. The fire motif is also present on the woodcut underneath, namely as the funeral pyre, and because of the tautologically linked artistic medium: wood(cut). In the *Ring* cycle, the fire is a leitmotif and key element of its finale, but it can also be associated with Germany's recent past: the Nazi's brutal burning of books, their bombings, and their ideas of purgatory-like (racial) cleansing.

In Kiefer's art, the natural elements, including fire, have played a major role: not only as motifs but also as materials and tools. Fire for Kiefer is a symbol of transformation that is both a source of energy and destruction: it can turn wood into ashes, it can glow and warm, damage and purify. In *Brünhilde*, fire alludes to the warrior queen's tragic fate in Wagner's opera, while, at the same time, bringing a catharsis that represents hope and seems to return peace to the Rhine – and to the world.

Lena Fritsch

38

URD, WERDANDI, SKULD (DIE NORNEN) (THE NORNS), 1981

In cold grey tones, ranging from very light to dark grey, combined with white and a dash of red, this oil painting presents a strongly smoking pile of burning tree branches and ash. The background suggests an empty landscape with mountains. The abstracted style and the smokiness of the scene convey a mysterious feel. In black letters on

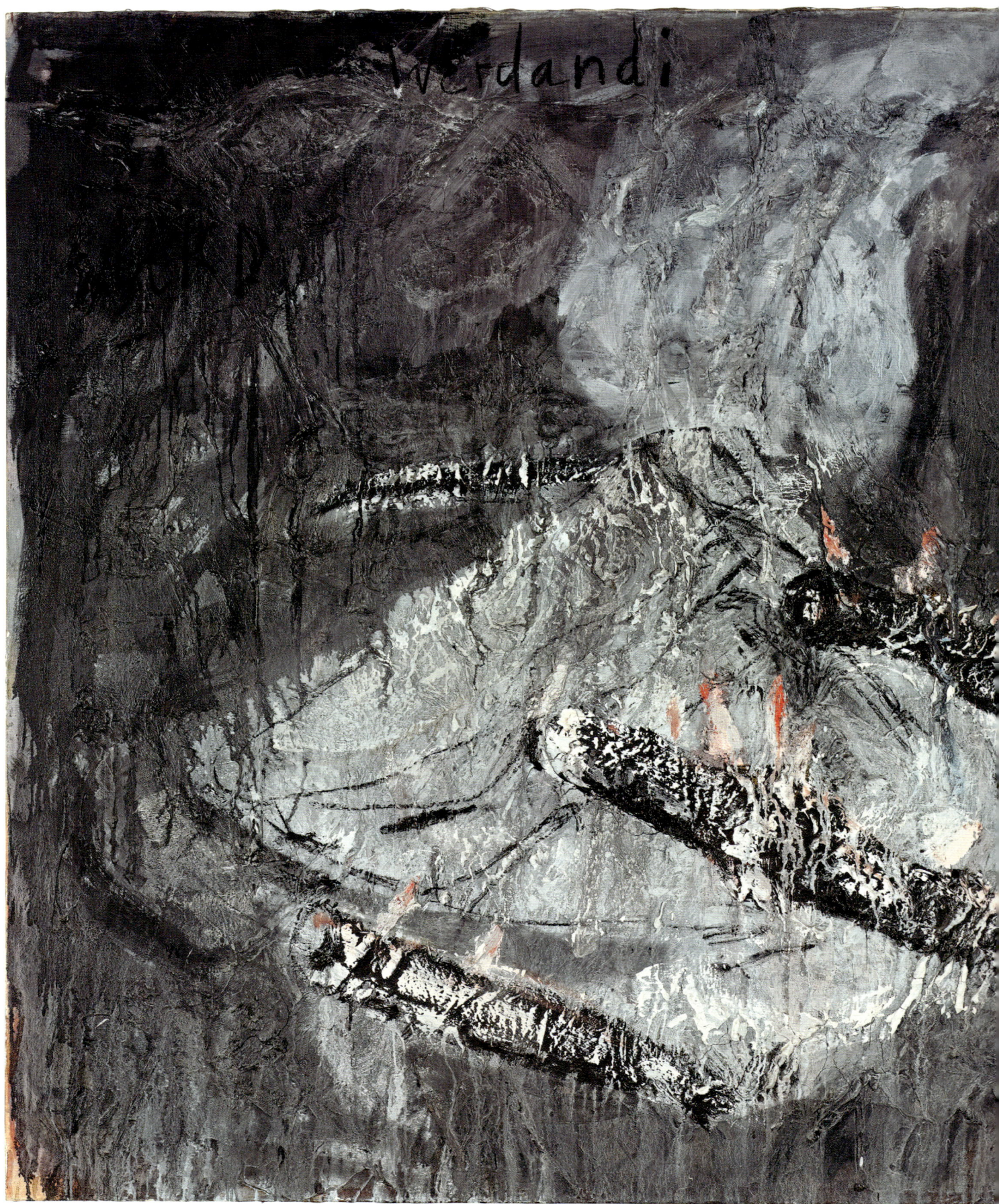

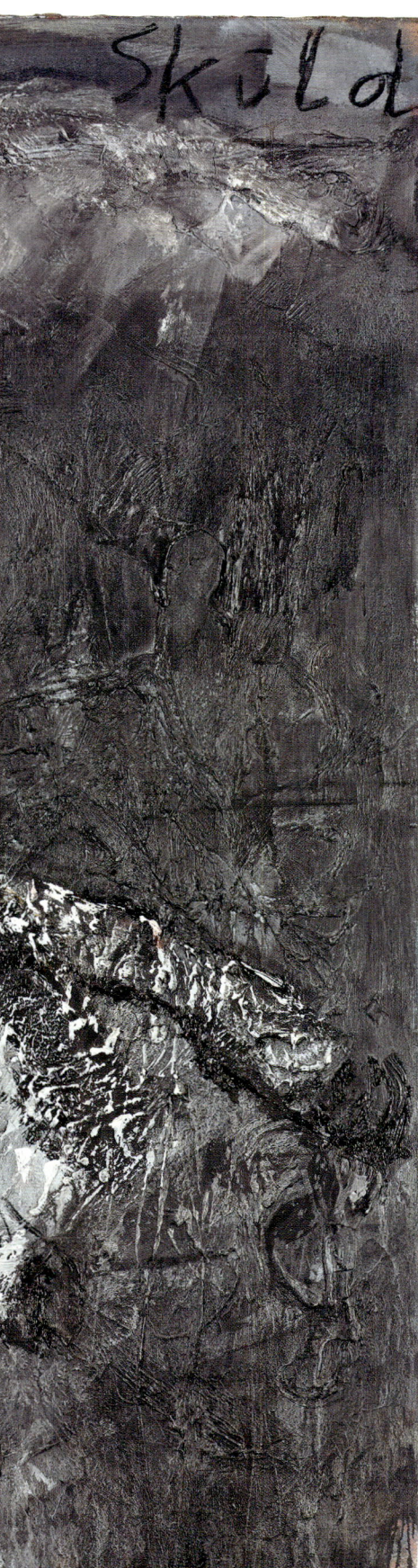

URD, WERDANDI, SKULD (DIE NORNEN) (THE NORNS), 1981
Oil on canvas
170 × 190 cm
Hall Collection

MARGARETHE – SULAMIT
(MARGARET – SHULAMITE), 1981
Watercolour on paper
42 × 56 cm

Hall Collection

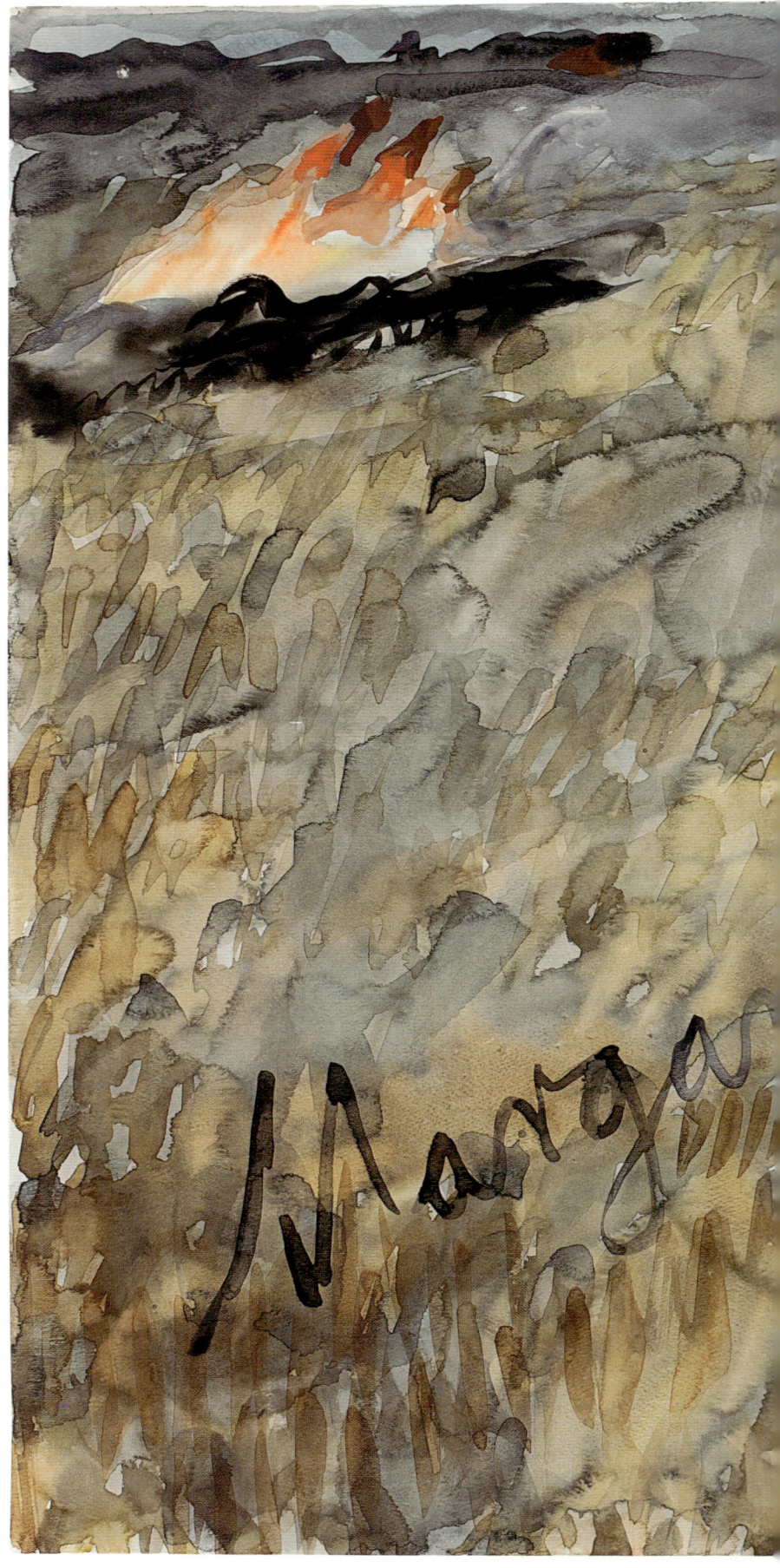

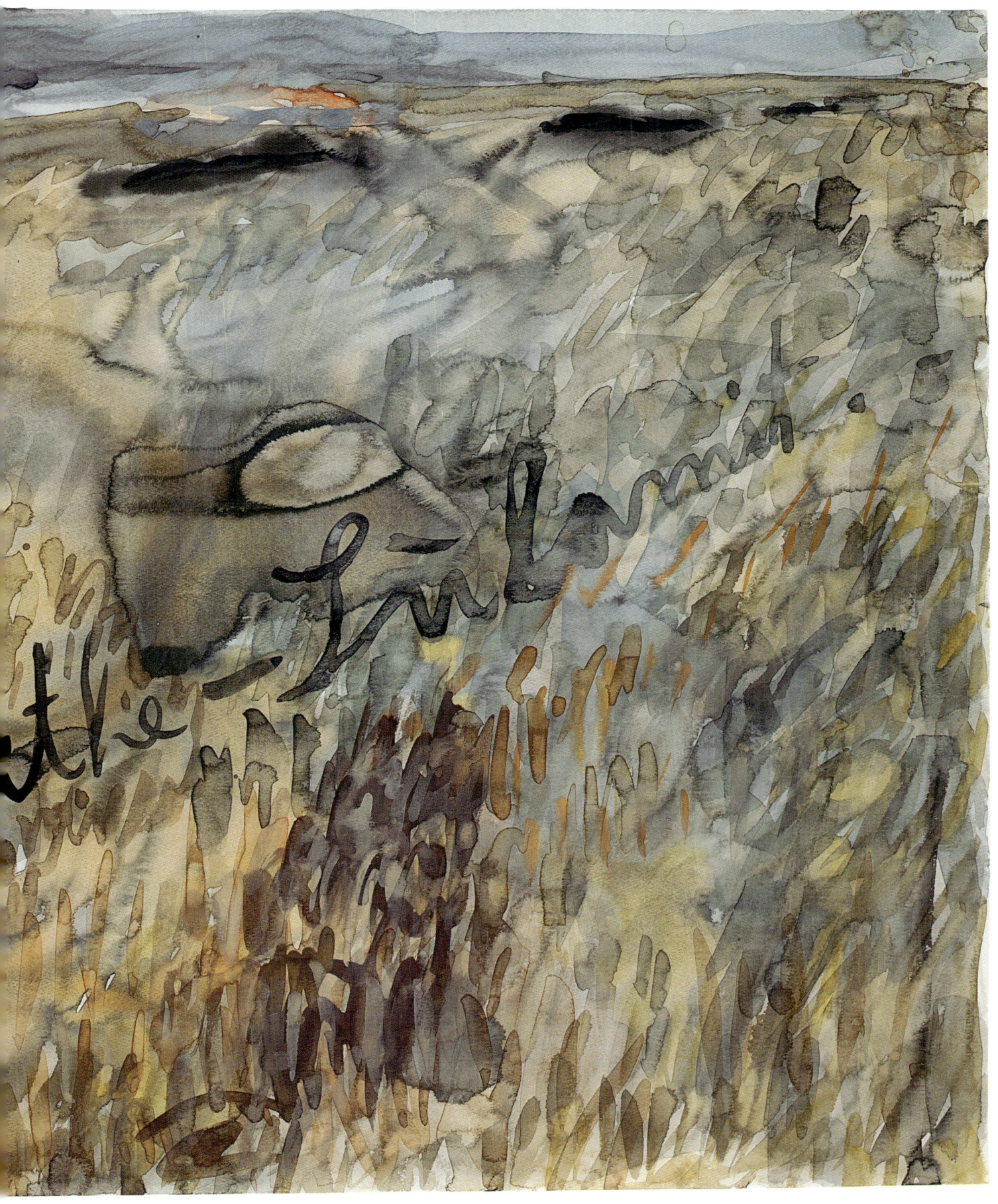

Black milk of daybreak we drink it at sundown
we drink it at noon in the morning we drink it at night
we drink it and drink it
we dig a grave in the breezes there one lies unconfined
A man lives in the house he plays with the serpents he writes
he writes when dusk falls to Germany your golden hair
  Margarete
he writes it and steps out of doors and the stars are flashing he
  whistles his pack out
he whistles his Jews out in earth has them dig for a grave
he commands us strike up for the dance

Black milk of daybreak we drink you at night
we drink you in the morning at noon we drink you at sundown
we drink and we drink you
A man lives in the house he plays with the serpents he writes
he writes when dusk falls to Germany your golden hair
  Margarete
your ashen hair Shulamith we dig a grave in the breezes there
  one lies unconfined

He calls out jab deeper into the earth you lot you others sing now
  and play
he grabs at the iron in his belt he waves it his eyes are blue
jab deeper you lot with your spades you others play on for the
  dance

the left and top of the painting it reads 'Urd', 'Werdandi' and 'Skuld'.

Urd, Werdandi and Skuld are the names of the three 'Norns', goddesses who are responsible for shaping the course of fate in Norse mythology, the complex Nordic religious framework that was upheld around the Viking Age. The Norns are thought to represent the past, present, and future, although it has been argued that, etymologically, the names do not imply a temporal distinction in a chronological sense.[79] In the 'Völuspá' poem, one of the most important primary sources that tells the story of the creation of the world, the Norns draw water from a sacred well to nourish the Yggdrasil life tree at the centre of the cosmos. There are also accounts about them spinning, measuring, and cutting the thread of life for gods and men. In Scandinavian and German art works from the nineteenth and twentieth centuries, they are often depicted as female figures beneath the Yggdrasil tree. For example, in a 1901 charcoal painting by German artist and illustrator Gottfried Ferdinand Carl Ehrenberg (1840–1914; p.181), Urd is painted as an old woman, carving runes into a staff so that the past does not disappear from memory. Young Skuld, sitting next to her, gazes into the future with a serious face. Her upper body is wrapped in a transparent veil, suggesting uncertainty. Above these two in the middle of the composition and facing the viewer directly with an earnest facial expression stands Verdandi, symbolising the present. She is depicted as a beautiful virgin figure wearing a winged helmet over her long blonde hair. Armed with a dagger, she also holds flowers in each hand.

Here in Kiefer's paintings, the Norns are not represented as female figures but symbolised by fallen branches from Yggdrasil, slowly burning, smoking, and turning into ashes. Eventually, new life will form from the ashes. Referencing the natural forces of plants and fire, the circle of life is visualised in its most elemental sense.

During the Third Reich, the National Socialists misappropriated Norse mythology and iconography, viewing it as a repository of Germanic culture and values that had been erased forcibly, including by the influence of Christian religion and culture. It was wrongly believed to corroborate ideologies of a pure Aryan ancestral race and the need for a war.[80] Following the Second World War, North Germanic folklore was therefore viewed as dangerously linked to National Socialism and removed from school curricula. Representative of Kiefer's approach at the time, the painting *Urd, Werdandi, Skuld (Die Nornen)* challenges the contemporary taboo around Norse mythology, looking at it afresh and trying to neutralise and liberate it from the association with Nazi ideologies. In Kiefer's abstracted painting, the past, present, and future are coming together symbolically, pointing at a non-chronological concept of time that perhaps goes beyond human understanding.

Lena Fritsch

39

MARGARETHE – SULAMIT (MARGARET – SHULAMITE), 1981

Anselm Kiefer's watercolour painting presents us with a wide field of gold-beige straw mixed with watery grey hues. In the background, black lines and small orange flames suggest fires. A thin grey section at the top of the painting indicates a smoky sky, conveying a dark atmosphere. It appears as if parts of the straw field have burnt, while others are still burning. Two names are scrawled across the work in diluted black letters: 'Margarethe – Sulamit'.

The title of the work cites two figures from French poet and translator Paul Celan's poem 'Todesfuge' ('Death Fugue'; *c*.1945). The reference would be understood widely in Germany by Kiefer's generation (and all following generations) as the poem has been part of our school curriculum. Paul Celan, one of the most important figures in German-language literature of the post-war era, was born into a German-speaking Jewish family in Bukovina, a region then part of Romania and earlier the Austro-Hungarian Empire. He was interned in a labour camp in Romania in 1942 – the same year his parents were murdered in a concentration camp in Trisnistria. In 1948 Celan exiled himself via Vienna to Paris, where he committed suicide in 1970. 'Todesfuge', first published in 1948, became well known when it was included in Celan's second collection of poems in 1952, *Mohn und Gedächtnis* (p.190). Some 36 lines long, the complex and multi-layered poem deals with the Holocaust in compelling dark imagery, structurally reflecting a musical fugue that repeats and recombines key themes in rhythmic variations. When philosopher Theodor Adorno famously stated in his essay 'Kulturkritik und Gesellschaft' in 1949, 'writing poetry after Auschwitz is barbaric', this was widely read as a 'ban' on post-Holocaust poetry *in toto*;[81] Celan's 'Todesfuge' was soon to be viewed as the most famous example that proved him wrong.[82] However, as comparative literature professor John Zilcosky has recently argued, the two Jewish intellectuals, who communicated in letters and later also met in person, agreed on many issues. They shared a suspicion of poetry and a hope for a new language, believing that 'only a revolution in form could overturn dominant social structures' and uncover 'a critical poetic speaking that might not be barbaric after Auschwitz'.[83] Adorno expressed his admiration for Celan in his *Aesthetic Theory*, posthumously published in

1973, and even wrote that 'art may be the only remaining medium of truth in an age of incomprehensible suffering. As the real world grows dark, the irrationality of art is becoming rational, especially at a time when art is radically tenebrous itself'.[84]

Celan's 'Todesfuge' can be divided into four main parts, each of which begin with the oxymoron line *schwarze Milch der Frühe*', translated as 'Black milk of dawn', a metaphor for the daily cycle of suffering experienced by the speaker. The narrator uses the second-person plural to represent the voices of the victims in the concentration camps. They are pitched against a single blue-eyed man, who lives in a house of 'vipers', representing a German guard and 'master from Germany', who personifies the prisoners' death. In the second part of the poem, the line 'your golden hair Margarete' is counterpointed with 'your ashen hair Shulamith'. Margarete references the doomed heroine Gretchen in Johann Wolfgang von Goethe's *Faust*, while Shulamith is the bride of Solomon, whose eroticism is celebrated in the *Song of Songs* in the Old Testament. Both women have in common that they are depicted as beautiful, innocent, and lovingly devoted to begin with, and later as heartbroken. The women can be interpreted as metaphors for 'Aryan' Germans on the one hand, and Jews on the other. The ashen colour of Shulamith's hair not only references the Jewish woman's darker hair colour but also the systematic murdering of Jews in concentration camps.

Celan's poetry more generally, and 'Todesfuge' in particular, recurs in Kiefer's work. Kiefer has expressed his fascination with Celan's language repeatedly, and created over 30 works in different artistic media in the 1980s inscribed and titled *Margarete*; *Dein goldenes Haar, Margarete*; *Shulamith*, etc. This small-sized painting mentions both women and presents us with a straw field in which golden and ashy colours are blurred, as if to show the inextricably intertwined relationship between

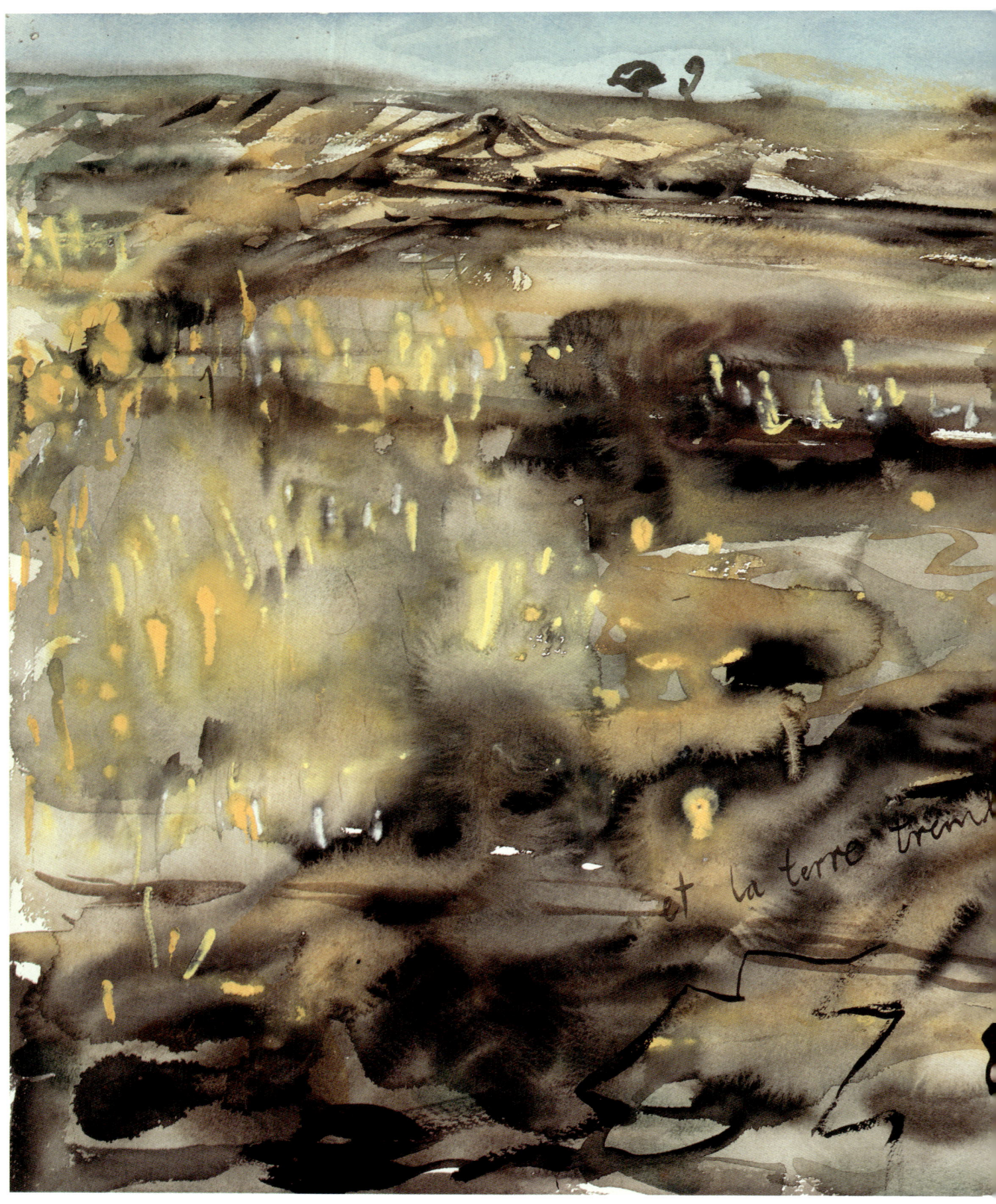

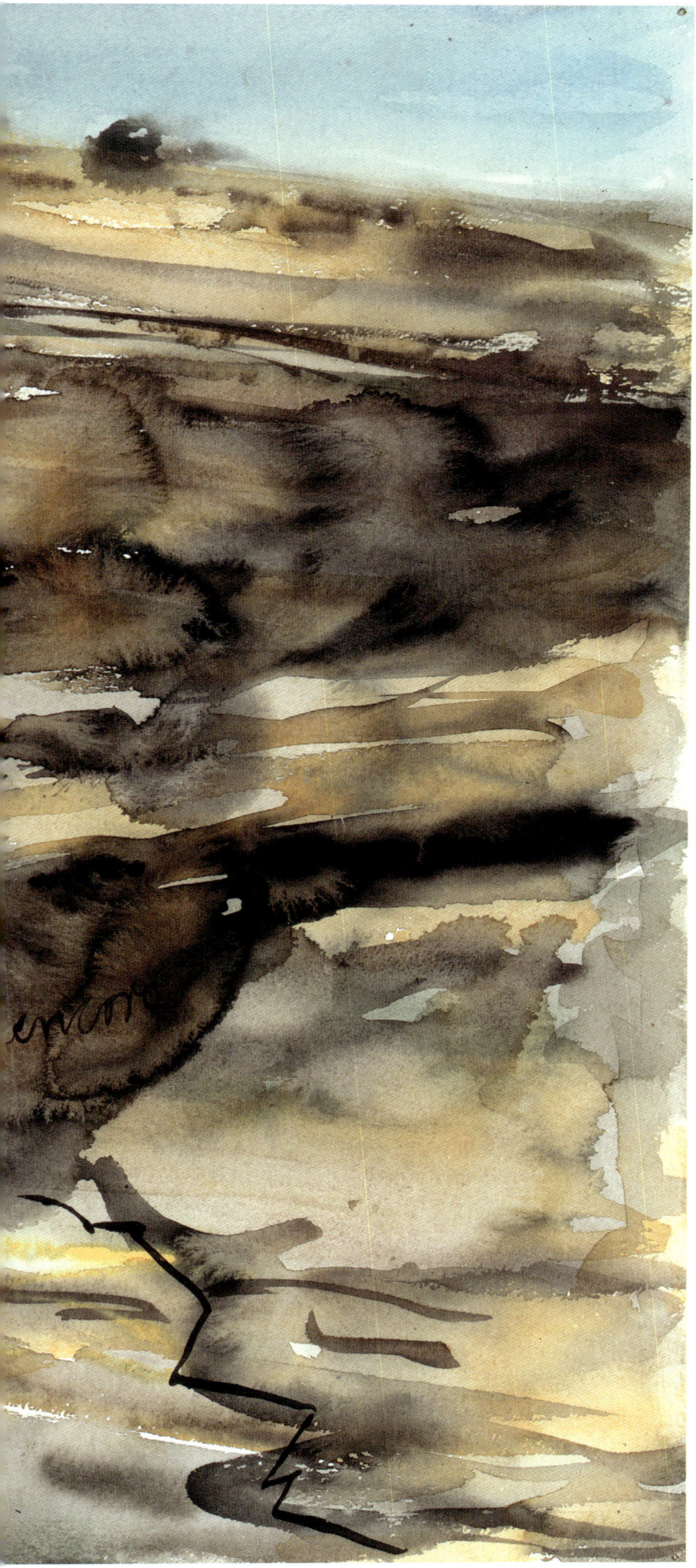

ET LA TERRE TREMBLE ENCORE (*AND THE EARTH STILL TREMBLES*), 1981

Watercolour on paper
49.5 cm × 64 cm

Hall Collection

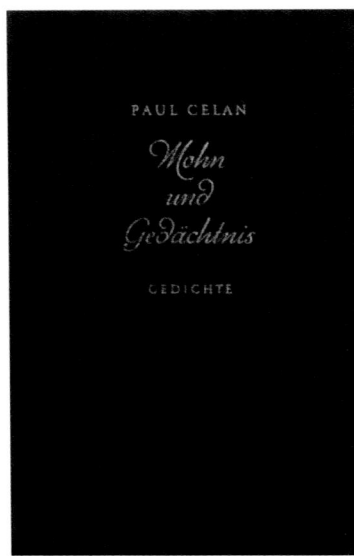

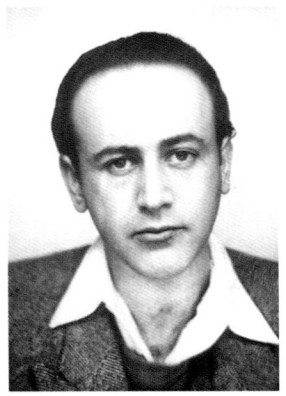

(left)
Paul Celan, Book cover of *Mohn
und Gedächtnis*, 1952
Stuttgart: Deutsche Verlags-Anstalt

(right)
Passport photo of Paul Celan, 1938

Margarete and Shulamith. Celan, as a Jew who wrote his compelling poetry in the German language, personifies this intertwined connection between 'German' and 'Jewish' that leaves the Nazi's forceful separation system ad absurdum.

Just like Adorno and Celan, Kiefer seeks to find a new artistic language after the horrors of the Holocaust. *Margarethe – Sulamit* focuses on straw, fire, and ash to create dark associative images in the viewer's mind that link with Celan's elegy. The gold-beige coloured straw not only represents Margarete's blonde hair but is also associated with the National Socialist's aesthetic ideal 'of a healthy German, who is able to cope with life'.[85] The fruitful fields link with the importance of the land in the German psyche, evident in Romantic paintings by Caspar David Friedrich, but also in 1930s works by painters such as Werner Peiner (1897–1984), whose work exemplifies Nazi ideologies of a return to honest, uncomplicated life in nature. At the same time, straw is also an important alchemical material in Kiefer's work, which he began to use in the 1980s, gluing it onto large canvas works.[86] Kiefer has described his interest in the material: '... an initially rigid substance, straw softens into a *materia prima* and ... changes into a dark matter ready to be received by the earth.'[87] The flames in the background of *Margarethe – Sulamit* and its ashy sections indicate the killing of Jews in concentration camps that Celan's poem alludes to. But the flames and ash also represent the transformative power of fire. The landscape in Kiefer's watercolour is in a process of change, suggesting the never-ending cycles of life.

This emotionally charged watercolour combines symbolic references to Celan's macabre poem that remind the viewer subconsciously of the most barbaric chapters of German history, with basic natural elements that point at the constant transitoriness and ephemerality of all being.

Lena Fritsch

40

ET LA TERRE TREMBLE ENCORE (AND THE EARTH STILL TREMBLES), 1981

Beige, brown, and watery-black lines and blurry patches come together in an abstracted wide landscape, suggesting a field or hill. A few zig-zag lines in the foreground convey an impression of broken land, contrasting with a thin section at the top of the watercolour, which presents us with a light-blue sky and small green elements in the background. In an artistic language comparable with *Margarethe – Sulamit* from the same year (pp.184–5), this painting exemplifies Kiefer's interest in landscapes that bear traces of major transformation and devastation. In very small brown letters, it reads in the lower part of the composition: '*et la terre tremble encore*', ('and the earth still trembles').

A contemporary earthquake in Southern Italy inspired this watercolour and seven similar works on paper and paintings. On 23 November 1980 a severe earthquake hit Irpinia with a moment magnitude of 6.9, killing and injuring thousands of people, leaving 250,000 people homeless, and destroying countless historical buildings in the area. Damage spread far from the epicentre, affecting Salerno and Naples, where dozens of structures were levelled. Art dealer Lucio Amelio (1931–1994) invited 66 artists to create work responding to the catastrophe for an exhibition titled *Terrae Motus*, in Naples. The show became the nucleus for a small collection and museum of contemporary art.[88] For the exhibition, Kiefer created an oil and clay on canvas painting in 1982 titled *(Waterloo) et la terre tremble encore*. In much larger size and with a strong sculptural, three-dimensional feel, the painting features a

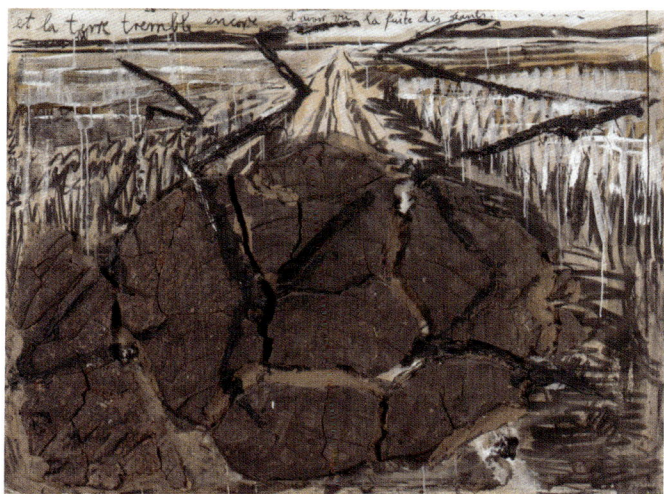

Anselm Kiefer
(Waterloo) et la terre tremble encore, 1982
Oil, acrylic, charcoal and clay on canvas
130 × 170 cm

devastated landscape with similar zig-zag lines like in our watercolour, representing broken land.

Combined with the words 'Waterloo, Waterloo', the same inscription '*et la terre tremble encore*' can also be found on other paintings from 1981 and 1982, for example on a large-sized oil, acrylic, clay, and charcoal painting, *Waterloo, Waterloo, et la terre tremble encore*, 1982, in the collection of the Frankel Foundation, US. The sombre work references the violent Battle of Waterloo on 18 June 1815, fought on a wide battlefield south of Brussels, between the French troops of Napoleon Bonaparte (1769–1821) and the Allied armies commanded by the Duke of Wellington from Britain, and General Blücher (1742–1819) from Prussia. Violent thunderstorms and heavy rain made the fights (and resulting battlefield landscape) even more devastating. The French defeat ended 23 years of war, beginning with the French Revolutionary wars in 1792 and continuing through the Napoleonic wars. British army major W. E. Frye described the bloody aftermath on 22 June 1815:

> This morning I went to visit the field of battle, which is a little beyond the village of Waterloo, on the plateau of Mont-Saint-Jean; but on arrival there the sight was too horrible to behold. I felt sick in the stomach and was obliged to return. The multitude of carcasses, the heaps of wounded men with mangled limbs unable to move, and perishing from not having their wounds dressed or from hunger, as the Allies were, of course, obliged to take their surgeons and waggons with them, formed a spectacle I shall never forget.[89]

Whether relating to a post-earthquake or a post-battlefield landscape, what is striking about *Et la terre tremble encore* is that it presents us in typical Kiefer style with the quiet aftermath of a devastating event. Reverberating with the violence it has witnessed, we can imagine that the deserted earth still trembles, only gradually calming down to recover from all the forceful damage it has experienced. In soft and watery colours, this intimate watercolour conveys a unique and timeless, dark beauty of destruction, while also indicating a peaceful sense of catharsis, leading to renewal and restoration in the future.

Lena Fritsch

41

DER RHEIN (THE RHINE), 1982

'I have grown up on the Rhine, the border river. But even then, it was more than a geographical border. Thinking about it now, there are roots that lose themselves at the barrier to the inaccessible space, a space that, in a wonderful way, is always empty, due to the incongruency between dream and fulfilment. As a child, of course, I didn't have any idea about this country named France. There were lines of poplar trees, beginnings of streets, but behind all this, there was an empty space, not yet populated for me, which then later had to be filled.'[90]
– Anselm Kiefer

For centuries, the Rhine was viewed as a German national symbol while, at the same time, also providing a political and cultural border to France. During the Romantic era and its emotive idealisation of nature, countless travelogues by writers such as Friedrich Hölderlin (1707–1843), Heinrich Heine, and Lord Byron (1788–1824), as well as paintings by J.M.W. Turner (1775–1851; p.194) helped develop a fascination with the beauty of Rhine landscapes. Composer Richard Wagner raised a musical monument for this 'Rhine romanticism' through his opera cycle *Der Ring des Nibelungen*, located along the Rhine.

41

DER RHEIN (THE RHINE), 1982

Collage of woodcuts on canvas with acrylic and
shellac
168 × 124 cm

Hall Collection

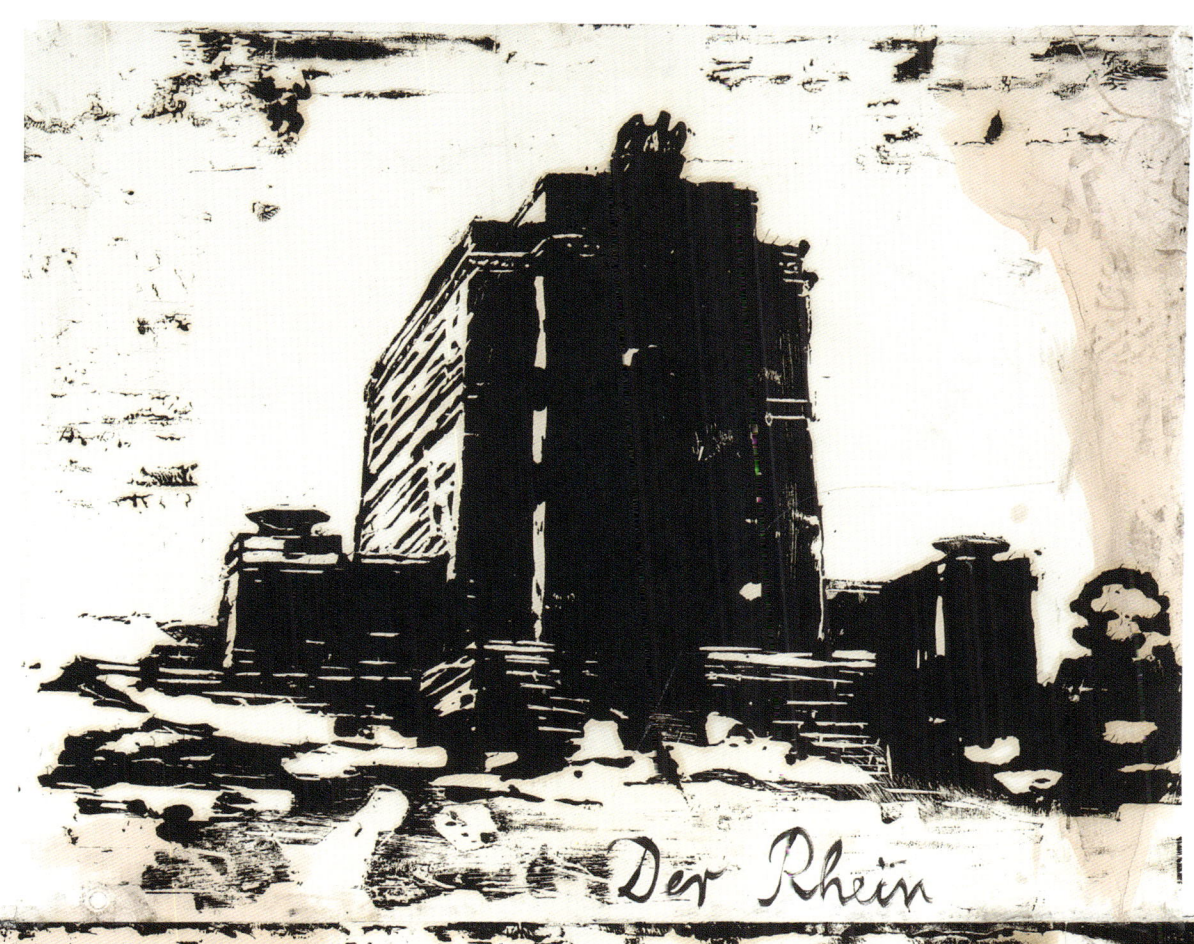

Der Rhein

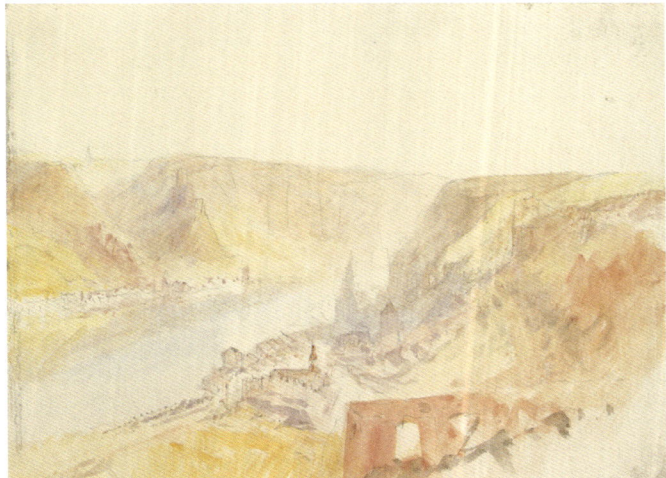

J.M.W. Turner (1775–1851)
*On the Rhine: looking over Sankt Goar
to Katz, from Burg Rheinfels*
Watercolour over graphite on wove paper,
18.1 × 23.7 cm

Kiefer, however, is also concerned with the political and war-associated challenges that have always been linked with the Rhine. The complex history and mythology of Germany is mirrored in the motifs of Kiefer's works. In the *Rhein* series, Kiefer intertwines Rhine landscapes with architecture. His works merge a built culture – including bunkers and National Socialist buildings – with culturally and historically charged nature. The German Reich commissioned for its military and representative buildings architects that were favoured by Adolf Hitler: Paul Ludwig Troost (1878–1934), Albert Speer (1905–1981), who was later to become National Socialist Minister of Armaments and War Production, and his protégé Wilhelm Kreis (1873–1955). The depicted buildings reference plans for the new museum quarter in Berlin as well as the military sites of two historic lines of defence: the Atlantic Wall was built by the German regime as of 1942 along the complete north-western coast of Europe to protect them from an Allied invasion; the Maginot Line was already constructed in the 1930s in France along its eastern borders between the Mediterranean Sea and the Belgian border. It was named after the minister of defence, André Maginot (1877–1932). Kiefer uses the sky, traditionally dedicated to gods and holy figures, in order to question the hierarchies of ideologies and socio-political systems. He shows the emblems and temples of a destructive power, critically challenging their space in the pantheon, questioning their meaning and symbolism. In doing so, Kiefer voids the architecture in his *Rhein* pictures, removing the original glorification symbolism.

The black and white contrast of the composition and the thin painterly revision work support the transformation of the paper into the all-engulfing space of air. The materials will change their structures and colours over the course of time due to light and temperature – Kiefer includes time deliberately as creative means that allude to the permanent change of everything. Kiefer's memories of his childhood and the current that as a border river between France and Germany already then stimulated his imagination, do not mean that he really understood the concept of a frontier as a child. Over the years, however, for Kiefer, the Rhine has become a symbol of the changeable quality of water that can confine as well as exclude, as the boundary lines continuously shift and change. As a border river, the Rhine is eventually a visible sign that all borders are illusions.

As of the 1970s, Kiefer has integrated woodcuts into his complex work, mostly creating monumental paper collages composed of different woodcut pictures. Each work is unique: the individual woodcuts are all printed by hand, and they mostly merge with acrylic, oil, and shellac paint into large-sized compositions. They are either combined from and onto paper or mounted on canvas. In 1974 Kiefer began to explore the material of wood itself as an expression of myth and history – the 'German forest' physically becomes part of the artistic process, and the paper is often placed directly onto the coloured wood planks.[91] Kiefer has explained:

> ... sometimes I also used black paint as glue. By the way, I liked using bad paper. Of course, I didn't have much money at the time, but I also appreciated the quality of cheap paper, partly also blotting paper.[92]

The soft wood of linden trees was always his favourite. Kiefer's grandfather was a carpenter and had left him old, well-stored wood, which adds an autobiographical layer to the material of wood in Kiefer's work.

> I was intrigued by the sawmill in Fillingen at my grandmother's; even today, I can still hear its sounds. It was an accumulation of energy: warmth, piled wood, woodcuts. I always thought I should one day buy a sawmill.[93]

Woodcut is fascinating to Kiefer in enabling him to try something that first appears impossible, transforming an inflexible material, wood, into the depiction of floating water or snow, covering its original form through creating, changing it into a new one. In terms of their contents, the early works mostly use Germany and its dense history, mythology, and culture as a starting point for complex, innovative visual messages.

Antonia Hoerschelmann
Translated from the German by Lena Fritsch

42

INNENRAUM (INTERIOR), 1982

Kiefer's paintings of deserted buildings from the early 1980s were based on photographs of projects by Albert Speer, Paul Ludwig Troost, Wilhelm Kreis, and other architects of the Nazi regime. Speer, Hitler's favourite architect, was responsible for the Reich Chancellery among other buildings in Berlin, as well as the Nazi Party rally grounds at Nuremberg. Troost, who died in 1934, built a number of Nazi buildings in Munich, including the Haus der Deutschen Kunst. Kreis worked with Speer on his ostentatious plans for the redesign of Berlin and also designed (but never realised) gigantic memorials, cemeteries, and mausolea for the German war dead throughout the Reich.

Innenraum (1982) is related to two much larger paintings: the first, also called *Innenraum* (1981) is in the Stedelijk Museum in Amsterdam; the second, entitled *Dem unbekannten Maler* (*To the Unknown Painter*; 1982), is in the Museum Boijmans Van Beuningen in Rotterdam (p.198). The former depicts an interior hall in Hitler's Reich Chancellery in Berlin, while the latter resembles one of the two *Ehrentempel* (Temples of Honour) in Munich, erected by the Nazis in 1935 to house the sarcophagi of Party members who had been killed in the failed Beer Hall Putsch more than a decade earlier.

In *Dem unbekannten Maler* and *Innenraum* (the watercolour included here), a dark silhouette of a painter's palette is shown mounted on an object resembling a tomb in the centre of the space. The natural form of the palette, its gracefulness and fragility, is in stark contrast to the overbearing severity and rigid order of the architecture. More tragically, the palette also appears to suggest the idea of the painter – as opposed to the National Socialist – as martyr. Helpless in the face of aggressive historical forces, the artist who did not comply with Nazi directives or whose work was considered 'degenerate' would be banned from exhibiting, teaching, or even working and thus became a non-person, 'unknown'. Others went into exile; those who couldn't, who happened to be Jewish, were transported to camps and murdered.

Kiefer's use of perishable materials such as straw and paper from his own woodcut collages, and the violent processes to which he subjects them, including burning and slashing, give the canvas a tangibly distressed surface. This not only evokes the destruction of the Chancellery and other Nazi monuments but symbolises the hubris and catastrophe of the Third Reich. Whether it also implies a desire on the artist's part to entirely obliterate his imagery is debatable. Kiefer would not have been unaware of the regret expressed at the time by certain revisionist architects that many of the best surviving examples of the stripped, Classical style favoured by Hitler were blown up by the Allies after the war, the *Ehrentempel* among them. The viewer, too, cannot help but experience a feeling of morbid fascination for this grandiose architecture, the doomed descendant of the Romantic Classicism of Schinkel and von Klenze. It is thanks to Kiefer's genius that

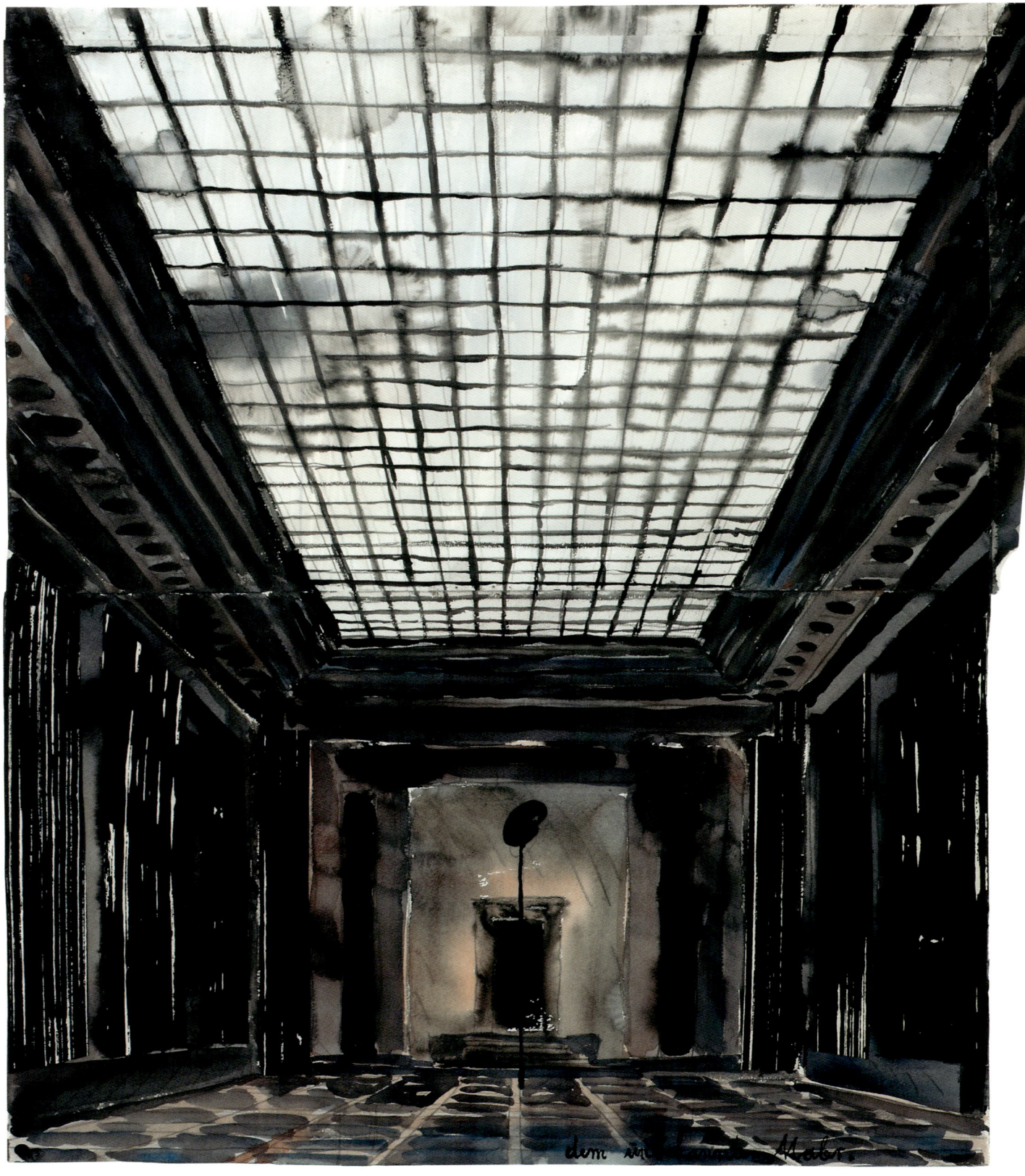

INNENRAUM (INTERIOR), 1982
Watercolour and graphite on paper
77.5 × 68.5 cm
Hall Collection

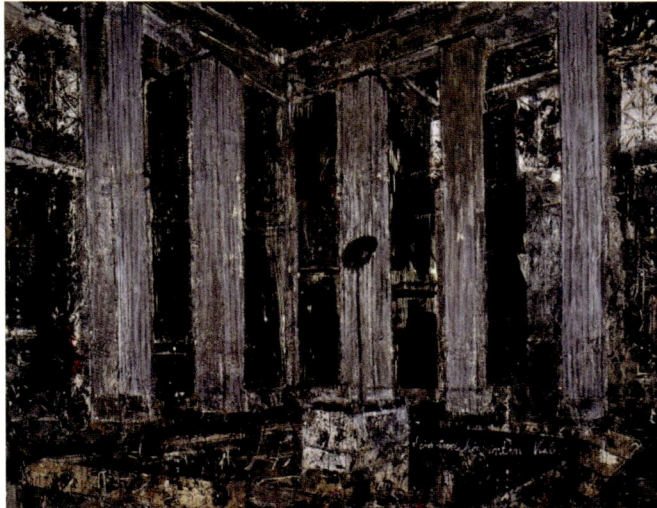

Anselm Kiefer
Dem unbekannten Maler
(*To the Unknown Painter*), 1982
Oil, acrylic, emulsion, straw and
woodcut on paper on canvas,
281 × 341.5 cm

his paintings allow such contrary emotions, such as repulsion and attraction, to co-exist.

Kiefer's art of this period is redolent of German Romantic iconography, nowhere more so than in his sweeping but defiled historical landscapes and 'apocalyptic' architectural visions that seem to emulate, but simultaneously undermine, the concept of the sublime. What he seems to be saying is that, in order to face up to being a German in the post-war, post-Holocaust age, one must understand the innate appeal to the German Romantic psyche of mysticism and the non-rational. And, crucially, in order to understand the Romantic mythology that the Nazis distorted for nationalistic purposes, one may find it necessary to suspend disbelief, to surrender temporarily to its allure – as millions did between 1933 and 1945. Only then can there be any hope of the evil being exorcised.

Richard Calvocoressi

43/44

DIE BLÄTTER FALLEN (THE LEAVES ARE FALLING), 2017–23

UND IN DEN NÄCHTEN FÄLLT DIE SCHWERE ERDE (AND AT NIGHT, THE HEAVY EARTH IS FALLING), 2017–23

Dominated by round shapes in warm hues of brown, gold, and beige, and complemented by small turquoise-green elements and black handwriting, Anselm Kiefer's new abstracted paintings convey an organic and natural feel. Shiny leaves and thick paint elevated from the large canvases create a sense of three-dimensionality, and of the leaves floating and falling endlessly in a timeless space.

The titles of both paintings, *Die Blätter fallen* (*The leaves are falling*) and *Und in den Nächten fällt die schwere Erde* (*And at night, the heavy earth is falling*) reference the poem 'Autumn' (1902, p.199) by Austrian writer Rainer Maria Rilke. In this work, Rilke describes the transience of life through the image of falling autumn leaves. Through the repetition of the word 'falling', the poem conveys a strong sense of uncontrollable movement and loss, first symbolised by the falling leaves and then, through the use of the first-person plural, representing the falling of all humans. The feeling of disconnection and decay depicted in the first three stanzas is juxtaposed with the final stanza, in which 'Someone' whose 'infinitely calm' hands hold up the falling, provides a sense of hope. At the time this poem was written, Rilke had moved to Paris to write a monograph on Auguste Rodin. With his wife and daughter still in Berlin, he struggled with a sense of alienation in the new, large city. 'Autumn' mirrors the existential and philosophical anxieties prevalent in early twentieth-century modern European literature, while also representing the author's Christian faith: not only is 'Someone' a direct reference to God, but the stars and the space/skies ('*Himmeln*' in the German original) also point at Christian iconography. Above all, however, the work can be interpreted as a timeless description of our fear of loneliness and ephemerality as we age, with the autumn leaves personifying human mortality and representing nature's endless cycles of transience.

The variety of materials that Kiefer uses in these two paintings is representative of his art today. The major role that the medium of photography has played in Kiefer's work – as inspiration, archive, and artistic medium – was recently showcased for the first time in the exhibition

'Autumn'
Rainer Maria Rilke, 1902

The leaves are falling, falling as if from far up,
as if orchards were dying high in space.
Each leaf falls as if it were motioning "no".

And at night, the heavy earth is falling
away from all other stars in the loneliness.

We're all falling. This hand here is falling.
And look at the other one ... It's in them all.

And yet there is Someone, whose hands
infinitely calm, hold up all this falling.[96]

Anselm Kiefer. Photography at the Beginning, at the Lille Métropole Musée d'art moderne, d'art contemporain et d'art brut, 2023–4. Here, a photograph is used as the foundation of the works, combined with the classic painting materials of oil, acrylic, shellac, and emulsion. Typical of Kiefer's work since the mid-1980s, this is complemented by string and lead, the latter a material that has long fascinated him for its different characteristics and applications, ranging from alchemists trying to turn it into gold to medical professionals using it to shield patients from the harmful consequences of X-rays. These materials add a sculptural element to the works. The paintings also include sediment from an electrolysis process, which points at Kiefer's fascination with the uncontrollable side of materials and their transient nature. The shellac as well as lead and electrolysis sediment all show how the artist has embraced the mutability and decay of artistic materials as part of his works: even after the paintings have been finished, they have a 'life' of their own and continue to change.

The two works here and another recent painting concerned with Rilke's poem 'Herbsttag' ('Autumn Day') were selected by Anselm Kiefer for this exhibition and book specifically to complement his early works. The new paintings represent a sense of continuity as well as development in his oeuvre. The use of text as part of the paintings and the reference to literature, particularly in the German-language, has remained an important part of Kiefer's art since the very beginning. His concern with historical, cultural, and personal memory, as reflected in many of his early works, is visible in the new paintings too. The continued interest in nature as a 'screen' that people's cultural, religious, and spiritual thoughts can be projected onto, is as obvious in these paintings as it was in his landscape paintings of the 1970s and 1980s. Focusing on his upbringing in Germany and the post-war issues of

his own country at the beginning of his career, however, Kiefer's work has grown in a variety of historical, cultural, and spiritual directions. In the past 50 years or so, his work has opened up and spread into different artistic spheres, with Kiefer's commercial success enabling him to create uniquely monumental works and large-scale projects, many of which can be seen as part of a *Gesamtkunstwerk*. Now almost 80 years old, Kiefer's artistic interest in the themes of transience and mortality, that Rilke's poems describe so elegantly, can be viewed as a reflection on the artist's own life. *Die Blätter fallen* and *Und in den Nächten fällt die schwere Erde* convey a personal sense of melancholy, while representing the senior artist's strong art of his autumn years.

Lena Fritsch

45

WER JETZT KEIN HAUS HAT (WHOEVER HAS NO HOUSE NOW), 2023

In this symbolistic Christian poem from 1902, Austrian writer Rainer Maria Rilke captures the spirit of early autumn (p.206). First published in his collection of poems *Das Buch der Bilder* in the same year, the text encompasses three stanzas with a growing number of verses that depict the gradual change of seasons. The iambic pentameter of the poem only begins after the exclamation 'Lord' ('*Herr*') at its very beginning, drawing attention to the narrator's emotional addressing of God in a plea-like prayer. Seasonal images, metaphors and adjectives associated with time all convey a strong sense of transience: 'sundials', 'shadows', 'the wind', 'fruits', 'vine', 'wine', 'final', and 'dry leaves' that are 'blowing'. Similar to Rilke's poem 'Autumn' (above), 'Autumn Day' also develops

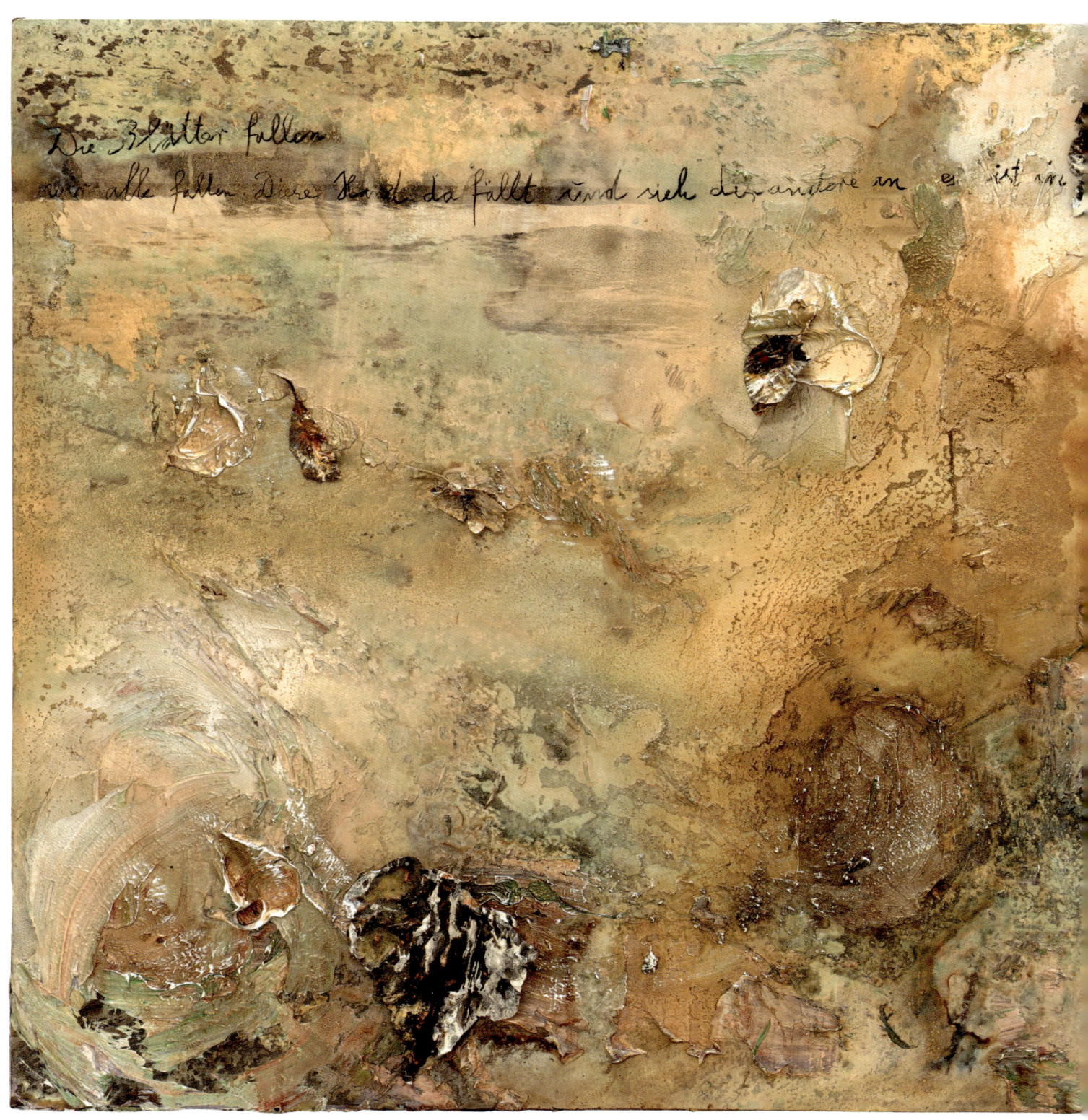

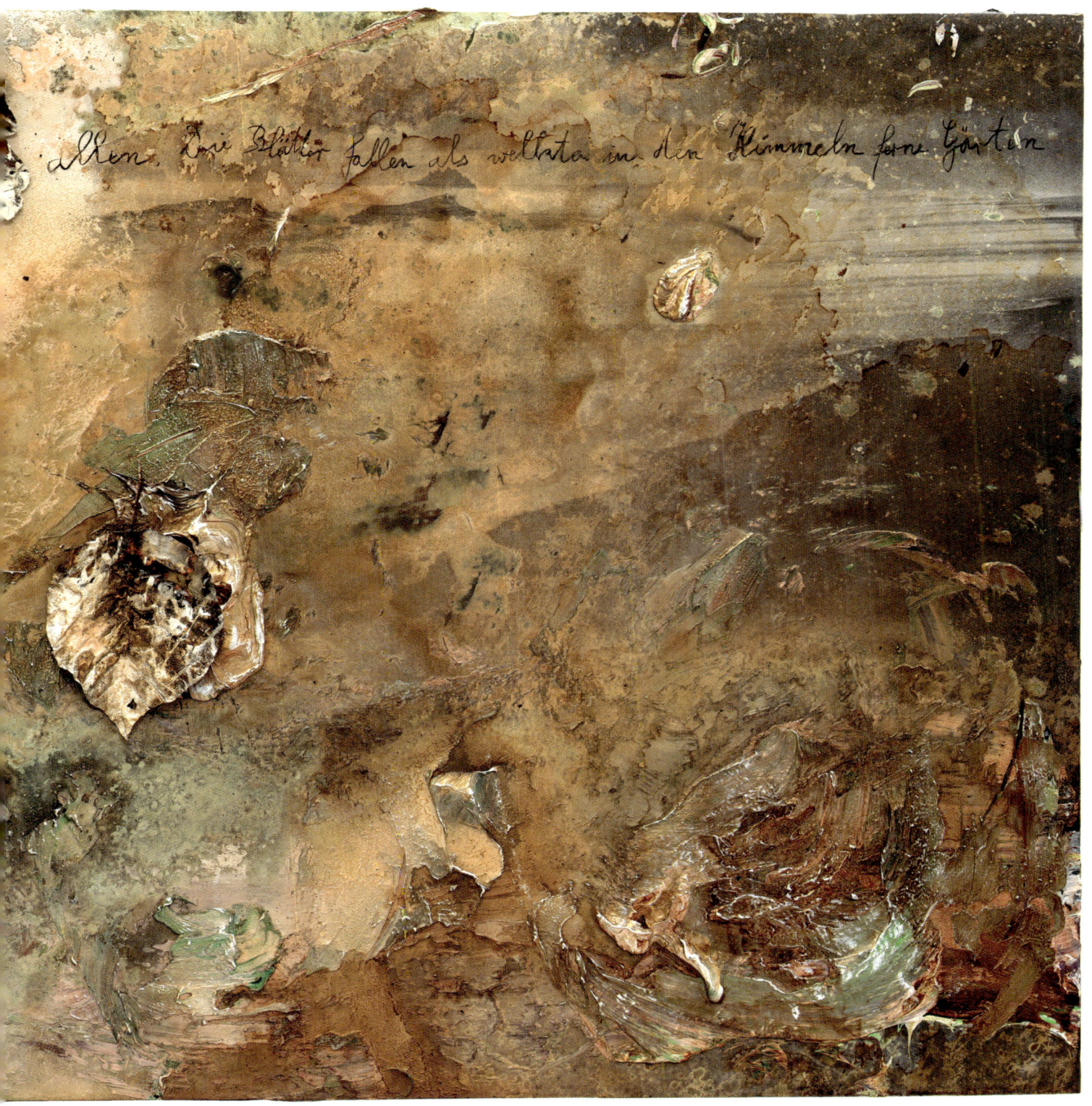

Allen. Die Blätter fallen als welkten in den Himmeln ferne Gärten

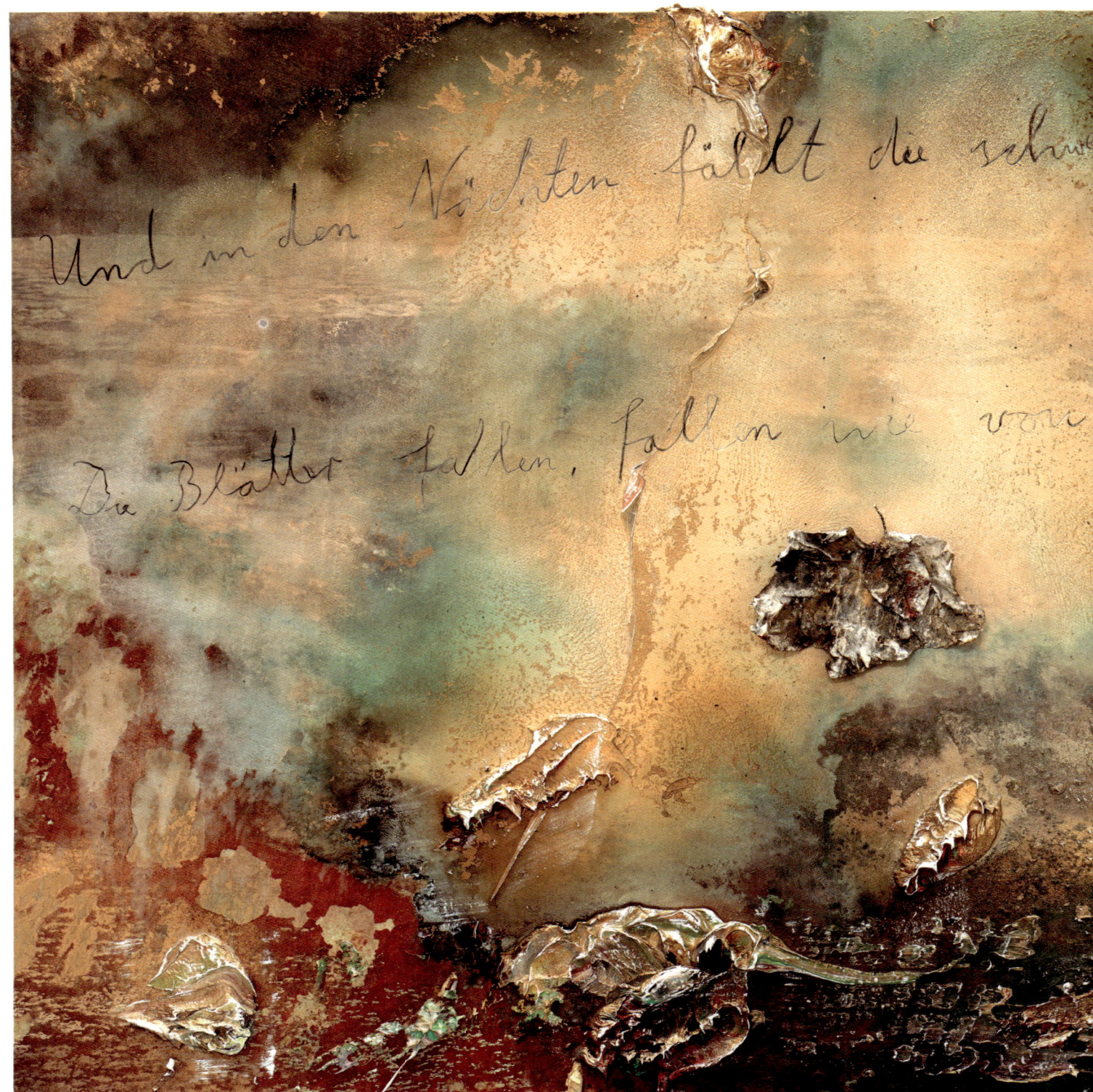

Und in den Nächten fällt die schwe

Die Blätter fallen, fallen wie von

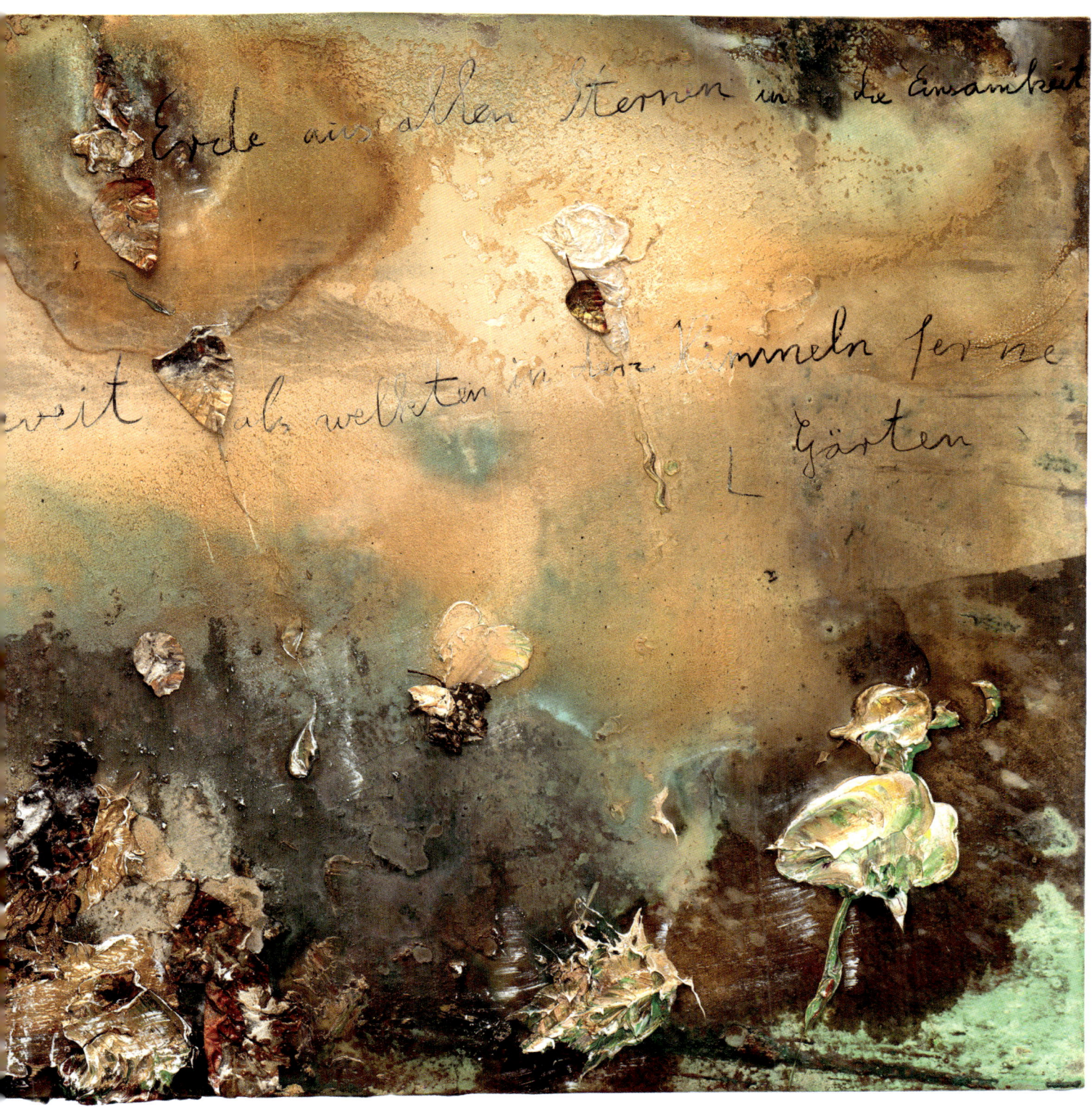

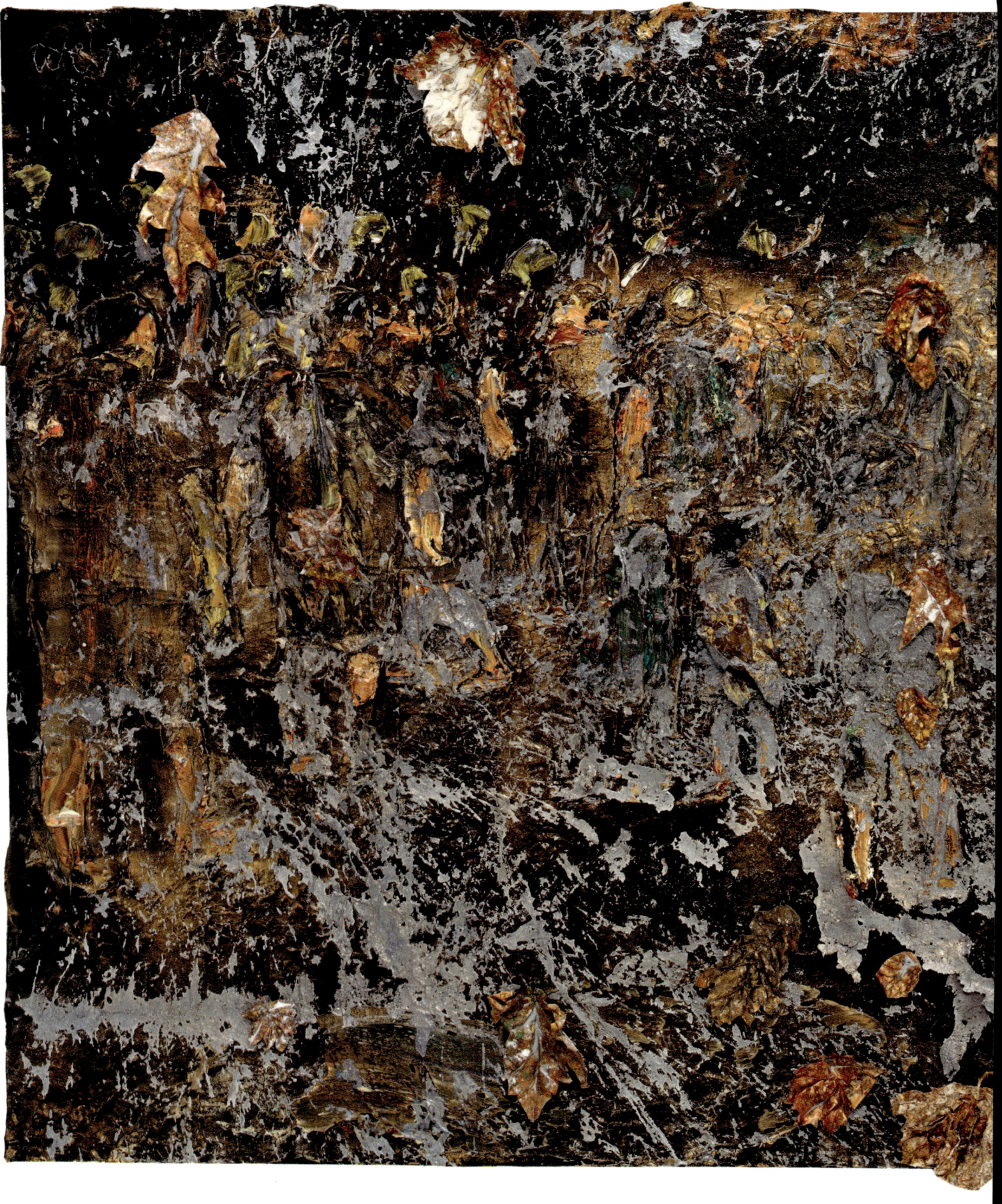

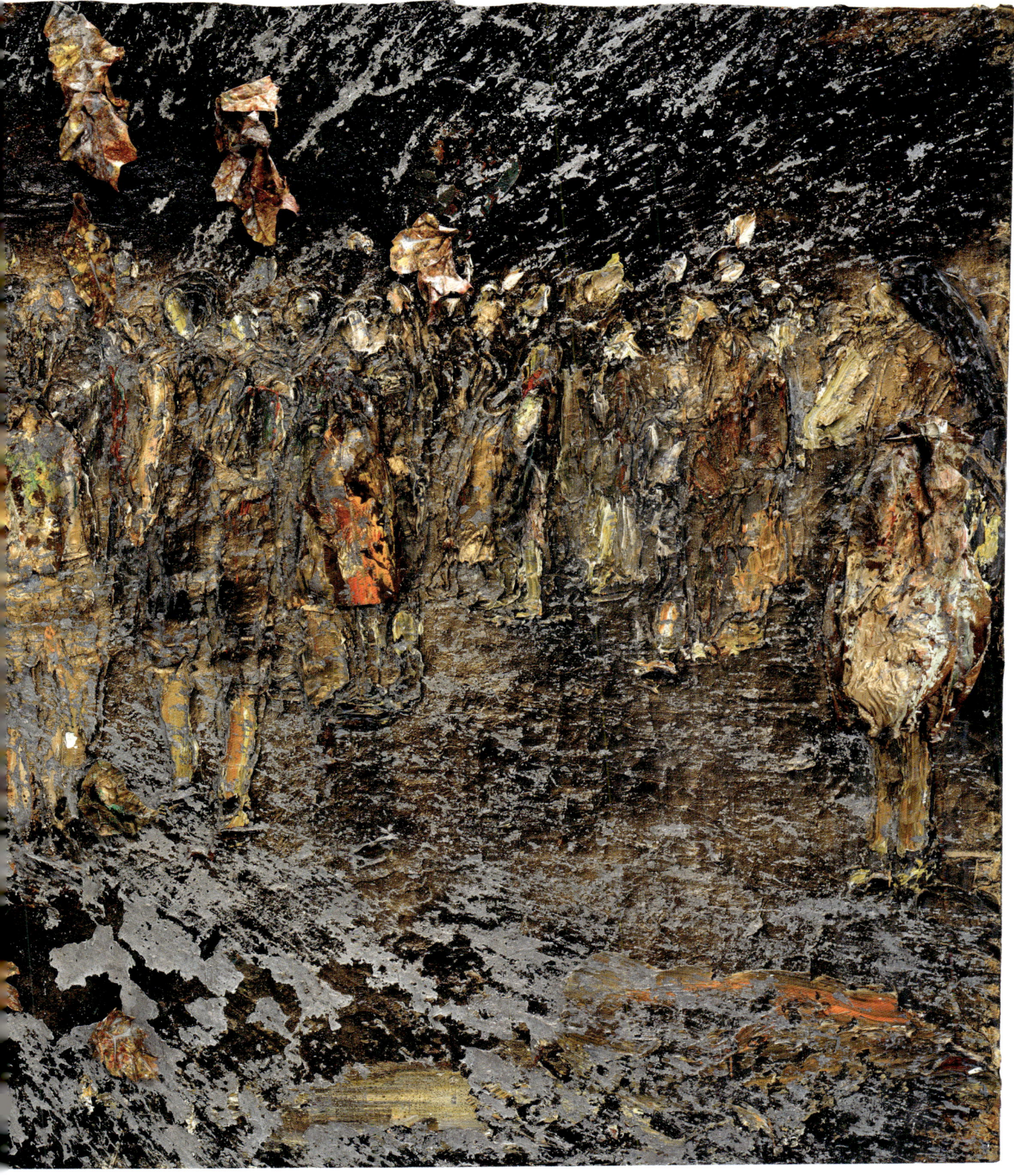

'Autumn Day'
Rainer Maria Rilke, c.1902

Lord: it is time. The huge summer has gone by.
Now overlap the sundials with your shadows,
and on the meadows let the wind go free.

Command the fruits to swell on tree and vine;
grant them a few more warm transparent days,
urge them on to fulfillment then, and press
the final sweetness into the heavy wine.

Whoever has no house now,
will never have one.
Whoever is alone will stay alone,
will sit, read, write long letters through the evening,
and wander the boulevards, up and down,
restlessly, while the dry leaves are blowing. [97]

from vividly describing nature to focusing on the human condition; the images of nature relate to the inside of man and his emotions. The third stanza links the present with the future, anticipating and stressing that 'whoever has no house now, will never have one'.

Anselm Kiefer's 2023 painting, *Wer jetzt kein Haus hat* (*Whoever has no house now*), references the third stanza of Rilke's poem in a dramatic way. The work is dominated by black, gold, grey, and glowing brown tones, featuring shimmering leaves on top of a densely populated canvas with multiple layers of thick paint and lead. Compared to his other recent works inspired by Rilke's 'Autumn' lyrics, *Die Blätter fallen* and *Und in den Nächten fällt die schwere Erde* (pp.200–3), this painting conveys a more energetic, wild, and dense impression. The emulsion, acrylic, oil, and shellac paint are complemented by the lead and string in a composition that appears endless, reminiscent of a leaf-covered forest ground, glittering beautifully on a warm and bright autumn day. On the top left side of the painting its title is handwritten thinly in chalk, adding an element of elegant fragility to the otherwise compact work.

The painting manages to translate Rilke's words into a dynamic visual language that suggests dry leaves blowing in the wind, while also conjuring a feeling of human restlessness, wandering alone in nature. It links to Kiefer's early paintings concerned with landscapes and a long tradition of Romanticism in German culture – including the work of such artists as Caspar David Friedrich and Phillip Otto Runge, who painted sublime encounters with nature in the late eighteenth century, often indicating a pantheistic faith – and German-language poems by authors ranging from Johann Wolfgang von Goethe to Rilke, who have used descriptions of nature to mirror human emotion.

Just like Rilke's poem, Kiefer's opaque painting also has different layers of meaning: not only can it be interpreted as a visual exploration of an autumn day in nature, but it can also be viewed as an homage to Rilke's beautiful poem and his elaborate art of writing. In the context of Kiefer's own life, it references his experiences of solitude, passionately dedicating his life to art. With regards to human life, autumn generally represents maturity and old age. Kiefer is aware of his temporal limitations: the melancholic title of the painting points at his own, tireless art production while growing old. Transience, the key theme of Rilke's poem, has been a major motif and characteristic of Kiefer's art for a long time, using perishable materials and techniques that enable his works to develop and transform even after they have left his studio for private or institutional collections. *Wer jetzt kein Haus hat*, featuring shellac, lead, and string, will probably not only outlive the artist but continue to change endlessly in a manner that is as restless as the artist himself.

Lena Fritsch

43 (pp.200–1)

DIE BLÄTTER FALLEN
(THE LEAVES ARE FALLING), *2017–23*

Emulsion, acrylic, oil, shellac, sediment
of an electrolysis, lead and string on
photograph mounted on canvas
126 × 250 cm

44 (pp.202–3)

UND IN DEN NÄCHTEN FÄLLT
DIE SCHWERE ERDE
(AND AT NIGHT, THE HEAVY EARTH
IS FALLING), *2017–23*

Emulsion, acrylic, oil, shellac, sediment
of an electrolysis, lead and string on
photograph mounted on canvas
126 × 250 cm

45 (pp.204–5)

WER JETZT KEIN HAUS HAT
(WHOEVER HAS NO HOUSE NOW), *2023*

Emulsion, acrylic, oil, shellac, lead, string
and chalk on canvas
190 × 330 cm

Collection of the artist

NOTES

1   Grey, Tobias, 'Anselm Kiefer: An Act of Remembrance', *Financial Times*, 6 January 2022.

2   Kiefer, Anselm, 'Occupations' ('*Besetzungen*'), *Interfunktionen* 12 (1975), pp.133–44.

3   Benjamin Buchloh cited in Mehring, Christine, 'Continental Schrift: The Story of *Interfunktionen*', *Artforum* 42, 9 (2004), p.179.

4   Adriani, Götz, *Baselitz, Richter, Polke, Kiefer: The Early Years of the Old Masters* (Dresden, 2019), p.239.

5   Anselm Kiefer in an interview with Alain Elkann, 16 January 2022, https://www.alainelkanninterviews.com/anselm-kiefer/ [accessed 20 April 2024].

6   Kiefer has expressed his respect for Caspar David Friedrich's work repeatedly, for example in an interview with Christian Weikop on 8 October 2013, quoted in Weikop, Christian, 'Forests of Myth, Forests of Memory', in Kathleen Soriano (ed.), *Anselm Kiefer* (London, 2014), p.32.

7   When using the term 'national identity' I understand this as a methodological construct that defines a set of cultural, social, and political features that could characterise Germany and distinguish it from other nations. These features are not only based on real facts but also on an imagined historical, cultural, and ethnic commonality, as argued by Benedict Anderson, who defines the 'nation' as an 'imagined community'. See Anderson, Benedict, *Imagined Communities: Reflections on the Origin and Spread of Nationalism* (London and New York, 1991).

8   Canetti, Elias, *Crowds and Power* (New York, 1978), p.173.

9   See also Sabine Schütz, who argues that Kiefer was familiar with such paintings. Schütz, Sabine, *Anselm Kiefer. Geschichte als Material. Arbeiten 1969–1983* (Köln, 1999), pp.214–20.

10   For a detailed analysis of *Ewiger Wald* see Lee, Robert G. and Sabine Wilke, 'Forest as Volk: *Ewiger Wald* and the Religion of Nature in the Third Reich', *Journal of Social and Ecological Boundaries* 1, 1 (Spring 2005), pp.21–46.

11   Heske, Franz, *German Forestry* (New York and Haven, 1939), pp.180–81.

12   Schama, Simon, *Landscape and Memory* (New York, 1995), p.10.

13   Weikop (2014), p.47.

14   Rosenthal, Nan, *Anselm Kiefer. Works on Paper in the Metropolitan Museum of Art* (New York, 1998), p.40.

15   Email correspondence between the author and Atelier Anselm Kiefer, April 2024.

16   Wilde, Oscar, 'The Nightingale and the Rose' [1888], East of the Web, https://www.eastoftheweb.com/short-stories/UBooks/NigRos.shtml [accessed 2 May 2024].

17   Stein, Gertrude, *Geography and Plays* [1922], The Project Gutenberg, 10 August 2010, https://www.gutenberg.org/files/33403/33403-h/33403-h.htm [accessed 2 May 2024].

18   Mansfield, Katherine, 'The Garden Party', [1922], The Project Gutenberg, 10 July 1998, https://www.gutenberg.org/files/1429/1429-h/1429-h.htm#chap02 [accessed 15 July 2024].

19   Stonely, Peter, 'Garden Party to Prison Cell: Oscar Wilde in Reading', Reading Museum, 20 November 2017, www.readingmuseum.org.uk/blog/garden-party-prison-cell-oscar-wilde-reading [accessed 2 July 2024].

20   Peake, Fabian, *Through a Window, Poems and Drawings* (Manchester, 1996), http://www.fabianpeake.co.uk/poetry/10.htm [accessed 2 May 2024].

21   Gibson, Robin, *Painting the Century, 101 Portrait Masterpieces 1900–2000* (London, 2000), p.82.

22   See Rosenthal, Mark, *Anselm Kiefer* (Chicago and Philadelphia, 1987), p.26.

23   Interview with the artist from April 1986, cited in Rosenthal (1987), p.26.

24   For a detailed analysis of Newton's use of the word 'emanation' see also Schliesser, Eric, 'Newtonian Emanation, Spinozism, Measurement and the Baconian Origins of the Laws of Nature', *Found Sci* 18 (2013), pp.449–66.

25   Kiefer, Anselm, 'Der nicht messbare Raum', *ZEIT Magazin* 49 (1988), p.8. Translated by the author.

26   Interview with Anselm Kiefer in Auping, Michael, *Anselm Kiefer: Heaven and Earth* (Fort Worth, 2005), p.172.

27   'Akademische Schinken, Rheinischer U-Boot-Krieg', *Der Spiegel*, 16 July 1948, https://www.spiegel.de/politik/akademische-schinken-a-80a589b2-0002-0001-0000-000044417748? [accessed 30 March 2024].

28   Ibid.

29   For more details on the cult see also Halsberghe, Gaston H., *The Cult of Sol Invictus* (Leiden, 1972).

30   White, Claretta, *Dancers in Action: How To #87* (California, undated c.1965), p.13.

31   Hall Art Foundation, *Anselm Kiefer: Frühwerk* (Derneburg, 2022), p.186.

32   This oft-cited statement, which became a dictum in German post-war cultural discourse, is part of a longer sentence in which Adorno talks about the dialectics of barbarism and culture/cultural critique. See Adorno, Theodor W., 'Kulturkritik und Gesellschaft' [1949], in Theodor W. Adorno, *Gesammelte Schriften, Band 10.1: Kulturkritik und Gesellschaft I* (Frankfurt, 1977), p.30.

33   Clearwater, Bonnie, 'Regeneration', in Norman Rosenthal, *Anselm Kiefer: Works from the Hall Collection* (New York, 2016), p.38.

34   See also the chapter about palettes in Arasse, Daniel, *Anselm Kiefer* (London and New York, 2014), pp.99–117.

35   Two years later, in 1976, Kiefer painted a flower still life with the same title, *Still Life is Exciting*. This painting is now in a private collection.

36   As quoted in Hall Art Foundation (2022), p.135.

37   For more information about Erna Lendvai-Dircksen see Schmölders, Claudia, 'Das Gesicht von Blut und Boden. Erna Lendvai-Dircksens Kunstgeographie', in Paula Diehl (ed.) *Körper im Nationalsozialismus: Bilder und Praxen* (Munich, 2006), pp.51–78.

38   Weiss, Matthias, 'Vermessen – fotografische Menscheninventare vor und aus der Zeit des Nationalsozialismus', in Ingeborg Reichle and Steffen Siegel (eds), *Maßlose Bilder: Visuelle Ästhetik der Transgression* (Munich, 2009), pp.359–77.

39   Eva König and Atelier Anselm Kiefer in an email to Lena Fritsch, 4 June 2024.

40   Rosenthal (1987), p.51.

41   Georg Baselitz in conversation with Andy Hall. See Hall Art Foundation (2022), p.140.

42   Ibid. p.192.

43   Hay, J. Stuart, *The Amazing Emperor Heliogabalus* (London, 1911), p.124.

44   Goldsworthy, Adrian, *How Rome Fell: Death of a Superpower* (New Haven, 2009), p.81; Sidebottom, Harry, *The Mad Emperor: Heliogabalus and the Decadence of Rome* (London, 2022).

45   A new publication by Australian literary scholar Peter Morgan describes George's circle and his poetry, arguing that through his writings George created a sense of connectedness and imagined possibilities of liaison, friendship, and community among homosexual men that did not exist before. See Morgan, Peter, *Stefan George: The Homosexual Imaginary* (Oxford, 2024).

46   Zimmermann, Rainer E, *Ernst Bloch: das Prinzip Hoffnung* (Berlin, 2016), p.99. Translated from the German by the author.

47   Adorno's statement is part of a longer sentence in which the philosopher talks about the dialectics of barbarism and culture/cultural critique. See Adorno (1977), p.30.

48   Named after the goddess Sati, who self-immolated because of her father Daksha's humiliation of her and her husband Shiva.

49   Anselm Kiefer as cited in Dermutz, Klaus, *Die Kunst geht knapp nicht unter. Anselm Kiefer im Gespräch mit Klaus Dermutz* (Berlin, 2010), p.240.

50   Ibid., p.192.
51   Ibid., p.99.
52   Ibid., p.250.
53   Ibid., p.142.
54   Ibid., p.119.
55   See also Melzer, Christien and Georg Josef Dietz, *Holzschnitt: 1400 bis heute* (Berlin 2022).
56   This is in contrast to *intaglio* printmaking techniques, whereby the printed lines are cut in the – mostly metal – matrix. Therefore, etchings and engravings, for instance, need to be printed under high pressure so the design can be transferred when the paper is pressed into the inked lines.
57   Landau, David and Peter Parshall, *The Renaissance Print 1470–1550* (New Haven and London, 1994), pp.21–3.
58   Parshall, Peter (ed.), *The Woodcut in Fifteenth-Century Europe*. Studies in the History of Art 75: Center for Advanced Study in the Visual Arts Symposium Papers 52 (New Haven and London, 2009), pp.9–15.
59   Thiem, Gunther, *German Woodcut in the Twentieth Century* (Stuttgart, 1984).
60   Hyman, James, 'Anselm Kiefer As Printmaker: A Catalogue, 1973–1993', *Print Quarterly* 14 (March 1997), pp.42–67; Hoerschelmann, Antonia (ed.), *Anselm Kiefer: The Woodcuts* (Vienna, 2016), pp.53–7.
61   Hyman (1997), p.45.
62   Hoerschelmann (2016), p.56.
63   Hall Art Foundation(2022), pp.91–3, 193. Hyman (1997) does not list these two series, but he acknowledges that his catalogue raisonné is provisional. He was neither aware of all existing prints nor of their different versions.
64   For an extensive list of sitters in Kiefer's woodcut portraits, see Rosenthal (1987) p.157, note 31.
65   Gachnang, Johannes and Theo Kneubühler, *Anselm Kiefer: Bilder und Bücher* (Bern, 1978).
66   The text, transcribed in full by the author: '*Lieber Jonny! Hier die ersten Hölzer. Gottfried Keller, einmal von der / Seite und einmal von vorne. Morgen kommen Ludmilla und Betty dran (Gottfrieds Freundinnen). Neben weiteren Köpfen sind auch noch Berge und Wildbäche zu schneiden. Den Wald, den ich habe, kann ich ja nicht für die Schweiz nehmen. / Die Zigarren kamen hier gut an. Schmecken sehr gut. Leider habe ich nur noch eine halbe Kiste. Bei dem Verbrauch müsste ich wohl wieder auf die Volkhavanna (Panatelas) umsteigen. Viele herzliche Grüße, Dein Anselm.*'
67   Ganzer, Karl Richard, *Das deutsche Führergesicht: 200 Bildnisse deutscher Kämpfer und Wegsucher aus zwei Jahrtausenden* (Munich, 1935).

68   Ibid., p.168.
69   Bartrum, Giulia, *Albrecht Dürer and His Legacy* (London, 2002), pp.77–91; Kuhlemann, Ute, 'Celebration of Dürer in Germany in the Nineteenth and Twentieth Centuries', in Bartrum (2002), pp.39–60.
70   Hoerschelmann (2016), cat. nos 24 and 28.
71   *Portrait of Maximimilian I* from around 1513–19 and *Portrait of Ulrich Varnbüler* dated 1522; see Bartrum (2002), cat. nos 267 and 163.
72   Ganzer (1935), p.54. Albrecht Dürer, *Portrait of Maximilian I*, 1519, oil on linden wood, 74 × 62 cm, Kunsthistorisches Museum, Vienna, inv.GG 825.
73   Walter Benjamin wrote about Klee's *Angelus Novus* repeatedly, most famously in *Über den Begriff der Geschichte* (*Theses on the Philosophy of History*), 1940. See Arendt, Hannah (ed.), *Illuminations: Essays and Reflections: Walter Benjamin* (New York, 1969), pp.253–64.
74   Anselm Kiefer in Zutter, Jörg, 'Drie vertegenwoordigers van een nieuwe Duitse schilderkunst', *Museumsjournaal Serie* 23, 1 (February 1978), p.61.
75   Edwards, Cyril, *The Nibelungenlied: The Lay of the Nibelungs* (Oxford, 2010), p.34.
76   Hall Art Foundation (2022), p.189.
77   For a detailed analysis of Kiefer's prints and a list of major early works, see Hyman (1997), pp.42–67.
78   Abteilung für Volksbildung im Magistrat der Stadt Berlin unter beratender Mitarbeit der Kammer der Kunstschaffenden und des Kulturbundes zur demokratischen Erneuerung Deutschlands [1946], *Verzeichnis der auszusondernen Literatur*, p.4, https://archive.org/details/AbteilungFuerVolksbildungDerStadtBerlinVerzeichnisDerAuszusondernndenLiteratur1946187S [accessed 9 April 2024].
79   For more details about the Norns see Bek-Pedersen, Karen, *Norns in Old Norse Mythology* (Edinburgh, 2011).
80   The idea of Norse mythology and the Vikings representing a Germanic monoculture (that Neo-Nazis worldwide still often refer to) can easily be proven wrong. The Viking's extensive travelling around the world and trade routes extending from Canada to Afghanistan led to a fusion of genes and cultures.
81   This statement, which became a dictum in German post-war cultural discourse, is part of a longer sentence in which Adorno talks about the dialectics of barbarism and culture/cultural critique. See Adorno (1977), p.30.
82   See Zilcosky, John, 'Poetry after Auschwitz? Celan and Adorno Revisited', *Deutsche Vierteljahrsschrift für Literaturwissenschaft und Geistesgeschichte, 2005–12* 79, 4 (2005),

pp.670–91.
83   Ibid, p.673.
84   Adorno, Theodor W., *Aesthetic Theory*, (trans.) C. Lenhardt (New York, 1984), p.27.
85   Meier, Cordula, *Anselm Kiefer: Die Rückkehr des Mythos in der Kunst* (Essen, 2013), p.111.
86   On Kiefer's use of landscapes metaphorically and as material in works relating to Paul Celan's poem, see also Schütz (1999), pp.290–312.
87   Kiefer, Anselm, *Art Will Survive its Ruins. Anselm Kiefer at the Collège de France* (Paris, 2011), p.275.
88   Kiefer's painting and the other works were incorporated into the Terrae Motus collection at the Fondazione Amelio – Instituto per l'Arte Contemporanea in 1982. The collection is now held at the Reggia di Caserta near Naples.
89   Frye, W. E., *After Waterloo: Reminiscences of European Travel 1815–1819* (London, 1908), https://www.gutenberg.org/ebooks/10939 [accessed 16 April 2024].
90   Anselm Kiefer as cited in his acceptance speech given on the occasion of the *Friedenspreis des Deutschen Buchhandels 2008*, www.friedenspreis-des-deutschen-buchhandels.de [accessed 28 May 2024].
91   Weikop, Christian, 'Forests of Myth, Forests of Memory', in Soriano (2014), pp.30–47. See also Hyman (1997) and Hyman, James, 'Anselm Kiefer As Printmaker, II. Alchemy and the Woodcut, 1993–1999', *Print Quarterly* 17, 1 (March 2000), pp.26–42.
92   Anselm Kiefer in conversation with the author in Paris, October 2015.
93   Ibid.
94   Richard Wagner, Brünhilde's libretto in Act III, at the end of *Götterdämmerung*, https://www.murashev.com/opera/Siegfried_libretto_English_Act_3 [accessed 3 May 2024].
95   Celan, Paul, 'Death Fugue', in *Poems of Paul Celan*, (trans. with an introduction by) Michael Hamburger (New York, 1989), pp.60–3.
96   Rilke, Rainer Maria, 'Autumn' [1902], in *Selected Poems of Rainer Maria Rilke: A Translation from the German and Commentary by Robert Bly* (New York, 1981) p.89.
97   Rilke, Rainer Maria, 'Autumn Day' [1902], in *The Selected Poetry of Rainer Maria Rilke*, (trans.) Stephen Mitchell (New York, 1982), p.11.

CONTRIBUTORS

Lena Fritsch is the Curator of Modern and Contemporary Art at the Ashmolean Museum, Oxford and responsible for exhibitions, displays, and acquisitions of international art. She teaches at the University of Oxford, V&A, and SOAS, London. Previously, she was a curator at Tate Modern, London and Hamburger Bahnhof, Berlin. Her recent publications include *Ashmolean NOW: Pio Abad* (2024), *Ashmolean NOW: Flora Yukhnovich × Daniel Crews-Chubb* (2023), *Tokyo: Art & Photography* (with Clare Pollard, 2021), *A.R. Penck: I Think in Pictures* (2019), *Ravens & Red Lipstick: Japanese Photography since 1945* (2018 and 2024), and *Giacometti* (with Frances Morris, 2017). She holds a PhD in art history from Bonn University and also studied at Keio University, Tokyo.

Stephanie Biron is the Assistant Director for Exhibitions and Programming at Kunstmuseum Schloss Derneburg. She contributed to the publication accompanying the museum's exhibition, *Anselm Kiefer: Frühwerk* (2022–3) and has a master's degree in art history from Hunter College, New York.

Richard Calvocoressi is an art historian and curator. He was an Assistant Keeper at Tate, London, Director of the Scottish National Gallery of Modern Art, and Director of the Henry Moore Foundation. In 2015 he joined Gagosian. His publications include *Anselm Kiefer: Morgenthau Plan* (2013), *Bacon Moore: Flesh and Bone* (with Martin Harrison, 2013), and *Georg Baselitz* (2021). He has known Anselm Kiefer since the early 1980s, when he was responsible for Tate acquiring Kiefer's 1973 *Parsifal* triptych.

Harriet Häußler holds a PhD in art history from the Ruhr-Universität in Bochum, Germany. Since 2009 she has been teaching and publishing widely about the art market and art of the twentieth and twenty-first centuries. She has authored numerous books and articles, including her thesis *Anselm Kiefer: Die Himmelspaläste* (2004) and her most recent book entitled *The Creators of the Art Market: From the Beginnings in Antiquity to Digitalisation in the Present Day* (2024). Häußler is a regular speaker at art market conferences and advises museums, artists, galleries, and auction houses. She is also a certified Systemic Business Coach.

Antonia Hoerschelmann studied art history, archaeology, and philosophy at the University of Vienna. Her first exhibitions and publications focused on Vienna at the turn of the century, and she also conducted research projects on art in the inter-war and post-war periods. Since 1992, she has been the Curator of Modern and Contemporary Art at the Albertina Museum, Vienna. Her numerous publications and exhibitions include projects about Egon Schiele, Oskar Kokoschka, Edvard Munch, Maria Lassnig, Arnulf Rainer, Georg Baselitz, and Martha Jungwirth. In 2016 at Albertina, she curated the first major exhibition dedicated to Anselm Kiefer's woodblock prints.

Liz Rideal is an artist and writer living in London. Professor at the Slade School of Fine Art, she has received a Leverhulme Fellowship, British Academy Award, and Scholarship at the British School at Rome. Her publications include books on self-portraiture, portraiture, and the best-selling title *How to Read Paintings* (2014). Rideal has exhibited widely in museums and galleries in Europe and America with three solo shows in New York. Her artwork is held in public collections worldwide, including Tate, London, Museet for Fotokunst, Denmark, the Philadelphia Art Museum, and the Metropolitan Museum of Art, New York. www.lizrideal.com

Lisa Saltzman is a Professor of the History of Art and the inaugural Emily Rauh Pulitzer '55 Chair in Modern and Contemporary Art at Bryn Mawr College. She is a specialist in post-war and contemporary art, as well as the history and theory of photography. Saltzman is the author of *Anselm Kiefer and Art after Auschwitz* (1999), *Making Memory Matter: Strategies of Remembrance in Contemporary Art* (2006), *Daguerreotypes: Fugitive Subjects, Contemporary Objects* (2015), and the co-editor, with Eric Rosenberg, of *Trauma and Visuality in Modernity* (2006). Her work has been widely anthologised and translated. Educated at Princeton and Harvard, she has been awarded fellowships from the Radcliffe Institute of Advanced Study, Clark Art Institute and Guggenheim Foundation.

Sabine Schütz is an art historian and art critic focusing on modern and contemporary art. She has worked as a curator at various German museums and has taught art theory and art history at the University of Cologne. Her publications include *Anselm Kiefer: Geschichte als Material 1969–1983* (1999), and numerous texts on Georg Baselitz, Tracey Emin, Gerhard Richter, David Salle, and many more. She lives between Germany and France.

An Van Camp is the Christopher Brown Curator of Northern European Art at the Ashmolean Museum, Oxford. Most recently, she curated *Bruegel to Rubens: Great Flemish Drawings* (Oxford, 2024) and co-curated *Young Rembrandt* (Leiden and Oxford, 2019–20). Before joining the Ashmolean in 2015, she was Curator of Dutch and Flemish Drawings and Prints at the British Museum, where she co-curated *Drawing in Silver and Gold: Leonardo to Jasper Johns* (Washington and London, 2015). She is also a member of the Editorial Board of *Print Quarterly* and *Master Drawings*.

Christian Weikop is Professor of Modern and Contemporary German art at the University of Edinburgh. He has published extensively on twentieth-century German art, including publications on Anselm Kiefer for international art institutions, namely Royal Academy, London (2014), Tate, London (2016), Nationalgalerie, Berlin (2019), Studies in Photography, Edinburgh (2022), and the LaM, Lille (2023).

CHRONOLOGY

CHRONOLOGY
THE EARLY YEARS

Autobiography from 'Anselm Kiefer', at the Bonner Kunstverein,
12 March–24 April 1977

Detailed chronology compiled by Stephanie Biron and originally published
in *Anselm Kiefer – Frühwerk (Early Works)* by the Hall Art Foundation
in conjunction with the related exhibition at Kunstmuseum Schloss
Derneburg, 2022–3.

1945 **8 March 1945, born in Donaueschingen; Grandmother; Ruins;
      black forests**
      Anselm Kiefer is born in Donaueschingen on 8 March 1945 in the
      basement of a hospital. For the first six years of his life he lives with his
      grandmother. Kiefer describes the area where he was brought up as one
      destroyed by the war. His grandfather dies when he is three years old and
      subsequently he visits the grave daily with his grandmother. She teaches
      him 'Maikäfer, flieg' ('Cockchafer Fly'), a German folk song with lyrics that
      describe a father at war.

1951 **Moved to the parents' in Ottersdorf; Primary school; Heaven-Hell;
      Rhine; Alluvial Forest; Border**
      At the age of six, Kiefer moves to live with his parents in Ottersdorf, near
      the Black Forest and the Rhine; he attributes the two styles of landscapes
      as a significant influence on his work. Baden is occupied by the French,
      and the Rhine acts as a division between the two countries. This division
      is palpable to Kiefer at this age. His father, who had been an officer in
      Nazi Germany, is not permitted to work as a teacher immediately after the
      war. He encourages his son to paint, and many of Kiefer's early childhood
      paintings and drawings are still in the possession of the artist today.
      His early influences were Paul Klee and Willi Baumeister. He is raised
      Catholic, practices as an altar boy, and learns the Latin Mass by heart.

1954 Kiefer makes his first book at nine years old, an illustrated retelling of
      stories including 'Sinbad the Sailor' and 'Genoveva'.

1956 **Secondary School in Rastatt; Rilke; Rodin**
      Kiefer begins secondary school at the Ludwig-Wilhelm-Gymnasium,
      Rastatt, Baden. He reads poetry in school, including 'Spaziergang' ('A
      Walk') by Rainer Maria Rilke, 'Todesfuge' ('Death Fugue') by Paul Celan,
      and various poems by Stefan George. At the age of fourteen or fifteen
      he hears Richard Wagner's *Lohengrin* on the radio. Around the same
      age he also copies a painting by Vincent van Gogh.

1961 At the age of sixteen, Kiefer makes, among other drawings, a charcoal
      portrait of his grandmother, which he later includes in the composition

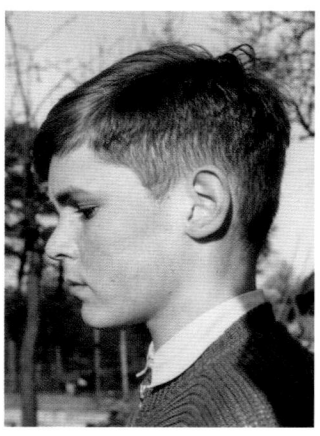

Anselm Kiefer, 1958

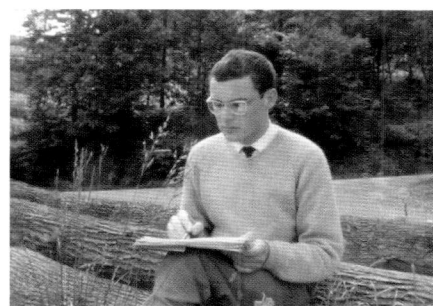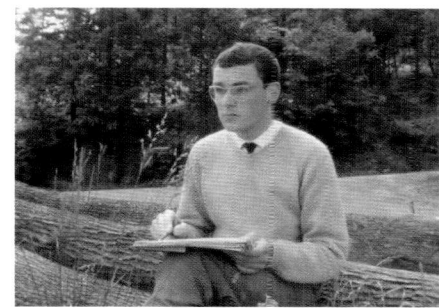

for *Landschaft mit Kopf* (1973). As an adult, he refers to his grandmother as '*eine Art Mutterersatz*', a kind of 'mother substitute'.

1963 Jean-Walter-Prize; Van Gogh; Holland; France
Kiefer is a recipient of the Bourse Zellidja, a scholarship for high-school students, started by architect Jean Walter, to embark on a month-long study trip on the theme of their choice. For his project, Kiefer proposes and completes a tour that follows in the biographical footsteps of Van Gogh. The trip includes Holland, Belgium, Paris, and the south of France. While in Paris, he is permitted to visit the atelier of Christian Dior and subsequently makes various figure sketches. In the south of France, he works for a few weeks for a farmer in Fourques, near Arles. Kiefer produces an illustrated journal with sketches of landscapes and portraits from this trip and considers becoming a writer. He receives the Jean Walter Prize for this travel journal: he was the first German student to do so.

1965 Qualifying exam; Italy; Sweden; Study of Law and French; Freiburg
Kiefer begins studying law and Romance (Neo-Latin) languages in Freiburg. He plans to be an artist but, at this time, does not think it necessary to attend an art academy.

1966 Paris; Haute Couture; Le Corbusier (La Tourette); Art studies under Peter Dreher, Freiburg
At the age of 21, Kiefer spends three weeks at the Dominican Order priory of Sainte Marie de la Tourette, outside of Lyon, studying the architecture of Le Corbusier and participating with the monks in daily prayer. He begins his formal art school training with the painter Peter Dreher at the School of Fine Arts of Freiburg. During his early years at the school, Kiefer experiments with ephemeral work, including food materials, much of which he destroys. Through Dreher, he meets the artist Rainer Küchenmeister, who had been imprisoned in the Moringen youth concentration camp. Kiefer sources material from *Tagebuch eines Frontsoldaten*, a magazine collected by his father, later using it in a project titled *Die Überschwemmung Heidelbergs* (1969).

1969 Art studies under Horst Antes, Karlsruhe; Motorcycle; Marble; Jean Genet; Huysmans; Ludwig II of Bavaria; Paestum; Adolf Hitler; Julia; Paintings: Heroic Landscapes
After transferring from Freiburg, Kiefer begins study with the artist Horst Antes at the Academy of Fine Arts, Karlsruhe. Antes accompanies him on trips, initiating introductions to Sigmar Polke and Gerhard Richter in Düsseldorf, and George Segal and Louise Nevelson in New York. Kiefer is also included in a group exhibition titled 'Klasse Antes' at the Galerie Zelle in Reutlingen, and in the annual exhibition of the Deutscher

Künstlerbund (Association of German Artists), Hanover. While in school, he listens, for the first time, to a record with speeches by Adolf Hitler, and begins to inquire more closely about Germany's recent fascist past. In the summer, he travels through Switzerland, France, and Italy to historic sites, where he takes photographic self-portraits parodying the Nazi salute in his father's Wehrmacht uniform in what he calls *Besetzungen* (*Occupations*). From the photographs, Kiefer develops thematically related work in other media, including artist's books such as *Für Jean Genet*, which was originally acquired by Georg Baselitz and is now in the Hall Collection. In his books, paintings, and watercolours, Kiefer begins adding handwritten inscriptions. He meets his first wife, Julia, and has his first solo exhibition at the Galerie am Kaiserplatz in Karlsruhe, invited by gallerist Helmut Rehme.

1970   Own books on heroic allegories, Occupations, holes in the sky; State examinations, German Academic Scholarship Foundation; Study with Joseph Beuys, Düsseldorf; Paintings on Trinity, Quaternity, above-below, I—You
Following completion of his studies and receipt of a scholarship from the Studienstiftung des deutschen Volkes (German Academic Scholarship Foundation), Kiefer starts meeting with the artist Joseph Beuys for informal discussions. The sporadic meetings last through early 1973, during which time Beuys encourages Kiefer in his actions and performances and disagrees with any interpretations of neo-fascism. Kiefer submits the *Besetzungen* photographs as part of his final portfolio for his degree in Karlsruhe, supported by his professor Peter Dreher. He exhibits artist books in a group exhibition titled '100 Artistes dans la Ville', in Montpellier. To draw attention to the books and this conceptually new medium, he includes a large painted self-portrait, *Heroische Sinnbilder (Selbstporträt),* depicting himself in his father's uniform and performing the '*Sieg Heil*' salute. For a short period, until 1974, Kiefer stops making artist's books.

1971   Marriage to Julia; Odenwald; Wood; Grain; Richard Wagner; Son Daniel; Winter Spring Summer Fall; Watercolours
After marrying, Kiefer and Julia move to Hornbach in the Odenwald, a small village east of Mannheim, where she takes a job as a teacher. Comments and a reserved reception by the villagers, along with the area's economic decline caused by redistricting after the war, will inspire Kiefer's projects including *Ausbrennen des Landkreises Buchen*. The couple have their first child, Daniel. Kiefer spends most of his time working in the attic studio space of a former schoolhouse built in 1930, and the imagery of both the studio space and the wood grain with which it is permeated begin to populate his work. He paints the forest landscape and works often with watercolour. His paintings also begin to incorporate names from Norse mythology (*Nibelungenlied*). In December, Kiefer joins one of Beuys's actions, *Rettet den Wald* (*Save the Woods*), in Grafenberger Woods, Düsseldorf. Beuys's performance was organised in reaction to a proposed plan to clear part of the woods for country-club tennis courts. Kiefer's participation in the performance is documented in the photograph, *Save the Woods*. Here, Kiefer is pictured standing next to Beuys together with approximately 50 students and disciples, who theatrically sweep the woods with birch brooms as a symbolic gesture to expel the bourgeoisie.

1972   Kiefer continues meeting with Beuys. During this time, he develops work for exhibitions in subsequent years, resulting in a prolific period of new subjects between 1973 and 1974. He continues working with watercolour,

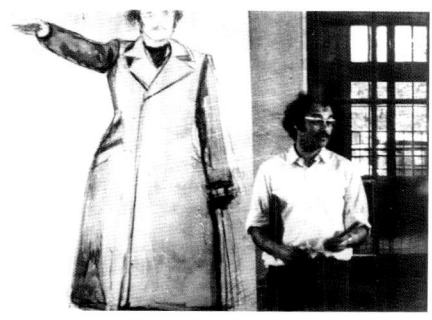

Kiefer paints *Heroische Sinnbilder*, 1969

producing works like *Vor Oskar Wilde für Julia*, completed the following year. Kiefer begins a series of large-scale works of the attic space in Hornbach, including *Holzraum* (*Wooden Room*), measuring 3 meters in height, now in the collection of the Museum of Modern Art New York, and later, *Der Nibelungen Leid* (*The Sorrow of the Nibelungs*; 1973).

1973 **Boulder-rock; Baselitz; Nibelung; Parsifal; Michael Werner**
Kiefer exhibits his work in the group exhibition '14 mal 14', curated by Klaus Gallwitz at the Staatliche Kunsthalle Baden-Baden. Georg and Elke Baselitz are introduced to his work, and after buying all the work in the exhibition they become his first collectors in Germany. One of the works acquired from that exhibition is *Ich – Du* (1971), a group of paintings with inscriptions to Julia and Daniel. Kiefer later visits Baselitz in Osthofen and then in Derneburg. At Beuys's recommendation, he meets gallerist Michael Werner, who would later introduce him to the artists A. R. Penck, Marcel Broodthaers, and James Lee Byars, and the work of French intellectuals including Alain-Fournier, Maurice Blanchot, and Georges Bataille. Werner hosts Kiefer's first exhibition at the gallery, 'Nothung', in which Wagner's opera *Parsifal* is symbolised in the form of a fallen sword. The Swiss curator Johannes Gachnang invites Kiefer to exhibit at the Goethe-Institut in Amsterdam, in an exhibition titled 'Der Nibelungen Leid'. Early collectors include Martin Visser and Martijn Sanders.

1974 **Works of the scorched earth; Heliogabalus; Johnny; Stefan George; Norwegian light; Hans Henny Jahn *(sic)*; Sick art; How To Paint**
Following a working relationship with Gachnang, Kiefer inscribes and dedicates many of his works to 'Johnny'. He often rolls and sends new work to Gachnang in Amsterdam by train from Germany. Inspired and amused by '*How To*' manuals produced and distributed in North America, Kiefer makes the *How to Paint* series. The paintings in the series, with compositions that feature a painter's palette, were acquired by Baselitz and are now in the Hall Collection. Other subjects include Norwegian lights, *Heliogabal* (1974–5; which Kiefer presents at the Rotterdam Arts Foundation), *Stefan!* and *Stefan II* (1975), and *Kranke Kunst* (*Sick Art*) (1974). Kiefer exhibits again at Galerie Michael Werner in a solo exhibition titled 'Malerei der verbrannten Erde'.

1975 **Thirty years old; Created books: Ausbrennen (Cauterization), Versenken (Sinking), Verholzen (Lignifying), Versanden (Covering with Sand); Mushrooms; Daughter Sarah**
When Kiefer is 30 years old, photograph excerpts from the *Occupations* series are published for the first time in *Interfunktionen*, a journal on art theory published in West Germany and edited by Benjamin Buchloh. It would be the publication's final issue, and Buchloh later became a staunch critic of Kiefer's work. Kiefer continues making books with growing interest in alchemy. The burning of the pages, which Kiefer works on in the basement of his home in Hornbach, becomes material to the conceptualisation of works like *Ausbrennen des Landkreises Buchen* (1974). He stages naval battles in a bath filled with water for photographs that serve as a template for the series *Unternehmen Seelöwe*. Anselm and Julia's daughter, Sarah, is born.

1976 **Siegfried forgets Brunhild; Maria; The essential is not yet done**
Kiefer focuses on the subjects Siegfried and Brunhild, characters from Wagner's opera cycle *Der Ring des Nibelungen* (*The Ring of the Nibelung*), and exhibits these works at Galerie Michael Werner in Cologne. This theme, and in particular the final scene of the opera, *Götterdämmerung*, in which Brunhild throws herself onto a pyre,

becomes the subject of various paintings and watercolours. Kiefer makes work with reference to Mary, mother of Christ, whose name he would later incorporate in work titles including *Ave Maria*, *Maria in den Dornwald ging* (*Mary walks amid the thorns*) and *Maria im Rosenhag* (*Madonna of the Rose Bower*). In the continuing *Scorched Earth* painting series, *Unternehmen "Trappenfang"* is completed – a landscape with dredged pathways inspired by the German initiative to take the Kerch peninsula at the eastern end of Crimea. Kiefer's autobiography ends with the suggestion that he still has work to accomplish.

1977   The first retrospective of Kiefer's work is held at the Bonner Kunstverein, for which the autobiography is assembled. He is represented in *documenta 6* with the inclusion of a few artist's books. He begins the *Wege der Weltweisheit* woodcut series and sends the first six portraits struck from the block to Gachnang, with an inscribed letter describing his progress:

> 'Dearest Jonny! Here are the first woodcuts. Gottfried Keller, once from the side and once from the front. Tomorrow Ludmilla + Betty come (Gottfried's female friends). Besides other heads, there are still mountains and mountain torrents to cut. The forest that I have, I cannot take for Switzerland.'

The letter suggests the productivity on the woodcuts is so massive that Kiefer cannot bring them all to Bern in the following year. Meanwhile, Kiefer explores imagery of the painter's palette in a series titled *Donauquelle*, and paints subjects inspired by Norse mythology, including *Yggdrasil* (1978). Galerie Michael Werner opens another exhibition of his work the same year ('Ritt an die Weichsel'). Kiefer begins a large woodcut series titled *Grane*, in which the horse in Wagner's opera *Götterdämmerung* becomes central to the composition.

1978   A solo exhibition at Kunsthalle Bern is organised by Gachnang. In the catalogue's introduction, Gachnang explains a commitment to Kiefer's work, and a decision to change the exhibition to focus on two recent series: *Wege der Weltweisheit* and *Noch ist Polen nicht verloren*. The former collages the individual woodcut portraits of cultural figures including Martin Heidegger, Rainer Maria Rilke, and Friedrich Gottlieb Klopstock, among others, and is the subject of a separate exhibition at the Galerie Maier-Hahn in Düsseldorf. The exhibition in Bern includes early books exhibited for the first time (including *Für Jean Genet*), along with paintings from the *Engel* and *Unternehmen* series. Kiefer completes a multiple book with 25 unique painted covers, titled *Die Donauquelle*, that is published as an edition by Galerie Michael Werner.

1979   Kiefer has two solo exhibitions in the Netherlands, one at the Stedelijk Van Abbemuseum in Eindhoven (in which *Landschaft mit Kopf* (1973) is included), and a second presenting books at the Galerie Helen van der Meij in Amsterdam. His working relationship with Michael Werner ends after the Eindhoven exhibition. He continues developing subjects including *Urd, Werdandi, Skuld (Die Nornen)* (1981) and *Ritt an die Weichsel* (1980–81).

1980   Klaus Gallwitz curates the German Pavilion of the Venice Biennale, pairing Kiefer's work in presentation with Baselitz. Kiefer is 35 years old. The four actions inspiring his participation, *Verbrennen Versenken Verholzen Versanden*, are first mentioned in his autobiography in 1975, quoted herein. Alongside his paintings, Baselitz presents his first

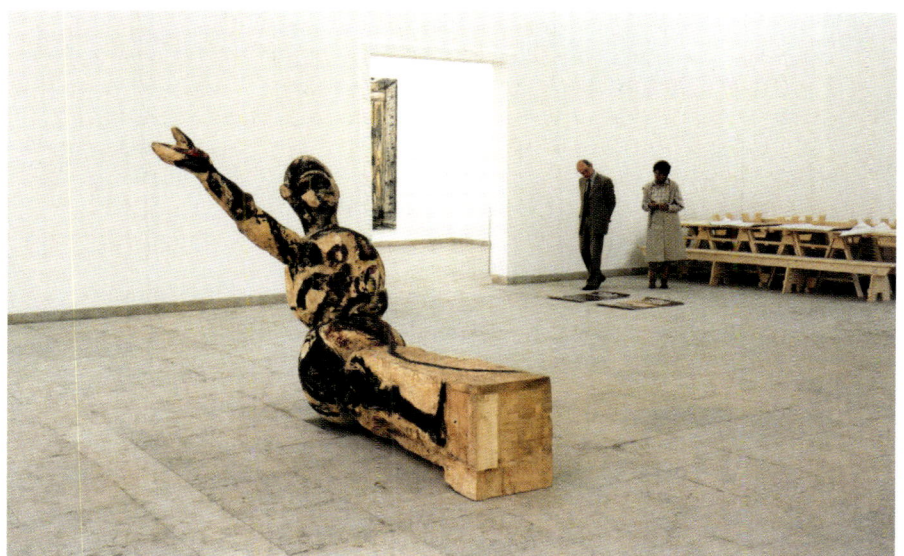

sculpture, *Modell für eine Skuptur* (1979/80), a reclining figure carved in wood with its arm raised. Kiefer includes *Wege der Weltweisheit* (1977), the large woodcut in the Hall Collection, among other works. He has additional solo exhibitions at three institutions – Mannheimer Kunstverein, Württembergischer Kunstverein Stuttgart, and the Groninger Museum, Netherlands, in which his paintings, books and photographic works are presented.

1981   Kiefer's work is included in the prestigious group exhibition at the Royal Academy of Arts, London, titled 'A New Spirit in Painting' and curated by Norman Rosenthal, Christos Joachimides, and Nicholas Serota. He has seven solo exhibitions, including those with gallerists Six Friedrich, Paul Maenz (who shows Kiefer's work in Germany regularly until 1989), and Marian Goodman (the first to exhibit his work in the US). Kiefer's paintings and watercolours notably focus on the Margarete-Shulamith refrain from the poem 'Todesfuge' by Paul Celan, a poem Kiefer first encountered as a teenager. He is similarly inspired by the poetry of Victor Hugo. At the same time, Kiefer incorporates the interior halls of buildings made prominent under the National Socialist Party, including those designed by Albert Speer, in works such as *Innenraum* or those dedicated *Dem unbekannten Maler* (*To the Unknown Painter*). He acquires a factory building in the town of Buchen in Baden-Württemberg, which will allow the scale of his work to increase.

1982   In woodcuts titled *Der Rhein*, Kiefer combines the imagery of German National Socialist architecture with the river, occasionally incorporating portraits from the *Wege der Weltweisheit* series. He develops from the architecture series the imagery of an impaled palette, referring to the personified assemblage as *Dem unbekannten Maler*. His solo exhibition, including paintings and books, opens at the Whitechapel Gallery in London, and he has five solo exhibitions at galleries, including Mary Boone in New York. Kiefer is on the precipice of a new gallery relationship with Anthony d'Offay, and a touring retrospective in the US, after which he becomes commercially successful. He will expand his studio practice in 1988 to include a former brick manufacturer in Höpfingen, and eventually acquire the La Ribaute, a silk factory in Barjac in 1992, formally leaving Germany for France.

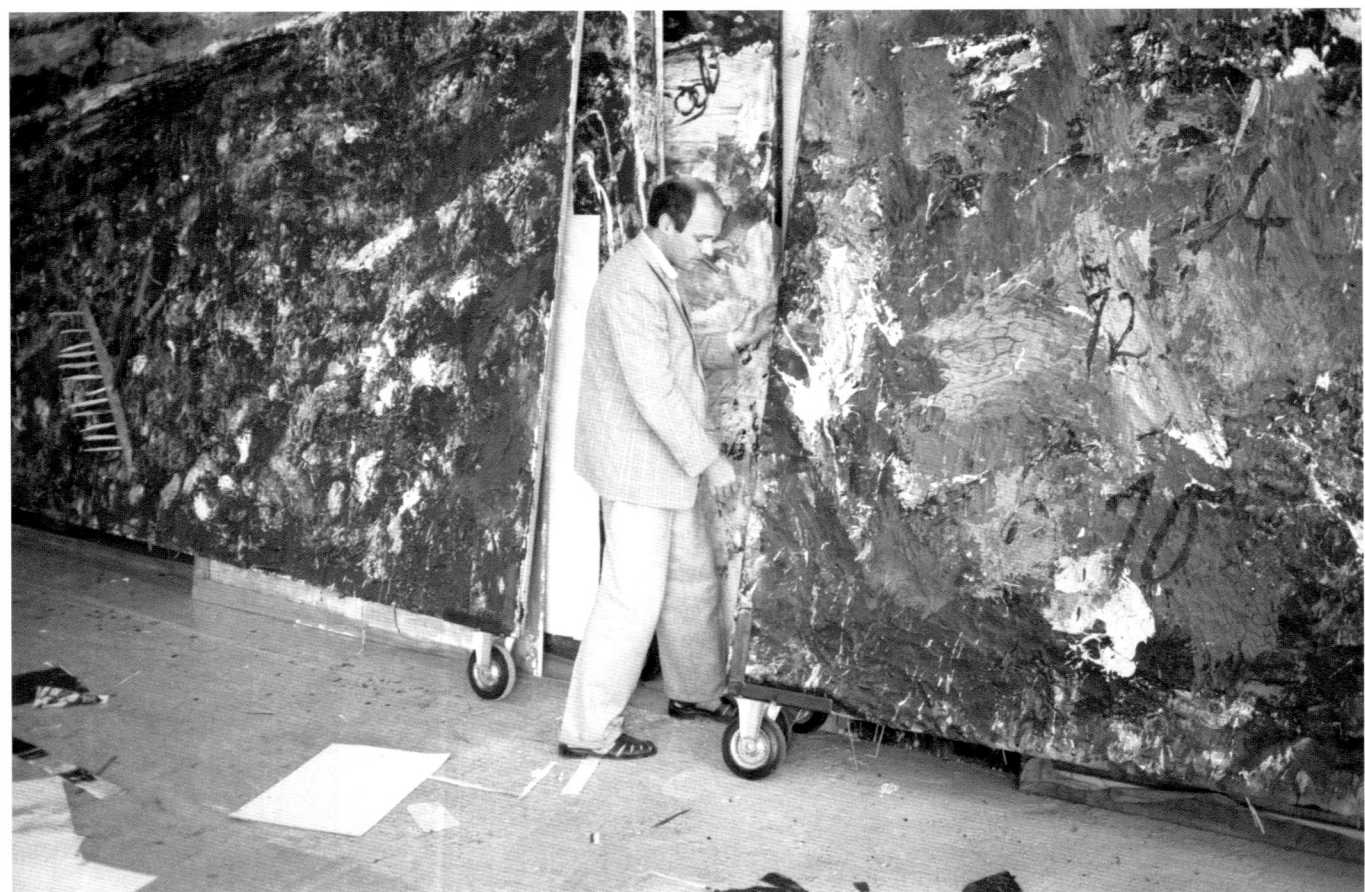

Anselm Kiefer in his studio,
August 1982

Sources

Adriani, Götz, *Baselitz, Richter, Polke, Kiefer: The Early Years of the Old Masters* (Dresden, 2019)

Baselitz, Georg, 'Georg Baselitz im Gespräch mit Andy Hall', interview with Andy Hall, 12 July 2022

Chauveau, Marc, *Anselm Kiefer à La Tourette* (Paris, 2019)

Clearwater, Bonnie, 'Regeneration', in *Anselm Kiefer: Works from the Hall Collection* (New York, 2017), pp.29–53

Gachnang, Johannes and Marianne Schmidt-Miescher, *Anselm Kiefer: Bilder und Bücher* (Bern, 1978)

Hecht, Axel and Werner Krüger, 'Venedig 1980: Aktuelle Kunst made in Germany', *Art: Das Kunstmagazin* 6 (June 1980), pp.40–53

Jocks, Heinz-Norbert, 'Anselm Kiefer. Das Taktile und das Intellektuelle', *Kunstforum* 238 (2016), pp.222–37, https://www.kunstforum.de/artikel/anselm-kiefer-6/ [accessed 14 July 2024]

Kiefer, Anselm, 'Painting with the Poets', interview with Alain Elkann, 22 November 2021, https://www.alainelkanninterviews.com/anselm-kiefer/ [accessed 14 July 2024]

Kiefer, Anselm, 'Café Deutschland im Gespräch mit der ersten Kunstszene der BRD: Anselm Kiefer', interview with Franziska Leuthäußer, Café Deutschland, Städel Museum, 26 January 2016, https://cafedeutschland.staedelmuseum.de/gespraeche/anselm-kiefer [accessed 14 July 2024]

SWR Retro, 'Jean-Walter-Preis für Anselm Kiefer', SWR-Abendschau, Erstausstrahlung, 24 June 1964, https://www.ardmediathek.de/video/swr-retro-abendschau/jean-walter-preis-fueranselm-kiefer/swr/Y3JpZDovL3N3ci5kZS9hZXgvbzExNzA0MTk [accessed 14 July 2024]

Von Stetten, Dorothea and Evelyn Weiss, *Anselm Kiefer* (Bonn, 1977)

Weikop, Christian, 'Forests of Myth, Forests of Memory', in Richard Davey, Kathleen Soriano and Christian Weikop, *Anselm Kiefer* (London, 2014), pp.30–47

Weikop, Christian, '"Occupations": A Difficult Reception', in *Heroic Symbols 1969 by Anselm Kiefer* (London, 2016), https://www.tate.org.uk/research/in-focus/heroic-symbols-anselm-kiefer/difficult-reception-occupations [accessed 14 July 2024]

Anselm Kiefer: Early Works
14 February to 15 June 2025

Copyright © Ashmolean Museum, University of Oxford, 2025

Lena Fritsch, Christian Weikop, Liz Rideal, Sabine Schütz, Lisa Saltzman, Antonia Hoerschelmann, An Van Camp, Harriet Häußler, Richard Calvocoressi, and Stephanie Biron have asserted their moral rights to be identified as the authors of this work.

British Library Cataloguing in Publications Data
A catalogue record for this book is available from the British Library

ISBN: 978-1-910807-64-4

p.8: *Wer jetzt kein Haus hat* (*Whoever has no house now*), 2023 (detail)

Copy-edited by Lizzy Silverton
Designed by Ocky Murray
Printed and bound in the UK by Belmont Press

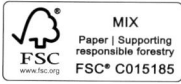

For further details of Ashmolean titles please visit:
www.ashmolean.org/shop

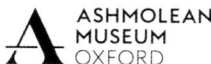 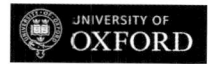

Presented in partnership with the Hall Art Foundation

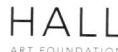

HALL
ART FOUNDATION

Supported by:

Patrons of the Ashmolean Museum

WHITE CUBE

Photo Credits for Works from the Hall Collection:
Tom Powel Imaging: pp.17–25, 79–93, 95, 98–109, 133–43; Mark-Woods.com: pp.45, 110; Steven Brookes Studio: pp.26–7, 34–5, 48, 58–9, 67, 68, 196; Adam Reich: pp.31, 40–1, 71, 74, 97, 122, 146–51, 153, 172–3, 174–5; Roman März: pp.128–9; Henner Rosenkranz: pp.56–57; Arthur Evans: pp.166, 171.

All works by Anselm Kiefer from the Hall Collection with the exceptions of:

p.10 © Till Brönner

p.13 Photograph by Volker Diehl. Courtesy of Volker Diehl

p.28 Alte Nationalgalerie, Berlin (NG 9/85)

p.29 Photograph courtesy of Gagosian gallery

p.32 © Anselm Kiefer

p.33 (left) Image copyright the Metropolitan Museum of Art/Art Resource/Scala, Florence (1995.14.2)

p.33 (right) Image copyright the Metropolitan Museum of Art/Art Resource/Scala, Florence (1995.14.4)

p.37 Photograph by Daniel Blau

p.42 State Museum Schwerin

p.43 Lex-Film, Albert Graf von Pestalozza

p.47 Image copyright the Metropolitan Museum of Art/Art Resource/Scala, Florence (1995.14.10)

p.51 Image copyright the Metropolitan Museum of Art/Art Resource/Scala, Florence (2000.96.3)

p.54 (left) © National Gallery, London (NG6322)

p.54 (right) Collection Kröller-Müller Museum, Otterlo, the Netherlands, formerly in the Visser collection, acquired with support from the Rembrandt Association, partly thanks to the Prins Bernhard Cultuurfonds. Photograph by Tom Haartsen

p.55 (left) Bavarian National Museum, Munich

p.55 (right) © Gerhard Richter. Lidice Gallery, Lidice, Czech Republic

p.60 Maisons de Victor Hugo, Paris, Wikimedia Commons

p.61 (left) GRANGER - Historical Picture Archive/Alamy Stock Photo

p.61 (right) Shakeyjon/Alamy Stock Photo

p.64 © Ashmolean Museum, University of Oxford

p.72 (left and right) Published by Walter T. Foster, California c.1965

p.73 (left) Published by Walter T. Foster ('How to Draw' series) c.1960s

p.73 (right) National Gallery of Art, Washington DC, US, Gift of Mrs John W. Simpson

p.76 (left and right) Published by Walter T. Foster, California c.1965

p.77 Frankfurt a.M: Umschau Verlag

p.94 © Anselm Kiefer

p.112 Saint Louis Art Museum (58:2001). Gift of Mr and Mrs John Wooten Moore

p.113 Historic Images/Alamy Stock Photo

p.120 Photography by Jochen Littkemann. Private Collection

p.121 (left) Bastion of Saint Roch, Wikimedia Commons

p.121 (right) Collection Kröller-Müller Museum, Otterlo, the Netherlands, formerly in the Visser collection, acquired with support from 56 private persons and the Ministry of Education, Culture and Science. Photograph by Tom Haartsen

p.124 Fandom Wiki

p.125 Neue Pinakothek, Munich. Photograph by Blauel/Gnamm – ARTOTHEK

p.130 Freiburg: Herder

p.144 Minneapolis Institute of Art, US. The Ethel Morrison Van Derlip Fund, 1965

p.145 © Ashmolean Museum, University of Oxford

p.155 (left) © Ashmolean Museum, University of Oxford

p.155 (right) Gift of Fania and Gershom Scholem, Jerusalem, John Herring, Marlene and Paul Herring, Jo Carole and Ronald Lauder, New York Collection The Israel Museum, Jerusalem B87.0994. Photograph ©The Israel Museum, Jerusalem by Elie Posner

p.161 Wikimedia Commons

p.164 Atelier Albrecht

p.165 Collection Städel Museum, Frankfurt am Main, photograph: Galerie Thaddaeus Ropac, Salzburg. BPK-Bildangentur

p.168 Wikimedia Commons

p.169 Image copyright the Metropolitan Museum of Art/Art Resource/Scala, Florence (1995.14.36)

p.176 (left) Digital image, the Museum of Modern Art, New York/Scala, Florence (184.1996)

p.176 (right) Munich: Deutscher Volksverlag

p.177 bpk/Deutsches Historisches Museum/Indra Desnica

p.180 Collection Kröller-Müller Museum, Otterlo, the Netherlands, formerly in the Visser collection, acquired with support from 56 private persons and the Ministry of Education, Culture and Science. Photograph by Tom Haartsen

p.181 (left) Wikimedia Commons

p.181 (right) Ivy Close Images/Alamy Stock Photo

p.190 (left) Stuttgart: Deutsche Verlags-Anstalt

p.190 (right) Wikimedia Commons

p.191 Terrae Motus collection of Caserta. By permission of the Ministry of Culture

p.194 © Ashmolean Museum, University of Oxford

p.198 Museum Boijmans, Rotterdam (3070 MK)

pp.200–05 © Anselm Kiefer

p.214 Atelier Anselm Kiefer

p.215 SWR Abendschau, 1963. Archive number 71511, ESD: 24.06.1064

p.219 Th. Moeller

p.220 Photograph by Volker Diehl. Courtesy Volker Diehl